GI100630660

Using PageMaker® 4
for the PC
Third Edition

Using PageMaker® 4
for the PC
Third Edition

Martin S. Matthews
and Carole Boggs Matthews

Osborne **McGraw-Hill**

Berkeley New York St. Louis San Francisco
Auckland Bogotá Hamburg London Madrid
Mexico City Milan Montreal New Delhi Panama City
Paris São Paulo Singapore Sydney
Tokyo Toronto

Osborne **McGraw-Hill**
2600 Tenth Street
Berkeley, California 94710
U.S.A.

Osborne **McGraw-Hill** offers software for sale. For information on trans-
lations, software, or book distributors outside of the U.S.A., please write
to Osborne **McGraw-Hill** at the above address.

This book is printed on recycled paper.

Using PageMaker® 4 for the PC, Third Edition

Copyright © 1991 by Martin S. Matthews and Carole Boggs Matthew.s
All rights reserved. Printed in the United States of America. Except as
permitted under the Copyright Act of 1976, no part of this publication may
be reproduced or distributed in any form or by any means, or stored in a
database or retrieval system, without the prior written permission of the
publisher, with the exception that the program listings may be entered,
stored, and executed in a computer system, but they may not be reproduced for publication.

34567890 DOC 9987654321

ISBN 0-07-881629-7

Acquisitions Editor: Liz Fisher
Technical Reviewer: Jeff Nelson
Copy Editor: Barbara Conway
Proofreaders: Jeff Green, Ann Spivack
Word Processor: Lynda Higham
Composition: Bonnie Bozorg
Production Supervisor: Kevin Shafer
Cover design: Bay Graphics Design, Inc.

Information has been obtained by Osborne **McGraw-Hill** from sources believed to be reliable. However,
because of the possibility of human or mechanical error by our sources, Osborne **McGraw-Hill**, or others,
Osborne **McGraw-Hill** does not guarantee the accuracy, adequacy, or completeness of any information and
is not responsible for any errors or omissions or the results obtained from the use of such information.

To Michael Boggs Matthews
Born April 5, 1986
A wonderful, new challenge to our working schedules
and our lives!

And he continues to be
as he approaches his second birthday.
— Second Edition

Little did we know!
(now age four and a half)
— Third Edition

Contents at a Glance

Contents

Acknowledgments

There are a number of people whom we would like to recognize for their assistance in producing the various editions of the books *Using PageMaker for the PC*.

First, we'd like to thank several individuals within Aldus. Mark Craemer, Kerri McConnell, Carolyn Bakamis, and Vicki Farmer were all extremely helpful with the first edition. Mark and Carolyn also played a large role in the second edition, as did Michael Sherwood and Tim Hennings. Craig Danuloff and Freda Cook were helpful in the third edition.

The newsletter produced in Chapter 7 is an actual quarterly, *The Orator*, published by Opinion Movers for The Churchill Club. Rich Karlgaard, of Opinion Movers, who is a founder of The Churchill Club, gave us permission to use the newsletter in this book and graciously provided us with information and materials.

Frank Stapleton, of McPherson's, provided a similar service in giving us permission to use his catalog, McPherson's Wholesale Art Supplies/Graphic Arts/Drafting and Engineering, as the sample project in Chapter 8.

Introduction

PageMaker for the PC has proven its ability to uniquely combine ease-of-use with tremendous production capability. As a result, it has become an important tool for producing newsletters, brochures, forms, catalogs, manuals, and many other publications usually sent to a commercial typesetter. Many people have found that it truly enhances their ability to communicate and reduces their costs.

Now, with the release of PageMaker 4, PageMaker's ease-of-use and production capability are significantly improved. The new Story Editor provides many word processing features like search and replace and spell checking within PageMaker. Expanded graphic and typographic controls such as the ability to adjust type size and leading by 1/10 point and attaching graphics to text enhance PageMaker's ease-of-use, as does the linking of text to its original word processing file. PageMaker's new table of contents and index generators, as well as multi-publication printing and Table Editor, are significant new capabilities. Whatever PageMaker was, it is now an exceptionally powerful product that can easily be put to use.

As easy as PageMaker is to use, and even to learn, we have found that there are many desktop publishing concepts that require explanation to users who are unfamiliar with publishing. Also, there are many shortcuts and tricks to using PageMaker. This book has been written to provide the necessary explanations and to demonstrate the many short cuts and tricks to unleashing the power of PageMaker 4.

If you have recently purchased the PC version of PageMaker or are contemplating doing so, *Using PageMaker 4 for the PC* was written for you. With it you will learn how to perform page composition using PageMaker to create professional-quality documents. *Using PageMaker 4 for the PC* will help you, whether you are new to PageMaker or are acquainted with it and want to use it to produce more advanced publications. You may or may not be an experienced computer user.

The exercises and examples used in this book are actual business forms and publications chosen to illustrate realistic and comprehensive uses of

PageMaker. In creating them you will learn the scope of capabilities that are available in PageMaker. The book is not a tutorial as such. It is a step-by-step guide to creating the examples presented here. However, as you create the examples, you will learn about PageMaker.

The book offers ample explanation and visual support of exactly what is occurring as you create the examples. You will be shown what to expect on the screen through hundreds of screen images that accompany the narrative. In the narrative we explain what is happening, consider the implications, and point out your options at each step.

You will learn how to bring text and graphics into PageMaker from applications such as WordPerfect, Microsoft Word, Micrografx Designer, and 1-2-3. This doesn't mean that you must use those applications in order to use this book. Rather, you select the chapter (using the index) that explains how to bring in the text or graphics from your particular word processor or graphics program; then you use those details in performing the integration for whatever chapter you want. In truth, working with the various packages is very similar from PageMaker's standpoint. The primary challenge is knowing what to do with the material once it is in PageMaker.

This book complements the PageMaker tutorials and documentation by continuing where they leave off. We have assumed that you have installed PageMaker and been through the tutorials. However, if you have not, pay particular attention to the first three chapters of this book to learn the basics of PageMaker, Microsoft Windows, and desktop publishing

How This Book Is Organized

Using PageMaker 4 for the PC is organized into three parts, each containing increasingly advanced applications of PageMaker. Although the projects are separate and can be created independently of each other, you will get a good overall understanding of PageMaker's capabilities by creating all of them. However, you can also concentrate on just those examples that you are interested in developing for yourself.

Part I is more of a tutorial than the rest of the book. It explains the basic concepts of using PageMaker so that you comfortably can handle the remaining chapters even if you have not read the PageMaker tutorial. In Part I we discuss the essential elements of desktop publishing, Microsoft Windows (required to operate PageMaker), and PageMaker. If you are already familiar with the concepts of Windows and PageMaker, simply scan the first three chapters to review the basics and terminology. If you are new to PageMaker, carefully read Part I so that you will be able to get more out of the other chapters. In Part I you will create an advertising flyer using PageMaker.

In Part II we address three common needs of businesses: creating business forms, advertising brochures, and formal financial reports—all of which benefit from looking as though they were professionally prepared. These applications, more advanced than the one you create in Part I, use most of the basic capabilities of PageMaker.

In Part III we demonstrate how to create a newsletter and a catalog—both advanced uses of PageMaker. Of course, you will not create the complete publications; however, you will create enough of them to learn and use the more advanced features of PageMaker.

Here is a synopsis of each chapter.

What This Book Contains

In Chapter 1 we discuss desktop publishing and compare it to traditional publishing. You will quickly learn the essential concepts and terminology that are important in understanding PageMaker.

In Chapter 2 you will become acquainted with Microsoft Windows 2.0 or 386 and the mouse, both of which are required for working with PageMaker. Again, important terminology and concepts that apply to PageMaker are explained.

In Chapter 3 you will learn the fundamentals of using PageMaker by actually creating an advertising flyer. You will be led through the production more slowly and with more guidance than you will be in later chapters.

Chapter 4 illustrates how to use PageMaker to create a sales order form. Custom forms that have a "typeset" look add a professional touch to most business documents.

In Chapter 5 you will create a two-page advertising brochure containing columns. The text for the brochure will be taken from WordPerfect and then placed into the PageMaker publication. A graphic will be brought in from Micrografx Designer.

Chapter 6 illustrates how to "dress up" financial reports that you may want to show people outside your own company. You will compose these formal, multipage documents with word processing text from Microsoft Word, a financial worksheet from Lotus 1-2-3, and graphs from 1-2-3.

In Chapter 7 you will build a newsletter, one of the most popular uses of PageMaker, containing three to four columns per page. You will bring graphics and text in from several packages and place them in the publication. Chapter 7 uses the autoflow and style sheet features, as well as the Story Editor, new to PageMaker 4.

Chapter 8 demonstrates how to create a catalog. The text will come from Microsoft Word and the graphics from Micrografx Designer and a scanner. You will use several advanced functions and learn how to lay out pages efficiently.

Equipment and Software You Need

You will need an IBM PC AT, IBM PS/2, or compatible computer with an Intel 80286, 80386, or 80486 microprocessor to use PageMaker with this book. Your computer must have at least 2MB of memory (more is useful because of the needs of PageMaker).

You must have a hard disk drive of at least 20MB. We assume that you have one hard disk and one floppy drive.

You need VGA, 8514/A, Hercules, or compatible display and adapter that allows you to see higher-resolution graphics on your screen.

To get printed output of professional quality, a laser printer or a PostScript device is necessary. The predominant printer for the PC is the Hewlett-Packard (HP) LaserJet Series II or LaserJet III, although there are many other laser printers on the market, including several new PostScript devices. Dot matrix printers lack the quality of laser printers.

Finally, on the equipment side, you must have a mouse or Windows-compatible pointing device. The primary choice is between a Microsoft Mouse and a Mouse Systems mouse.

On the software side, you must have a PC or MS-DOS operating system, DOS 3.1 or later. You will also need Microsoft Windows 3.0, under which PageMaker 4 operates. And, of course, you need PageMaker 4 for the PC.

This book was written on an IBM PC AT compatible with an Intel 80386 processor. The screen illustrations were produced with a VGA video adapter running in monochrome mode using software from SymSoft Corporation and Anderson Consulting and Software. If you are using a different video adapter or a different VGA mode, your screen may differ slightly from the screen images shown in this book. An HP LaserJet Series II with a LaserMaster Series III Professional controller was used for printing the camera-ready art.

Typographical Conventions

Using PageMaker for the PC employs several typographical conventions that make it easier to use. These are as follows:

- **Bold** type is used when you are instructed to enter text from the keyboard.

- Keys from the keyboard are presented in small capital letters; for example, ENTER and ALT. A hyphen (-) between keys means to press the keys simultaneously. A comma (,) indicates a separate keypress. For example, SHIFT-F8, 2 means "press SHIFT and F8 simultaneously, then press 2."

To the extent practical, we have followed the typographical and naming conventions used in the PageMaker manuals. Most importantly, terms such as *click, drag, choose,* and *select* are presented here as they are in the PageMaker manuals.

About the Authors

Martin S. Matthews and Carole Boggs Matthews are partners in Matthews Technology, a firm providing consulting, training, and seminars on computer topics to large and small firms nationwide. They assist companies and individuals in selecting and installing computer systems, advise in the design and development of software, and conduct training sessions and seminars. The Matthews combine expertise in computing with solid business experience. Both have been managers and vice presidents as well as systems designers and developers for a variety of companies. Between them, they have more than 45 years of computer experience. *Using PageMaker 4 for the PC* is a result of a 14-year association with many different aspects of the printing and publishing industries. Among the Matthews' 14 computer-related books are *AppleWorks Made Easy* (three editions), *WordStar Professional: The Complete Reference, Using 1-2-3 Release 3,*

Works for the PC Made Easy, Q&A Made Easy, PageMaker 4 for the Macintosh Made Easy, and *Excel Made Easy, IBM PC Version* (all published by Osborne/McGraw-Hill).

DISK ORDER FORM

Save Time and Effort—Increase Accuracy

The word processing and graphic files used to build the publications in this book as well as the finished publications are available on disks. The disks are not required to build the publications, but by using the disks you can save the time and effort of typing the input and also eliminate the possibility of introducing errors.

The files are available on 360KB or 1.2 MB 5 1/4" diskettes for the IBM PC AT or 720 KB 3 1/2" diskettes for the IBM PS/2 and 100% compatible computers. If you have a different format or computer, contact us and we will attempt to accommodate you.

Be sure that your input is accurate and avoid the inconvenience of typing the detail by purchasing these disks. Save time and explore PageMaker now.

To order, complete the form on the reverse side and return it to Matthews Technology with your payment. Please allow up to four weeks for delivery.

To: Matthews Technology
           P.O Box 967
           Freeland, WA 98249

Please send me the disk set indicated for *Using PageMaker 4 for the PC, Third Edition*. My check for $29.95 is enclosed (U.S. funds on a U.S. Bank). (Washington state residents add 7.8% sales tax for a total of $32.29.)

____Four 360 KB 5 1/4" disks   ____One 1.2 MB 5 1/4" disk.
____Two 720 KB 3 1/2" disks

Send to:

Name:_____

Company:_____

Street:_____

City:_____State:_____ZIP:_____

Phone:_____

RETURN POLICY:

Returns are accepted only if a disk is defective. In that case, return the disk within 15 days and you will be sent a replacement disk immediately.

Osborne/McGraw-Hill assumes NO responsibility for this offer. This is solely an offer of Martin S. Mattews and Carole Boggs Mathews, and not of Osborne/McGraw-Hill.

The PageMaker Environment

Part I, composed of Chapters 1, 2, and 3, introduces you to PageMaker and its environment. It is more of a tutorial than the rest of the book so that all readers, regardless of prior experience with computers and PageMaker, are brought to a common level of understanding before the more advanced features of PageMaker are introduced.

Chapter 1 defines and explains some publishing terms and concepts necessary to understanding PageMaker. It acquaints you with the steps necessary to create a document using desktop publishing. Chapter 2 introduces you to Microsoft Windows, under which PageMaker operates. In Chapter 3 you use PageMaker to create an advertising flyer. Page-Maker's basic menus and operating concepts are thoroughly explained with many illustrations of the screen.

If you are already familiar with Windows and PageMaker, simply scan Part I to review the terminology and concepts and to become familiar with some of the changes in PageMaker 4 and Windows 3. If you are new to PageMaker, plan to spend more time with Part I because it is the foundation for the later chapters.

1 *Desktop Publishing And PageMaker*

Desktop publishing is a most appropriate term for producing high-quality publications from desktop computers. When Paul Brainerd, president and founder of Aldus Corporation, the publisher of PageMaker, coined the phrase, he envisioned an inexpensive desktop computer system that would perform most of the functions of expensive typesetting and layout. Desktop publishing is *page makeup* (typesetting plus layout) at a moderate cost. It is the ability to do at your desk what you previously sent out to design, typesetting, and layout services or didn't have printed due to the high cost.

Two major advantages of desktop publishing are the reduced cost of producing quality publications and the ability to produce them in-house. The net result is that the quality of business publications substantially improves.

Desktop publishing with PageMaker allows you to design a publication, add text, graphics, and *design elements* (lines, boxes, and so on), and then print it with a quality close to professional typesetting. PageMaker takes desktop publishing a step further by making these functions relatively easy to learn and perform, allowing many more people to use it.

In producing a publication with PageMaker, you may use a laser printer for both proofing and final printing, thus completing the full publishing cycle on desktop equipment. Or, after completing the creation and page makeup with PageMaker, you might use a commercial typesetting machine or an *imagesetter* (which produces camera-ready text and graphics) and an offset printing press for the final steps. In both instances you have used desktop publishing for the critical creation and makeup functions. In the second case, for reasons of either quality or volume, you have chosen to complete the process with traditional means. You have still saved money and time, and you have maintained greater control of the project.

Even though desktop publishing is easier and less expensive than traditional publishing, it still includes all the traditional steps. Because publishing deals with the production of printed material, it includes everything from simple memos to letters, forms, reports, flyers, brochures, magazines, pamphlets, manuals, catalogs, directories, and even complex, multivolume books. No matter how simple or complex the publication, it requires the same steps to produce. Obviously the steps are more significant in some cases than in others.

The steps are planning, design, content creation, page makeup, and printing. In the following paragraphs you'll look at each of these in detail.

Planning

Planning is concerned primarily with the content (in general terms), the schedule, and the budget. In planning you determine what goes into a publication, who will perform the various tasks, how long each task takes, and how much the publication will cost. Planning a simple memo is easy: you have text on a single subject, you will write it yourself in 20 minutes, and the cost will be minimal. However, a monthly newsletter containing up to 15 articles by different writers, with a number of illustrations and a fixed schedule and budget, can require substantial planning.

There is little difference in planning for a publication produced with traditional techniques and one produced with PageMaker. In each case planning is very important. If, upon starting a publication, you pause to answer the questions of what, who, when, and how much, you will find the remaining publishing tasks much easier.

Design

Once you have planned the content of a publication, you can determine how to display it on the pages. Traditionally this is the domain of the designer, whose objective is to produce a unique publication that is both attractive and easy to read. To achieve this, the designer considers all visual elements, from the overall appearance of the publication to the type size for subheadings. This includes such elements as the number and size of columns; the typefaces and their sizes; the use and placement of design elements; and the appearance of titles, headings, subheadings, and captions.

Design can be broken down into a series of steps: establishing the design constraints, determining the master and regular page layouts, selecting the type, and determining the use of design elements. These steps are basically the same for both traditional and desktop publishing, although some factors may differ. Let's look at each.

Establishing Design Constraints

In the planning phase you determined the budget and schedule constraints. Design constraints are of a physical nature, created primarily by the equipment used to produce the publication. For example, your typesetting machine or laser printer has a limited number of type styles and sizes. The printing press or laser printer used to print the publication is limited both in the size of paper it can handle and the area of the paper that can be printed upon (called the *image area*). To print a multipage publication, you may choose a large printing press on which several pages are printed together on a single large sheet. This sheet is then folded down to the individual page size, and the folded edges are trimmed off so the pages can be turned. The size limitations of the folding and trimming machines determine the final page size (called the *trim size*). Finally, paper comes in predetermined sizes. If you design a publication larger than a standard size, you must print on the next larger size (probably more expensive) and then trim off the excess (also adding to the cost).

Your choice of desktop publishing hardware and software also influences your design options. If you use a laser printer for both proofing and printing, you have one set of typeface, paper size, and image area constraints. If you use a commercial imagesetter and offset press, you have another set of constraints. In any case, you must consider these requirements in your design.

Establishing the constraints of your chosen production equipment is a mandatory first step in a publication's design. These constraints determine the outer boundaries within which you design the publication. You need to know these limits before you can proceed.

Determining the Master Page Layout

In designing a multipage publication, you want most, if not all, of the pages to reflect a common design. To do this with PageMaker, you design a *master page* (or pages) that contains the elements common to most pages. Among the common elements are page size, margins, number and size of columns, a layout grid of the margins and column edges, and the use of facing pages. Headers, footers, page number location, and common design elements such as lines between columns also can be placed on the master page.

PAGE SIZE Your first decision in designing a master page involves the page size. The previously determined design constraints set the outer limits. Now within those limits you must determine the final page size. The standard 8 1/2 by 11-inch letter size is often appropriate. However, paper size does not necessarily constrain page size. You may want to consider other sizes, depending on your publication and how you will produce it. You may paste up several pieces to create a single page (called *tiling*), or you may have several pages on a single piece of paper, as shown in Figure 1-1.

MARGINS Once you know the page size, you can determine the image area. This is the area inside the margins of a page in which you place the material to be printed. To determine the image area, simply set the margins on the four sides of the page—top, bottom, inside, and outside, as shown in Figure 1-2.

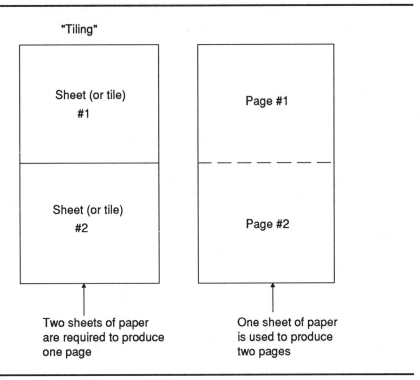

Figure 1-1.　*Two methods of paging*

Again, the constraints of your equipment and software will influence your decision on margins. Other factors also play a part. For example, the type of page binding influences the inside margin or *gutter*. You can also use margins, such as a particularly large outside margin, as part of the distinctive style of the publication.

COLUMNS　Most newspapers, magazines, newsletters, brochures, and many books have multiple columns on a page because most people find a narrow column is easier to read. In designing the master page, you determine the number and size of the columns to appear on a page. PageMaker lets you create up to 20 columns per page; however, except for forms or special-purpose publications, you rarely use more than three or four columns.

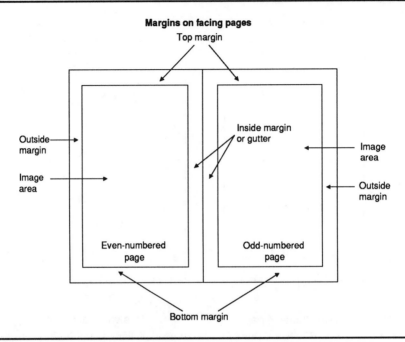

Figure 1-2.   *Locating the four margins*

You also determine the amount of blank space between columns. A space of 1/4 inch or 6 millimeters is common, but there are no hard rules. Finally, you may have columns of equal or unequal size, depending on your needs and styling considerations. Figure 1-3 shows some examples.

LAYOUT GRID   In building a master page using PageMaker you automatically create a *Layout Grid.* This is a set of nonprinting dotted lines on the screen image of a page to assist in lining up text and graphics. The margins and column edges (called *column guides* by Aldus) form the foundation of the grid. In addition, you may add other nonprinting guides to assist in page makeup. For example, if you want all chapter heads to start on line 10, you might place a horizontal ruler guide there to remind you. Such a guide does not prevent you from placing text above line 10 on some pages.

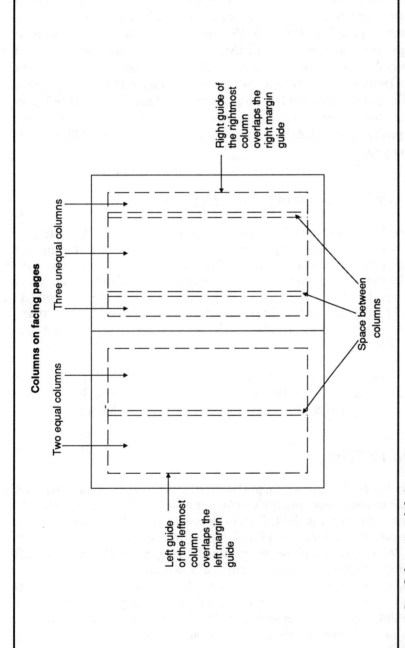

Figure 1-3.   Columns and their components

FACING PAGES   If you print on both sides of a page in a multipage publication, you will have *facing pages*—left and right pages beginning with pages 2 and 3, as shown in Figures 1-2 and 1-3. You may want to create separate master pages in this situation because there can be a number of differences between the left and right pages. For example, the left and right margins need to be reversed because the inside margin, where the publication will be bound, is on the right side of the left page and on the left side of the right page. Also a header, footer, or page number may be positioned toward the outside of each page, which is a different side on facing pages.

Determining the Detail Page Layout

Once you have established the master page or pages, you lay out each regular page by customizing a master page layout. First, you make a mock-up of the publication by determining the length of the text and the size and number of photos or graphics. You create a *rough* of the publication by placing the text and graphics on each page as you want them. In PageMaker you can use shading of various densities to represent text and graphics. You may create several roughs before settling on a final detailed layout. This final layout is called a *dummy* (or a *comp,* for comprehensive layout).

With PageMaker you might want to use the actual text and graphics to create the roughs. Using the actual content is not much harder than placing shading, which is one advantage of desktop publishing.

Selecting Type

A major element in designing a publication is selecting the type to be used. You must consider not only the *typeface* or design of the type but also the *size, style* (whether it is light, Roman or medium, bold, or italic), and the spacing between letters (including *kerning*—the special spacing between certain letter pairs) and between lines (*leading*). Finally, you need to consider the alignment, or *justification,* of the type.

Whether you are doing traditional or desktop publishing, you must select a typeface and determine its size, style, spacing, and justification. The available typefaces depend upon the equipment you are using. You determine these when establishing the design constraints.

TYPEFACES You select a typeface because you like how it conveys your message to the reader. Your choice depends on the effects you want to achieve. Some typefaces are easier to read or more distinctive than others. Most designers believe that typefaces with small extra strokes (called *serifs*) on the ends of the letters are easier to read in large blocks of text. A common example of such a face is Times Roman. It and its derivatives are used in many newspapers, magazines, and books. A more modern typeface, without the extra strokes (called *sans serif*), can be very distinctive and clean looking. Sans serif typefaces, such as Helvetica, are commonly used in advertising and on business cards and stationery. Figure 1-4 shows examples of typefaces similar to Times Roman and Helvetica.

An individual publication should not have too many different typefaces. Three or four are normally considered the limit. This provides one face each for the text, titles, headings, and captions on charts or tables. Within a single typeface, you have Roman or medium weight, bold, and italic styles, as well as varying sizes. Again, however, do not use too many sizes or your publication will become hard to read. (The word *font* is frequently confused with the word typeface. A typeface is one particular design or

---

This is a serif typeface similar to Times Roman.
TIMES ROMAN times roman
abcdefghijklmnopqrstuvwxyz
ABCDEFGHIJKLMNOPQRSTUVWXYZ
1234567890-=\`[];',./~!@#$%^&*()_+|{}:"<>?

This is a sans serif typeface similar to Helvetica.
HELVETICA helvetica
abcdefghijklmnopqrstuvwxyz
ABCDEFGHIJKLMNOPQRSTUVWXYZ
1234567890-=\`[];',./~!@#$%^&*()_+|{}:"<>?

Figure 1-4. *Examples of typefaces similar to Times and Helvetica*

face, independent of size; a font is a typeface of a given style, size, and orientation.)

TYPE SIZE   Type size is measured in *points*. One point equals 1/72 inch. Points are measured from the top of the ascenders (the top of the letter "k" or "b," for example) to the bottom of the descenders (the bottom of a "p" or "y"). PageMaker 4 for the PC supports type sizes of 4 through 650 points, in increments of 1/10 point. Your printer and its available fonts may limit your selection of type sizes. Normal text in books, newspapers, and newsletters ranges from 9 to 12 points, with titles and headlines larger and "fine print" smaller. Selected examples of sizes from 6 to 72 points are shown in Figure 1-5.

HORIZONTAL SPACING   The horizontal spacing of letters determines how long a line is. Line length is called the *column width* and normally is measured in either inches or *picas*. There are 12 points to a pica and approximately 6 picas to the inch. Horizontal spacing is a function of the size of individual letters and the spacing between them. Because almost all published material uses *proportionally spaced* typefaces (where a "w" takes more space than an "i"), letter size is the most important factor in spacing. Second, in addition to the normal spacing between words, extra space can be added between both letters and words to lengthen lines so their right edges align (*justifying* the lines). Space is often taken away between certain letter pairs to improve their appearance (called kerning). Kerning is a function of the typeface and whether you are using upper- or lowercase. For example, a lowercase "t" and "y" or a lowercase "f" and "o" can both be kerned in certain typefaces. PageMaker uses kerning lists of letter pairs for this purpose. In addition, PageMaker offers manual kerning so you can add or take away space from any letter pair.

The extent of your concern with horizontal spacing depends on how you want your publication to read and look. Right-justifying your text may make it look better but it may not be easier to read. You can justify by adjusting the space between words, or, to make the text look more professional, you can justify a line by adjusting the space between characters.

PageMaker 4 has several commands that allow you to change the horizontal spacing of a line. First, if you are using a PostScript, Hewlett-Packard Laseret III, LaserMaster, or similar printer that uses scalable fonts, you can adjust the width of a character from 5 percent to 250 percent of its normal width. This makes the character itself, not the space around

6-point type

8-point type

10-point type

12-point type

18-point type

24-point type

36-point type

48-point type

60-point ty

72-point t

Figure 1-5.   *Selected examples of type sizes from 6 to 72 points*

This 24-point type at a 100% or "normal" width

This 24-point type at a 70% width

This 24-point type at a 130% width

Figure 1-6.   *Character width*

it, wider or narrower, as shown in Figure 1-6. Second, you can adjust the space between characters with six *tracking* settings, from very loose to very tight, as shown in Figure 1-7. Third, you can adjust the range over which you are willing to let PageMaker automatically adust the word and letter spacing when justifying and hyphenating a line.

Fonts are designed with a specific character and word spacing, and with a kerning table for the special spacing between certain pairs of characters. To justify a line or to provide for the grammatical hyphenation of a word, PageMaker may adust this designed letter and word spacing. You can control the limits within which it does this: You can set word spacing from 0 to 500 percent, with 100 percent being the designed word spacing. And you can set letter spacing from -200 percent to 200 percent, with 0 being the normal letter spacing.

The tracking applied to this 12-point unjustified type is called "No Track." The tracking applied to this 12-point unjustified type is called"No Track."

The tracking applied to this 12-point unjustified type is called "Very Loose." The tracking applied to this 12-point unjustified type is called "Very Loose."

The tracking applied to this 12-point unjustified type is called "Loose."The tracking applied to this 12-point unjustified type is called "Loose."

The tracking applied to this 12-point unjustified type is called "Normal."The tracking applied to this 12-point unjustified type is called "Normal."

The tracking applied to this 12-point unjustified type is called "Tight." The tracking applied to this 12-point unjustified type is called "Tight."

The tracking applied to this 12-point unjustified type is called "Very Tight."The tracking applied to this 12-point unjustified type is called "Very Tight."

Figure 1-7. *Tracking or spacing between characters*

VERTICAL SPACING   Vertical spacing between lines of type is called leading (pronounced "ledding"). The term comes from the days of lead type when literally more lead was added to the top and bottom of a line of type to adjust the spacing between lines. Today leading refers to the total height of a line, from the top of the tallest characters in the line to the top of the tallest characters in the line below. Leading, like type, is measured in points. Normally you talk about leading in relation to the type size. For example, 10-point type with 11-point leading is described as 10/11 ("ten over eleven"). A 10/10 leading is really no leading; it is just the normal vertical spacing of a given font. As the leading increases, space is added

---

This is 12-point type with 12-point leading. It is called "12/12." Effectively this means that there is no leading.

This is 12-point type with 14.4-point leading. It is called "12/14.4." This is what PageMaker provides with its default "Auto" leading.

This is 12-point type with 16-point leading. It is called "12/16." The spread between the lines begins to look unattractive.

This is 12-point type with 10-point leading. It is called "12/10." This is "negative" leading, in which the lines begin to overlap.

Figure 1-8.   *Examples of different leading*

between lines. For good readability of normal text, the leading should be one or two points greater than the type. PageMaker's "Auto" leading feature initially provides leading of 120 percent of the type size—for instance, 10/12 or 12/14. However, you can change the "Auto" leading percentage and also manually specify leading in 1/10-point increments, including negative leading (10/8, for example), for special effects. Figure 1-8 shows examples of varying amounts of leading.

In PageMaker 4 you can choose between two methods of applying leading: "Proportional" leading, which places proportional amounts of space above the tallest ascender and below the lowest descender, and "Top of caps" leading, which places all the space below the lowest descender. These options are demonstrated in Figure 1-9. Previous versions of Page- Maker provided only "Proportional" leading, which is also the traditional method of applying leading. "Top of caps" leading applies the same amount of space, but in a way that is more easily measured because there is a fixed point from which to measure—the tops of capital letters.

This is an	This is an
example of	example of
"Proportional"	"Top of caps"
leading	leading
applied to 18-	applied to 18-
point type	point type
with 160%	with 160%
(29-point)	(29-point)
leading.	leading.

Figure 1-9. *"Proportional" vs. "Tops of caps" leading*

ALIGNMENT   Text can be aligned on either the left or right margin, on both margins (justified), or in the center of the page (centered). In this country almost all text (except for titles, headings, and captions) is left-aligned. Because the Western eye is used to reading from left to right, left-aligned text is easier for us to read. Longer blocks of text prove easier to read when both the left and right margins are aligned. Right alignment and centering are used only in special circumstances, such as in titles and captions. PageMaker 4 has added the "Force justify" command to force the justification of the last line of a paragraph. Figure 1-10 shows examples of left-aligned, right-aligned, centered, justified, and force-justified paragraphs.

Using Design Elements

The final step of the design process is to specify the use of design elements. These are the lines, boxes, rectangles, and bullets that separate and emphasize the text. In traditional publishing, design elements are hand-drawn or transferred from Zipatone sheets and are placed on the final, camera-ready copy. In desktop publishing, and in PageMaker in particular, most of these elements are created with the computer on either the master or detail page layouts.

Use design elements with caution. Lines, boxes, and bullets used appropriately are effective in enhancing the appearance and readability of a publication. Overuse or misuse, however, is distracting and can mar an otherwise good publication. The ease with which design elements are applied in the desktop publishing environment has sometimes led to their overuse.

Content Creation

The purpose of a publication is to disseminate the writing and graphics that make up its content. The planning and design work preceding content creation and the production steps following it only support the central functions of writing, drawing, and photographing the actual material. However, this book, which is about PageMaker, concerns primarily design

This is an example of normal letter
and word spacing that PageMaker
uses with 12-point type that has been
left-aligned.

This is an example of normal letter
and word spacing that PageMaker
uses with 12-point type that has been
right-aligned.

This is an example of normal letter
and word spacing that PageMaker
uses with 12-point type that has been
centered.

This is an example of normal letter and
word spacing that PageMaker uses with
12-point type that has been justified.

This is an example of normal letter and
word spacing that PageMaker uses with
12-point type that has been force
j   u   s   t   i   f   i   e   d   .

Figure 1-10.   *Types of alignment*

and production. It addresses the creation phase only to the extent that text
and graphics must somehow be brought into a publication. Therefore, the
discussion of content creation is limited to considerations necessary for

transferring text, graphics, and photos or other noncomputer-generated material to the desktop publishing environment.

Generating Text

Almost all text to be published with PageMaker is first written on a word processor. The word processing files are then transferred to and used by PageMaker. But PageMaker can also get text directly from the keyboard. Let's look at both of these methods of generating text.

WORD PROCESSING PACKAGES   There are considerable differences in how word processing packages code formatting information in their files. (Formatting information includes margins, indents, carriage returns, tabs, and type specifications.) To be efficient, PageMaker must both read the files and pick up as much of the formatting information as possible. PageMaker does not handle all word processing packages, so check to see if yours produces files that PageMaker can use. As of this writing, Page-Maker 4 for the PC works with DisplayWrite 3.0 to 5.0, Microsoft Word 4.0 to 5.5 and Word for Windows, MultiMate Advantage II, Samna AMI PRO, Windows Write (3.0 only), WordPerfect 4.2 to 5.1, WordStar 5.0 through 6.0, XyWrite III Plus 3.53, and packages such as Volkswriter 3 and WordStar 2000 that can create Document Content Architecture (DCA) files. This list is constantly changing, so check the latest Aldus literature if your word processing package is not listed here. PageMaker also supports ASCII (unformatted and SMART ASCII) text files.

To see how PageMaker interprets the formatting codes from your word processor, make a sample file in your word processor, using the formatting conventions you will need. Do this before you begin to write. Then transfer the sample file to PageMaker to see how it handles the formatting conventions.

As you use the word processor, keep in mind the planned column width in PageMaker, as well as any anomalies you find in the sample file. You might use identical column widths in both the word processor and Page-Maker to avoid problems. For example, a 1-inch indent in a 6-inch column in the word processor might make sense. However, a 1-inch indent in a narrower column, a 2-inch column, for instance, is not appropriate.

PageMaker ignores some formatting elements in all word processing packages. Among these are right margins (right indents are usually picked up), footnotes, headers, and footers. See the PageMaker manuals for more information on how PageMaker works with your word processor.

DIRECT ENTRY   For small amounts of text, such as captions, titles, and headings, direct keyboard entry into PageMaker is easier than using a word processor. Also, you often are not aware of all the captions or other supporting text needed until you are doing the final page makeup. Using direct entry, you can place the text exactly where you want it, and PageMaker 4's new story editing features make direct text entry into PageMaker almost as easy as using a word processing program. On the other hand, with a word processor you can contain the captions, titles, and headings in several small files and place them individually, or you can "cut" an item from a single file and then "paste" it around the publication.

Creating Graphics

In traditional publishing, figures or illustrations come from one of two sources: hand-drawn art and photographs. Both are produced separately from the text and must be pasted on during final page makeup. Desktop publishing still employs these two sources of figures and illustrations (generically called *graphics*). In addition, art can be created with a computer and transferred directly to the desktop publication. Photographs and similar materials also can be used in this way by being *scanned*—read by a machine that converts the image into computer-usable form.

Most graphics come into PageMaker in the size in which they were created. Once in PageMaker, they can be shrunk or expanded to fit the space allocated. Drastically changing their size, however, affects the clarity of the final image. In PageMaker you can also *crop* a graphic (cut it off in two dimensions) to fit the space allocated. Although you cannot erase part of a graphic, you can cover it over or mask it with "paper" colored shading. You can also use PageMaker's drawing tools to enhance the image.

A number of different types of programs can be used to produce graphics within a computer. PageMaker can read directly four types of graphics disk files produced by these programs: *paint-type* (or bit-mapped) graphics files, *draw-type* (or object-oriented) files, Encapsulated PostScript (EPS) files, and scanned images in the Tag Image File Format (TIFF). The following paragraphs further describe each of these types of files.

PAINT-TYPE GRAPHICS   Paint-type graphics create drawings with a series of dots or *bits* that are either turned on or off (a process known as *bit-mapping*). On the screen these bits, called *pixels,* are the smallest addressable unit. The number of pixels per square inch determines the clarity or *resolution* of what you see and depends on the type of display adapter and monitor that you have. On a laser printer the quality of the final printed image varies with the number of dots per square inch that it prints. Most desktop laser printers currently print 300 dots per inch (dpi). Because of differences in resolution between the screen (normally much less than 300dpi) and the printer, you may notice differences in the clarity of the image produced by each.

Computer applications that generate paint-type graphics include Microsoft Windows Paint, PC Paint, PC Paintbrush, and Publisher's Paintbrush. Use these applications for sketches and other freehand work that would traditionally be done by an artist or illustrator.

DRAW-TYPE GRAPHICS   Draw-type graphics use drawing commands to create the image. For example, a command might be "draw a line between points A and B." Draw-type graphics are produced in the same way on both the screen and the printer. Consequently, the screen and printer images look very much alike.

Draw-type applications include CorelDraw, Micrografx Designer, Lotus 1-2-3, and Excel. These applications are best used for precise, geometrical shapes, such as mechanical drawings and charts produced with a straightedge and compass, as well as many other forms of drawing.

ENCAPSULATED POSTSCRIPT (EPS)   Encapsulated PostScript is a file format created by Adobe Systems that describes a graphic or text object using the PostScript language. Most graphics programs that can drive a PostScript printer also produce EPS files. EPS is really a special draw-type file format.

SCANNED IMAGES   Scanned images are created by a *scanner,* which is a computer-peripheral device into or onto which an image is placed to produce the same image in the computer. Using a scanner, you can import an image from drawings, as well as from color or black-and-white photographs. The resolution of the image both on the screen and when printed is a function of the capabilities of the scanner, its software, your display card, and your printer. The scanned image is never as clear as the original photograph. Therefore, you may want to use scanned images only to create a dummy for sizing and placement and then have a commercial printer use the actual photo in the final printing. High-resolution scanner files can be quite large, taking considerable disk space and slowing down printing. Consider using low resolution files in scanning if the images are only for sizing a dummy.

Files produced by scanners must either use a TIFF, a special format created for scanners, or be created through a compatible graphics application, such as PC Paintbrush. Scanners that create files PageMaker can read include those produced by Canon, Datacopy, DEST, Hewlett-Packard, Logitech, MicroTek, and Ricoh.

Linking Text and Graphics Files With PageMaker Files

Placing or importing a text or graphics file into a PageMaker 4 publication automatically creates a link between the original text or graphics file and the PageMaker file on which you are working. This allows the PageMaker publication to reflect any changes made to the original document. It also requires that the original files remain accessible to the PageMaker file for as long as you want to maintain the link.

When you place a text file in a PageMaker publication, a complete copy of the text file is transferred to the PageMaker file, and a link is automatically established with the original file. If the original file is changed, the PageMaker publication automatically can reflect the changes (with or without an alert that the change has taken place), or you can be notified that the original document has changed and then choose whether to include that change in the PageMaker publication.

When you place a graphics file in a PageMaker publication, you can choose whether to transfer the complete file to the publication. If you choose not to transfer the complete file, only a low-resolution copy of the image is stored with the publication. This saves file space and reduces PageMaker's processing time. On the other hand, if the PageMaker file cannot find the complete graphics file, you cannot print the graphics file at full resolution.

Files or parts of files that are pasted onto a PageMaker publication by means of the Clipboard from a source other than another PageMaker publication have no link to their original document. Files that are transferred from one PageMaker publication to another by means of the Clipboard have their original link transferred, if it existed.

PAGE MAKEUP

Page makeup combines the traditional functions of typesetting and layout—the final two steps before printing. Typesetting is simply reproducing a manuscript with the correct type and spacing. Traditionally, the typeset manuscript is printed onto long ribbons of photographic paper, called *galleys,* that are then cut and pasted onto finished pages; then photos and line drawings are added, followed by the design elements, headings, and page numbering. The layout process requires considerable skill and much patience—especially if major changes are introduced late in the process. With the advent of desktop publishing, this process is easy and requires less skill. Additionally, major changes can be handled with less effort.

Desktop publishing has also changed the order of the functions. Because the text is already in galley form when it comes from the word processor, in the first step of page makeup you place the text and graphics onto the page layout. Then you select the desired type fonts (if this has not been done in the word processor). Finally, you adjust the layout and apply any remaining design elements.

Page makeup in a desktop publishing environment, then, has three subsidiary steps: placing text and graphics, font selection, and adding the finishing touches.

Placing Text and Graphics

At first you will probably spend most of your time in PageMaker placing text and graphics. How well you build the layout grid and create the text and graphics determines how easily the placement process goes. With experience you can spend a high proportion of your time planning and designing. Placing text and graphics, however, will always be a major part of desktop publishing, just as it is in traditional publishing.

In traditional publishing you first paste up text, leaving open spaces for the graphics; then you paste up the graphics. With desktop publishing it is easier first to place and size the graphics and then to "flow" the text around them. You will be doing a great deal of this in the publications that follow. Therefore, we will delay discussing the methods and techniques for placing text and graphics until you can actually see the results as you build the publications.

Font Selection

Typesetting in traditional publishing requires retyping a manuscript into a typesetting machine. As the text is entered, the typesetter adds special commands to change fonts and type styles and to establish column widths and text indentation. Generally, the text is proofread both before and after it is typeset. With desktop publishing, the manuscript is typed only once into a word processor, so it needs to be proofread only once—before being transferred to PageMaker. The only remaining typesetting tasks are to identify font changes and to establish column widths. Because in Page-Maker column sizing is part of page layout, it is not considered a typeset-ting function. The only remaining typesetting task is to identify the fonts you want to use—hence the change in terms to "font selection" for what is, in traditional publishing, all of typesetting.

Font selection is determining which typeface, size, and style to use and where. You may even be able to do this in your word processor. For example, with most word processors you can identify bold and italic styles. You should do as much formatting as you can in the word processor. You then will have less to do with the text in PageMaker, and the original word processing file will have many of the properties of the finished PageMaker publication.

PageMaker works with a wide variety of printers and the fonts that are available for them. The fonts generally include a variety of typefaces, styles, and sizes. Among the typefaces are serif faces—such as Times Roman, Century Schoolbook, Garamond, and Palantino—as well as sans serif faces—such as Helvetica, Futura, and Avant Garde. There may also be sets of special symbols such as Symbol and Zapf Dingbats. All of the typefaces listed so far are proportionally spaced. Most sets of typefaces also have a *monospaced* face, such as Courier, in which all of the characters are the same width. The name of a typeface can be copyrighted, but not the typeface itself. You will, therefore, see a typeface or a very close copy of it called a number of different things. For example, Times Roman is called Dutch, News Serif, and Times, and Helvetica is called Swiss and Sans. Most typefaces come in four styles; Roman or medium weight, bold, italic, or oblique, and bold italic.

Depending on the printer and the fonts you are using, PageMaker 4 lets you print scalable typeface and style combinations in any size from 4 to 650 points, in 1/10-point increments. They can also be printed either vertically (*portrait,* or tall, orientation) or horizontally (*landscape,* or wide, orientation). Therefore, you can choose from a large number of fonts when using printers with scalable fonts (see Appendix B for a discussion of scalable fonts).

Many typefaces and styles are stored on a disk connected to either your computer or your printer. These are sometimes called *soft fonts* and can be transferred to the printer (*downloaded*) either manually or automatically. Many vendors offer soft fonts that you can download to your printer. Two of these are Adobe Systems, the creators of PostScript, and Bitstream. Soft fonts can take up a lot of disk space, and downloading them at the time of printing can add substantially to your printing time. Appendix B further discusses fonts and laser printers.

Adding the Finishing Touches

After you have placed the text and graphics and selected the type, you need to make corrections to the layout and add any final design elements. For example, you might want to emphasize your graphics with separating lines on the top and bottom.

This is the cleanup phase. You want to catch remaining errors, look for text or graphics improperly aligned, and, in general, correct any unsatisfactory facet of the layout. Look for pages that are "too busy"—those with too many design elements. Design elements should lead the reader's eye easily and effectively. If they are not doing that, they are not working.

Throughout the desktop publishing process, print your publication frequently to see how it looks. While you are adding the finishing touches, this becomes doubly important. You may have a WYSIWYG (what you see is what you get) screen image, but it is still almost impossible to visualize the final product without printing it several times.

PRINTING

Considering the amount of effort preceding it, printing is anticlimactic. If you are producing your final product on a laser printer, you simply choose the "Print. . ." command once more, perhaps increasing the number of copies. If you are printing the final product on a printing press, however, you must take the output of your laser printer or imagesetter to a printer and have it "run off." In either case, there is little for you to do in the printing phase—it is the final step in creating your document. In desktop publishing, printing is important only in completing the publishing cycle.

The following chapters discuss each publishing step in greater depth as it relates to actually producing a publication. Before you get into the actual projects, let's briefly look at Microsoft Windows.

2 *Using Windows And the Mouse*

PageMaker is a Windows application, which means that PageMaker requires Microsoft Windows for it to run. Windows provides the interface between you and PageMaker—the way PageMaker tells you on the screen what it is doing, and the way you tell PageMaker what to do. This chapter acquaints you with some of the essentials of Microsoft Windows 3. You may never use all of Windows' capabilities and tools, but in becoming acquainted with them, you will appreciate the additional power in the PageMaker environment.

This chapter is more of a tutorial than the rest of the book. It proceeds more slowly in order to establish a common ground for using this book and PageMaker. If you are already familiar with Windows and using a mouse, simply scan the chapter to verify that you know the vocabulary used here and the basic operating procedures used in Windows 3.

Introducing Windows

PageMaker is designed to run under Microsoft Windows, an extension of the MS-DOS operating system. This is desirable for several reasons, but primarily because Windows offers a standard environment for all programs or *applications* that run under it. This environment consists chiefly of a standard screen display, or *visual interface,* that you use to communicate with Windows applications. Once you have learned to use Windows, you will find that working with the various applications that run under Windows, including PageMaker, is very similar.

Windows also provides a way to transfer information among applications, such as from Word for Windows or CorelDraw to PageMaker. Through this feature (called the Clipboard), you can easily move a Word document or a Corel drawing to a PageMaker publication.

Windows allows you to simultaneously load more than one application into memory and to switch among them with minimal effort. You can work with a word processor, a graphics application, and PageMaker all at the same time. Of course, the degree to which this can be done depends on the amount of memory in your computer.

Finally, Windows provides a set of applications—handy tools that include the following:

Calculator	A calculator program for adding, subtracting, dividing, and multiplying numbers
Calendar	A scheduling program for jotting down your appointments and commitments
Cardfile	A list-management program
Clock	A clock that can be displayed on-screen at all times
Notepad	A program that lets you keep notes, reminders, and other memos handy
Paintbrush	A graphics program
PIF Editor	A special editor for PIF files
Recorder	A means of recording and playing back sets of keystrokes, or macros
Terminal	A communications program that lets you connect via a modem and telephone lines to another computer
Write	A word processing program

As a result of operating under Windows, PageMaker has all these tools available to it on demand.

The quickest way to learn about Windows is to start using it. If you have not already done so, turn on your computer now and start Windows. If you have not already installed Windows, refer to Appendix A, "Installing Windows and PageMaker," which tells you how to do it. When you have completed the installation and your mouse is connected, return here.

How you start Windows depends on how you installed it. If you followed the instructions in Appendix A and the suggestions in the Windows Setup program, you will have put the Windows directory in the path statement of your AUTOEXEC.BAT file along with the program name, WIN. This automatically starts Windows when you start or boot your computer. If you did not change your AUTOEXEC.BAT for Windows, you must tell DOS which directory contains Windows by using the "CD" (Change Directory) command. Using WINDOWS3 as the Windows directory, enter the command **CD\WINDOWS3**. Once you have done that, direct the computer to start Windows by typing **WIN**.

The Windows Screen

When you start Windows 3, you first see something like the screen shown in Figure 2-1, if you installed Windows with the instructions in Appendix A. Depending on how you installed Windows and whether you have more or fewer Windows applications, your screen may look different. The screen shown in Figure 2-1 has two windows, both of which have several standard features that appear in most windows of Windows 3. The top line, or *title bar,* contains the title of the window. In this case the two windows are the Program Manager and Windows Applications.

On the left end of the title bar is a box named the Control-menu box. This contains a *menu* of window options that are always available. You use this menu to perform such operations as moving, sizing, or closing a window.

On the right end of the title bar are two buttons, Minimize and Maximize, that you use to change the size of the window.

Below the title bar in the Program Manager application window is the *menu bar.* The menus available (File, Options, Window, and Help) apply only to the Program Manager. The menus displayed in the menu bar change as the contents of the window changes.

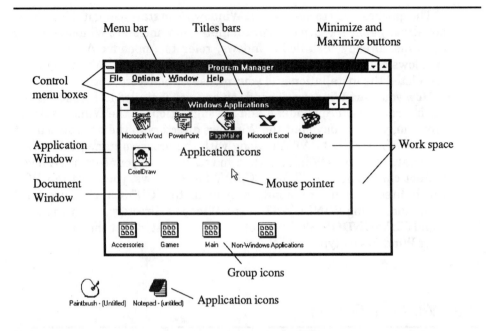

Figure 2-1.   *Windows 3 startup screen*

Below the menu bar is the document window or *workspace,* which contains the document or information currently being worked on. At the bottom of the workspace (see Figure 2-1) are graphic symbols, called *group icons,* that represent four groups of programs you can use.

At the bottom of the screen, below the Program Manager window, is an area called the *icon area.* In Figure 2-1 it has two icons in it, for the Paintbrush and Notepad applications. When you have started an application such as Notepad or Paintbrush but then temporarily set it aside while you do something else, the application becomes an icon. You can activate a program, move it, or deactivate it with the icon. When an application is inactive, its icon is stored in the icon area.

Several indicators show where you are on the screen. First, the *active window*—the one you are currently working in— is indicated by the title bar and border filled in with normally a dark color and light letters. Both the Program Manager and Windows Applications windows are active in Figure 2-1. Second, the *selected object* or objects—what your next action will affect—is highlighted as is the Aldus PageMaker program icon in Figure 2-1. In this case the program name is reversed, white or light-colored letters on a black or dark-colored background. The third indicator is the arrow in the Windows Applications window. This is the *mouse pointer,* which tells you where the mouse is pointing. All three indicators change as you work. The varying symbols tell you something about the task being done. You will see examples later on.

Using the Mouse

Although Windows allows you to use either the mouse or the keyboard to enter commands, the mouse greatly increases the power of Windows. It is strongly recommended that you use a mouse, and most instructions in this book assume such use. The keyboard occasionally does offer a shortcut, so these plus general rules for using the keyboard will be covered.

The mouse is used to move the pointer on the screen. You can *select* an object by moving the mouse until the pointer is on top of it (pointing *on* it) and then pressing the mouse button. Using the mouse in this way allows you to choose, for example, an option on a menu. A mouse can have one, two, or three buttons. Only one button is used by Windows, while Page-Maker uses two buttons. By default, the button used by both Windows and PageMaker is the left button; however, you can change the default to another button. You may want to make this change if you are left-handed. Whichever button you use, it is called the *main mouse button* in this book. The second button used by PageMaker is the right button by default and is called the *secondary mouse button.*

Mousing Around

If you move the mouse across a flat surface such as a table or desk, the mouse pointer (arrow) on the screen also moves. Practice moving the mouse as follows:

1. Place your hand on the mouse. The button(s) should be under your fingers with the cord leading away from you.

2. Move the mouse now, without pressing a mouse button, and watch the pointer move on the screen. If you run out of room while moving the mouse, simply pick it up and place it where there is more room. Experiment with this now.

3. Move the mouse to the edge of your work surface. Then pick it up and place it in the middle of your work surface, and move it again in the same direction.

Watch how the pointer continues from where the mouse was picked up. The arrow changes to a double-headed arrow when you point on the border of the window (move the mouse slowly over the border). This tells you that the pointer is on the border. If you press the mouse button here, you can size the window, as you will see shortly.

This book uses the standard Windows terminology to guide you in using the mouse. These terms and your actions are as follows:

Term	Action
Press	Hold down a mouse button
Release	Quit pressing a mouse button
Point on	Move the mouse until the tip of the pointer is on top of the item you want
Click	Quickly press and release a mouse button once
Double-click	Press and release a mouse button twice in rapid succession
Click on	Point on an item and click
Drag	Press and hold a mouse button while you move the mouse (to move the highlight bar within a menu to the desired option, to move an object in the work area, and to highlight contiguous text you want to delete, move, or copy)
Select	Point on an item and click (the same as "click on")
Choose	Drag the pointer (and the corresponding highlight bar) to a menu option and release a mouse button

After the upcoming demonstrations of these terms, this book assumes that you know them. For example, the instruction "Select the File menu and choose the Run option" indicates that you should point on the word "File" in the menu bar, press and hold the mouse button while moving the mouse toward you to drag the highlight bar down to the "Run" option, and then release the mouse button. Practice using the mouse to perform some of these actions:

1. *Point on* the PageMaker icon by moving the mouse (and the corresponding pointer) until the pointer is resting on it.

2. *Select* the PageMaker icon by *clicking*—quickly pressing and releasing the mouse button once while pointing—on it. The title bar beneath the icon becomes highlighted, indicating it is selected.

3. *Drag* the PageMaker icon to the lower-right corner of the Windows Applications window. First point on the PageMaker icon, and then press and hold the mouse button while moving the mouse until the pointer and the icon move to the lower-right corner of the window, as shown in Figure 2-2.

4. *Drag* the PageMaker icon back to its original position.

5. *Click* on the Minimize button—the downward pointing arrowhead in the upper-right corner of the Windows Applications window. The

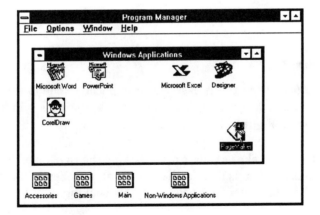

Figure 2-2.   *PageMaker icon moved to the lower-right corner*

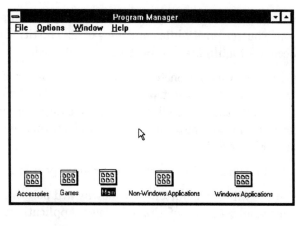

Figure 2-3.   *Windows Applications window closed to a group icon*

window closes and becomes another group icon, as is illustrated in Figure 2-3.

6. *Double-click* on the Accessories group icon in the lower-left corner of the Program Manager window. The Accessories window opens, as shown in Figure 2-4.

It sometimes takes a couple of tries to get the rhythm of double-clicking. A frequent problem is double-clicking too slowly. You will see later in this chapter how to adjust the speed of double-clicking.

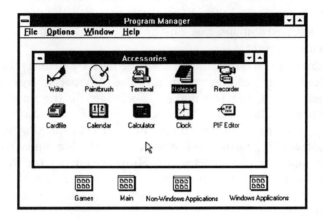

Figure 2-4.   *Accessories window open*

Using Windows

A *window* is an area of the screen that is assigned a specific purpose. There are two types of windows: *application windows,* which contain running programs or applications such as PageMaker, and *document windows,* which contain a document used with an application, such as a PageMaker publication. An application window may contain one or more document windows. The Accessories and Windows Applications windows that you have been looking at on your screen are document windows, whereas the

Program Manager window is an application window. You can tell an application window by its menu bar, which a document window does not have. Both types of window have a title bar with the window title in the middle, a Control-menu box on the left, and Minimize and Maximize buttons on the right.

Windows can be quite small (about 1/2 by 1 1/2 inches minimum), they can fill the screen, or they can be any size in between. By clicking on the Maximize button, you can make the window fill the screen. When you maximize a window, a new button, called the *Restore button,* appears in place of the Maximize button. If you click on the Restore button, you return the window to its size just before you clicked the Maximize button. As you have already seen, if you click on the Minimize button, the window shrinks to an icon at the bottom of the screen. Then, by double-clicking on an icon, you can return it to an open window that is the size it was when you minimized it.

You can make an open window any intermediate size by dragging on the border of the window. When you place the mouse pointer on top of the border around the window, the mouse pointer becomes a double-headed arrow. By pressing the main mouse button while you see the double-headed arrow and dragging the border, you can change the window size. By dragging on any side, you can change the size of the window in one dimension. By dragging on a corner, you can change the size of the window in two dimensions.

Finally, both an open application window and an application icon can be dragged anywhere on the screen. A document window can be dragged only within its application window. To drag an open window, point anywhere on the title bar of the window, except on the Control-menu box or the Minimize or Maximize buttons, and drag it where you want it. To drag an icon, point anywhere on the icon and drag it.

Practice using some of the window-sizing features with these instructions:

1. Click on the Maximize button in the far upper-right corner of the Accessories window. The Accessories window expands to fill the Program Manager window.

Notice that the title bar has changed. The title now reads "Program Manager - [Accessories]," which tells you that the Accessories window has filled the Program Manager window. Also note that the Control-menu box in the title bar is for the Program Manager while the Control-menu box in the menu bar is for the Accessories window. The menu bar belongs to the Program Manager.

2. Click on the Restore button that now appears just under the Maximize button. The Accessories window returns to its former size.

3. Click on the Maximize button of the Program Manager window. It expands to fill the screen.

4. Click on the Restore button of the Program Manager window, and the window shrinks to its former size.

5. Point on the lower-right corner of the Accessories window border. A double-headed arrow appears if you are precisely on the border.

6. Drag the lower-right corner toward the lower-right until the Accessories window is about one and one-half times its former size.

7. Drag the lower-right corner toward the upper-left until the Accessories window is about one-quarter its former size before it was enlarged, as shown in Figure 2-5.

8. Point on the title bar of the Accessories menu (anywhere but the Control-menu box and the Minimize and Maximize buttons).

9. Drag the Accessories window to the lower-right corner of the Program Manager window. Note that you cannot get out of the Program Manager window.

10. Drag the Program Manager window around the screen.

11. Click on the Minimize button of the Program Manager window. It closes to an icon at the bottom of the screen.

12. Double-click on the Program Manager icon. Notice how the Program Manager and Accessories windows open in the same location in which they closed.

13. Drag both the Accessories window and the Program Manager window back to their original positions, as shown in Figure 2-5.

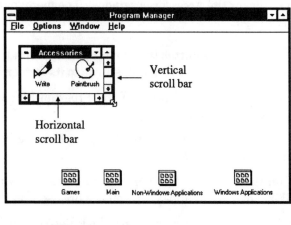

Figure 2-5. *Shrunken Accessories window*

Using Scroll Bars

A window on the screen is just that—an opening through which you can see something displayed. If what is displayed is very small, a small window can adequately display it all. If what is displayed is very large, the largest window you can create (one that covers the entire screen) may not be large enough to display it all. In that case you can horizontally or vertically move or *scroll* what the window contains.

Imagine that you are reading a billboard by looking through a stationary knothole in a high fence close to the billboard. You must move the billboard from left to right to read a full line on it, and you must move the billboard from top to bottom to read all of the lines. The *scroll bars* perform the same function for a Windows window. The scroll bars move the area being displayed (not the window itself) up or down (vertically) or left or right (horizontally).

Each of the two scroll bars has three mechanisms for moving the area being displayed. First, there are four *scroll arrows,* one at each end of each scroll bar. By clicking on one of the scroll arrows, you can move the display area in the direction of the arrow by a small increment—one line vertically. Second, there are two square *scroll boxes* in the scroll bars. By dragging a scroll box you can move the display area by a corresponding proportional amount. Third, there are the scroll bars themselves. By clicking on the scroll bars (in areas other than the scroll arrows and scroll boxes), you can move the display area in the direction corresponding to where you clicked by the height or width of one window.

Use the reduced Accessories window and the following instructions to try out the scroll bars:

1. Click on the down scroll arrow at the bottom of the vertical scroll bar. Notice that the display area moved up to display the information below that previously shown. Notice, also, that the scroll box has moved down in the scroll bar.

The position of the scroll box in the scroll bar represents the approximate position of the area displayed within the overall area. When the vertical scroll box is at the top of its scroll bar, you are looking at the top of the overall area. When the horizontal scroll box is at the left end of its scroll bar, you are looking at the left edge of the overall area. When both scroll boxes are in the middle of their scroll bars, you are looking at the middle of the overall area.

2. Click on the right scroll arrow several times until the scroll box is at the far right of the horizontal scroll bar. Your screen should look like Figure 2-6.

3. Click on the horizontal scroll bar on the left of the scroll box until the scroll box is at the far left of the scroll bar. Notice how it takes fewer clicks to move over the length of the scroll bar.

4. Drag the vertical scroll box a small amount toward the middle of the scroll bar. This allows you to move the display area in very precise increments.

The three scrolling mechanisms give you three levels of control. Clicking on the scroll bar moves the display area the furthest, dragging the scroll

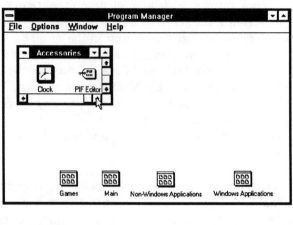

Figure 2-6.   *Accessories window scrolled to the lower-right corner*

box can move the display area in the smallest and most precise increments, and clicking on the scroll arrows moves the display area a small to intermediate amount.

Now that you can scroll the Accessories window, do so next to select an application.

Starting Applications

The Accessories window contains the icons for the various tools available in Windows 3. Each of these tools is an application that runs under Windows, just like PageMaker. To start an application you simply double-click on its icon. Do that next and work with several application windows.

1. Scroll the Accessories window until you can see the Clock icon.

2. Double-click on the Clock icon. The Clock application starts and opens a window entitled Clock, as shown in Figure 2-7.

The Clock's title bar and border are dark with light letters, while the Program Manager's title bar and border have become light with dark letters. This means that the Clock is now the active application while the Program Manager is inactive. (Your screen may differ slightly from the figures and illustrations shown in this book. That is due to the differences in displays, display adapters, and in the options you selected during Windows installation.)

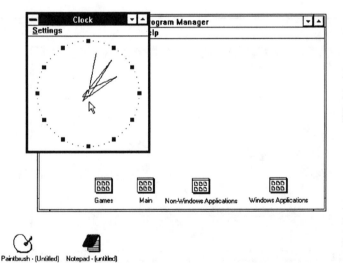

Figure 2-7.   *Clock window open*

3. Click on the Clock's Maximize button. The Clock window expands to fill the screen.

4. Click on the Restore button, and the Clock window returns to original size.

5. Drag the Clock window (by dragging on the Clock's title bar anywhere except the buttons or the Control-menu box) to the lower-right corner of the screen.

6. Click on the Accessories window to activate the Program Manager, scroll the Accessories window until you can see the Notepad icon, and then double-click on it. The Notepad application starts, and its window opens and becomes the active window, as shown in Figure 2-8.

7. Drag the Notepad window until it overlaps the Clock, if it did not originally. It should not completely cover the Clock.

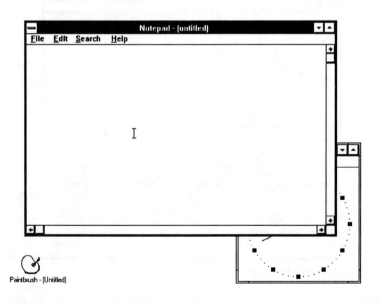

Figure 2-8. *Notepad window open*

8. Click on the Clock to activate it. Notice how it now overlaps the Notepad.

9. Click on the Notepad window to reactivate it, and then drag on the upper-left corner to reduce the size of the Notepad to about half its original size so you can see the Accessories window.

10. Click on the Accessories window to activate the Program Manager, scroll the Accessories window until you can see the Paintbrush icon, and then double-click on it. The Paintbrush application starts, and its window opens and becomes the active window.

11. Size the Paintbrush window so you can see the Clock, the Notepad, and the Program Manager windows, as shown in Figure 2-9.

You now have four applications running in Windows: the Program Manager, the Clock, the Notepad, and Paintbrush. Move them around, size

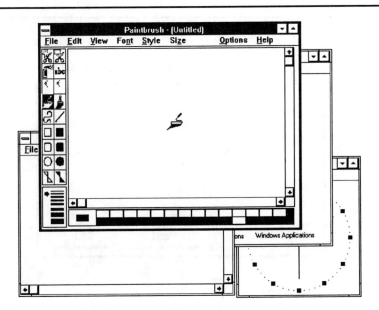

Figure 2-9.   *Paintbrush window added*

them in various ways, and activate first one and then another until you are comfortable working with multiple applications.

As you move the mouse among these windows, the mouse pointer changes. In the Paintbrush window the mouse pointer can be a paint roller, a dot, crosshairs, or several other shapes; in the Notepad window the pointer is an *I- beam;* and in the Clock and Program Manager windows the pointer is the familiar arrow. The pointer is telling you what can be done when it is in each of the various windows. With the dot in Paintbrush you can draw, while you can use the crosshairs to cut away part of a drawing. The I-beam is used with text and is thin enough so you can insert it between characters. When you click an I-beam you are establishing an *insertion point,* which determines where text you type is placed.

12. Click on the Minimize button of the Notepad, Clock, Paintbrush, and Accessories windows. The first three become application icons at the bottom of the screen, while the Accessories window becomes the now familiar group icon at the bottom of the Program Manager window, as shown in Figure 2-10.

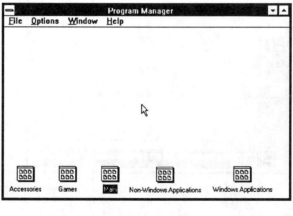

Figure 2-10.   *Application windows turned into icons*

Notice how the clock still tells time even though it has turned into an icon. This is generally true about application icons—they are running programs that are temporarily inactive. The only difference between an inactive window and an application icon is the amount of the screen they utilize and that you must double-click on an icon to activate it while you only need to click on an inactive window.

13. Drag the three application icons to reorder them or place them in other locations on the screen, just to see how you can do it. When you are done, drag them back to their original location and order, as shown in Figure 2-10.

Manipulating windows and their icons—by selecting, dragging, maximizing, minimizing, sizing, and scrolling—is one of the primary functions of the Windows environment. Practice these techniques until they are second nature. You will use them often. Another primary function of the Windows environment is the use of menus.

Using Menus

Menus are the primary device you use to give instructions to Windows and its applications. MS-DOS, by itself, is command oriented—you type commands at a system prompt. In Windows you give commands by making a choice on a menu. The menus that are available to you at any given time are shown in the menu bar. By clicking on a menu name—that is, by selecting a menu—you open a menu. By clicking on a menu option—that is, choosing an option—the option performs its function.

Menu options can represent several different functions. Often when you choose a menu option you tell the application to carry out a command, like save a file or copy something. Other menu options allow you to set parameters or defaults for the items you are working on, like selecting the size of a page to be printed or the color of an object. Still other menu options are themselves menus—in other words, selecting a menu option opens another menu. This is called *cascading menus*.

Look at several menus now and get a feel for how they operate with these instructions:

1. Click on the Program Manager File menu. It opens as shown here:

The Program Manager File menu has eight options. Several of the options ("Move..." and "Copy...", for example) are dimmed, while others are not (not in the illustration, but on your screen). Dimmed options are not available in the context of what you are doing. For example, if you do not have an open file in the current window's workspace, you cannot save a file from that window, and the "Save..." option is dim. Many of the options, such as "New...", "Copy...", and "Run...", have ellipses (...) after them. When you select such an option, a *dialog box* opens. A dialog box is a place for you to provide further information or answer questions about the option you selected. For example, if you asked to save a file but you have never provided the application with a filename, a dialog box opens asking you for the filename.

2. Click on "New..." in the File menu. A dialog box opens, asking if you want to add a new application to a group or whether you want to add a new group and what to name the program or group.

3. Click on "Cancel" to close the dialog box.

4. Click on the File menu again, and then on "Properties..." and "Run..." to look at their dialog boxes. Click on "Cancel" in each case to close the dialog box.

5. Click on the Options, Window, and Help menus in succession to look at each of them.

In the Window menu one of the listed windows has a check mark to the left of it. This means that window is currently active. One of the options of the Window menu allows you to choose the active window. When you click on your choice, a check mark is placed beside it so that the next time you open the menu you can tell which is active.

Notice that several options on the menus have a series of keystrokes to the right of their names. These are *shortcut keys*. By pressing these keys you may directly choose the menu option without first opening the menu.

Using Dialog Boxes

As you have seen, dialog boxes are a means of providing information about an option you have chosen. The dialog boxes you just looked at are rather

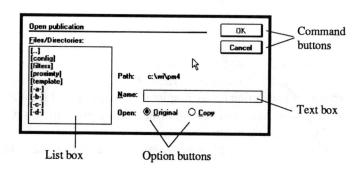

Figure 2-11.　*The Open publication dialog box*

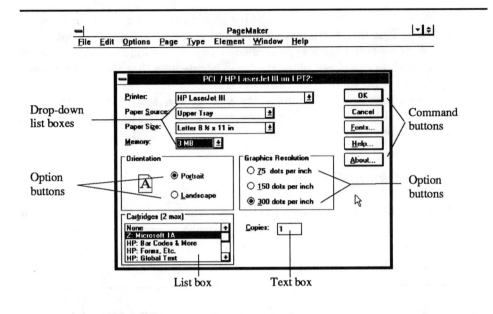

Drop-down list boxes

Command buttons

Option buttons

Option buttons

List box   Text box

Figure 2-12. *The Printer setup dialog box*

simple, with only a couple of items. Some dialog boxes can be very complex, with many different components. Windows uses several types of components to gather different types of information. These components are shown in the dialog boxes displayed in Figures 2-11, 2-12, and 2-13. These dialog boxes are used in PageMaker for opening files, setting up a printer, and setting up a page.

The various dialog box components and their usage are as follows:

Component	Usage
Check boxes	To select several items from among a series of options. Click on as many check boxes as desired to select those options. When selected, a check box will contain an "X"; otherwise the box is empty.
Command button	To take immediate action; for example, to close a dialog box, to cancel a command, or to open another or expand the current dialog box. Clicking on a

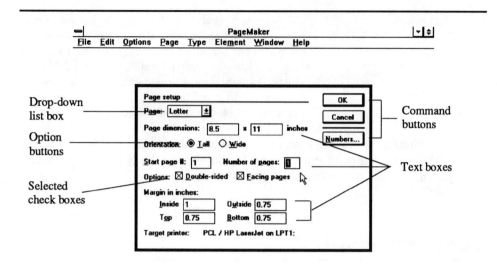

Figure 2-13. *The Page setup dialog box*

command button activates it. "OK," the most common command button, is used to close a dialog box. An ellipsis (...) indicates that a command button opens another dialog box, and a double greater-than symbol (>>) indicates a command button expands the current dialog box.

Drop-down list boxes   To select normally one item from a list in a constrained space. The current selection is shown. Clicking on the arrow that is to the right opens the drop-down list box. Click on the option that is desired, possibly using the scroll bar first.

List boxes   To select normally one item from a list. The current selection is highlighted. Click on the option desired, possibly using the scroll bar first.

Option buttons   To select one item from a set of mutually exclusive options. A selection is changed by clicking on another option.

Text boxes   To enter text, such as a filename. The mouse pointer
                                    turns into an I-beam in a text box. Clicking the mouse
                                    in a text box places an insertion point, and any text
                                    typed follows the insertion point. Without clicking an
                                    insertion point, any existing text in a selected text box
                                    is replaced by anything typed. The DEL key removes
                                    existing selected text in a text box.

Dialog boxes provide a very powerful and fast means of communicating
with Windows and its applications. It is important that you know the terms
just discussed and are comfortable using dialog boxes.

Using the Keyboard

You can do almost everything (except enter text) with a mouse, but in
several instances the keyboard provides a shortcut. You have seen how
several menu options have direct shortcut keys. You can also choose any
of the other menu options with a general keyboard procedure. You can open
any menu by pressing ALT (you do not have to hold it down) followed by the
underlined letter in the menu name. After pressing ALT you can also use
LEFT ARROW and RIGHT ARROW to highlight a menu name, and then use
DOWN ARROW to open the menu and highlight an option. After a menu is
open you can choose an option by typing the underlined letter in the option
name, or by highlighting the option with the direction keys and pressing
ENTER. ENTER can also be used to open a menu once you have highlighted
the menu name, and the F10 function key can be used in place of ALT to
initiate the process. To cancel a menu selection and return to the workspace, press ALT or F10 a second time or press ESC twice. To cancel a menu
selection but stay in the menu bar so another menu selection can be made,
press ESC.

Give the mouse a rest for a moment and access several menu options
using the keyboard as follows:

1. Press ALT-F to open the Program Manager File menu.

2. Type **R** to select the Run option. The Run dialog box opens.

3. Press TAB to move among the various fields in the dialog box, and then press ESC to cancel the dialog box, close the File menu, and deactivate the menu bar.

In general, to move around in a dialog box, you first press TAB to move through the major groups of options (normally from left to right and top to bottom), or use SHIFT-TAB to reverse the direction; alternatively, press *and hold* ALT while pressing the underlined letter in the option or group name to move directly to that option or group. Then use the direction keys to highlight an option within a group, and press SPACEBAR to make the final selection of the option. Finally, press ENTER to complete and close the dialog box. To leave a dialog box without making any changes, canceling any effect it might have, press ESC.

4. Press F10 to reactivate the menu bar.

5. Press RIGHT ARROW twice to move to the Window menu.

6. Press ENTER to open the Window menu, then press DOWN ARROW four times to highlight the second group of applications.

7. Press ENTER to select the highlighted menu item, close the menu, return to the workspace, and open the selected group window.

8. Click on the Minimize button of the open group window to shrink it once again to an icon.

Using the Control Menu

The Control menu, located in the upper-left corner of most windows and icons and some dialog boxes, allows you to perform many other Windows functions with the keyboard that you have previously learned to perform with the mouse. There are some differences among Control menus but, for the most part, the options are the same.

1. Click on the Control-menu box or press ALT-SPACEBAR to open the Control menu shown here:

The options available in this Control menu and their functions are as follows:

Option	Function
Restore	Restores the window to its size prior to its being minimized or maximized
Move	Allows you to use the keyboard to move the window
Size	Allows sizing the window with the keyboard
Minimize	Minimizes the window size to an icon
Maximize	Maximizes the window size, normally to fill the screen
Close	Closes the window
Switch To...	Switches among the currently running applications and allows rearrangement of their icons and windows

Additional options that are available on other Control menus are as follows:

Option	Function
Edit	Opens an Edit menu with four options (non-Windows applications in 386 enhanced mode only):
	Mark Allows you to select text to be copied to the Clipboard
	Copy Copies text to the Clipboard
	Paste Copies the contents of the Clipboard to the insertion point in the active document window
	Scroll Scrolls the active document window
Next	Switches to the next open document window or document icon (on document windows only)
Paste	Copies the contents of the Clipboard to the insertion point in the active document window (real and standard mode only)
Settings	Allows you to enter settings for multitasking (non-Windows applications in 386 enhanced mode only)

Try several of the Control menu options now using the keyboard and these instructions:

2. Press DOWN ARROW to highlight "Move", and press ENTER to choose it. The pointer becomes a four-headed arrow.

3. Press one or more of the direction keys to move the window in the direction you choose. An outline shows you where you are going.

4. When the outline of the window is where you want it, press ENTER. Should you want to cancel the move, press ESC before pressing ENTER.

5. Press ALT-SPACEBAR to reopen the Control menu of the Program Manager (the active window).

6. Press DOWN ARROW twice to highlight "Size", and press ENTER to choose it. The pointer becomes a four-headed arrow.

7. Press one arrow key to select one side whose size you want to change, or press two direction keys simultaneously to select two sides whose sizes you want to change. (Pressing two direction keys simultaneously is the same as selecting a corner with the mouse.)

8. Press one or two arrows until the window is the size you want it, and then press ENTER. Should you want to cancel the sizing, press ESC before pressing ENTER.

9. Press ALT-SPACEBAR to reopen the Program Manager Control menu.

10. Type **X** to choose "Maximize." The Program Manager window expands to fill the screen.

11. Press ALT-SPACEBAR to open the Program Manager Control menu, and press ENTER to choose "Restore." The Program Manager window returns to original size.

12. Press ALT-SPACEBAR again, and type **N** to choose "Minimize." The Program Manager window shrinks to an icon.

13. Press ALT-ESC to cycle through the various application icons (or windows if any were open). When you have reached the Program Manager again, press ALT-SPACEBAR to open the Control menu.

14. Press ENTER to choose "Restore." The Program Manager window reopens at its last size and location.

15. Press CTRL-F6 or CTRL-TAB to cycle through the various document (group) icons (or windows, if any are open).

16. When you reach Main, press ALT-- (hyphen) to open the Main group Control menu.

17. Choose "Restore" by pressing ENTER since "Restore" is already highlighted. Your screen should look like that shown in Figure 2-14.

Notice that to open Control menus and to cycle through windows and icons, you use different key combinations for application windows than you do for document windows. Use ALT-SPACEBAR to open an application window Control menu, and use ALT-ESC to cycle through application windows and icons. Use ALT-- (hyphen) to open a document window Control menu, and use CTRL-F6 or CTRL-TAB to cycle through the document windows and icons in the active application window.

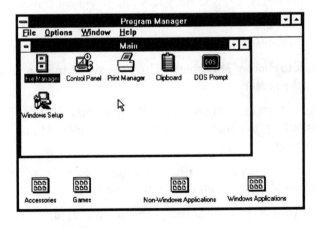

Figure 2-14.   *Main group displayed in the Program Manager window*

One important Control menu option you have not tried yet is "Close". In most windows, "Close" simply closes the window. With the Program Manager, "Close" closes Windows and returns you to DOS. You will do that later in the chapter. Once the Control menu is open, you can choose "Close" in the normal ways: by clicking on it, by highlighting it and pressing ENTER, or by typing **C**. You can choose "Close" with the Control menu closed by double-clicking on the Control-menu box or by pressing ALT-F4. The other Control menu options ("Switch To...", "Edit...", "Next", "Paste", and "Settings...") are not relevant to PageMaker and thus are beyond the scope of this book.

The keyboard and the Control menu are important adjuncts to the mouse. But they should be viewed as that and not the other way around. With Windows and PageMaker the mouse is by far the most effective and expeditious way to do most things. For that reason, this book usually has instructions for the mouse. Keyboard instructions normally are given only for shortcut keys when you are already typing on the keyboard.

Using the Main Group Applications

The Main application group, which should currently be displayed on your screen, includes the following six applications:

Application	Function
File Manager	To view and manipulate files (replaces MS-DOS Executive in previous versions of Windows).
Control Panel	To set defaults such as color, double-click speed, and date and time.
Print Manager	To manage the queuing and printing of files.
Clipboard	To display the contents of the Clipboard.
DOS Prompt	To provide a DOS command-line prompt at which any DOS command can be entered. Type **exit** to return to Windows.
Windows Setup	To make changes to the hardware and software configuration you are using with windows.

Take a brief look now at two of these applications that are of value with PageMaker: the Control Panel and the File Manager.

Setting Defaults
With the Control Panel

The Control Panel is the primary place in Windows where you set the parameters or defaults that tell Windows how you want a number of different functions handled. Open the Control panel now and look at the options.

1. Double-click on the Control Panel icon. The Control Panel opens as shown here:

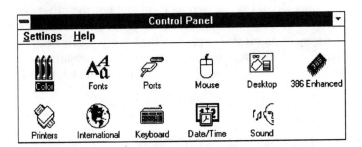

The Control Panel consists of 10 to 12 functions, each with its own icon, for which you can set defaults. The icons and the functions they set are as follows:

Icon	Functions Set
Color	Colors associated with the various parts of the screen
Fonts	Fonts available for both screen and printer(s)
Ports	Communications parameters used with serial ports
Mouse	Behavior of the mouse, including the double-click rate, the speed the pointer moves across the screen, and whether the left or right mouse key is the main mouse button
Desktop	Characteristics of the screen or "desktop," including the cursor blink rate, the presence or absence of a "magnetic" grid to better align objects, and the patterns used for various areas
Network	Parameters applicable to your network (available only if you are using a network)
Printers	Parameters applicable to your printer(s), including ports assigned, paper size and orientation, graphics resolution, and the identification of the default printer

Icon	Functions Set
International	Formats for numbers, currency, dates, and time
Keyboard	Keyboard repeat rate
Date/Time	System date and time
Sound	Presence or absence of the warning sound or beep
386 Enhanced	Sharing of peripheral devices and system resources in multitasking environment (available only if you are using 386 enhanced mode)

You can set any function by selecting the appropriate icon (double-click on it) and then entering the necessary parameters in the dialog box that opens. Try that now by setting the double-click rate of the mouse.

2. Double-click on the Mouse icon in the Control Panel. The Mouse dialog box opens, as shown here:

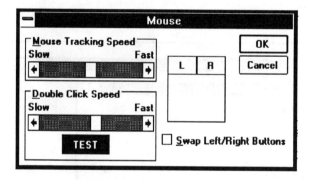

3. If you are left-handed and want to make the right mouse button the main mouse button, click on the check box at the bottom of the screen labeled "Swap Left/Right Buttons." To reverse this you must now click with the right mouse button.

4. Double-click on the "Test" command button. If the button darkens, the double-click speed is set correctly.

5. If the Test button does not darken, you must change the speed. Click on either the "Slow" or "Fast" scroll arrow, whichever is correct for you, and try double-clicking again.

6. Repeat steps 4 and 5 until the double-clicking speed is set correctly.

7. When you are done with the Mouse settings, click on "OK" to close the dialog box and return to the Control Panel window.

On your own, look at the other Control Panel functions. You will find you can do a lot to tailor Windows to your tastes. Unless you want to change something, click on "Cancel" in each dialog box so you cannot change anything inadvertently.

8. When you are done with the Control Panel, double-click on the Control Panel Control-menu box in the upper-left corner. This will close the Control Panel and return you to the Main group window of the Program Manager.

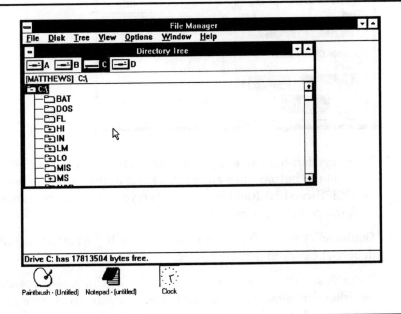

Figure 2-15.   *File Manager and root directory tree*

Creating a Directory With the File Manager

The File Manager provides all of the customary DOS file-handling commands, such as COPY, DELETE, and RENAME, as well as a number of file manipulation tools that have only been available with such packages as Xtree and PC Tools. Open the File Manager now, and create a new directory named PUB to store your PageMaker publications.

1. Double-click on the File Manager icon in the Main group window of the Program Manager. The File Manager window opens, and a directory tree window for your root directory also opens, as shown in Figure 2-15.

The directory tree provides a very powerful way of viewing and working with your directories and their files. In the initial view of your directories, you will see an alphabetical list of all of the subdirectories under your root directory. Each of the directories are represented by a file folder. The root directory's file folder has a minus sign in it, which means that if you click on the root directory's file folder, you will collapse all of the subdirectories into the root directory. Some of the other file folders have plus signs in them, which means that they have subdirectories, and if you click on them their subdirectories open, as shown here:

Other directory file folders are empty, which means they do not have subdirectories under them. You may open and list the files and subdirectories in any directory by double-clicking on the folder icon. For example, when you double-click on the DOS directory folder, you get this directory window:

```
📁[..]                    📄 COUNTRY.SYS          ☐FC.EXE              ☐
📄4201.CPI                ☐DEBUG.COM              ☐FDISK.EXE           📄
📄4208.CPI                ☐DISKCOMP.COM           ☐FILESYS.EXE         ☐
📄5202.CPI                ☐DISKCOPY.COM           ☐FIND.EXE            📄
📄ANSI.SYS                📄DISPLAY.SYS            ☐FORMAT.COM          ☐
☐APPEND.EXE               ☐DOSSHELL.BAT           ☐GRAFTABL.COM        ☐
☐ASSIGN.COM               📄DRIVER.SYS             ☐GRAPHICS.COM        ☐
☐ATTRIB.EXE               ☐EDLIN.COM              📄GRAPHICS.PRO        ☐
☐BACKUP.COM               📄EGA.CPI                ☐GWBASIC.EXE         ☐
☐CHKDSK.COM               📄EMM386.SYS             📄HIMEM.SYS          ☐
☐COMMAND.COM              ☐EXE2BIN.EXE            ☐IFSFUNC.EXE         📄
☐COMP.COM                 ☐FASTOPEN.EXE           ☐JOIN.EXE            📄
```

In a directory window, of which you can have as many as you like, you can select or highlight files you want to move, copy, rename, or delete. For moving and copying, have both the source and destination directories open and visible. Point on the file icon you want to move or copy. Then to move a file, press and hold ALT while dragging the file icon from the source directory to the destination directory. To copy a file, press and hold CTRL while dragging the file icon. If you wish to move, copy, rename, or delete several files at one time and the files are listed sequentially, click on the first filename, and then press and hold SHIFT while clicking on the last filename in the sequence. If you want to select several files that are not in sequence, press and hold CTRL while clicking on each item. To cancel a selected item, press and hold CTRL while clicking on the item. To delete or rename files, select the files and then choose the appropriate command from the File menu.

The File menu provides access to several other file functions, as you can see in Figure 2-16. Among these functions is creating a directory. Use the "Create Directory..." command now to create a directory called PUB to store your PageMaker publications.

2. Click on the File Manager File menu to open it.

3. Click on "Create Directory..." to choose that option. The Create Directory dialog box opens, as shown here:

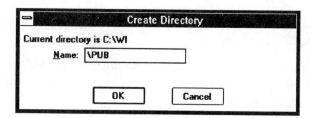

If you are in the directory under which you wish to create a new subdirectory, all you would need to type is the new subdirectory name. Otherwise you need to type the full pathname of the new subdirectory.

4. Type **pub** or, if necessary, precede it with the pathname, as in **c:\wi\pub**. (You may have already done this in Appendix A.)

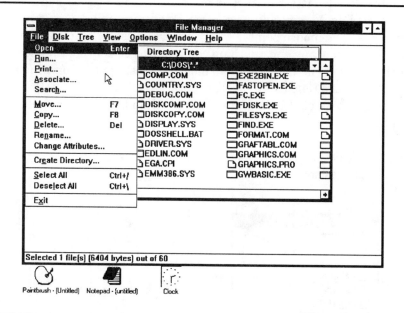

Figure 2-16.   *File Manager File menu*

5. Press ENTER to close the dialog box, create the directory, and return you to the File Manager window.

6. When you are done with the File Manager, double-click on its Control-menu box to close it and return you to the Main group window of the Program Manager.

Getting Help

Windows 3 on-line help is very extensive and context sensitive— it tries to provide specific help about what you are doing. You can get help by several methods. The fastest method is to press F1. You'll get an index for using help. In PageMaker, and most other Windows applications, you can also press F9. The mouse pointer will become a question mark, which you can click on something and anything you want to get help on. Another method of getting help is to use the Help menu on most application windows. You can access the Help menu by either clicking on it or pressing ALT-H. Do that next, and look at the Program Manager Help facility with these instructions:

1. Click on Help in the menu bar. The Program Manager Help menu opens, as shown here:

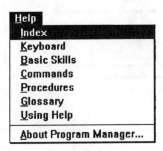

Most Help menus within Windows 3 have the same set of options. These options and the information they provide are as follows:

Option	Information Provided
Index	Topics covered in alphabetical order
Keyboard	Keys used to perform various functions
Commands	Explanations of all commands
Procedures	Descriptions of procedures to accomplish various functions
Using Help	Tutorial on how to use Help
About	Information about the application and your system resources

For example, if you want information about the keys used with menus, proceed with these steps:

2. Click on Index. A window appears, as shown in Figure 2-17, asking you to choose between the Program Manager help index and Windows help index.

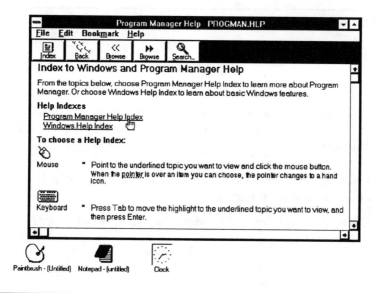

Figure 2-17. *Index to Windows and Program Manager Help*

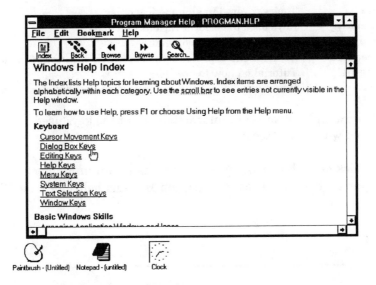

Figure 2-18.   *Windows Help Index window*

In help windows you make a choice by clicking on the underlined topic. When the pointer is pointing on a topic that can be chosen, it becomes a pointing hand.

3. Click on "Windows Help Index". The Windows Help Index window opens, as shown in Figure 2-18.

4. Click on "Menu Keys". The Menu Keys help window opens, as shown in Figure 2-19.

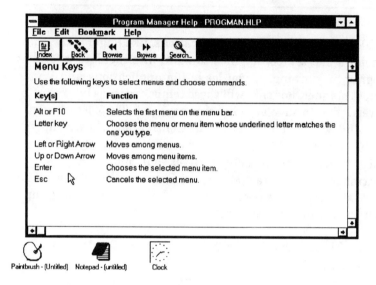

Figure 2-19.   *Menu Keys help window*

The command buttons at the top of a help window return you to the index, retrace the path you have taken to get to the current help window, allow you to browse through related topics either before or after the current topic, or allow you to search for a topic.

5. Use the "Help" command buttons on your own to review the Windows 3 Help facility.

6. When you are done reviewing "Help" double-click on the Control-menu box to close Help. You return to the Main group window of the Program Manager.

Leaving Windows

Windows 3 and many of the applications, like PageMaker, that run under Windows use temporary files to store intermediate information as the program is running. If you leave the applications and Windows in the correct manner, not only will these temporary files be erased, but you will be reminded to save any files you have not. The correct manner to leave any window is to double-click on its Control-menu box. Simply do this until you are out to the DOS prompt and you have correctly left Windows. Then, and only then, you can safely turn off your computer.

Arrange your Program Manager window the way you want it to be when you next use Windows—with the Windows Applications group open—and then leave Windows with these instructions:

1. Double-click on the Control-menu box of the Main group window to close it.

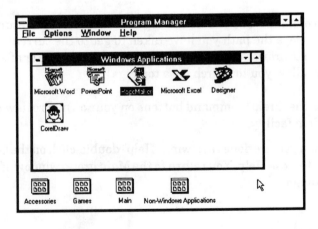

Figure 2-20. *Program Manager and Windows Applications windows in final position*

2. Double-click on the Windows Applications group icon to open it.

3. Size and position the two windows and icons in those windows (not the icons at the bottom of the screen) so they look approximately like Figure 2-20.

4. Double-click on the Program Manager Control-menu box. You will be asked to confirm you want to leave Windows and save the current Windows configuration. (If you do not want to save the current Windows configuration, click on the check box to remove the "X".) Click on "OK" to proceed with leaving Windows. You return to the DOS prompt.

This chapter has laid a foundation on which you can now begin to add specific knowledge of PageMaker. Windows is not a simple subject, but it provides a very powerful framework that is fully utilized by PageMaker. You now have enough knowledge of that framework to use it in PageMaker. You'll do that in Chapter 3 as you build a flyer.

3 *Getting Started With a Flyer*

In this chapter you'll use PageMaker to create a flyer, the most basic of advertising pieces. This gives you an opportunity to review the basic functions of PageMaker before proceeding to more advanced features. The purpose of a flyer is to inform people about a subject as succinctly as possible. A flyer is rarely longer than one page, although it may be printed on both sides. The flyer you create here is the one-page, single-sided publication shown in Figure 3-1.

There are many different ways to create a flyer, from writing it by hand to printing it in four colors. Here you'll produce a single-color flyer with a shaded rectangular border and a line across it. Also, you'll use three fonts to produce the text (or *copy*).

PageMaker is an excellent tool for building a flyer because you can create the complete publication without using other applications. You can draw the rectangle, apply the shading, draw the line, and produce the copy in three fonts, all within PageMaker. You can produce the copy in a word processor and then "place" that copy on the flyer using PageMaker; however, it is easier to produce a small amount of copy within PageMaker and save having to switch between applications.

CREATIVE
DESIGNS

Creative Designs specializes in the design, production, and promotion of all forms of printed material.

Creative Designs uses the latest in computer technology to design the initial layouts, typeset the necessary copy, and perform the final page composition. We then use the latest in four-color presses and bindery equipment to produce the highest quality work obtainable. In addition, we have extensive direct mail marketing and fulfillment services available.

Creative Designs can help you with any of the following:

- BOOKS
- MANUALS
- BROCHURES
- NEWSLETTERS
- BUSINESS PLANS
- ANNUAL REPORTS
- BUSINESS FORMS
- FLYERS
- POSTERS
- CATALOGS
- PAMPHLETS
- NEWSPAPERS
- PRESENTATIONS
- MAILING LABELS
- OR ANYTHING THAT CAN BE PRINTED

Call us at 1-800-555-5000 (nationwide) or stop in at our new plant at 1900 Westwind Avenue, Oceanside, WA 98999.

Figure 3-1. *The finished flyer*

Planning and Designing the Flyer

Because the flyer is fairly simple, planning it is also simple and straight-forward. The content is basic information about the capabilities and products of a hypothetical company named Creative Designs. You can produce the flyer in a couple of hours. Except for your time and the overhead associated with using the computer, your only direct cost is the printing. If you print the flyers on a laser printer, the cost is 4 to 6 cents per page, depending on how you amortize the printer. That is fairly expensive for larger volumes. If you want to print several thousand copies, you can take the output of the laser printer master page to a commercial printer and have it printed on an offset press for considerably less cost per page.

The design is not very complex either. Your design constraints are the limitations of the fonts that you have available and the 8 1/2 x 11-inch page size of a laser printer. These are not absolute limitations—there are ways around them; however, for this flyer the 8 1/2 x 11-inch page size and your fonts should be adequate. Because you have a single page, you need not design a master page. The regular page has a shaded, rounded corner rectangle with a line across it. The text consists of a company name, a descriptive body, and a bulleted list of products. The company name is 60-point sans serif typeface, such as Helvetica or Gill Sans, in a bold italic style with 66 points of leading (spacing between lines). The body text is a 12-point serif typeface, such as Times Roman or Times New Roman, in a medium weight with PageMaker's automatic leading (12,14.4), and the bulleted list of products is an 18-point sans serif typeface, such as Helvetica or Gill Sans, in a bold style, with automatic leading (18/21.6).

The actual fonts that you use are not critical. Your purpose here is to practice putting together the flyer and to get an idea of what it looks like. The only consequence of using different fonts is that the letter spacing may be different than that shown here. The Adobe Times New Roman and Gill Sans that are shipped with PageMaker 4 are used in this book and work well for this flyer, but you may choose to use other fonts.

Once you have planned and designed the flyer, your primary remaining tasks are to create the text and make up the page. To do that, you must first bring up PageMaker. Before beginning the actual work on the flyer, however, take a brief look at PageMaker's menus and other facilities.

Starting PageMaker

If you have not installed PageMaker, turn to Appendix A, "Installing Windows and PageMaker," and follow the instructions to complete installation.

Once you install Windows and PageMaker, you have directories on your hard disk for each of these products. If you followed the instructions in Appendix A, you have a Windows directory named WI and subdirectories for Windows itself (W3) and for PageMaker (PM4). In addition, if you followed the instructions in either Appendix A or Chapter 2, "Using Windows and the Mouse," you have created another subdirectory under WI named PUB to hold the publications produced using this book. The instructions in this and the remaining chapters assume that you are using this directory scheme. If you choose to use a different scheme, you must make the necessary corrections to the instructions.

Use your normal method of starting your computer, Windows, and PageMaker. (You can refer again to the startup discussion in Appendix A if necessary.) When PageMaker comes up you should see the PageMaker application window shown in Figure 3-2.

Now that you are in PageMaker, let's review the menus before starting on the flyer.

Reviewing PageMaker's Menus

The PageMaker application window shown in Figure 3-2 uses the standard Windows format that you saw in Chapter 2. At the top of the screen is a title bar with a Control-menu box on the left and the Minimize and Maximize buttons on the right. Below that is the work area, where the publication that you are working on will be displayed.

The eight PageMaker menus allow you to direct PageMaker to do what you want. The menus function like they do in other Windows applications. You select a menu by pointing on it with the mouse pointer and then pressing the main mouse button (normally the left button). You choose a menu option by either clicking on it or holding the main mouse button down, and then dragging the pointer downward until the menu option you want is highlighted and releasing the button. You can also use the standard

Figure 3-2.   *The PageMaker application window*

ALT key combinations to select a menu and shortcut keys to invoke some of the menu options.

The following paragraphs discuss each of the menus and most shortcut keys. As you read, select the menu being discussed and view it on your own screen. Notice that some options are dark, while others are dim. You can choose only the dark options at this time. The dim options are available only under certain circumstances (for example, you need an active publication to choose "Save"). The individual options are explained as they are used. Here they are just introduced.

File Menu   The File menu contains the standard Windows options: "New...", "Open...", "Save", and "Print...". In addition, PageMaker has "Close" to close the current publication but keep PageMaker active, "Save as..." to name or rename a publication, "Revert" to load the last saved copy of the publication currently in the work area, "Export..." to save a text file from a publication to a word processor, "Place..." to pick up text or graphics created outside of PageMaker, "Links..." to reconnect or set options for the links joining a PageMaker publication with the text and graphic files that built it, "Book..." to group several publications into a book, "Page setup..." to establish primary page parameters such as size and margins, "Target printer..." to choose the printer you want to use, and "Exit" to close both a publication and PageMaker.

The "New...", "Open...", "Save", "Place...", "Print...", and "Exit" options have shortcut keys, which are shown in the menu as a caret (^) and the letters N, O, S, D, P, and Q. The caret represents the CTRL key. To use these shortcut keys, press and hold CTRL while typing an **n, o, s, d, p,** or **q.** In this book these commands are represented as CTRL-N, CTRL-O, CTRL-S, CTRL-D, CTRL-P, and CTRL-Q. The "Links..." option has a shortcut key shown in the menu as Sh^D. The "Sh" represents the SHIFT key. In this book the "Links..." shortcut is represented as SHIFT-CTRL-D.

File	Edit	Option	
New...			^N
Open...			^O
Close			
Save			^S
Save as...			
Revert			
Export...			
Place...			^D
Links...			Sh^D
Book...			
Page setup...			
Print...			^P
Target printer...			
Exit			^Q

Edit Menu The Edit menu has the standard "Cut", "Copy", and "Paste" commands to delete, copy, and move selected text or graphics. The shortcut keys for "Cut" and "Paste", SHIFT-DEL and SHIFT-INS, are used as they were in Windows. To cut out a word, for example, select it with the mouse and then press SHIFT-DEL. To move this item to a new location, move the insertion point to that location by clicking the mouse there and pressing

SHIFT-INS. To *copy* rather than *move* the item, choose "Copy" (or press CTRL-INS) instead of "Cut" (or SHIFT-DEL). Cut or copied items go into an area of memory known as the Clipboard, which allows them to be moved or copied onto either the current publication or another one. The "Clear" option, or the DEL key, lets you delete a selected item without putting it on the Clipboard. This preserves the current contents of the Clipboard, as a new item replaces the previous item; that is, the Clipboard holds only one item at a time.

The "Undo" option of the Edit menu is particularly useful. You can change your mind, canceling your most recent command, unless it deals with files, lines, or shading. If you have not selected or deselected an item or moved to another page, you can undo such actions as moving a block of text, cropping a graphic, or changing the page setup. Usually you must choose "Undo" *immediately* after the command in order to correct it.

The "Select all" option allows you to select all the text and graphics on a page. "Find...", "Find next", and "Change..." are used in the Story Editor (described later) to locate or replace text or formatting, and "Spelling..." activates the spelling checker in the Story Editor. "Preferences..." lets you choose the unit of measure—inches, millimeters, picas, ciceros, and several other elements. The "Edit story" option allows you to switch between layout and story views. The story view, new with PageMaker 4, provides access to the Story Editor, which gives you greater speed and several word processing tools not available in the normal layout view.

Edit	**O**ptions	**Pa**
Undo All Bksp		

Cut	Sh Del
Copy	^Ins
Paste	Sh Ins
Clear	Del
Select all	^A
Find...	^8
Find next	Sh^9
Change...	^9
Spelling...	^L
Preferences...	
Edit story	^E

Options Menu With the Options menu you can turn on or off several screen options, such as rulers and guides. You can also add column guides (using "Column guides"), lock the zero point ("Zero lock") and the guides ("Lock guides"), and control the manner in which text flows across columns and pages and around graphics ("Autoflow"). You can also turn on or off a magnetic property of guides and rulers with "Snap to guides" and "Snap to rulers". Finally, from the Options menu you can create either a table of contents ("Create TOC...") or an index ("Create index") and add to or show the index ("Index entry..." or "Show index..."). You use a number of these options later in this chapter where they are explained further.

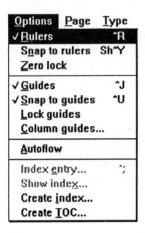

Page Menu The Page menu offers seven options for changing the page size in a window, from viewing a page that has been reduced to 25 percent of its normal size to viewing a full page, to viewing a part of a page that has been enlarged to 400 percent of its actual size. The Page menu also allows you to "Insert pages..." to and "Remove pages..." from a publication. With "Go to page..." or its shortcut key, CTRL-G, you can bring up a particular page. Finally, this menu allows you to turn on or off the display of items from the master page ("Display master items"), such as guides and headings, and to copy master guides to a new page.

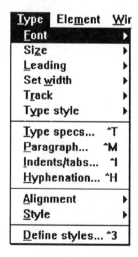

Type Menu   The Type menu allows you to select and change the typeface, size, and style. You control all aspects of type from this menu, including the leading, alignment, indents, tabs, hyphenation, and spacing. The Type menu is covered in some depth later in this chapter.

Element Menu   The Element menu controls the width and style of lines used in drawing lines, rectangles, circles, or ovals as well as the shade or pattern used to fill a rectangle or circle. Most of the suboptions below the first two options ("Line" and "Fill") on the Element menu are obvious except, possibly, the "None" option in the Line submenu and the "Paper" option in the Fill submenu. Occasionally (when you build the order form in Chapter 4, for example) you may want to add shading without a visible border or rectangle. To do this, draw a rectangle with the "None" line option and then add shading. "Paper" shading is an opaque absence of any shading that covers up what is beneath it. You will see how it is used later in this chapter.

Additional options on the Element menu include "Bring to front" and "Send to back", which allow you to change the relative position of a selected item; "Text rotation...", to rotate selected text in 90-degree increments; "Text wrap...", to control how text wraps around graphics; "Image control...", to control the contrast on scanned graphics; "Rounded corners...", to change the degree of rounded corners on rounded-edge rectangles; "Define colors...", to define the colors to be applied to graphics and text; and "Link info..." and "Link options...", to maintain the links set up between a publication and the individual text and graphic files used to create the publication.

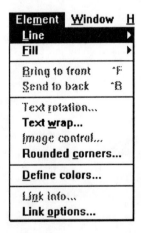

Window Menu   The Window menu provides the means of turning on or off several ancillary windows and other features, such as the "Toolbox,"

"Scroll bars", "Style palette", and the "Color palette". You'll work at length with the Toolbox later in this chapter. The Window menu also allows you to arrange several icons.

Help Menu The Help menu is the gateway to PageMaker's extensive on-line help system. This system not only provides help on every command and many topics, but also provides help on using Help. Select the Help menu now, choose "Index...", and click on "Using PageMaker Help". Read the screen that appears, and click the downward-pointing arrow to read the complete article. You can get context-sensitive help (help that is related to whatever you are doing) at almost any time by simply pressing SHIFT-F1. The mouse pointer will turn into a question mark that you can click on a menu option or some other item on the screen to get help on that item. Double-click on the Control menu or choose "Exit" from the File menu to leave Help and return to what you were doing when you called Help.

The Help menu contains another option, "About PageMaker", that provides the PageMaker version number and other information about PageMaker.

Before you begin building the flyer, you have one more preliminary task to perform—the printer setup procedure.

Setting Up the Printer

PageMaker tries to display on the screen what it is going to print. To do this, it must know which printer you will use. PageMaker maintains a list of the printers that you specified when you installed Windows, and that list can include several printers. You therefore must specify the target printer for the publication that you are going to build. To do this, select the File menu shown here from the menu bar, and then execute the following steps.

1. Choose the "Target printer..." option. After selecting "File" in the menu bar, press and hold the main mouse button and drag the mouse down until "Target printer..." is highlighted, as shown in the next illustration. Then release the main mouse button.

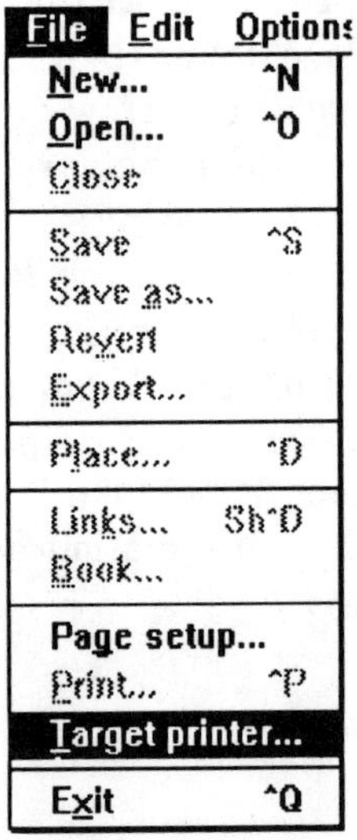

File	**Edit**	**Option**s
New...		^N
Open...		^O
Close		
Save		^S
Save as...		
Revert		
Export...		
Place...		^D
Links...		Sh^D
Book...		
Page setup...		
Print...		^P
Target printer...		
E**x**it		^Q

You see the list of printers that you established during installation. The illustration shows two printers installed. The HP LaserJet will be used here. If you have more printers than can be displayed in the list box, use the scroll bar beside the list to scroll to the printer you want (click on the downward-pointing arrow).

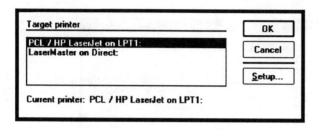

2. From the Target printer list box, using the scroll bar if necessary, double-click on the printer that you want to use or click on the Setup command button.

   The Printer specifications dialog box shown in Figure 3-3 opens. In this dialog box you describe the printer options that you will use in the publication. It displays the options for the HP LaserJet Series II. You will want to set your defaults to fit your printer.

3. Choose the appropriate settings for your printer by clicking the desired option buttons and making selections from the list boxes.

4. If you need to, click on the Fonts command button, and the Soft Font Installer appears.

   The Soft Font Installer gives you a means of storing fonts on floppies. With the small amount of space taken up by the new scalable fonts used by the Adobe Type Manager (ATM), you should not have to do that.

5. When you are done with the Soft Font Installer, click on "Exit".

6. When you have completed printer setup, click on "OK".

7. Click on "OK" again to close the Target printer dialog box. You are now ready to begin constructing the flyer.

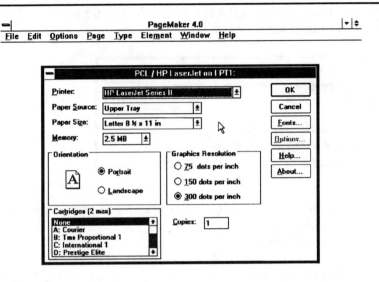

Figure 3-3.   *The HP LaserJet Printer specifications dialog box*

Creating the Layout

The first step in building the flyer is to create the layout grid. This is a
system of dotted lines that includes the margins and other guides that
appear on your screen but do not print. These guides help you place text
and graphics on a page. You begin the layout by creating a new publication
and establishing the page setup. To create a new publication, select File
and choose "New", as shown here:

```
File  Edit  Options
New...         ^N
Open...        ^O
Close

Save           ^S
Save as...
Revert
Export...

Place...       ^D

Links...      Sh^D
Book...

Page setup...
Print..        ^P
Target printer...

Exit           ^Q
```

Establishing the Page Setup

When you request a new publication, PageMaker displays the Page setup dialog box shown in Figure 3-4.

The Page setup dialog box allows you to determine the page size and orientation (whether the text is oriented horizontally or vertically on the page), whether the pages are double-sided, the number of pages (and how they are numbered), and the margin sizes. PageMaker has already filled in the dialog box with the default values. You can recognize the defaults by the highlighted option buttons (black dots in a circle), checked boxes, or the data in the text boxes such as the margins. For the flyer, you can accept the defaults except the margins. You don't want the double-sided option, which is the default, but the flyer only has one page, so it doesn't matter.

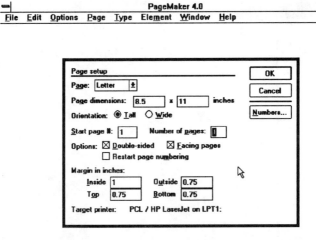

Figure 3-4.   *The initial Page setup dialog box*

The margins you will use for the flyer are 1 inch on either side and 1.25 inches on the top and bottom. Because the inside margin is already 1 inch, you must change only the other three. Follow these instructions to make those changes:

1. Point on and drag across the "0.75" in the Outside text box.

The "0.75" becomes highlighted, and when you next enter a value, it replaces the highlighted contents.

2. Type **1** and press TAB.

The pointer moves to the Top text box, the top margin is highlighted, and you can now change it.

3. Type **1.25** and press TAB to move to the Bottom text box.

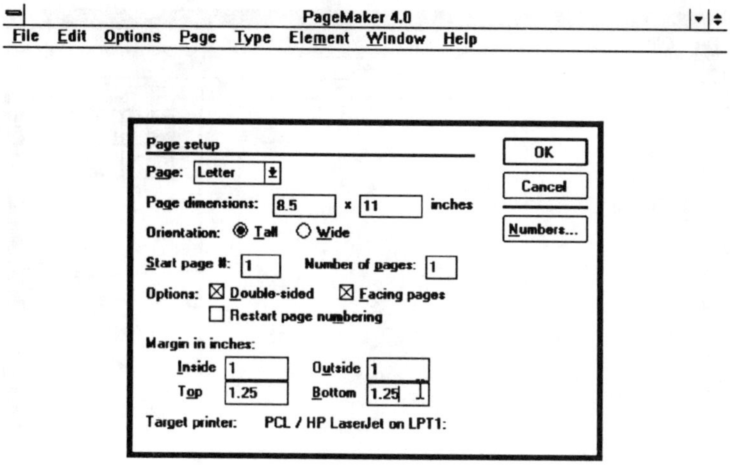

Figure 3-5.   *The final Page setup dialog box*

4. Again type **1.25**.

Your Page setup dialog box now looks like that shown in Figure 3-5.

5. Press ENTER or click on "OK" to complete the dialog box and return to the work area.

Upon returning, you see the outline of the flyer displayed in the center of the work area, as shown in Figure 3-6. The margins that you just set are shown as a dotted rectangle within that outline. The flyer has been sized so that you can see the entire page within the window. Recall that the Page menu offers several alternative sizes for viewing the publication. The current display allows you to see the total page on the screen (with the "Fit in window" option). The text in this view is very small, and most of it cannot be read; however, the page area displayed is large, allowing you to see the total page. The opposite extreme is the "400 percent size" option, which

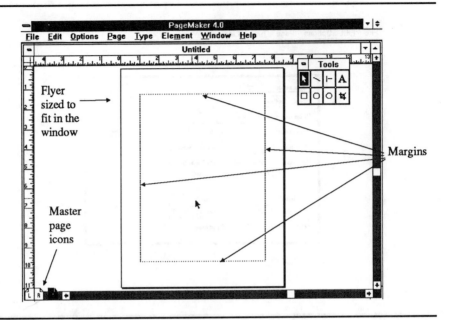

Figure 3-6.   *The flyer sized with "Fit in window"*

makes the text very large and the area very small, allowing you to see only a small portion of the page.

The area surrounding the flyer is called the *pasteboard*. You can use it as a temporary holding and work area by cutting and pasting or dragging items to and from the publication and the pasteboard. In the lower-left corner is a series of icons representing the master and regular pages. The page icons with an "L" and an "R" represent left-facing and right-facing master pages. You will not be using the master pages in this application, of course, because the flyer contains only one page. The regular page icon, containing the numeral 1, is the current page in the work area. You know that because the icon is highlighted. If you specify more pages in the Page setup dialog box, a numbered icon for each page appears (up to the limit of the screen). To switch back and forth between pages, click the appropriate page icon. Because there is only one page in the flyer, only one page icon appears.

In the upper-right corner of the work area is a window labeled "Tools". This Toolbox contains eight tools. The most commonly used tool is the *pointer* (or arrow) in the upper-left box that is highlighted. It is used for pointing and selecting items both in the work area and on the menus. The capital "A" in the upper-right box represents the *text tool*. It is used for adding, deleting, and editing text. Below the text tool is the *cropping tool*, which is used to trim the sides of a graphic. The other tools are used to draw straight lines, perpendicular lines, rectangles, rounded-corner rectangles, and circles or ovals. These tools are discussed at length in this and subsequent chapters.

The next step is to add and adjust the guides.

Adding Guides

PageMaker allows you to draw nonprinting lines on the page so you can precisely align text and graphics. These lines, which are easily moved, are most useful when placed according to exact measurements, as on a ruler. Both vertical and horizontal rulers are useful, and PageMaker has them, as shown in Figure 3-6. These are used to precisely place the guides on a page. As you move the mouse, you see a faint dotted line move in each of the rulers. The *zero point* on each ruler corresponds to the upper-left corner of the page. Consequently, the rulers give you the precise measurement of where the pointer is, regardless of where you move it on the page. When you change the image size, the rulers' dimensions change accordingly. Experiment with the rulers until you are comfortable with them.

Using the rulers, you can see how the margins exactly fit the measurements set in the page setup of 1.25 inches on the top and bottom and 1 inch on each side.

Column Guides   In addition to the margins, you may have columns for aligning text within the margins. PageMaker assumes that the margins you established are the edges of your text and places a default set of *column guides* in the left and right margins, creating between them one column equal in size to the page width, less the margins. In this case, however, the margins are the border around the text, and the actual text will be inside those margins. You use the column guides to specify where the actual text will be. Therefore, you need to move the column guides. Do that now with the following instructions:

1. Point on the left margin guide, which at this time also contains the column guide, and then press and hold the main mouse button.

A double-headed arrow appears, which allows you to move the column guide in either direction.

2. Drag the column guide to the right until the dotted line in the horizontal ruler reaches 1.75 inches, and then release the main mouse button.

3. Point on the right margin guide. Then press and hold the main mouse button while dragging the column guide to the left until the line in the horizontal ruler reaches 6.5 inches. Finally, release the main mouse button.

(These new column guides are not equidistant from the original margins because the shadow border requires a 0.25-inch offset.)

Ruler Guides   Besides column guides, you can use other guide lines for various purposes. Because you create these lines from the rulers, they are called *ruler guides*. On the flyer, you want a ruler guide for the line between the company name and the body of the flyer. Add this ruler guide as follows:

1. Point on the top or horizontal ruler. Press and hold the main mouse button until the double-headed arrow appears.

2. Drag a new ruler guide down until the dashed line in the left or vertical ruler reaches 3 1/4 inches. Then release the main mouse button.

When you have placed the column and ruler guides, your flyer should look like Figure 3-7.

The margin, column, and ruler guides constitute the initial layout grid for your flyer. You will add more guides later, but for now these will suffice. Now you can add the text.

Entering the Text

The text on the flyer consists of three segments: the company name, the body describing the company's capabilities, and a list of products. Each

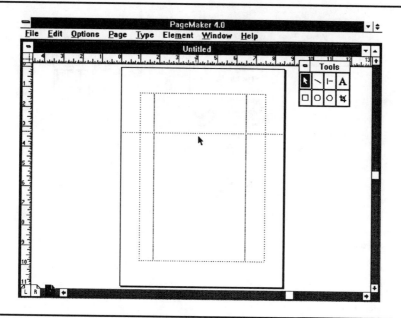

Figure 3-7. *Flyer with the three new guides*

segment uses a different font and spacing, so each is entered separately. Let's start with the company name.

Building the Company Name

To enter text with PageMaker, you need the text tool from the Toolbox. You will also use the text tool when you edit text. With this tool you can select text to cut and paste and to change its typeface, size, or style. To select the text tool:

Point on the text tool (the capital A) in the Toolbox, which is shown in Figure 3-7. Click the main mouse button.

The pointer becomes an I-beam when it is in the work area. As with Windows, when you click the main mouse button with the text tool, the *insertion point* (a vertical line indicating where the text you next type is placed) moves under (or very close to) the I-beam icon.

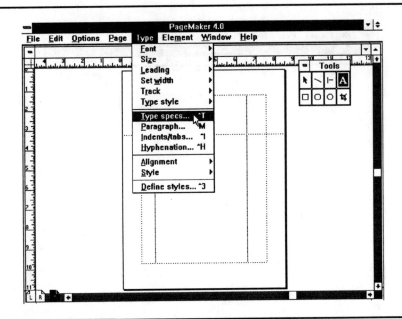

Figure 3-8.   *The toolbox with the text tool selected and the Type menu with "Type specs..."*
selected

Selecting the Type   Because you want the company name to be larger
and in bold type, you must change the type specifications. The type
specifications control the typeface, the type size (points), the type style
(bold, italic, and so on), the spacing between lines (leading), the letter
positioning (subscript and superscript), and the case (lower- and upper-
case). To change the type specifications, follow these instructions:

1. Select the Type menu, shown in Figure 3-8, and choose "Type specs...".
   The Type specifications dialog box opens.

2. Click on the downward-pointing arrow to the right of the "Font" text
   box. A list of typefaces appears, as shown here:

Use the scroll bar, if necessary, until you see "Gill Sans" or the sans serif font you want to use for the company name. Then click the main mouse button on that typeface to choose it.

To make the company name larger, you must increase the size of the typeface from the standard 12 points to 60 points.

3. Point on the downward-pointing arrow next to the "Size" text box and scroll through the list of point sizes until "60" appears. Then click on "60" to choose that point size. The number 60 appears in the "Size" text box.

4. Press TAB to go to the "Leading" text box. The word "Auto" is high-lighted.

5. Type **66** to change the leading from automatic (which would produce a leading of 72) to a leading of 66.

6. Click on both the "Bold" and "Italic" check boxes to choose those styles. An "X" appears in the boxes to indicate that they have been chosen.

7. Click on the downward-pointing arrow to the right of the "Case" text box. A list of case options appears. Click on "Small caps". Your dialog box should look like Figure 3-9.

8. Finally, click on "OK" to accept the type specifications as they now stand and to return to the work area.

Now that you have established the type specifications, you can enter the company name.

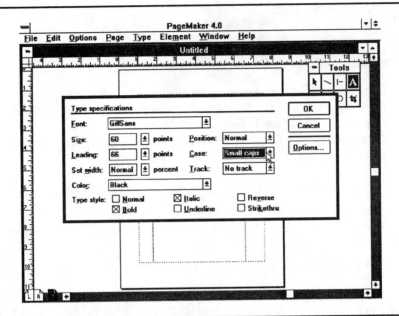

Figure 3-9.   *The final Type specifications dialog box for the company name*

Entering the Company Name   Entering the company name is straight-forward. First, use the mouse to place the insertion point where you want to begin typing, and then type the text. Enter the company name as follows:

1. Position the I-beam pointer to the right of the left column guide and slightly below the top margin, at about 2 inches on the vertical ruler (you can correct any alignment error later). Click the main mouse button. A flashing vertical line appears next to the left column guide representing the insertion point where the text will begin.

2. Type **Creative** and press ENTER. The word "Creative" appears on the flyer in bold italics, with small caps for the lowercase letters. The next line must be right-aligned to balance the two lines of the company name.

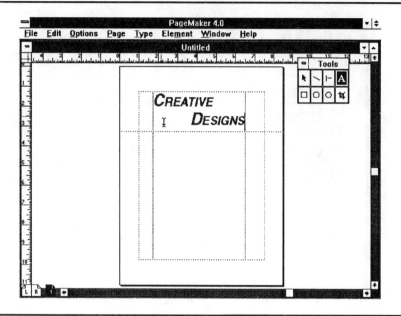

Figure 3-10.   *The flyer with the words "Creative Designs"*

3. Now press CTRL-SHIFT-R (press and hold both CTRL and SHIFT keys while typing **R**) to right-align the second line, and then type **Designs**. Your flyer should look like Figure 3-10.

Centering the Company Name   You may notice that the company name is not exactly centered in its area. In Figure 3-10 it is a little high. Yours may be the same, or too low, or too far to the left. PageMaker has an option that is normally very useful but here prevents you from exactly centering the company name. This option, called "Snap to guides", makes all non-printing guides (margins, column guides, and ruler guides) act like magnets. Whenever text or graphics, or even the pointer, nears a nonprinting guide, it is pulled to that guide.

To center the company name, select it with the pointer tool. Then turn off the "Snap to guides" option and move the company name with the mouse

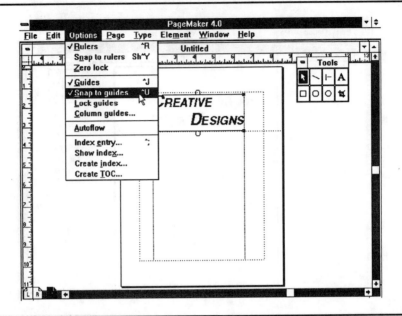

Figure 3-11. *The Options menu with "Snap to guides" selected and the company name selected on the flyer*

until you are satisfied with its position. The instructions to do that are as follows:

1. Click on the pointer tool in the Toolbox.

2. Point on the word "Creative", and click the main mouse button. This selects the two lines of the company name and provides *handles*—horizontal lines with loops in them like window shades—on either side of the company name, as shown in Figure 3-11. With these handles the company name can be moved.

3. Select the Options menu and choose "Snap to guides" to turn the guides off, as shown in Figure 3-11.

Now the company name will not be pulled toward one of the guides as it is moved about.

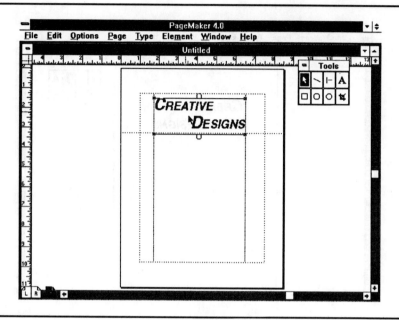

Figure 3-12. *The flyer with the company name centered*

4. Point somewhere in the middle of the company name. Then press and hold the main mouse button until a four-headed arrow appears.

5. Hold the main mouse button down, and move the company name around until it is positioned the way you want it. Then release the main mouse button. The final result looks something like Figure 3-12.

Don't be concerned that the final "s" in "Designs" overlaps the right column guide. It corrects itself when it is printed.

You now must restore the "Snap to guides" so that you can use the magnetic capability to precisely place text and lines for the balance of the flyer.

6. Select the Options menu and choose "Snap to guides" to turn the guides back on.

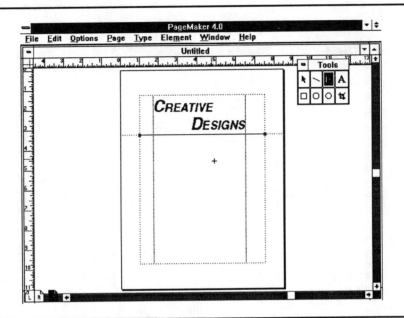

Figure 3-13.   *The flyer with the line in place*

Placing a Line   You want a line or rule, perpendicular to the margins, to separate the company name from the body of text. Use the perpendicular-line tool to draw a line from the left to the right margin. You must then look at the line width options in the Element menu to see if a different width is better. Follow these instructions:

1. Click on the perpendicular-line tool (just to the left of the text tool) in the Toolbox. The pointer changes to a *crossbar*.

2. Point the crossbar at the intersection of the left margin (*not* the column guide) and the horizontal ruler guide that separates the company name from the body of the flyer.

3. Press and hold the main mouse button while dragging the line across to the right margin, as shown in Figure 3-13. Do not release the button until you are satisfied with the position of the line.

If you do not see a line, it can be for one of two reasons: either you have accidentally turned on "Reverse line", which gives you a white line on a white background (turn it off by choosing "Reverse line" from the "Line" option of the Element menu), or, more likely, your line is hidden under the ruler guide. You can choose to have ruler guides on top ("Front") or underneath ("Back") of lines and other objects. If ruler guides are on top, they are easy to move and see; if they are underneath, the lines or boxes they are under are easy to move and see. There are arguments in favor of both positions—it is a question of personal preference. You can change the positioning of ruler guides by clicking on "Front" or "Back" under Guides in the Preferences dialog box reached from the Edit menu.

If the line is not the way you want it, press DEL to get rid of it and start over. Though you could go to the pointer tool, click on the line, and move it around the way you did the company name, the DEL method is easier here.

The little boxes at the end of the line indicate that it is selected. If you click the main mouse button, a new line is started and the original is

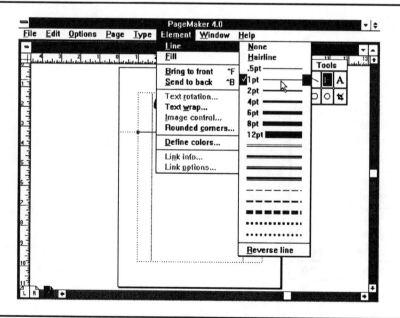

Figure 3-14.   *The Element menu with "Line" and "1 pt" selected*

deselected. Because you want to consider changing the width of the original line, it is important that it remain selected.

4. Look at the line width by selecting the Element menu and clicking the "Line" option to open the Line submenu. Review the options and, without changing the selection, release the main mouse button.

The 1-point line should already be selected as the default, as in Figure 3-14. This is a line width of 1/72 inch, which is acceptable for the flyer.

You now have done enough work to make it worthwhile to save your publication before continuing.

Saving the Publication   Because you may require several hours, or even days, to construct a publication, you should save it periodically. Then, if you have a power outage or make a major mistake, you can quickly recover by retrieving the copy on disk. Save the flyer now.

1. Select the File menu and choose "Save as...", as shown here:

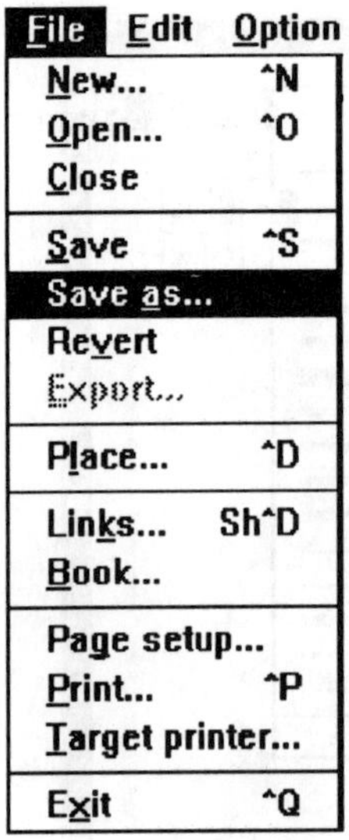

File	Edit	Option
New...	^N	
Open...	^O	
Close		
Save	^S	
Save as...		
Revert		
Export...		
Place...	^D	
Links...	Sh^D	
Book...		
Page setup...		
Print...	^P	
Target printer...		
Exit	^Q	

The Save publication as dialog box opens, as shown here:

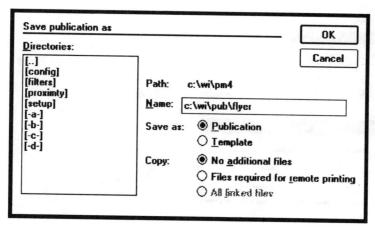

You can select a disk drive and directory (path) from the Directories list box by scrolling the list up or down until the path you want appears. Then select the path by clicking on it. Or you can simply type the path in the text box to avoid searching the list. Here you will do the latter. PageMaker lists the disk drive and directory that it thinks you want to use above the text box. If they are incorrect, enter the correct ones in the text box before entering the filename. Here, since the path is not correct, you need to enter the full path and filename of the publication. If you are using a different directory name, make the necessary changes in the following commands. The completed dialog box should look like this:

2. Type **c:\wi\pub\flyer** in the Name text box and press ENTER.

PageMaker automatically adds the extension .PM4 to publication files. Your publication is now saved. Notice that the name C:\WI\PUB\ FLYER.PM4 now appears in the title bar.

Intermission   You may want to take a break now and continue at a later time. To close PageMaker and Windows, follow these instructions:

1. Select PageMaker's Control menu and choose "Close", as shown here:

2. Select the Program Manager Control menu and choose "Close", as shown here:

3. Click on "OK" in the End session dialog box, as shown here:

Entering the Text Body

As you might imagine, entering the text body is straightforward. After specifying the type and selecting the text tool, you simply type the desired text. Although you go one step further to justify the text, that is all there is to it.

Continuing   If you are returning from a break, reload PageMaker and aopen the flyer publication. To do that, follow these steps:

1. Reload PageMaker following your normal procedure. The PageMaker copyright screen appears.

2. Select the File menu and choose "Open...", as shown here:

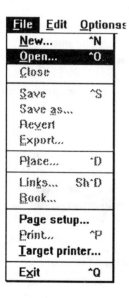

The Open publication dialog box appears as follows:

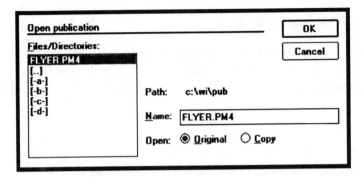

3. Double-click on the "[..]" in the "Directories" list box, scroll the list until you find the PUB directory or the directory you are using, and then double-click on that directory. The FLYER.PM4 publication appears in the list box.

4. Double-click on "FLYER.PM4" in the list box.

If you are using a different directory scheme than the one described in Appendix A, you may want to just type the full pathname and filename in the text box and press ENTER.

Your flyer will again appear in the PageMaker work area on your screen.

Getting Ready   Until now you have used a publication size in which a full page fits on the screen. This helps in creating the layout grid and entering the company name, which is very large. The text body, however, is normal 12-point type and is not readable at the size provided by the "Fit in window" option. Therefore, to enter the text body, you should enlarge the view you have of the page to full or actual size. Follow these steps:

1. Select the Page menu and choose "Actual size", as shown here:

```
 Page   Type   Element
 √ Fit in window        ^W
   25% size             ^0
   50% size             ^5
   75% size             ^7
   Actual size          ^1
   200% size            ^2
   400% size            ^4

   Go to page...        ^G
   Insert pages...
   Remove pages...

 √ Display master items
   Copy master guides
```

The flyer enlarges until a portion of it fills the work area.

2. Use the vertical and horizontal scroll bars to center the flyer with the company name just below the ruler, as shown in Figure 3-15. (Click on the arrows at the extremes of the scroll bars to move the image in small increments, or drag the scroll boxes to move the image by either larger amounts or finer increments until the image is correctly placed.)

To enter the text, you must select the text tool and specify the type. The text is entered in 12-point Times New Roman in medium or Roman style. You also want to use both upper- and lowercase.

3. Click on the text tool.

4. Select the Type menu and choose "Type specs...".

5. Click on the downward-pointing arrow to the right of the Font text box. A list of typefaces then appears. Use the scroll bar, if necessary, until you see "Times New Roman" or the serif font you want to use for the body text, and then click the main mouse button on that typeface to choose it.

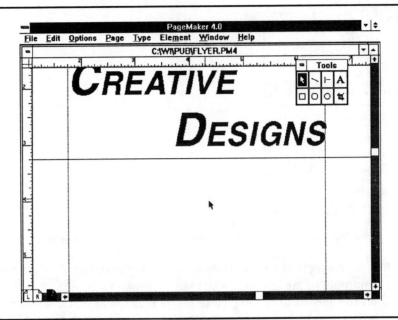

Figure 3-15. *The flyer enlarged to actual size*

6. Press TAB to go to the Size text box, type **12**, press TAB to go to the Leading text box, type **auto**, click on "Normal" in the Type style check box, click on the downward-pointing arrow to the right of the Case text box, and click on "Normal" in the list that appears. Your Type specifications dialog box should look like the one shown in Figure 3-16.

7. Press ENTER or click on "OK" to complete the type specifications.

Typing the Body   You must place the insertion point where you want the text to begin. Be careful. If you improperly locate the insertion point, your text may not appear where you want it or may not appear at all. Also, as you type, you may notice that PageMaker is slow to display the results. Your text is there (assuming that the insertion point was correctly placed);

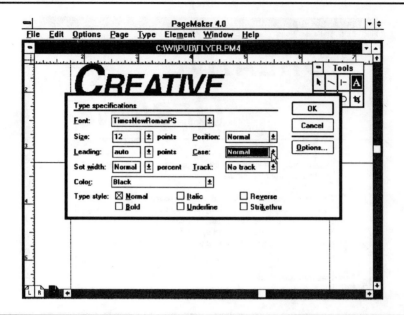

Figure 3-16. *Type specifications dialog box with the specifications for the text body*

pause and you will see it appear. Follow these instructions to type the body text.

1. Position the I-beam pointer against the inside of the left column guide so that the dotted line in the vertical ruler is at 3 3/4 inches, and then click the main mouse button.

The insertion point appears in the text area against the column guide. If the insertion point is to the left of the column guide, move it by repositioning the pointer and clicking the mouse button again.

2. Type the following three paragraphs. (Press ENTER twice at the end of each paragraph.) When you are done, your screen should look like Figure 3-17.

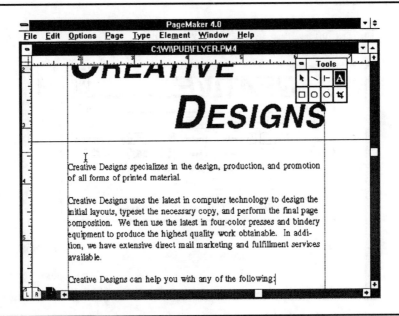

Figure 3-17.   *The first three paragraphs of the text body*

Creative Designs specializes in the design, production, and promotion of all forms of printed material.

Creative Designs uses the latest in computer technology to design the initial layouts, typeset the necessary copy, and perform the final page composition. We then use the latest in four-color presses and bindery equipment to produce the highest quality work obtainable. In addition, we have extensive direct mail marketing and fulfillment services available.

Creative Designs can help you with any of the following:

A fourth paragraph will be entered lower on the page to allow room for the product list. The fourth paragraph uses the same font and style as the first three. Again, be careful in positioning the insertion point.

3. Click on the vertical scroll bar below the scroll box to move the screen down until 8 inches on the vertical ruler approaches the middle of your screen.

4. Click the pointer at 8 3/4" on the inside of the left column guide. Then type the following:

   Call us at 1-800-555-5000 (nationwide) or stop in at our new plant at 1900 Westwind Avenue, Oceanside, WA 98999.

Justifying the Body   The paragraphs in Figure 3-17 look good, but for that final polished look, you'll want to justify them; that is, align them on the right as well as on the left. One of the beauties of PageMaker and laser printer technology is that justification looks almost as good as that done by a commercial typesetter. To justify, simply select the text and then choose the "Justify" option of the "Alignment" command under the Type menu. First justify the top three paragraphs and then, separately, the fourth, as follows:

1. Click on the vertical scroll bar *above* the scroll box in order to move the screen up.

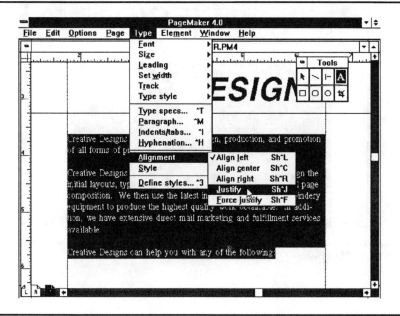

Figure 3-18.   *The first three paragraphs selected and the Type menu with "Alignment" and then "Justify" selected*

2. Place the pointer on the first letter of the first paragraph. Press and hold the main mouse button.

3. Drag the pointer just below the third paragraph and release the main mouse button. The first three paragraphs will be highlighted, as shown in Figure 3-18.

4. Select the Type menu, choose "Alignment", and then choose "Justify." The result will look like Figure 3-19.

5. Click *below* the scroll box to move back down to the fourth paragraph.

6. Position the pointer at the start of the fourth paragraph. Press and hold the main mouse button while dragging down past the second line, and then release the button.

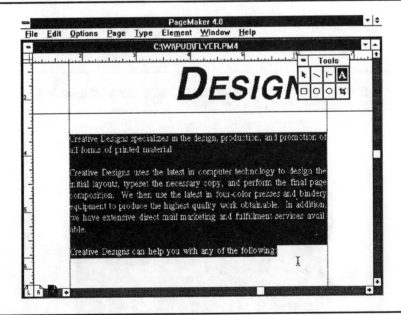

Figure 3-19.   *The effects of justification*

7. Select the Type menu, choose "Alignment", and then choose "Justify."

Listing the Products

Between paragraphs 3 and 4 of the text body, you will list two columns of products. You could use tabs or spaces to indent and separate the two columns, but aligning the columns and keeping them that way may be difficult. Another solution is to establish two columns with PageMaker's column guides. Do that now.

1. Select the Options menu and choose "Column guides...", as shown here:

```
Options  Page  Type
√ Rulers           ^R
  Snap to rulers  Sh^Y
  Zero lock
√ Guides           ^J
√ Snap to guides   ^U
  Lock guides
  Column guides...
  Autoflow
  Index entry...   ^;
  Show index...
  Create index...
  Create TOC...
```

```
Column guides                          OK

                                       Cancel

Number of columns:      2

Space between columns:  .25   inches
```

The Column guides dialog box opens so you can specify the number of columns and how much space to leave between them.

2. Type **2** in the "Number of columns" text box.

3. Press TAB to move to the "Space between columns" text box and type **.25**. Then press ENTER to return to the work area.

Notice that there are two new column guides in the center of the flyer, but your original column guides have moved back under the margins. You must move them out again and position the center guides. Do that now.

4. Click on the pointer tool in the Toolbox.

Next you'll move the column guides from under the margins. You may not be able to see both of the margins on the screen. If so, use the horizontal scroll bar to adjust the display so first one and then the other is visible in the next two steps.

5. Point on the left margin. Press and hold the main mouse button while dragging the column guide to the 2" mark. Then release the button.

6. Point on the right margin. Press and hold the main mouse button while dragging the column guide to the 6" mark. Then release the button.

7. Point on the right center column guide and drag it (both center column guides will move) to the 4 1/8-inch mark on the horizontal ruler. Your screen should look like Figure 3-20.

8. Now save your work by using the shortcut keys, CTRL-S (press and hold CTRL while typing **S**).

Typing the List   Now that the columns are in place, you can type the list of products without worrying about the alignment. The font for the list will be 18-point Gill Sans in bold and small caps. You again make these changes through the Type menu, as follows:

1. Select the Type menu and choose "Type specs...". The Type specifications dialog box opens.

Figure 3-20.   *The final column guide position*

2. Click on the downward-pointing arrow to the right of the Font text box. A list of typefaces appears. Use the scroll bar, if necessary, until you see "Gill Sans" or the sans serif font you want to use for the list of products. Then click the main mouse button on that typeface in order to choose it.

3. Press TAB to go to the Size text box, type **18**, click on "Bold" in the Type style check box, click on the downward-pointing arrow to the right of the Case text box, and click on "Small caps" in the list that appears. Your Type specifications dialog box should look like the one shown here:

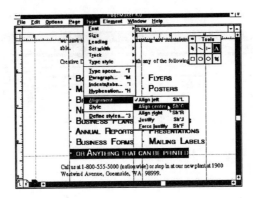

4. Press ENTER to return to the work area. Before typing, you must place the insertion point again.

5. Click on the text tool.

6. Position the I-beam against the inside of the far left column guide and click the main mouse button at 6 1/4 inches on the vertical ruler.

Each line begins with a bullet. To produce a bullet, press CTRL-SHIFT-8 simultaneously. After the bullet, type an *en space,* a fixed-width space equal to one-half of the point size being used. The en space is generated by pressing CTRL-SHIFT-N simultaneously. Press ENTER at the end of each line, and put an en space between words, except in the last line, where you should use normal spaces. Don't worry that the last line overlaps the fourth paragraph. That will be corrected.

7. Type the following list:

   ■ **Books**

   ■ **Manuals**

   ■ **Brochures**

   ■ **Newsletters**

   ■ **Business Plans**

   ■ **Annual Reports**

   ■ **Business Forms**

   ■ **or Anything that can be printed**

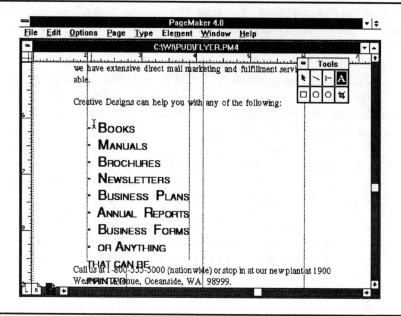

Figure 3-21.   *The left column filled in*

Your screen will look like the one shown in Figure 3-21.

8. Position the I-beam against the inside of the left guide of the right column and click on 6 1/4 inches, and then enter this list:

   ■ Flyers

   ■ Posters

   ■ Catalogs

   ■ Pamphlets

   ■ Newspapers

   ■ Presentations

   ■ Mailing Labels

Adjusting the Last Item   Because the "or Anything" item in the first
column takes several lines, it overlaps the fourth paragraph. To correct the
"or Anything" item, make it one line that spans both columns. To do this,
you must "cut" the item from the list of products and "paste" it back. Then
you place a *selection box* around it and enlarge the selection box so that it
is the same width as the sum of the two columns. Finally, you'll center the
item in the box at the bottom of the list. To make these adjustments, follow
these instructions:

1. Drag down a horizontal ruler guide and place it against the bottom
    edge of the words "or Anything." You will use this to reposition the line
    when you bring it back.

2. Drag the I-beam across all lines of the "or Anything" item in the left
    column to highlight it, as shown in Figure 3-22. Press SHIFT-DEL to cut
    it away from the rest of the column, and press BACKSPACE to move the
    insertion point up one line.

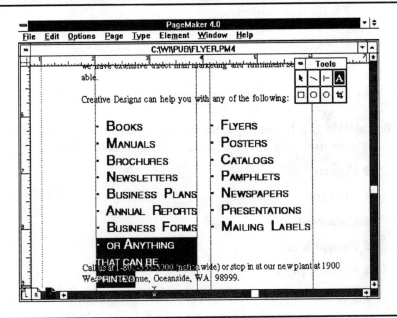

Figure 3-22.   *Both columns filled in and the last item selected*

3. Click the I-beam against the inside of the far left column guide at 8 3/8" on the vertical ruler.

4. Press SHIFT-INS to paste the "or Anything" item back onto the flyer.

The "or Anything" item can now be expanded and centered.

5. Click on the pointer tool.

6. Click anywhere on the "or Anything" item.

A selection box forms around the text. Now you must enlarge the selection box to the width of the two columns—4 inches. Notice that the lines above and below the text have small square boxes at each end. These are handles, which you can use to change the width of the selection box.

7. Point on one of the right-hand handles of the selection box. Press and hold the main mouse button while dragging the handle until it is on top of the rightmost column guide at 6" on the horizontal ruler.

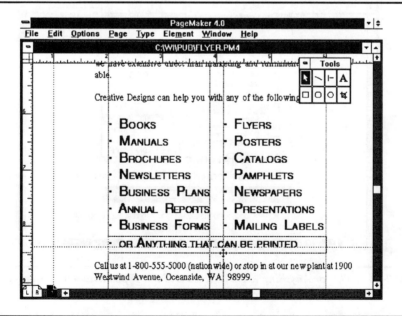

Figure 3-23. *The selection box stretched across both columns*

8. Point in the middle of the selection box, and drag it up or down until it is just sitting on the horizontal ruler guide you place under the original item. Be careful not to move it left or right. Your screen should look like that shown in Figure 3-23 when you are done.

You have now stretched the selection box to fill both columns. If you center the item in the box, it is centered between the two columns. Now do that to finish the text entry.

9. Click on the text tool.

10. Select the "or Anything" item by dragging across it.

11. Select the Type menu, choose the "Alignment" option, and then choose "Align center", as shown in Figure 3-24.

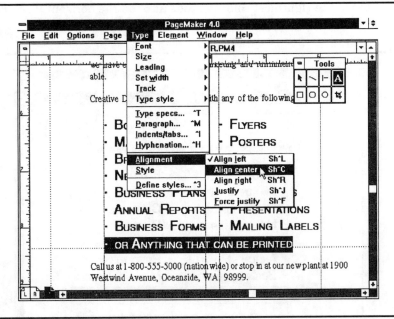

Figure 3-24.   *The "or Anything" item selected and the Type menu with "Alignment" and "Align center" selected*

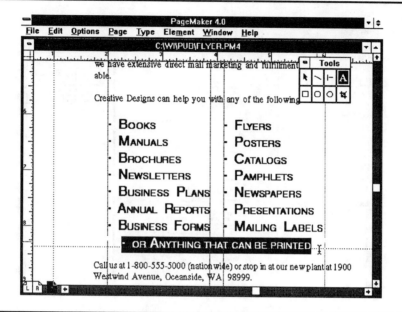

Figure 3-25. *The final list of products*

When you are done, your screen should look like the one in Figure 3-25. This completes the entry of the text.

Before proceeding, reduce the size of the flyer so that it again fits in the window, and then save it again.

12. Select the Page menu and choose "Fit in window".

13. Select the File menu and choose "Save". The screen appears as in Figure 3-26.

This might be a good time to take another break. If you want to do that, use the earlier instructions for closing and reopening PageMaker and the flyer publication. Otherwise, continue and construct the border around the text.

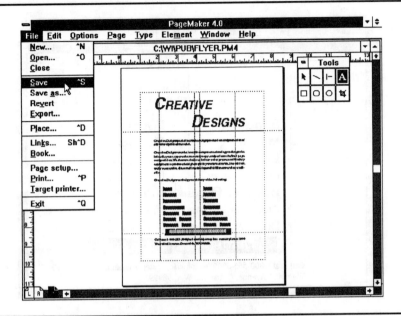

Figure 3-26. *The full flyer and the File menu with "Save" selected*

Constructing the Border

The border around the text consists of two rounded-corner rectangles
slightly offset from one another. The purpose of this is to use the right
rectangle to create a shadow effect by filling the area between the rectangles with black shading (look again at Figure 3-1). Although in PageMaker
only complete rectangles or circles can be shaded, not a small portion of
one as we want here, PageMaker makes each rectangle a layer and allows
them to be "stacked" on top of one another. If the right rectangle is shaded
"Solid" and is on the bottom, and the left rectangle is shaded "Paper" and

is stacked on top, you get the effect you want. The text, which is another layer (actually a series of layers), must be on top of the stack to be readable.

Building the First Layer

PageMaker's "Snap to guides" option (which causes the guides to act as magnets) is both a help and a hindrance in placing the rectangles. Two sides of each rectangle are on the margins, and the magnetic attraction is beneficial. However, the other two sides are free of the margins but close enough to them for the magnetic attraction to interfere. To overcome this problem, you must carefully position the free end by using the rulers. Let's start with the leftmost rectangle—the one that will end up on top. It uses the top and left margins as guides and is 1/4 inch away from the bottom and right margins. The steps used to create and place the first rectangle are as follows:

1. Select the rounded-corner tool (the second tool from the left in the bottom row). The pointer becomes a crossbar.

2. Place the crossbar on the intersection of the top and left margins. The crossbar is attracted to the intersection and should stick there easily.

3. Press and hold the main mouse button while dragging the pointer diagonally toward the opposite corner. A rectangle begins to form.

4. Drag the pointer until the dotted line in the horizontal ruler reaches 7.25 inches and the dotted line in the vertical ruler reaches 9.5 inches. Then release the main mouse button. Your flyer should look like the one shown in Figure 3-27.

PageMaker provides various degrees of rounded corners and shading. Therefore, to complete your first rectangle you must choose the type of rounded corner that you want, and then apply the "Paper" shading. Because this rectangle is currently on top of the stack, once the shading is applied it covers up the text layer beneath it. So you must move the shaded

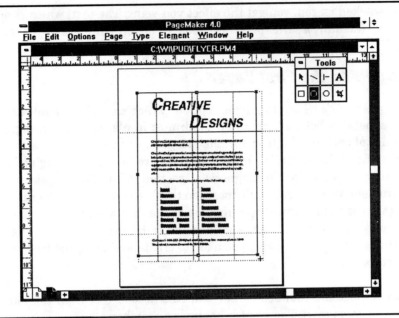

Figure 3-27.   *The flyer with the first rectangle selected*

rectangle down, under the text on the stack, or "send it to the back." The
following instructions explain how to perform those functions:

1. Select the Element menu and choose "Rounded corners..." as shown
   here:

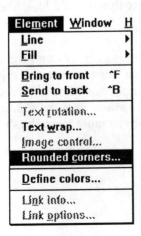

The Rounded corners dialog box opens, as shown here:

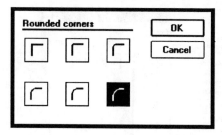

2. Click on the bottom-right option button for the most rounded of the corners, and press ENTER or click on "OK".

3. Select the Element menu, choose "Fill" and then "Paper", as shown in Figure 3-28. The shaded rectangle will cover the text.

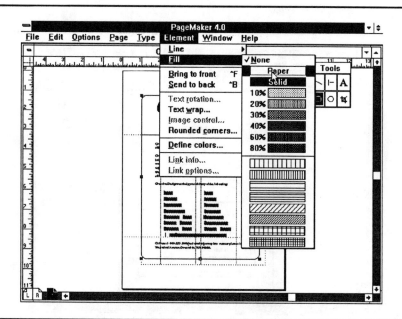

Figure 3-28.   *The Element menu with the "Fill" and "Paper" options selected*

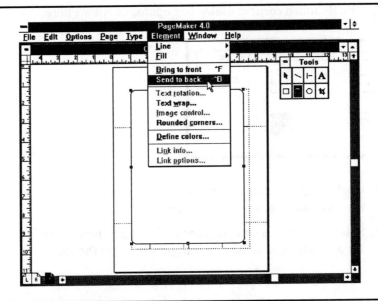

Figure 3-29.   *The shaded rectangle covering the text and the Element menu with "Send to back" selected*

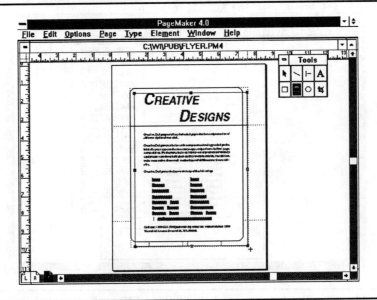

Figure 3-30.   *The flyer with the second rectangle in place*

4. Select the Element menu and choose "Send to back", as shown in Figure 3-29. The text reappears on top of the rectangle.

Building the Second Layer

The second layer is very similar to the first, except that it is offset to the right and shaded black. The instructions to build it are as follows:

1. Place the crossbar pointer 1/4 inch in from the top and left margins. The dotted line in the horizontal ruler reads 1.25 inches, and the one in the vertical ruler reads 1.5 inches.

2. Press the main mouse button and drag the pointer diagonally toward the opposite corner, to the intersection of the bottom and right margins. Then release the main mouse button. Your flyer should look like that shown in Figure 3-30.

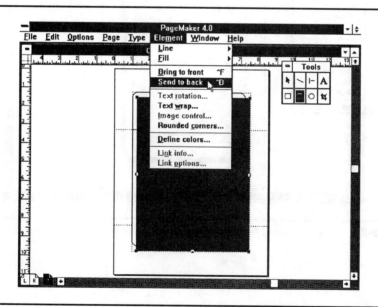

Figure 3-31.   *The second shaded rectangle covering the text and the Element menu with "Send to back" selected*

3. Select the Element menu and choose "Rounded corners...".

4. Click on the bottom-right option button and press ENTER.

5. Select the Element menu, choose "Fill", and then choose "Solid". The text again is covered up, as shown in Figure 3-31.

6. Select the Element menu and choose "Send to back."

The text reappears, and the shadow effect is present. This is a good spot to save your handiwork.

7. Select the File menu and choose "Save", as shown in Figure 3-32.

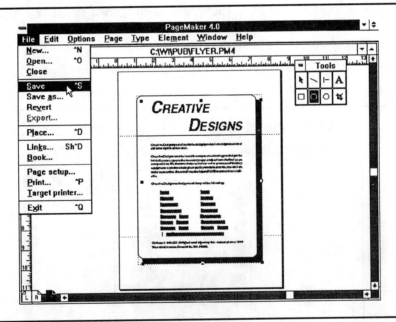

Figure 3-32. *The completed flyer and the File menu with "Save" selected*

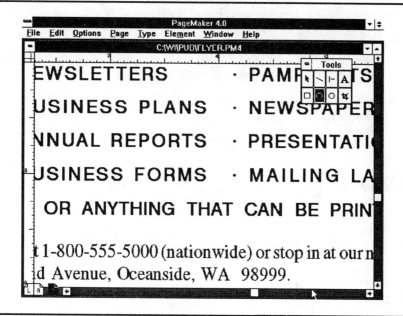

Figure 3-33.   *A part of the flyer at "200% size"*

Except for cleaning up and printing, the flyer is now complete.

Cleaning Up and Printing

The cleanup consists of scanning the flyer for mistakes or imperfections. To do this "under a magnifying glass," you first change the page size to 200 percent. Finally, you print the publication and then save it one more time.

1. Select the Page menu and choose "200% size". Your screen should look like the one in Figure 3-33.

2. Use the vertical and horizontal scroll bars to scan the flyer, checking for mistakes: misspellings, unaligned text, and so on.

3. Return to the Page menu, choose "Fit in window", and click on the pointer tool.

4. Select the File menu and choose "Print...", as shown here:

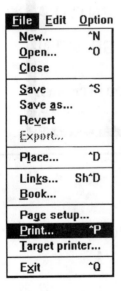

The Print dialog box opens up, as shown in Figure 3-34.

5. Accept all the defaults by clicking on "OK". Several message boxes open up to tell you the status of the printing.

6. When the printing is complete (it may take a while), save the file one more time by pressing CTRL-S.

7. Finally, end the session by selecting the File menu and choosing "Close", as shown in Figure 3-35.

This chapter has covered a lot of ground. If some features and options remain unclear, don't worry about it. You'll have a chance to work with them in more detail in later chapters.

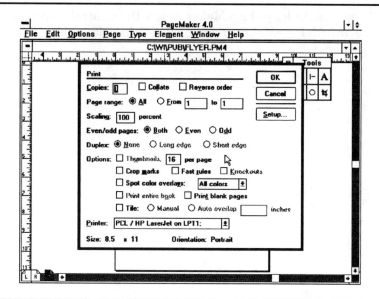

Figure 3-34. *The Print dialog box*

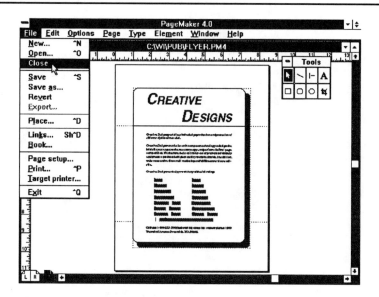

Figure 3-35. *The File menu with "Close" selected*

If you wish to leave PageMaker, select the Control menu, and choose "Close" in both PageMaker and Windows. Otherwise, continue on to create an order form.

II *Basic PageMaker Publications*

Part II illustrates three common uses of PageMaker: a business form, a sales brochure, and a formal financial report. To create them you use the capabilities of PageMaker and thus become increasingly familiar with how to use this desktop publishing tool. Having completed Part I, you'll find that Part II is faster, with less explanation of commands and features with which you are already familiar. However, when new techniques are introduced, the pace is somewhat slower again—although not to the degree you experienced in Part I. From now on, you will find yourself moving through the applications as an experienced PageMaker user.

Chapter 4 offers a sales order form because most organizations use forms, many of which must be custom designed. Building this form serves as an example of how you would create other business forms using PageMaker. You'll use PageMaker's line- and box-drawing tools, the multiple-column feature, and column shading to achieve a typeset look.

Chapter 5 shows how to create a threefold, double-sided brochure—a commonly used technique for obtaining professional-looking brochures. You'll use PageMaker's landscape orientation to place text from WordPerfect, lines, and a drawing or graphic from Micrografx Designer. Of course, you can use other word processing and graphics packages if you want.

Chapter 6 creates a set of formal financial statements, such as you might show to stockholders, a bank, or prospective investors. You combine Lotus 1-2-3 spreadsheets and graphs with Microsoft Word 5 text to build these formal statements, although you could easily use other spreadsheets and word processors.

4 Making a Sales Order Form

In this chapter you create the Sales Order form shown in Figure 4-1. In building the form you incorporate several features that allow the Sales Order form to look as if it came from a commercial printer. For example, the form uses several different type styles and sizes. The line widths also differ. The form uses multiple columns (one, two, and six columns) to organize its contents. Two of the columns are shaded.

You can easily use these same techniques to create a variety of business forms. Once you have seen how easy it is to create the Sales Order form, you will want to create other forms with PageMaker. As you build this form, you may want to modify it to satisfy your specific needs. However, in order to follow the exact instructions, please delay your modifications until you have completed the chapter. Many of the instructions depend on precise measurements and character lengths.

Planning and Designing the Form

Your first step is to plan and design the Sales Order form. You must decide now what text labels and data you want on the form and how they are to

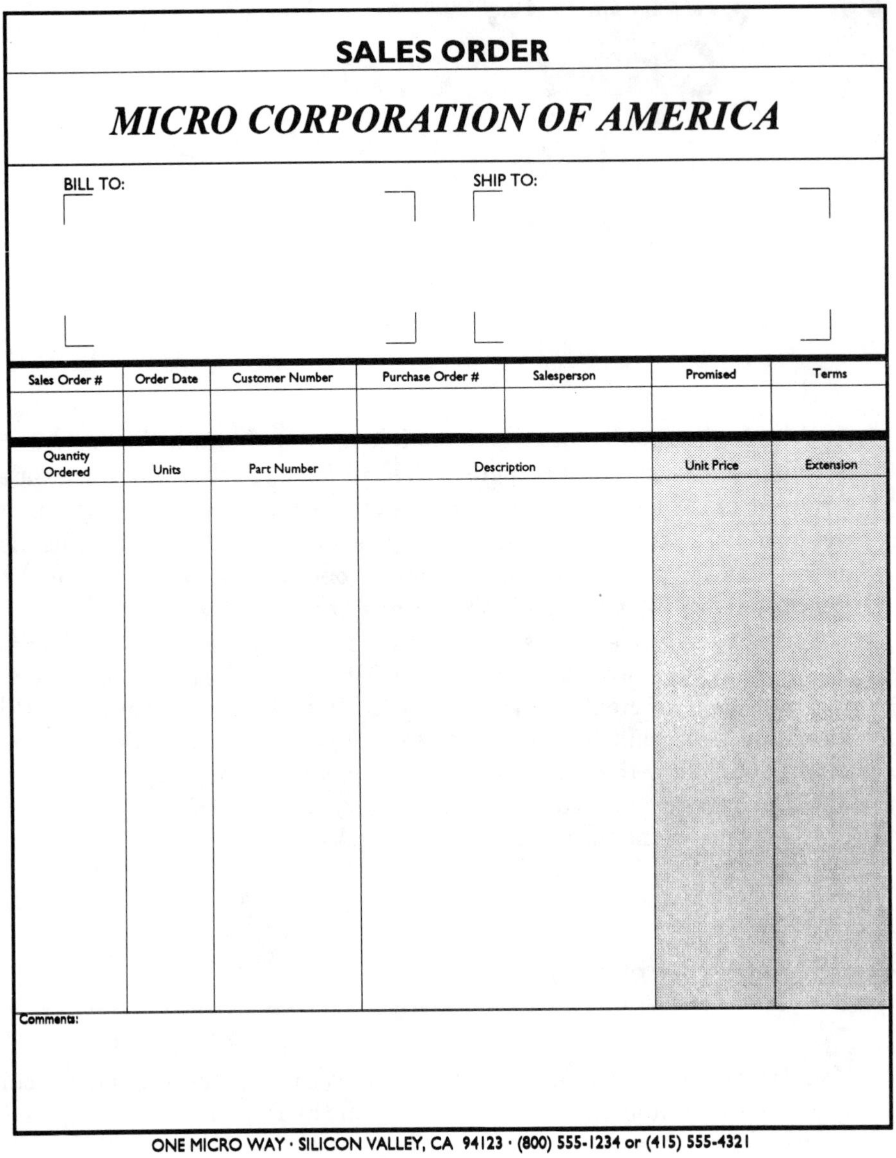

SALES ORDER						

MICRO CORPORATION OF AMERICA

BILL TO:

SHIP TO:

Sales Order #	Order Date	Customer Number	Purchase Order #	Salesperson	Promised	Terms

Quantity Ordered	Units	Part Number	Description		Unit Price	Extension

Comments:

ONE MICRO WAY · SILICON VALLEY, CA 94123 · (800) 555-1234 or (415) 555-4321

Figure 4-1.   *Printout of the finished Sales Order form*

be laid out on the page. For instance, to determine what labels and data you need on the form, you want to answer these questions: What information do I want to collect with the form? Who will use the form? How will it be used?

Information to Be Collected

In this case the questions have been answered for you. The primary use of the sales order is to record customer orders. The form is used by salespersons to take down information from customers as they order. The order may come in by telephone or in person. After the Sales Order form is completed, the contents are entered into the computer, where other departments use the information to fill the order and bill the customer.

The information includes the billing and shipping addresses for the accounts receivable and shipping departments. Critical information about the order is collected, such as the sales order number, order date, customer number (assuming there is one), the customer's purchase order number, the name of the salesperson collecting the information, and the terms of the order. Then the order is itemized, and the quantity ordered (and in what units), the part number of the item, a description, the unit price quoted, and the extended price (unit price times quantity) are listed. These last two items are not filled in by the salesperson, so they are shaded on the form to remind them to leave that area blank. With this information, the order can be collected in a warehouse, shipped to the recipient, and then billed.

After the information is defined, it must be laid out on the page with lines, fonts, and shading added to it. The organization and design of the page is shown in Figure 4-2. Notice how the design features add interest and readability to the form.

Lines

One way to organize the parts of the form is to use different line widths. For example, imagine how the boxes in the middle of the form (containing "Sales Order #" and so on) might be lost without the heavier lines, which cause them to stand out. In addition, because the lines gradually get wider as you look down the page, your eye automatically attends to these important details rather than to the customer bill-to and ship-to informa-

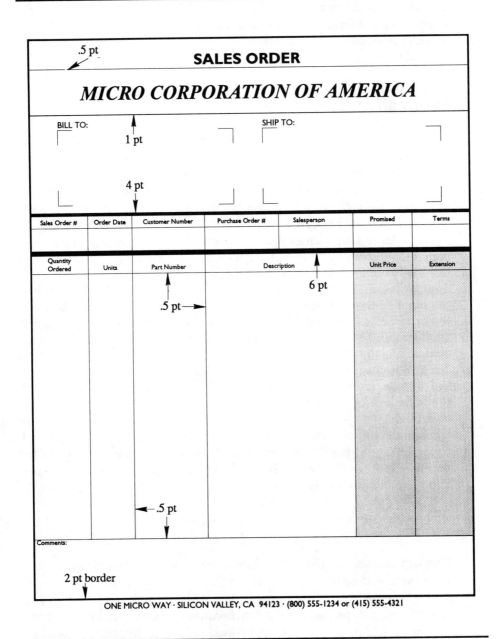

Figure 4-2.   *Line widths on the Sales Order form*

tion, which is already easy to see because of its location and spacing on the page.

Figure 4-2 shows the five line widths that are used. The line forming the border around the sales order is 2 points wide; beneath the form title, 0.5 point; beneath the company name, 1 point; beneath the bill-to and ship-to information, 4 points; beneath the detail boxes, 6 points; the column dividers, 0.5 point; and beneath the columns, 0.5 point.

Fonts

Selecting different fonts (type styles and sizes) is another way for you to differentiate the areas of the form and enhance the appearance of the document.

This book assumes that you have the Adobe Gill Sans, Times New Roman, and Symbol typefaces that are included in the PageMaker 4 package. You do not have to use these typefaces; you can use any sans serif typeface in place of Gill Sans and any serif typeface in place of Times New Roman. For the sake of brevity, throughout this and succeeding chapters, Gill Sans and Times New Roman or their equivalents are referred to as Sans and Times, respectively.

The Sales Order form uses four fonts: the form title is 18-point Sans Bold; the company name (which is to be emphasized), 24-point Times Bold Italic; the return address and the bill-to and ship-to labels, 10-point Sans; and the rest of the text, 8-point Sans. Figure 4-3 shows these fonts.

Shading

Shading lends interest to the form, as you can see in Figure 4-3. The "Fill" option of the Element menu has several suboptions for shading an area. You can choose "Solid" or "Paper" shades as you did in Chapter 3, or you can choose a density to vary the darkness (or lightness) of the shaded area. Also, you can choose one of eight patterns for the background instead of shading. In this chapter you use 10 percent shading, which is dark enough to be noticed, but light enough to show the Unit Price and Extension entries.

Having completed the planning and design for the Sales Order form, you are now ready to begin building it.

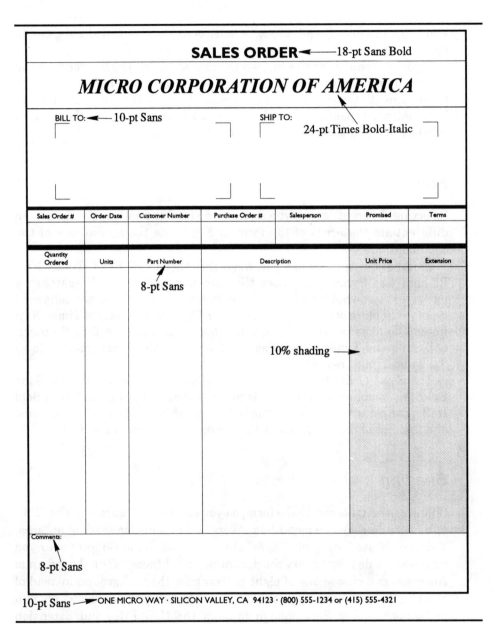

Figure 4-3. *Fonts and shading on the Sales Order form*

Setting Defaults

Before getting started, start your computer and load PageMaker. As soon as you have done that, return here. If you have difficulties, return to Appendix A and review the steps.

Your first step is to set up your printer and establish the document defaults.

Setting Up the Printer

Setting up your printer before you actually begin creating the document is important because the screen image depends on your printer selection. PageMaker tries to make the screen image as close to the actual printed image as it can. The visual images of fonts and special effects depend on what your printer can print. For example, if your printer cannot print a font of 24 points and you specify that size in your document, the screen image defaults to the nearest size that the printer can print.

In addition to assuring the correct screen image, you must change (or verify) some of the options. The orientation of the Sales Order form is "Portrait", which is vertical on the page, as opposed to "Landscape", which is horizontal. Also, you want the "300" dpi (dots per inch) option for the printer resolution.

Follow these steps to set up your printer:

1. Choose "Target printer..." from the File menu.

   A dialog box displays the list of printers installed for Windows.

2. Double-click on the printer that you want to use for the Sales Order form. If you do not see it, use the scroll bar to find it. If the printer is already highlighted, you can just click on "Setup".

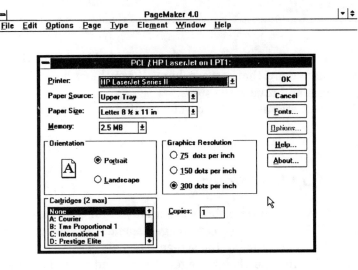

Figure 4-4. *Options set for the target printer*

The screen displays additional options in a dialog box, as shown in Figure 4-4.

3. Verify that these settings are correct: "Letter 8 1/2 x 11 in" for Paper Size, "Portrait" for Orientation, and "300 dots per inch" for Graphics Resolution. If one or more are not set, make the necessary adjustments.

4. When all settings are as you want them, click on "OK" twice.

Next you will set the defaults for the publication.

Establishing Defaults

You also want to set the defaults for the overall type of document and its size. You do this by filling in the Page setup dialog box. This allows you to specify the size of the page, its orientation—whether vertical or horizontal ("Tall" or "Wide")—whether it is double-sided and has facing pages, the number of pages in the publication, and what margins you are using as the default.

To set the page specifications, follow these steps:

1. Choose "New..." from the File menu.

The Page setup dialog box is displayed. Scan the box and note which options need to be changed. The Page dimensions option is "8.5" x "11" inches, which is what you want. The Orientation is "Tall" (vertical)—also what you want. However, the "Double-sided" and "Facing pages" options are checked, and the Sales Order form has only one side. In addition, the margins are too wide for the Sales Order format. You must change these options as shown in Figure 4-5.

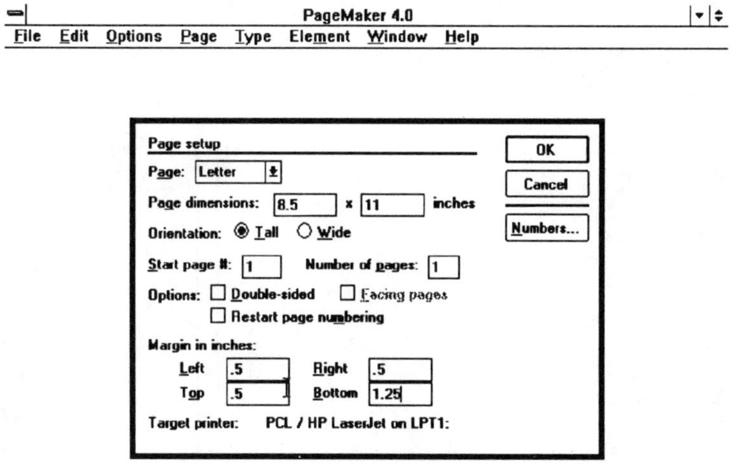

Figure 4-5.   *Options changed for Sales Order page setup*

2. Turn off the "Double-sided" option by clicking the check box.

This also turns off the "Facing pages" option, because you cannot have facing pages without a double-sided page.

3. Drag across the Left margin number and type **.5** to reset it, and then press TAB to advance the insertion point to the Right margin.

4. Type **.5**, and then press TAB to advance the insertion point to the Top margin.

5. Type **.5**, and then press TAB to advance the insertion point to the Bottom margin.

6. Type **1.25**, and then press ENTER to complete the dialog box.

Your screen shows the page outline with the dotted margin guides within it, as shown in Figure 4-6.

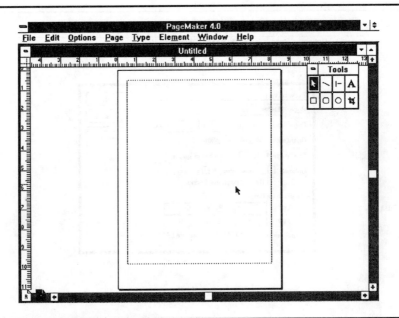

Figure 4-6.   *The Initial page setup*

In the upper-right corner is the Toolbox, which you will use often. The pointer tool (the arrow) is currently selected, as indicated by the highlighted background.

Now that the page setup is completed, you can set the rest of your defaults.

Setting Up Ruler Guides

When rulers are turned on, as they are in Figure 4-6, they appear on the top (the horizontal ruler) and left side (the vertical ruler) of the screen. Within them are faint, dotted lines that move as the mouse pointer is moved. You can track the insertion point exactly by noting its position on the scale marks of the rulers. From the rulers you can drag ruler guides, the longer dotted lines used to further define the areas of the Sales Order form. By lining up the ruler guides to exact scale marks, you can precisely place text, lines, shading, and graphics.

If your rulers are not turned on, do so now.

Choose "Rulers" from the Options menu.

Setting Line Width Default

You must set the default for line width with the pointer tool or a drawing tool *before* drawing a line, a box, or a circle. If you wait until after drawing the object, you are not setting the default but merely the size of the line you just drew. For example, if you first select a 2-point line width with the pointer tool and then draw a box, it is 2 points. If you then draw a line and, before deselecting it (by clicking the mouse elsewhere), change the line width to 1 point, the next line you draw reverts to 2 points by default.

Most line widths in the Sales Order form are 0.5 point wide. To make that your default,

Choose ".5pt" from the "Line" option of the Element menu, as shown in Figure 4-7. The default line width is now set for most of your lines.

Setting Type Specifications

Setting the defaults for the type specifications works the same way as the line defaults. The defaults are the type specifications you set either with

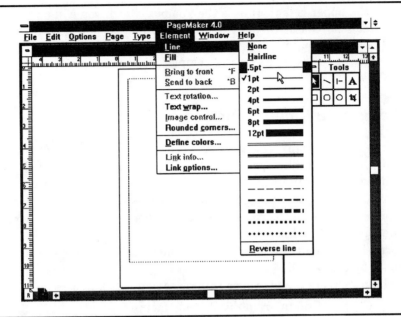

Figure 4-7. *Setting line width default to ".5pt"*

the pointer tool or, prior to establishing the insertion point, with the text tool.

Setting the type specifications defaults defines the characteristics of the type most commonly used in the Sales Order form. You may recall from Figure 4-3 that the most common type is 8-point Sans. You can use a shortcut technique to get to the type specifications. Although you could choose the "Type specs..." option from the Type menu, try pressing two shortcut keys. To set the type specifications, follow these steps:

1. Press CTRL-T (for "Type specs...").

The Type specifications dialog box is displayed.

2. Click on the downward-pointing arrow to the right of the Font text box. Use the scroll bars to scroll the list of typefaces until "Gill Sans" or the

sans serif typeface you want to use is visible. Click on the typeface you want for a default and press TAB to move to the type Size text box.

3. Type **8** to set the type size at 8 points.

4. Verify that Set width, Type style, Position, and Case are set to "Normal"; that "Auto" appears in the Leading text box; that Color is set to "Black"; and that Track is set to "No Track".

5. When the dialog box is complete, as shown in Figure 4-8, click on "OK" or press ENTER to tell PageMaker that you are finished with the "Type specs..." option.

The alignment is another aspect of the type for which you want to establish a default. Most of the text in the Sales Order form is centered.

6. Choose "Align Center" from the "Alignment" option of the Type menu, or use the shortcut key CTRL-SHIFT-C.

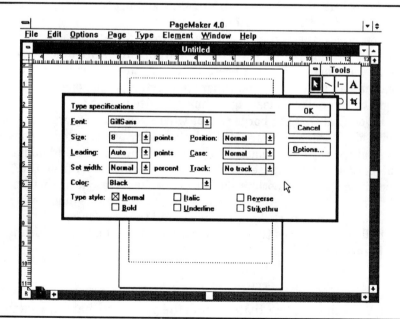

Figure 4-8. *The default Type specifications dialog box*

Your type defaults are now set and you can begin placing guide lines. You can change the specifications for a particular entry (and preserve your document defaults) by drawing a line or setting an insertion point *before* changing the specifications for that entry.

Entering the Border And Horizontal Lines

The Sales Order form uses many lines to define the various areas. You can enter these lines now. First you define the outline of the form. Then you place several ruler guides to help you determine where the actual lines are to be drawn within the form.

From Chapter 3 you recall the benefits of "Snap to guides". This option gives guide lines a magnetic property that attracts the pointer as it nears them and allows you to match up your pointer to a given location. You will find this feature useful here. However, you must turn off "Snap to guides" to perform another task later.

You create the border of the Sales Order form by placing a rectangle around the page, exactly where the margin guides are now located. To do this, you place the square-corner tool at the upper-left corner of the margins and then drag the expanding rectangle diagonally to the lower-right corner before releasing the main mouse button.

If you find that the border is not where you want it, press the DEL key while the border lines are still selected (they are selected as long as the lines of the rectangle contain tiny boxes at the corners and midpoints). If the border becomes deselected, select the pointer tool from the Toolbox, click it on the top or bottom sides to select the rectangle again (the left and right sides of the box work if you first move the column guides from beneath the margins before clicking on them), and then continue.

Follow these steps to build the border line of the form, which is shown in Figure 4-9.

1. Select the square-corner tool.

2. Place the crossbar that replaced the pointer so that it is exactly in the upper-left corner of the margins. (Notice how "Snap to guides" helps you by attracting the pointer to the margins.)

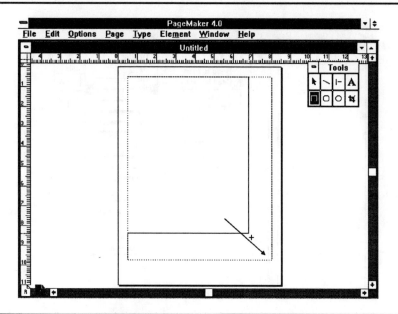

Figure 4-9.   *Building the border line*

3. Drag the rectangle diagonally to the lower-right corner of the margins.

4. Release the main mouse button when the rectangle exactly covers the margins.

    While the box is still selected, you can specify the 2-point line width, as shown in Figure 4-10.

5. Choose "2pt" from the "Line" option of the Element menu.

Placing Ruler Guides
And Drawing Lines

Now you can place the ruler guides for the seven horizontal lines. These help you exactly place the actual horizontal and vertical lines of the form.

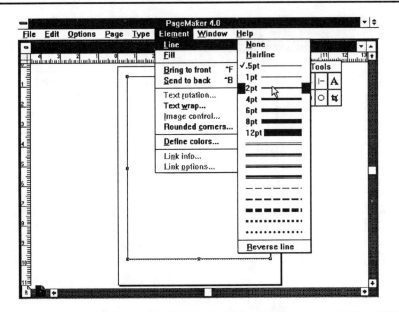

Figure 4-10.   *"Line" option from the Element menu with the line width set to "2pt"*

Notice that as you position the lines, the scale marks on the rulers disappear when the moving dotted line in the rulers is exactly over them. Similarly, the crossbar seems to disappear when it is exactly lined up over a ruler guide line.

You are currently looking at a "Fit in window" view on the screen. This lets you see the whole page on one screen, but you cannot see any particular part of it in much detail. For instance, look at the horizontal and vertical rulers. They are divided into sixteenths, and you will be placing some of the lines on the eighths scale marks. Since you cannot see them very clearly, you may not be able to precisely place the guides on the marks. That is all right because you can correct the positioning later in an "Actual size" view.

Follow these steps to place the ruler guides:

1. Select the pointer tool and click on the document Maximize button to get the largest possible full document image.

2. Press the main mouse button on the horizontal (top) ruler, and drag a ruler guide to 1 inch on the vertical ruler.

3. Drag a second ruler guide to 1 3/4 inches on the vertical ruler.

4. Drag a third ruler guide to 3 3/8 inches.

5. Drag a fourth ruler guide to 3 5/8 inches.

6. Drag a fifth ruler guide to 4 inches.

7. Drag a sixth ruler guide to 4 3/8 inches.

8. Drag a seventh ruler guide to 8 3/4 inches.

When you complete these steps, your screen looks like Figure 4-11. Now draw the actual horizontal lines on the form.

9. Select the perpendicular-line tool to the immediate left of the text tool.

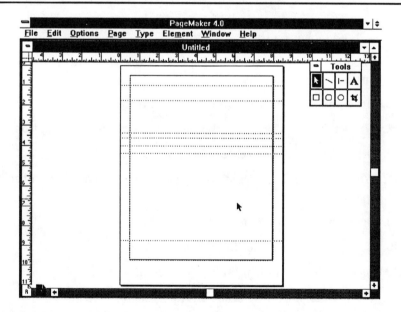

Figure 4-11. *Horizontal ruler guides on the form*

10. Place the crossbar on the intersection of the first horizontal ruler guide (at 1.0 inch on the vertical ruler) and the left margin. Press the main mouse button and draw a line to the right margin guide. Make sure that the new line is exactly over the ruler guide before releasing the main mouse button.

If the line has been incorrectly placed, press DEL before it is deselected, that is, before you click the main mouse button on a different line. You can tell that it is selected because the ends of the lines have tiny boxes on them. If it becomes deselected before you can delete it, you must select the pointer tool, click on the incorrect line to select it (you may have to move the guide lines up or down before the actual line, which lies under the guide lines, can be selected), press DEL to delete the line, and then select the perpendicular-line tool once again before continuing.

Before the line is deselected, you should also check that the line width is correct. It should be the default 0.5 point.

11. Select the "Line" option of the Element menu and verify that ".5pt" is checked.

12. In the same way as you did for step 10, draw the second horizontal line at 1 3/4 inches on the vertical ruler.

13. Choose "1pt" from the "Line" option of the Element menu before the line is deselected.

14. Draw the third horizontal line at 3 3/8 inches.

15. While the line is selected, choose "4pt" from the "Line" option.

16. Draw the fourth horizontal line at 3 5/8 inches.

17. While the line is selected, verify that ".5pt" is checked on the "Line" option.

18. Draw the fifth horizontal line at 4 inches.

19. Choose "6pt" from the "Line" option.

20. Draw the sixth horizontal line at 4 3/8 inches.

21. Verify that ".5pt" is checked on the "Line" option.

22. Draw the seventh horizontal line at 8 3/4 inches.

23. Verify that ".5pt" is checked on the "Line" option.

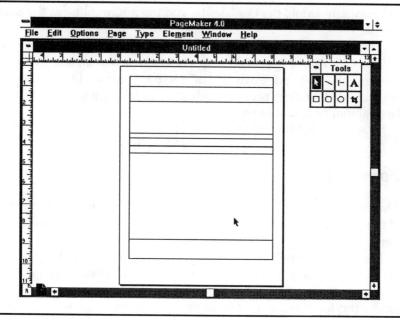

Figure 4-12.   *The Sales Order form with all necessary horizontal lines*

24. Select the Options menu and choose "Guides" to turn off the ruler
guides to allow you to look at the lines you have drawn.

Your screen should look like Figure 4-12.

You have successfully entered all the horizontal lines for the Sales Order
form. Continue even if you can tell that some of the lines need adjusting;
you can do this later. Now you must enter the text.

Entering Noncolumnar Text

In Figure 4-1 you can see that four areas of the Sales Order form may be
considered to be one column wide: the areas containing the title of the form,

the company name, the Comments, and the address line at the bottom of the page.

It is important to enter the single-column text before placing the column guides. Otherwise, PageMaker tries to keep the text all within the current column, causing text (such as the company name) to wrap around on several lines. So first proceed with the single-column text, and then the two-column text, and so on.

First you enter the form title.

Form Title

The title of the form is "Sales Order." You want to place this in the top area of the form. As you recall from the design discussion, the type is 18-point Sans.

The current default of "Snap to guides", which causes the guide lines to act as magnets as the pointer gets close to them, is usually helpful because the magnetic property helps you repetitively line up the pointer with the guide. But for entering text it hinders you by causing the centering to be off. One of your first tasks is to disable "Snap to guides".

Follow these steps to enter the title:

1. Choose "Guides" from the Options menu to turn them back on and "Snap to guides" in the Options menu, causing them to be disabled (no check mark beside it).

At this point you want to change to "Actual size" so you can enter the text more accurately. Although you could choose the "Actual size" option from the Page menu, you will use a shortcut method of varying the screen image size by pressing CTRL-1.

When you expand the screen image to actual size, the view that you see depends on what was highlighted or selected when you pressed CTRL-1. The object highlighted or selected becomes the center of the screen in actual size. Selecting what you want to see ahead of time saves you from having to position the screen with the scroll bars. Here you want to position the screen where you can see the top two bands of the screen.

2. Press and hold CTRL while clicking the mouse on the line you drew at 1 3/4 inches, thus selecting the second line. This line is in the center of the screen when you go to "Actual size."

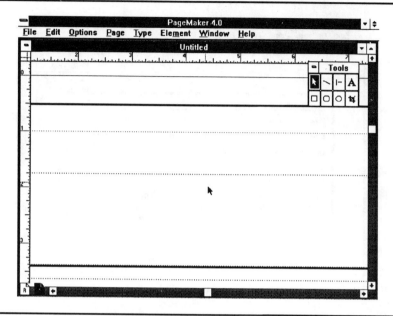

Figure 4-13.   *"Actual size" screen image before entering title*

Holding down CTRL while clicking assures that you select the line you drew, not the ruler guide on which you drew it. In the future, if you have trouble selecting an object, hold down CTRL while clicking on the object.

3. Select "Actual size" by pressing CTRL-1.

Your screen should look like Figure 4-13. If it does not, adjust it by using the scroll bars.

Now you can enter the text. The title will be centered because you have used that for the default alignment; that is, it will be centered between the right and left margins. However, you also want it to be centered between the top margin and the first horizontal line. To do this, you must click the pointer in the position where you want the letters to be typed—as close to the middle of the band as you can. You can do a final adjustment later.

4. Select the text tool (the one marked "A").

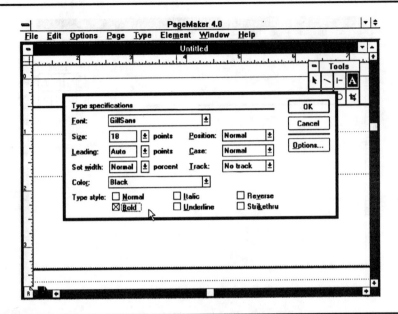

Figure 4-14. *The Type specifications dialog box showing "18pt" options*

5. Click in the top band of the page, close to the middle horizontally and at 7/8 inches on the vertical ruler.

6. Press CTRL-T for "Type specs".

7. Press TAB, type **18** for the Size, and click on "Bold" for the Type style in the Type specifications dialog box, as shown in Figure 4-14.

8. Click on "OK" or press ENTER to complete the dialog box.

9. Press the CAPS LOCK key.

10. Type **SALES ORDER**.

You can see that the title, centered as the default specifies, is now on the page.

Name of Company

The company name is entered in the second band below the form title. Recall from the design discussion that the name is in 24-point Times, centered, and bold italic.

Follow these steps to enter it:

1. Click in the second band below the form title, at 1 3/8 inches on the vertical ruler and 4 1/4 inches on the horizontal ruler.

2. Press CTRL-T for "Type specs".

3. Click on the downward-pointing arrow to the right of the Font text box and use the Scroll bar to scroll the list of typefaces until "Times New Roman" or the serif typeface you want to use is visible. Click on that typeface and press TAB to move to the type Size text box and verify that Position and Case are "Normal" and that Leading is "Auto"; and then click on "OK."

4. Type **24** for the Size, click on "Bold" and "Italic" for the Type style.

5. Type **MICRO CORPORATION OF AMERICA**.

The page now contains the company name centered, in bold italic, and with the type specifications set forth in your design. Your screen should look like Figure 4-15.

Now skip to the bottom of the page and enter the company address.

Company Address

You next enter the company address on the last band of the page, just below the bottom margin. It is 10-point Sans and "Normal" Type style.

Between the street and city, and between the ZIP code and the phone numbers, you enter a bullet. In PageMaker this is done by pressing CTRL-SHIFT-8 (the 8 should be typed on the regular keyboard, not the numeric keypad). Place a space on either side of the bullet.

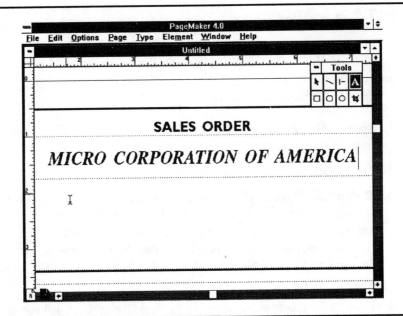

Figure 4-15.   *The completed title and company name*

Follow these steps to enter and edit the address:

1. Verify that the text tool is selected.

2. Adjust the screen by dragging the vertical scroll box two-thirds of the way down the bar so that you can see the last two lines of the form, as shown in Figure 4-16.

3. Place the I-beam in the last band of the page, between the bottom margin guide and the bottom of the page at about 2 inches on the horizontal ruler and 10 inches on the vertical ruler. The insertion point appears around 5 1/2 inches on the horizontal ruler, as shown in Figure 4-16. Click the main mouse button.

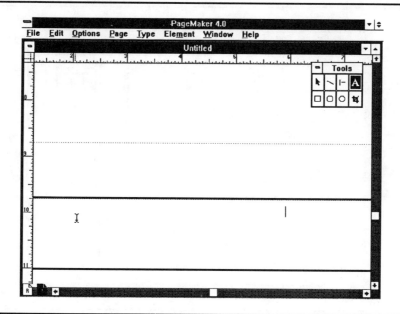

Figure 4-16. *The last two bands of the form*

4. Press CTRL-T for "Type specs...", press TAB, type **10** for the Size, and verify that the Font is "Sans", that Leading is "Auto", and that Type style, Position, and Case are "Normal". Click on "OK".

5. Type **ONE MICRO WAY • SILICON VALLEY, CA 94123 • (800) 555-1234 or (415) 555-4321**.

Figure 4-17 shows the result.

Sometimes when text is below the bottom margin, as in this case, it does not get properly centered. Check that next.

6. Select the pointer tool.

7. Click in the middle of the address text so that it becomes selected, as shown in Figure 4-18.

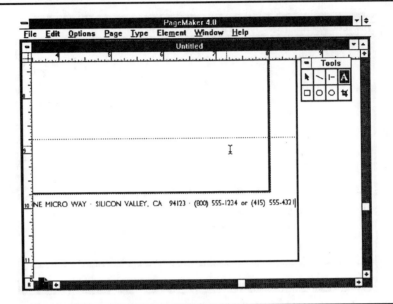

Figure 4-17.   *The address as it initially appears*

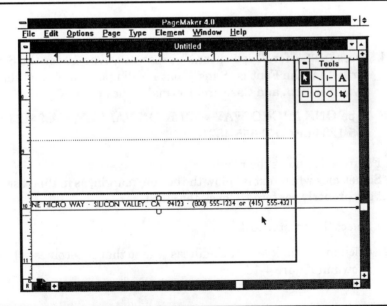

Figure 4-18.   *The address with a selection box around it*

A selection box (two lines, one above and one below the text) appears. The lines have "handles" on them and tiny boxes on each end of the lines that you can use to move the text. When you move them, the lines become a solid box.

8. Drag one of the tiny boxes on the right end of the lines until it is under the right margin guide at 8 inches on the horizontal ruler.

9. Adjust your screen by clicking on the horizontal scroll bar between the scroll box and the left scroll arrow. Then drag one of the tiny boxes on the left end until the selection box spans from margin to margin, as shown in Figure 4-19.

The lines and handles disappear when you select something else. For now, click the pointer in the pasteboard to see the text without the selection box.

You now enter the last of the single-column text—the Comments label.

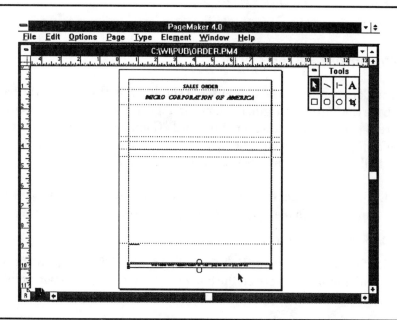

Figure 4-19.   *The address selection box extending from margin to margin*

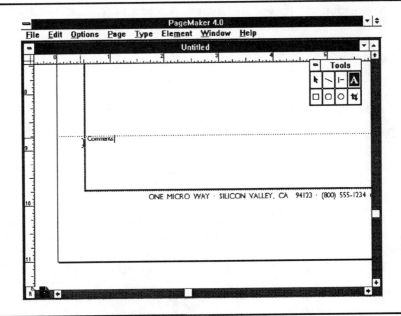

Figure 4-20. *"Comments" in the bottom band*

Comments Area Label

The Comments area label is entered similarly, in the band of the page just above the bottom margin, as shown in Figure 4-20. The type specifications are 8-point Sans. However, the word "Comments" is not centered; it is left-aligned with an en space separating it from the left margin.

Follow these steps to create the Comments label:

1. Use the horizontal scroll bar to position the screen so that the left margin is visible, as shown in Figure 4-20.

2. Select the text tool.

3. Click the I-beam in the bottom band, at 8 7/8 inches on the vertical ruler and anywhere on the horizontal ruler. The insertion point jumps to the center, but you will fix that next.

4. Press CTRL-SHIFT-L to left-justify the text.

5. Press CTRL-T for "Type specs".

6. Verify that the default type specifications are set on "Sans", "8" points, and "Normal" Type style, Position, and Case. Then click on "OK".

7. Press CAPS LOCK to release it.

8. Press CTRL-SHIFT-N to place an en space and type **Comments:**.

The text is left-aligned and should look like Figure 4-20. If it is not placed exactly as you want it, you can correct it soon.

9. To view the overall look of the form, press CTRL-W. The "Fit in window" view appears.

Although you cannot see the printing, you can see the positioning of the text within the bands. You may now want to correct some of the positioning of the text.

Correcting the Text Positioning

If you look closely at the positioning of the form title and the company name, you may discover that the text is not centered, either vertically or horizontally, exactly as you want it. For instance, it may be too close to an upper or lower line. Correct this as you did the address by selecting the text with the pointer tool, which produces a selection box with the handles around the text. Then move the text by pressing the main mouse button until a four-headed arrow appears and drag the text block into position.

Use the shortcut method of switching your screen image from "Fit in window" to "Actual size" and back. Recall that to do this you first select an object near the center of the area where you want the image to be centered and then press CTRL-1.

If the form title is not centered correctly, follow these steps to correct it:

1. Select the pointer tool.

2. Click on the company name and then press CTRL-1.

3. If necessary, arrange the screen with the scroll bars so that the form title is clearly visible.

4. Click on the form title so that a selection box appears around it.

5. Drag the selection box around until it is centered as you want it.

If the company name is not centered between the lines, follow a similar procedure to correct it. Check the comments and address as well.

When you are satisfied with your form, you need to restore "Snap to guides" and the screen size, as follows:

6. Click the main mouse button on the pasteboard to the right or left of the order form to clear the selected text (to get rid of the lines and handles).

7. Choose "Snap to guides" in the Options menu. A check mark appears next to the option.

8. Press CTRL-W to return to the "Fit in window" screen image.

You can now enter the vertical lines and fill in the labels of the form. But first you must save your work.

Saving Your Work

Now is a good time to save your Sales Order form to protect yourself against accidentally losing your work. Remember that \wi\pub is our pathname for the PageMaker publications subdirectory. If you have used a different pathname, change the following instructions accordingly.

To save your file with the shortcut technique, follow these steps:

1. Press CTRL-S for "Save".

2. When the dialog box is displayed, select the correct subdirectory and type **order** in the Name text box, as shown here:

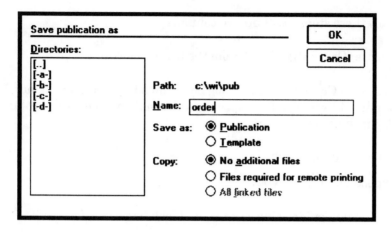

3. When you are satisfied with the name, press ENTER.

Now you are ready to enter the BILL TO:/SHIP TO: area of the form.

Entering BILL TO:/SHIP TO: Area

In Figure 4-1 you can see that the BILL TO:/SHIP TO: area can be visualized as two columns. And establishing two columns turns out to be the easiest way to create this area.

After setting up the two columns, you again place several ruler guides to define precisely where to put the corner brackets surrounding each address area.

Setting Up Two Columns

It is easy to set up columns with PageMaker. You simply specify the number of columns and the spacing between them in the dialog box that is displayed when you select the "Column guides" option in the Options menu. Once the column guides are placed on the page, you arrange them as you want and then draw the corner brackets.

Follow these steps to set up two columns:

1. Choose "Column guides..." from the Options menu.

You see the Column guides dialog box, which has boxes for the number of columns to be set up and the spacing between them. Specify two columns with 0.5 inch between them.

2. Type **2** and press TAB.

3. Type **.5** and press ENTER.

Your Column guides dialog box should look like this:

```
┌──────────────────────────────────────────────┐
│  Column guides _____    ┌──────────┐│
│                                    │    OK    ││
│                                    └──────────┘│
│                                    ┌──────────┐│
│                                    │  Cancel  ││
│                                    └──────────┘│
│  Number of columns:      ┌─────────┐           │
│                          │ 2       │           │
│  Space between columns:  │ .5 │  inches        │
│                          └────┘                │
│                                                │
└──────────────────────────────────────────────┘
```

You can see two column guides in the center of the page. These are the innermost delimiters of the two columns and are separated by the 0.5 inch that you specified. The left and right margins hide the outer column guides. Next you want to bring in the outer column guides so that the columns are narrower.

4. Select the Options menu and choose "Snap to rulers" to turn them on (checked).

5. Press and hold the main mouse button on the left margin to select the column guide there. A two-headed arrow appears.

6. Drag the column guide right to 1.0 inch on the horizontal ruler.

7. Similarly, drag the right column guide from under the right margin left to 7 1/2 inches on the horizontal ruler.

You have now created two columns with 1/2 inch on either side and 1/2 inch between them, as shown in Figure 4-21. Next you want to set up additional ruler guides to help place the corner brackets and text.

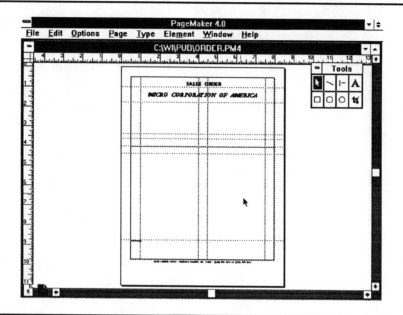

Figure 4-21.   *Column guides for two columns*

Entering Ruler Guides

You can now set up four horizontal ruler guides and four vertical ones. They are used when you draw the corner brackets.

As you drag the ruler guides from the two rulers onto the form, you know when you have placed them exactly on a mark because the dotted line in the ruler disappears when it is exactly over one of the scale marks.

To draw the horizontal ruler guides, follow these steps:

1. Point on the horizontal (top) ruler, and drag a horizontal ruler guide down to 3 1/4 inches on the vertical ruler.

2. Drag a horizontal ruler guide to 3 inches on the vertical ruler.

3. Drag a horizontal ruler guide to 2 1/4 inches.

4. Drag a horizontal ruler guide to 2 inches.

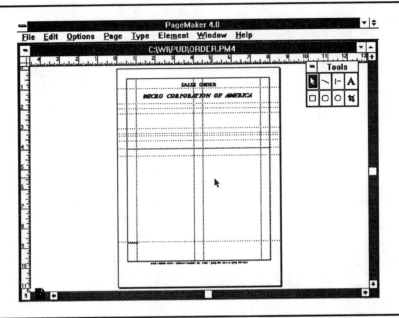

Figure 4-22.   *Horizontal ruler guides and columns for the BILL TO:/SHIP TO: area*

Your Sales Order form should look like the one shown in Figure 4-22. Now you can add the vertical ruler guides.

5. Point on the vertical ruler and drag a vertical ruler guide right until it reaches 7 1/4 inches on the horizontal ruler.

6. Drag another vertical ruler guide to 4 3/4 inches on the horizontal ruler.

7. Drag a vertical ruler guide to 3 3/4 inches.

8. Drag a vertical ruler guide to 1 1/4 inches.

Your finished screen should look like the one shown in Figure 4-23.

You must make sure the guide lines are precisely lined up; otherwise the corner brackets will be off and it will be apparent. To do this, you must return the screen to actual size and then adjust the lines so they are exactly

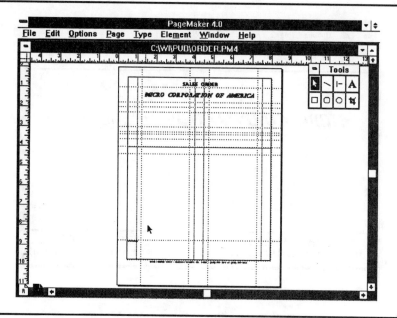

Figure 4-23.   *The completed vertical and horizontal ruler guides*

on the ruler scale marks. To see all of the horizontal ruler, you must hide the Toolbox temporarily.

9. Choose "Toolbox" on the Window menu to turn off the Toolbox.

10. Select the company name as the item to center around, and press CTRL-1.

11. If you need to, adjust your screen image with the scroll bars until your screen looks like the one shown in Figure 4-24.

12. Adjust the ruler and column guides so they are exactly at 2, 2 1/4, 3, and 3 1/4 inches on the vertical ruler and at 1, 1 1/4, 3 3/4, 4, 4 1/2, 4 3/4, 7 1/4, and 7 1/2 inches on the horizontal ruler.

Once your guide lines are precisely set up, the boxes formed by the lines will be perfectly square.

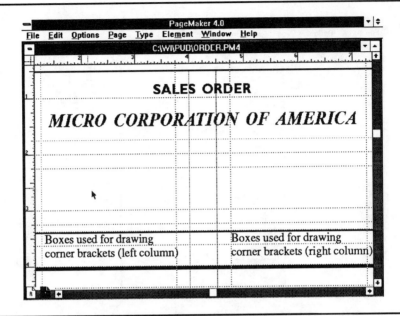

Figure 4-24.   *Actual size screen showing BILL TO:/SHIP TO: area*

Notice in Figure 4-24 that in each column there are four boxes surrounding a large rectangle formed by the guide lines. Two sides of each box are used to form the corner brackets; for example, on the top left box, the top and left sides of the box will be used for drawing the corner brackets. You can be comfortable that the corner brackets will be correctly drawn since the boxes are perfectly square.

Drawing BILL TO:/SHIP TO: Corner Brackets

You first draw the corner brackets for the left column by drawing two lines in each of the four boxes in the left column, as shown in Figure 4-24. You use the perpendicular-line tool for drawing. In choosing the tool you want, you use a shortcut (by pressing SHIFT-F3) because the Toolbox is not available on your screen. (You could put the Toolbox back on the screen,

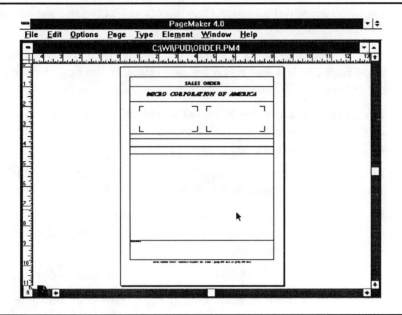

Figure 4-25.   *The eight corner brackets without guides*

choose the line tool, and then hide the Toolbox again, but that's too much work!) You must double-check that the default is correctly set for lines at 0.5 point.

To draw the lines, follow these steps:

1. Select the "Line" option of the Element menu and verify that the ".5pt" option is checked. If it is not, drag the highlight bar to it and release the main mouse button.

2. Press SHIFT-F3 for the perpendicular-line tool.

Notice the pointer becomes a crossbar. In the following instructions, use Figures 4-24 and 4-25 to assure yourself that you are drawing the lines in the appropriate locations.

3. Place the crossbar in the upper-left corner of the top left box at 1 inch on the horizontal ruler and 2 inches on the vertical ruler, and draw a

1/4-inch horizontal line along the top of the box to form the top of the corner bracket.

4. Place the crossbar in the upper-left corner of the top left box and draw a 1/4-inch vertical line down to the bottom of the box along the left guide line.

5. Place the crossbar on the lower-left corner of the bottom box at 1 inch on the horizontal ruler and 3 1/4 inches on the vertical ruler and draw a 1/4-inch vertical line to the top of the box.

6. Place the crossbar on the lower-left corner of the bottom box and draw a horizontal line across to the right side of the box.

7. Draw similar lines to form corner brackets on the upper-right box of the left column, beginning at 4 inches on the horizontal ruler and 2 inches on the vertical ruler.

8. Draw the corner bracket on the lower-right box of the left column.

9. Draw the four corner brackets in the right column in the same way.

Turn off "Guides" from the Options menu, and press CTRL-W for the "Fit in window" view. Your screen should look like the one shown in Figure 4-25 when you are done. Be sure to turn "Guides" back on and return to "Actual size."

Typing Text

Once you have drawn the corner brackets, you can type in the text. Because the default for alignment is still "Centered", you must change it so that the text is left-aligned. Use the shortcut method to do this. You also must verify and choose the type specifications for 10-point Sans.

   To enter the text, follow these steps:

1. Press SHIFT-F4 to get the text tool.

2. Place the I-beam above the upper-left corner bracket in the left column at 1 15/16 inches on the vertical ruler; then click the main mouse button.

3. Press CTRL-SHIFT-L to left-align the text (the insertion point relocates).

4. Press CTRL-T for "Type specs", press TAB, type **10** in the Size text box, and verify that the other defaults have not changed in the Type specifications dialog box; then click on "OK".

5. Press the CAPS LOCK key to turn on capital letters.

6. Type **BILL TO:**.

7. Move the I-beam to the right column above the upper-left corner bracket at 1 15/16 inches on the vertical ruler, and then click.

8. Press CTRL-SHIFT-L to left-align the text.

9. Press CTRL-T for "Type specs", press TAB, type **10** in the Size text box, and verify that the other defaults have not changed in the Type specifications dialog box; then click on "OK".

10. Type **SHIP TO:**.

Your screen should look like the one shown in Figure 4-26.

Before you continue, you should clean up the page by removing some of the ruler guides. You can identify which lines are the ruler guides because the lines contain wider spaced dots or are a different color than the column guides. Also, the ruler guides span from the top of the page to the bottom; the column guides, only between the top and bottom margins. Be careful not to accidentally move one of the other lines.

To remove the guides, follow these steps:

11. Press CTRL-W for "Fit in window".

12. Select the pointer tool by pressing F9.

13. Drag all of the horizontal and vertical guide lines (the ones with wider dot spacing that runs to the edges of the page) to the pasteboard before releasing the main mouse button.

When you are finished, your page should look like the one shown in Figure 4-27.

Note that the F9 shortcut key for the pointer is different from the other tool shortcut keys. F9 switches you between the tool you last used and the pointer. For example, if you are using the text tools and you press F9, you

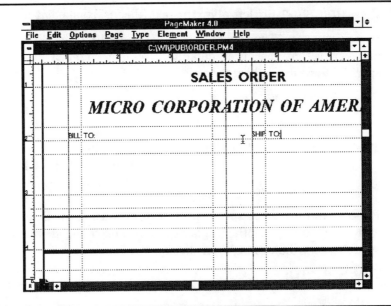

Figure 4-26. *The completed BILL TO: / SHIP TO: area*

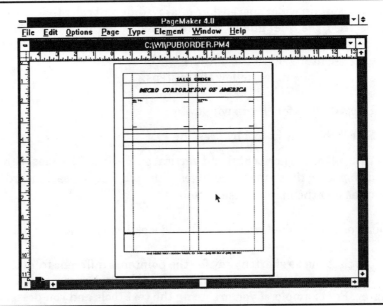

Figure 4-27. *Sales Order form after guide lines have been removed*

will get the pointer. If you press F9 again, you will be returned to the text tool.

You can now complete the Sales Order form by filling in the order detail area.

Building the Detail Area
Of the Form

The order details consist of two areas of information: a column area and a detail area. The column area is made up of six columns, each with a label box immediately above it. Above the column labels is the detail area. It contains a row of detail boxes, each having its own label box, as shown in Figure 4-1.

To define the order details, you first set up the six column guides with no spaces separating them. Then you draw the actual lines. Finally, you fill in the text and fill two of the columns with shading.

Setting Up Guide Lines
For Six Columns

Again, your first task is to set up and then arrange the column guides for the lines. Then you can use them to precisely draw the actual lines.

To place the column guides, follow these steps:

1. Verify that you are working with the pointer tool. If not, press F9.

2. Choose "Column guides..." from the Options menu.

3. When prompted by the dialog box, type **6** columns, press TAB, and type **0** inches. The Column guides dialog box should look like this:

```
┌─────────────────────────────────────────────────┐
│  Column guides                      ┌──────────┐  │
│  ────────────────────────────────   │    OK    │  │
│                                     └──────────┘  │
│                                     ┌──────────┐  │
│                                     │  Cancel  │  │
│  Number of columns:     ┌──────┐    └──────────┘  │
│                         │ 6    │                   │
│  Space between columns: │ 0    │    inches         │
│                         └──────┘                   │
└─────────────────────────────────────────────────┘
```

4. Press ENTER to complete the dialog box. (PageMaker inserts column guides at 1 3/4, 3, 4 1/4, 5 1/2, and 6 3/4 inches on the horizontal ruler.)

Because you need to be able to see the page with greater accuracy in order to place the guide lines, you will switch the screen to "Actual size" view. You want to be able to see the middle of the page.

5. Press CTRL-1 to return the screen view to "Actual size", and use the horizontal scroll bar so that you can see the middle of the screen as shown in Figure 4-28.

Now you arrange the column guides in the appropriate locations by dragging them to specific locations on the horizontal ruler.

6. Drag the far left column guide from 1 3/4 to 1 1/2 inches on the horizontal ruler.

7. Drag the next column guide from 3 to 2 1/4 inches.

8. Drag the third column guide from 4 1/4 to 3 1/2 inches.

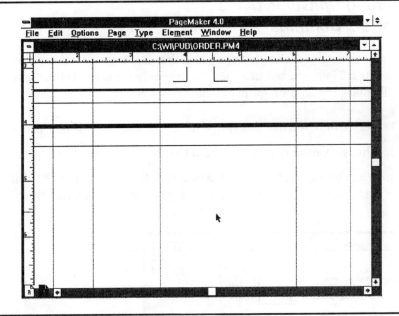

Figure 4-28.   *The adjusted column guides arranged to specifications*

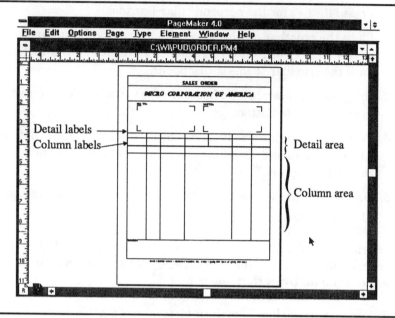

Figure 4-29. *The Sales Order form showing label areas for boxes and columns*

9. Drag the fourth column guide from 5 1/2 to 6 inches.

10. Drag the fifth column guide from 6 3/4 to 7 inches.

Your page now looks like the one shown in Figure 4-28.

11. Press CTRL-W to return to "Fit in window" view.

Next, you can draw the actual lines.

Drawing the Column Lines

As shown in Figure 4-29, the lines that you draw extend vertically from the horizontal line at 3 3/8 inches to the line at 8 3/4 inches above the Comments area. The end result is the definition of the order details, including both the initial detail area and the six columns. Both the detail boxes and the columns have label areas, as shown in Figure 4-29.

To draw the lines, follow these steps:

1. Press SHIFT-F3 for the perpendicular-line tool.

2. Place the crossbar on the top of the leftmost column guide, at 1 1/2 inches on the horizontal ruler and 3 3/8 inches on the vertical ruler, until the crossbar seems to disappear.

3. Drag the line down to 8 3/4 inches on the vertical ruler before releasing the main mouse button.

4. Verify that the line size is correct by selecting the "Line" option of the Element menu and seeing whether the ".5pt" option is checked. If not, choose that option.

5. Draw four other vertical lines for the four remaining column guides in the same way.

Notice that above the "Description" label in Figure 4-1 is an extra vertical line separating the "Purchase Order #" column from the "Salesperson" column. Draw that line now.

6. Draw a vertical line from the intersection of 3 3/8 inches on the vertical ruler and 4 3/4 inches on the horizontal ruler to 4 inches on the vertical ruler.

Your page should look like the one shown in Figure 4-30.

7. Save your work by pressing CTRL-S for Save.

Now you can begin entering the text.

Establishing Order Detail Boxes

As seen in Figure 4-29, you've established two areas with the horizontal and vertical lines: a detail area containing label boxes and detail boxes, and six columns, each with label boxes. You first fill in the labels in the detail area.

To place the text, you must work in "Actual size" mode. You will notice that it is not easy to exactly center text in the boxes. You must place the insertion point in the same place in each label area. Otherwise, your text may be centered between the right and left sides, but not between the upper and lower lines. If some of them are off center, it is obvious.

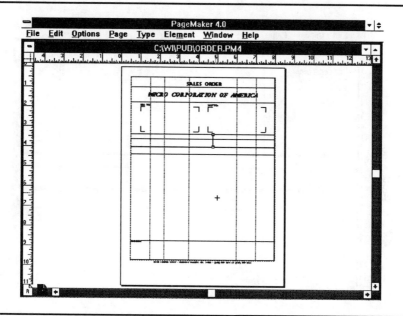

Figure 4-30. *The completed columnar lines*

To enter the text, follow these steps:

1. Press CTRL-1 to get the "Actual size" view of the page, and use the horizontal scroll bar to adjust the view so that you can just see the left margin.

The view should show the detail area in the middle of the screen, with the left margin slightly visible, as shown in Figure 4-31.

2. Press SHIFT-F4 or choose the text tool.

3. Place the I-beam in the label area of the upper-left detail area at 1 inch on the horizontal ruler and 3 9/16 inches on the vertical ruler; then click the main mouse button.

4. Turn off CAPS LOCK to return to lowercase.

5. Type in **Sales Order #**.

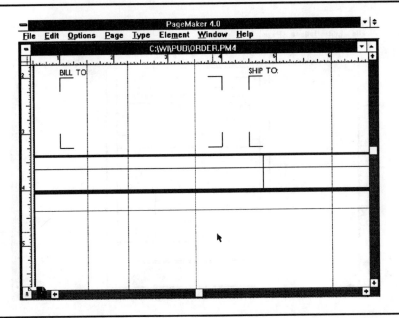

Figure 4-31. *The "Actual size" view of the detail boxes*

Your screen should look like the one shown in Figure 4-32.
Continue with the rest of the labels:

6. Place the I-beam in the next label box to the right, at 3 9/16 inches on the vertical ruler, and click the main mouse button.

7. Type in **Order Date**.

8. Move to the third detail label box, place the I-beam again at 3 9/16 inches, click, and type **Customer Number**.

9. In the fourth label box, place and click the I-beam as before. Then press CTRL-SHIFT-L to left-align the label, type two em spaces (a fixed width space equal to the full type size) by pressing CTRL-SHIFT-M twice, type **Purchase Order #**, press TAB, and type **Salesperson**.

10. Use the horizontal scroll bars to position the form, place the I-beam, and type **Promised** in the sixth label box.

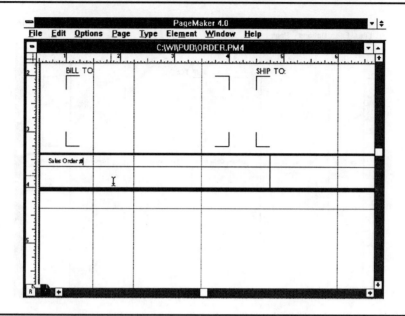

Figure 4-32.   *The first detail area filled in*

11. Type **Terms** in the seventh box.

    Your screen should look like the one shown in Figure 4-33.
    If some of your text is not centered between the upper and lower lines, you must adjust it by using the same technique that you used earlier to adjust the form title and company name. You can follow these quick steps if necessary to adjust any of the label text.

12. Drag down a horizontal ruler guide and place it just under the items you believe are correctly centered.

13. Select the pointer tool by pressing F9.

14. Click on the uncentered text.

15. When the text is seen inside the selection box, press the main mouse button until the pointer becomes a four-headed arrow, and then drag the text up or down until it is just sitting on the new ruler guide.

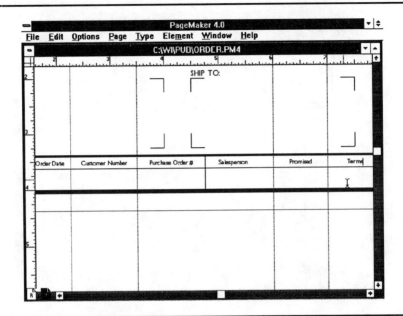

Figure 4-33. *All of the detail label areas filled in*

You can enter the column titles in a similar manner.

Entering the Column Titles

The label box for the first column contains two lines of text; the rest of the columns, only one. Consequently, the positioning of the I-beam within the first label box differs. Otherwise, the task is very similar to that of filling in the detail label boxes.

To enter the column labels, follow these steps:

1. Adjust your screen with the horizontal scroll bar to position the window so that the left margin is just visible.

2. If necessary, press F9 to return to the text tool.

3. Place the I-beam in the first label box above the far left column at 4 3/16 inches on the vertical ruler; then click.

4. Type **Quantity** and press ENTER.

5. Type **Ordered**.

6. Place the I-beam in the second label box at 4 5/16 inches on the vertical ruler, click, and type **Units**.

7. In the same way, placing the I-beam at 4 5/16 inches on the vertical ruler, type **Part Number** in the third box.

8. Type **Description** in the fourth box.

9. Type **Unit Price** in the fifth box.

10. Type **Extension** in the sixth label box.

Your screen should look like the one shown in Figure 4-34.

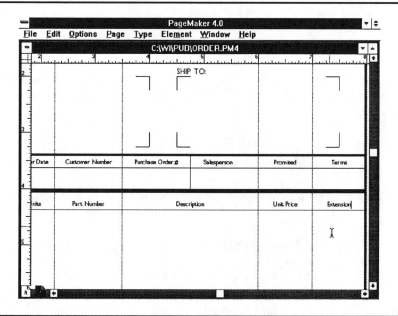

Figure 4-34.   *All labels entered*

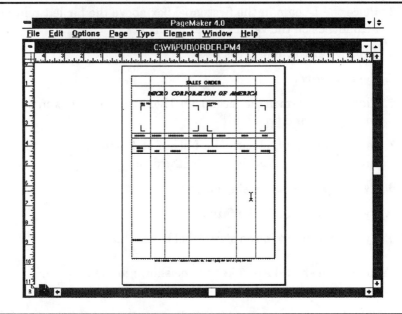

Figure 4-35. *The final order form before shading*

Again, you may have to center some of the text. If you need to do this, use the technique that you just used for adjusting the detail labels to move the text to where you want it.

11. Press CTRL-W to return the screen to the "Fit in window" view. Your screen should look like Figure 4-35.

Your final step is to supply the shading in the last two columns.

Shading Two Columns

The fifth and sixth columns are given 10 percent shading so that the sales staff leaves them blank. To shade an area, you must have a rectangle or oval to contain the shading; using the line tool to draw a rectangle with intersecting lines won't do. It must be a rectangle or oval made with their respective tools. Then you simply tell PageMaker to fill in the area with the shading of your choice. Because the columns are already defined by lines of their own, you will draw an invisible rectangle (one without lines) to hold the shading.

As you will recall from the flyer example in Chapter 3, PageMaker builds documents in layers. When you first draw the rectangle, it is on top of the stack of layers, which won't be a problem because its sides are invisible and it is empty. However, as soon as you fill in shading, the shaded rectangle covers up the text and column lines beneath it. You must place the shaded rectangle on the bottom of the stack, which allows the text and column lines to show up.

To add the shading, follow these steps:

1. Press F9 for the pointer tool.

2. Choose "None" in the "Line" option of the Element menu to draw a rectangle without visible lines.

3. Select the square-corner tool by pressing SHIFT-F5.

4. Position the crossbar on the upper-left corner of the Unit Price label box at 6 inches on the horizontal ruler and 4 inches on the vertical ruler.

When the crossbar is correctly positioned, the intersection beneath it disappears.

5. Drag the rectangle diagonally to the lower-right corner of the "Extension" column, at 8 inches on the horizontal ruler and 8 3/4 inches on the vertical ruler before releasing the main mouse button.

Before deselecting the box, select the shading.

6. Choose "10%" from the "Fill" option of the Element menu.

The columns are filled in with the shading, and everything under it has been covered up, as shown in Figure 4-36. You now send the top layer, the shaded rectangle, to the bottom of the stack, or to the back.

7. Choose "Send to back" from the Element menu.

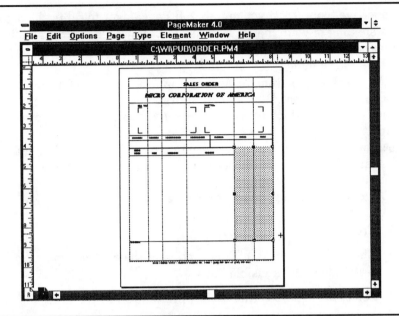

Figure 4-36. *Right two columns shaded before you choose "Send to back"*

The Sales Order form is now complete. Save your work.

8. Press CTRL-S for "Save".

The final product now appears on your screen. You may want to look at the whole Sales Order form in "Actual size" or even "200%" view and make any necessary adjustments.

Printing the Sales Order Form

Your Sales Order form is ready to be printed. Because you have already printed the flyer in Chapter 3, the instructions here are brief.

1. Press CTRL-P to print.

2. When the Printer dialog box is presented, verify that it is acceptable, and when your printer is ready, click on "OK".

Check that your Sales Order form is similar to that shown in Figure 4-1. If not, correct, save, and reprint it.

This concludes the building of the Sales Order form. You can use the techniques presented in this chapter to produce many forms for your own company or business. In addition, you can add graphics or a company logo if you want, as you see in the next chapter.

Chapter 5 demonstrates how to build a threefold, double-sided brochure.

5 *Creating a Brochure*

Brochures come in many forms. The one that you'll build in this chapter is a single sheet of 8 1/2 by 11-inch paper, printed on both sides and folded into thirds, as shown in Figures 5-1 and 5-2. It is the standard form of brochure used for direct mail solicitation. Its purpose is to provide information about the capabilities of a company—in this case, a firm engaged in desktop publishing.

You create the brochure with a combination of text entered in both PageMaker and WordPerfect to take advantage of the capabilities of each. It is easier to enter small amounts of text requiring special formatting or placement in PageMaker. However, it is easier to enter and edit larger blocks of text in a word processor, especially when indenting frequently. The single key used to indent in WordPerfect is preferable to the menu and dialog boxes that you must use in PageMaker. So here you enter the company name, product list, and address directly into PageMaker because they are short, use unique fonts, and are independently located on the brochure. You enter the balance of the brochure in WordPerfect, where you can easily indent, check the spelling, and perform other editing.

If you use a word processor other than WordPerfect (and it is supported by PageMaker), use it instead. Read through the WordPerfect instructions and duplicate them in your word processor. Also check the index of this book for the pages (if any) that discuss your word processor, and scan them to see if any specific instructions are needed to use your word processor with PageMaker for a project like this brochure.

Because some printers with limited memory may have a problem printing the brochure with graphics on it, you build the brochure in two stages. In the first stage you enter or "place" all text and one short line segment.

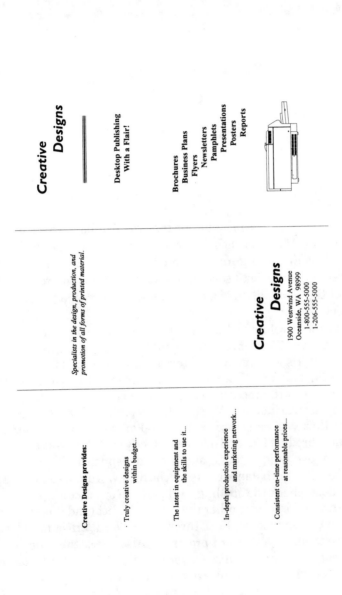

Figure 5-1. *The printout of page 1 of the finished brochure with graphics*

What can we do for you?

· Save Money...
We have highly efficient equipment and the skills necessary to produce the best quality products at the lowest prices -- benefits we pass on to you.

· Eliminate Hassle...
We are designers, managers, and skilled craftsmen who help you plan, design, produce, and promote your printed products. We understand the intricacies of typesetting, printing, bindery, and direct mail solicitation. We oversee the project from beginning to completion.

· Create Effective Publications...
A truly effective publication - one that accomplishes its purposes - is the only kind we produce: sales brochures that sell; training manuals that teach; and newsletters that inform. An effective publication is a sound investment.

How are our services used?

· Finding Answers...
What is the purpose of the publication? What is the audience? What copy, graphics, and photos are to be used? What size and shape is desired? What length is it? What color is appropriate?

· Setting Budgets and Schedules...
How much do you want to spend and when do you want the work completed? How can we help you stretch your dollars, giving you the best publication in the time you have to produce it?

· Planning and Design...
Based on your specifications we create a design and a production plan to meet your needs.

· Production and Promotion...
We use the latest equipment and specialized talents and skills to produce and promote your publication.

Who uses our services?

Big and small companies, public and private agencies, including architects, aerospace companies, banks, bakeries, contractors, CPA firms, doctors, hospitals, libraries, local governments, schools, universities, and wineries.

We will provide you a specific list of our customers in your industry if you request it.

We welcome all projects where quality, attention to detail, and creativity are of concern.

For outstanding results, let us assist you with your next project.

Figure 5-2. *The printout of page 2 of the finished brochure with graphics*

In the second stage you add several vertical lines and a graphic from Micrografx Designer. This allows you to see the effects of two schools of graphic design: one that favors simplicity in the brochure by not using graphics and another that espouses "completeness" and uses them.

Planning and Designing the Brochure

Planning for the brochure is reasonably simple. You may want to have a marketing or public relations person create the copy (or the first draft of it), but the brochure can easily be a one-person project. If you plan on printing a large quantity (anything over a hundred copies), you should produce only a set of originals on your laser printer and then take them to a commercial printer for the final product. During the planning, you should also consider the mailing costs and procedures for distributing the brochures.

The design begins with a single 8 1/2 by 11-inch standard letter-size piece of paper. You use both sides of the paper, considering each side a page. Each page is divided into three columns with a 1/2-inch margin on all edges. When the paper is folded, the columns become panels.

Three fonts are used in creating the brochure: the title (the company name) is set in 24-point Gill Sans bold italic type; the rest of the right column on the first page uses 14-point Times New Roman bold; and the balance of the brochure uses 12-point Times New Roman (medium weight), with the headings in bold. You may wish or need to use other typefaces, sizes, or styles to correspond with those you have available. The Times New Roman and Gill Sans typefaces were developed by Adobe Systems, Inc., and are included with PageMaker 4. For the remainder of this chapter Times New Roman or its serif equivalent is referred to as Times and Gill Sans or its sans serif equivalent is referred to as Sans. There are many other font vendors that you may also use. Appendix E lists the addresses and phone numbers of several of these. (See Appendix B for a discussion of laser printers and fonts.)

The graphic on the cover is created with Micrografx Designer. It is a line drawing of the HP LaserJet Series II. If you do not have Designer, you can use any other drawing package you have available. As with the word processor, look at the instructions given in this book for Designer, and then look in the index to see if your drawing package is discussed. While you can use a paint program, the results you get are different. Finally, if you do not wish to do a drawing, you can use any appropriate clip art (or click art) you have. Several vendors sell files of graphics that you can use in your publications. See Appendix E for a list of some of them.

The vertical lines or rules between columns are hairlines, the smallest line width available in PageMaker. Therefore, except for possible font or graphic substitutions, the brochure design is unaffected by system constraints.

Before bringing up PageMaker to create the brochure, look now at creating the text and graphics with WordPerfect and Micrografx Designer. If you do not want to enter the text and graphics files used to build the PageMaker publications in this book, you can buy a disk containing those files, as well as files containing the finished publications. See the order form in the front of the book.

Creating the Text and Graphics

Because the primary focus of this book is PageMaker, the following discussion only briefly examines what you do in WordPerfect and Micrografx Designer to create the text and graphics for this brochure. In particular you should notice the constraints that PageMaker places on files imported from these applications. If you are using a different word processor or drawing application, take a look at the chapter that discusses how those applications are used in addition to reading this section.

Entering the WordPerfect Text

Text brought into PageMaker from WordPerfect 5.1 retains almost all the formatting and style settings chosen in WordPerfect. For PageMaker to identify the text as a WordPerfect file, however, the file must have the extension WP5. For example, you will name this file BROCH.WP5. You therefore set the spacing, indents, tabs, typeface, type size, and type style within WordPerfect. When you transfer the document over to PageMaker, all this information goes with it.

Setting Up WordPerfect   It is important that the format settings are correctly set in WordPerfect because you'll use them in PageMaker. Start WordPerfect now, open a new document, and make the following settings:

1. Use the default tab setting of every 0.5 inch.

2. Use the default of full justification.

3. Use the default of inches as the measurement system.

4. Set the font to 12-point Times.

Text Entry   The actual text entry is straightforward. Just follow the annotation as to spacing and style shown in Figures 5-3 through 5-5. If you are using different copy on your brochure, make a reasonable guess on the spacing in WordPerfect, and then make any necessary corrections in PageMaker. The indents and character spacing are design choices for this copy. With different copy you may want another design. If you want your brochure to look like the one shown in Figures 5-1 and 5-2, you must enter the same number of returns and tabs and apply the bold and italic style where shown. The indented paragraphs use the standard 0.5 inch indent entered with F4, and the bullet character is character number 7 (applied by pressing ALT and typing **7** on the numeric keypad).

When you have finished entering the copy, save the file in your \WI\PUB directory with the filename BROCH.WP5. Finally, you may want to print the file.

Creating the Graphic With Micrografx Designer

Creating the graphic in Micrografx Designer is less demanding than entering the text in WordPerfect because, for the purpose of this exercise, all you want to do is place a graphic in a PageMaker publication. You don't care what the graphic is. With text, part of the objective is to have it

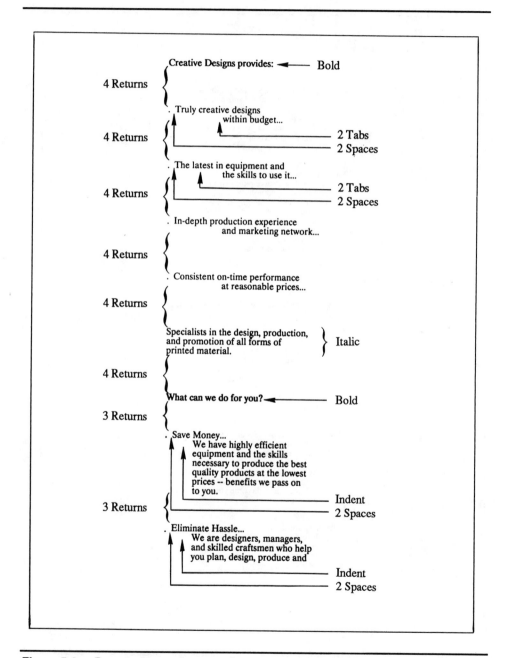

Figure 5-3. *Page 1 of text to be entered*

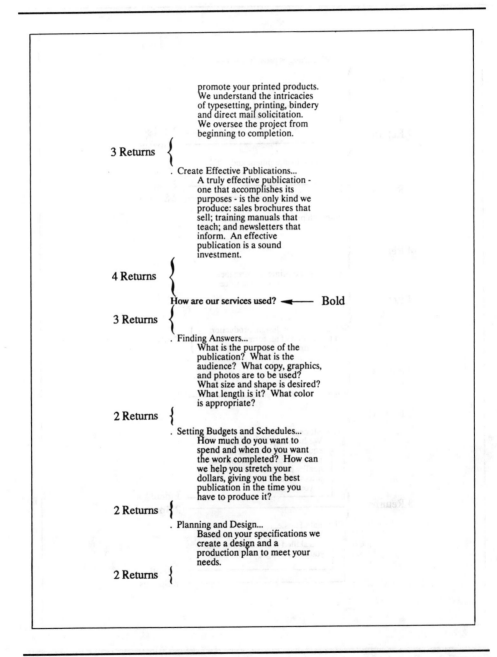

promote your printed products.
We understand the intricacies
of typesetting, printing, bindery
and direct mail solicitation.
We oversee the project from
beginning to completion.

3 Returns

. Create Effective Publications...
A truly effective publication -
one that accomplishes its
purposes - is the only kind we
produce: sales brochures that
sell; training manuals that
teach; and newsletters that
inform. An effective
publication is a sound
investment.

4 Returns

How are our services used? ◄—— Bold

3 Returns

. Finding Answers...
What is the purpose of the
publication? What is the
audience? What copy, graphics,
and photos are to be used?
What size and shape is desired?
What length is it? What color
is appropriate?

2 Returns

. Setting Budgets and Schedules...
How much do you want to
spend and when do you want
the work completed? How can
we help you stretch your
dollars, giving you the best
publication in the time you
have to produce it?

2 Returns

. Planning and Design...
Based on your specifications we
create a design and a
production plan to meet your
needs.

2 Returns

Figure 5-4. *Page 2 of text to be entered*

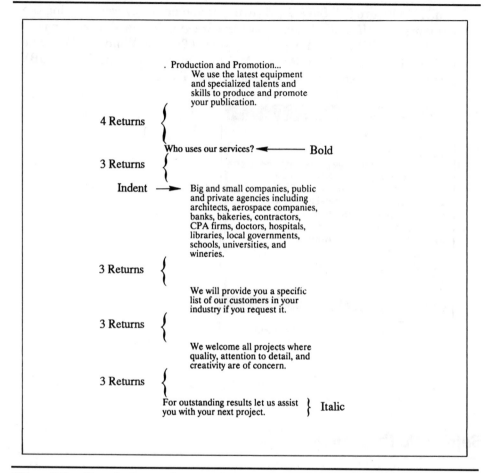

Figure 5-5. *Page 3 of text to be entered*

properly formatted. Therefore, you may want to take the time to create the drawing shown here, or you may want to substitute something else.

For whatever graphic you want to use or create, start Micrografx Designer, or the drawing package you want to use, and prepare the drawing now. When you are done you should have a drawing on your screen similar to Figure 5-6. Save the drawing as you normally would, using the filename HPLJII.DRW. Then export the drawing in one of three formats: Paintbrush (PCX), Tag Image File format (TIF), or Windows MetaFile (WMF). If you use the Windows MetaFile format and the \WI\PUB\ directory, your Export dialog box should look like this:

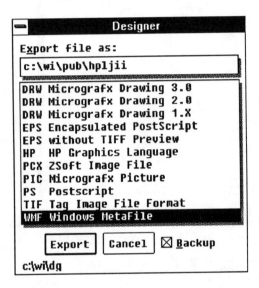

You are now ready to load PageMaker and begin building the brochure.

Setting Up the Brochure

You greatly simplify the remaining tasks when you correctly lay out the brochure and set the defaults appropriately before entering text or graphics. In addition, this setup phase helps you place the imported text correctly. The importance of this phase cannot be overemphasized.

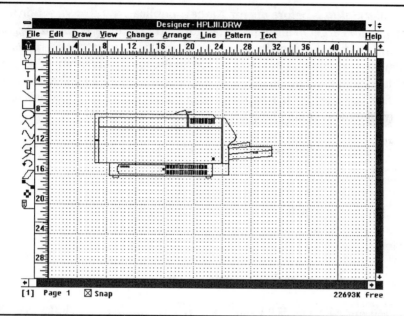

Figure 5-6.   *The Micrografx Designer screen with the completed HPLJII.DRW*

Establishing the Layout

The layout is governed by three dialog boxes: Target printer, Page setup, and Column guides. All three of these dialog boxes must be set and their settings agree for the brochure to be produced properly. For example, you must select both "Landscape" orientation in the Target printer dialog box and "Wide" orientation in the Page setup dialog box to rotate the page on the screen and to have it print properly. In landscape or wide orientation, the 11-inch edge of an 8 1/2 by 11-inch piece of paper is horizontal. The 11-inch edge is vertical in "Portrait" or "Tall" orientation.

Printer Setup Before opening a new publication, always set or at least check the Target printer dialog box for your printer. It is easy to forget this, but checking the printer setup is particularly important to remember if you are creating a publication in landscape orientation or if you are changing your font cartridge or paper size. It is a good habit to do this before you start each new publication. Load PageMaker now and open the Target printer dialog box using the following instructions:

1. Select the File menu and choose "Target printer...".

2. Double-click on the printer you want to use.

To get the Target printer dialog box, you can double-click on the printer name in the listing box or just click on "Setup" if the printer is already highlighted.

3. Click on the Landscape option button.

If you are using an HP LaserJet Series II, your printer dialog box should now look like the one shown in Figure 5-7.

4. Click on "OK" twice to return to the work area.

Page Setup The next step is to create a new publication and do the page setup. In addition to coordinating the printer's use of landscape mode with the wide orientation of the page on the screen, you must reset the margins and turn off the "Double-sided" option. Even though the brochure is double-sided, both sides have the same layout (margins, columns, and guides). So you can save time by defining the layout on one master page and having it apply to both pages. If you leave "Double-sided" turned on (an "X" is in the check box), PageMaker assumes that the two sides are different and you have two master pages, which defeats your purpose. Use the following instructions to define the page setup:

1. Choose "New" from the File menu.

2. Type **2** in the already-selected Number of pages text box.

3. Click on the "Wide" Orientation option button.

4. Click on the Double-sided check box to turn it off.

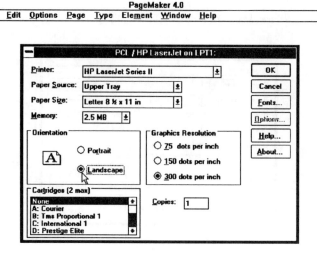

Figure 5-7.   *"Landscape" orientation turned on in the printer dialog box*

5. Drag across the "1" in the Left margin text box.

6. Type **.5**, and press TAB to move to the Right margin text box.

7. Type **.5**, and press TAB to move to the Top margin text box.

8. Type **.5**, and press TAB to move to the Bottom margin text box.

9. Type **.5** in the Bottom margin text box.

When you are done, your dialog box should look like the one shown in Figure 5-8.

10. Click on "OK" to return to the work area.

Column Guides   The brochure has three columns of text on each page. The space between the columns varies. The easiest way to handle this is to set up five columns on each page, with two of the columns serving as

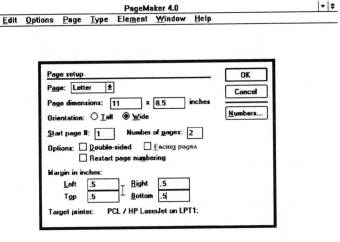

Figure 5-8. *The Page setup dialog box*

variable space between the text columns. In this way you can handle the varying widths without trying to move column guides as you are flowing text. The instructions to establish the columns and set the default widths follow. But first you need to set the unit of measure to be used on the rulers.

1. Choose "Preferences" from the Edit menu.

2. Click on the downward-pointing arrow to the right of the Measurement system text box, and then click on "Inches decimal".

3. Click on the downward-pointing arrow to the right of the Vertical ruler text box, and then click on "Inches decimal". Your Preferences dialog box should look like this:

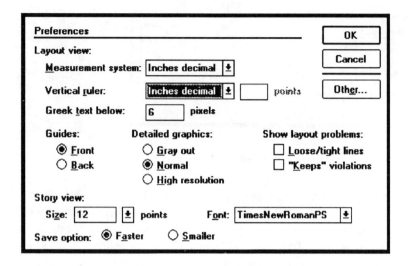

4. Click on "OK" to close the Preferences dialog box.

You will find that it is easier to work with the decimal scale than fractions when you are placing precise column and ruler guides.

5. Click on the master-page icon (the page icon with an "R" in it).

6. Choose "Column guides" from the Options menu to get the Column guides dialog box.

7. Type **5** in the "Number of columns" text box.

The space between columns does not matter because you have established additional columns for that purpose. Therefore, to avoid confusion, set the space between columns to zero.

8. Press TAB to move to the "Space between columns" text box and type **0**. Your Column guides dialog box should look like this:

```
┌──────────────────────────────────────────────────────────┐
│  Column guides _____   ┌────────┐  │
│                                               │   OK   │  │
│                                               └────────┘  │
│                                               ┌────────┐  │
│                                               │ Cancel │  │
│  Number of columns:      ┌─────────┐          └────────┘  │
│                          │5        │                      │
│  Space between columns:  │0│       │  inches              │
│                          └─────────┘                      │
│                                                           │
└──────────────────────────────────────────────────────────┘
```

9. Press ENTER to return to the publication.

Ruler Guides   Next you want to place two vertical ruler guides to divide the page into three equal panels. Because you will be moving the column guides, you must have a fixed point of reference to visually check on how the layout is coming. Later you will draw a hairline rule down these guides. You may find it difficult to achieve the placement of the ruler and column guides at the exact positions suggested. Come as close as you can in the current "Fit in window" view. When you go to "Actual size" view, you can refine the position and become more precise.

1. Drag a vertical ruler guide to 7.33 inches on the horizontal ruler.

2. Drag a vertical ruler guide to 3.67 inches on the horizontal ruler.

Adjusting Page 1   Once the master set of columns and guides is positioned, you can go to each page and adjust the column widths.

1. Click on the page 1 icon in the lower-left corner of the window to display page 1. Notice that the columns and two vertical ruler guides have been copied over from the master page.

2. Drag the leftmost column guide (between columns 1 and 2, as shown in Figure 5-9) from 2.5 to 3.3 inches on the horizontal ruler.

3. Drag the rightmost column guide (between columns 4 and 5) from 8.5 to 8.15 inches.

4. Drag the right margin guide from the right margin to 10.2 inches on the horizontal ruler. (Drag the Toolbox down by dragging on the title

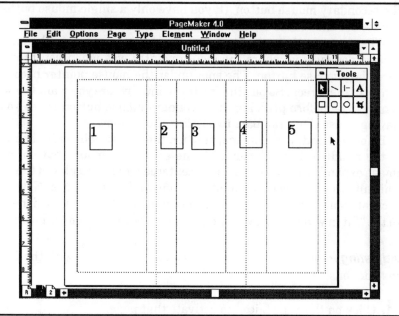

Figure 5-9.   *Column layout of page 1*

bar so you can see the ruler on the right. Restore the Toolbox to its original position when you are done.)

This completes the layout of the first page. Your screen should look like the one shown in Figure 5-9. If you would like to be very accurate, expand the image to "Actual size" view and adjust the lines exactly to the dimensions just given.

In this chapter you use a third method to switch between "Fit in window" and "Actual size" images of your publication. In Chapter 3 you accomplished this by choosing options on the Page menu. In Chapter 4 you used the CTRL-1 and CTRL-W shortcut keys. Here you vary the screen image by pressing the *secondary mouse button*. Normally this is the right mouse button. However, if you redefined the use of the mouse buttons so the left one is not the main mouse button, you must use the left mouse button as the secondary mouse button. (If you have only a single mouse button, you cannot use the mouse to vary the image.)

When you use the mouse to change to "Actual size" view, the image you receive depends on where the mouse pointer was when you pressed the secondary mouse button. The spot under the mouse pointer becomes the center of the screen. So positioning the pointer where you want the screen's center to be before pressing the secondary mouse button saves you from having to use the scroll bars to position the window.

Before expanding the image, position the mouse pointer in the top third of the middle column. Then click the secondary mouse button, and the image expands to actual size and is centered where you placed the pointer. This allows you to see the middle column and ruler guides. Now you can accurately adjust the column and ruler guides. When you are done, return to the "Fit in window" view by pressing the secondary mouse button again.

Adjusting Page 2   Next adjust the columns on page 2 with the following instructions:

1. Click on the page 2 icon to activate that page.

2. Drag the leftmost column guide (between columns 1 and 2) from 2.5 to 3.2 inches on the horizontal ruler.

3. Drag the next column guide (between columns 2 and 3) from 4.5 to 4.1 inches.

4. Drag the next column guide (between columns 3 and 4) from 6.5 to 6.9 inches.

5. Drag the rightmost column guide (between columns 4 and 5) from 8.5 to 7.8 inches.

Your second page should now look like the one shown in Figure 5-10. Again, if you wish more precision, expand to "Actual size" view and adjust the placement of the guides. Return to "Fit in window" view when you are done.

6. Click on the page 1 icon to return to that page.

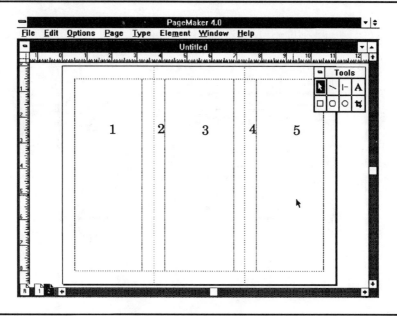

Figure 5-10.　*Page 2 with column and ruler guides in place*

Setting the Defaults

As a general rule, you should set all the defaults before starting work on a publication. This gives you a known starting place for all related functions, including text entry and drawing.

In earlier steps you set the printer and page defaults, chose the decimal-inch preference, and established the number of columns. These are all defaults. The only defaults remaining to be set are the type and line specifications and the method of alignment. Use the following instructions to set these remaining defaults.

1. Verify that the pointer tool is selected.

2. Press CTRL-T to open the Type specifications dialog box.

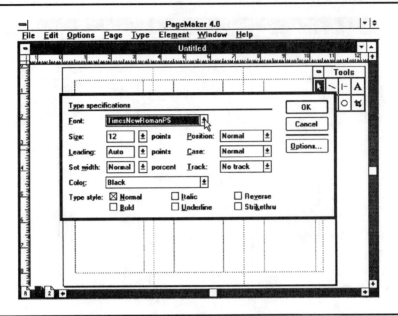

Figure 5-11. *The Type specifications dialog box with default settings*

3. Click on the downward-pointing arrow on the right of the Font text box. Click on "Times New Roman" or the serif typeface you want to use.

4. Confirm that the Size text box contains "12", that Leading is "Auto", and that Set width, Type style, Position, and Case are all set to "Normal".

Your Type specifications dialog box should look like the one shown in Figure 5-11.

5. Click on "OK" or press ENTER to complete the Type specifications dialog box.

6. Press CTRL-SHIFT-J to set "Justify" as the default alignment.

7. Choose "Hairline" from the "Line" option of the Element menu as the default line width.

This completes the setting of the defaults. Now go to the right column and enter the cover of the brochure.

Creating the Cover

The first page of the brochure contains three columns. When it is folded, the right column becomes the cover, the middle column becomes the back, and the left column becomes the inside flap—the first panel seen when the brochure is opened. The cover contains the company name at the top, a short line segment under the name, a slogan in the middle, and a list of products below the slogan. Later in this chapter you will place the graphic that appears at the bottom of the cover.

Each item on the cover—name, line segment, slogan, and product list—requires unique treatment and is therefore discussed separately in the paragraphs that follow.

Entering the Company Name

The company name consists of the words "Creative Designs." You enter these words on separate lines using 24-point Gill Sans bold italic type. (If you do not have this specific font, use any 24-point sans serif bold italic font that you have available. The italic type sets apart the company name from the rest of the cover.)

A design objective is to center the words "Creative Designs" between the fold and the edge of the page. To do this, you left-align the first word against a column guide 0.8 inch from the fold and right-align the second word against a column guide 0.8 inch from the edge of the page. You have already set the column guides appropriately, so you need only align the words. You use the "Actual size" view to perform these tasks. Use the following instructions to enter the company name and align it:

1. Position the mouse pointer at 8.5 inches on the horizontal ruler and 1.7 inches on the vertical ruler.

2. Press the secondary mouse button to expand to "Actual size" view.

The view should be centered where you placed the mouse button. Note the precision with which you can control the view.

3. Select the text tool.

4. Click to the right of the left column guide in the right column at 1.15 inches on the vertical ruler to position the insertion point.

5. Press CTRL-T to open the Type specifications dialog box.

6. Click on the downward-pointing arrow on the right of the Font text box. Click on "Gill Sans" or the sans serif typeface you want to use. Press TAB and type **24** in the Size text box and click on both "Bold" and "Italic" in the Type style check boxes, as shown in Figure 5-12.

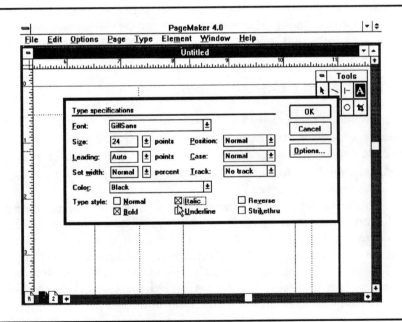

Figure 5-12. *The Type specifications dialog box with the title settings*

7. Press ENTER to return to the work area.

8. Press CTRL-SHIFT-L to select left alignment.

9. Type **Creative** and press ENTER.

10. Press CTRL-SHIFT-R to select right alignment.

11. Type **Designs** and press ENTER.

The company name should appear as shown in Figure 5-13. Don't worry if it seems that the final "s" in "Designs" looks cut off; it will be correct when it is printed.

Next you place the short line segment under the name.

Drawing a Line

The line segment under the name is a design element—an artistic touch to separate and emphasize the name. First you place one horizontal and

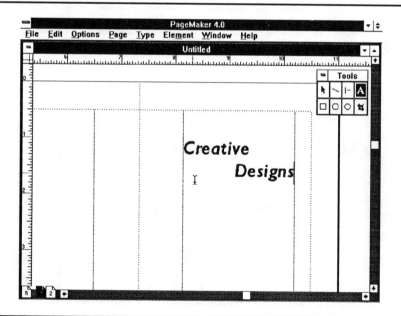

Figure 5-13.   *The "Actual size" view showing aligned company name*

two vertical ruler guides to establish where the actual line is drawn. After you draw the line, you select the kind of line you want from the "Line" option of the Element menu. The instructions for drawing the line are as follows:

1. Select the perpendicular-line tool.

2. Drag down a horizontal ruler guide and place it at 2.15 inches on the vertical ruler.

3. Drag over two vertical ruler guides. Place one at 9.95 inches and the other at 8.4 inches.

4. Draw a horizontal line from 8.4 to 9.95 along the ruler guide you placed at 2.15 inches on the vertical ruler, as shown in Figure 5-14.

5. While the line is still selected, open the "Line" option of the Element menu, and choose the triple line shown in Figure 5-14.

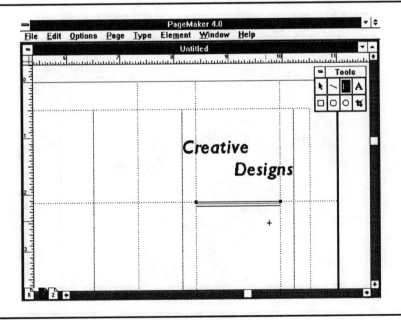

Figure 5-14. *Triple line segment under the company name*

If the line segment is deselected before you choose the line style from the "Line" option of the Element menu, you must reselect it. You can easily do that by changing to the pointer tool and then pressing and holding CTRL while clicking on the line segment with the main mouse button. If you do not press and hold CTRL while clicking, you select only the horizontal guide line.

You now must get rid of the vertical ruler guides so they do not interfere with entering the remaining text on the cover. Follow these steps:

6. Select the pointer tool (if it is not already selected).

7. Drag the vertical ruler guide at 8.4 inches off the right edge of the publication.

8. Drag the vertical ruler guide at 9.95 inches off the right edge of the publication.

Entering the Remaining Cover Text

The remaining text on the cover consists of a two-line slogan and a list of eight products. You place the insertion point before entering the text and reset the type specifications. To place the product list, you set a series of tab stops. Use these instructions to carry out those tasks and enter the remaining text:

1. Select the text tool.

2. Click to the right of the left column guide in the right column at 3 inches on the vertical ruler to place the insertion point.

3. Press CTRL-T to open the Type specifications dialog box.

4. Press TAB and type **14** in the Size text box. Click on "Bold" in the Type style check box, as shown in Figure 5-15.

5. Press ENTER or click on "OK" to close the dialog box.

6. Press CTRL-SHIFT-C to center the text.

7. Type **Desktop Publishing** and press ENTER.

8. Type **With a Flair!** and press ENTER.

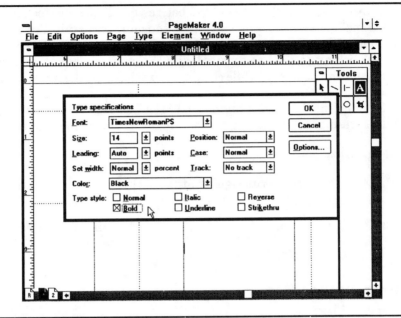

Figure 5-15.   *The Type specifications dialog box for the bottom of the cover*

9. Press ENTER four times to provide a separation between the slogan and the product list.

10. Press CTRL-SHIFT-L to left-align the products.

You want the list of products to be stairstepped across the page. You can do this in several ways, but the easiest method is to use tabs. Because the normal tab spacing at every half inch is too wide for this list, you must reset the tabs with the Indents/tabs dialog box. Setting the tab stops is a two-step process when you need accuracy, as you do here. Place the pointer on the tab ruler close to where you think you want to add a tab stop, and press and hold the main mouse button. Then move the tab left and right while watching the text box containing the exact tab setting. When that setting is correct, release the main mouse button. Follow these steps:

11. Press CTRL-I to get the Indents/tabs dialog box.

12. Press and hold the main mouse button at .20 inch on the tab ruler to create a new tab stop (the bent-arrow icon). Look at the text box in the center and above the tab ruler. If you need to, drag the tab stop left or right until the text box reads exactly 0.2. Then release the main mouse button.

13. Repeat step 12 to place a new tab stop at .35 on the tab ruler.

14. Drag the existing tab stop at .5 right to .55.

15. Place new tab stops at .70 and .90.

16. Drag the existing tab at 1.0 right to 1.05.

17. Place a new tab stop at 1.25.

The reason for the uneven tab stops (.15 inch and .20 inch between tabs) is that all tabs at .20 inch are too wide to fit in the space available, all at .15 inch are too narrow, and you can't set tabs in between. The Indents/tabs dialog box should look like this:

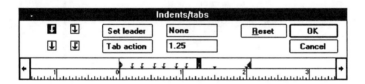

18. Press ENTER or click on "OK" to return to the work area.

19. Use the vertical scroll bar to adjust the screen image so that it extends from about 2.4 inches to about 6.5 inches on the vertical ruler. Maximize both your application and document windows if they are not already.

20. Type the following list of products (omitting the commas). After each product, press ENTER. On the second product press TAB once before typing the product, on the third product press TAB twice, and so on for the remaining products. The last item, "Reports," has seven tabs preceding it.

Brochures, Business Plans, Flyers, Newsletters, Pamphlets, Presentations, Posters, Reports

Figure 5-16 shows what the slogan and product list should look like in "Actual size" view when they are properly entered. Figure 5-17 shows the same thing in "Fit in window" view.

21. Click the secondary mouse button to go to the "Fit in window" view.

22. Press CTRL-S to save the brochure. The Save dialog box should appear.

23. Open the correct directory (\WI\PUB\ is used here) by double-clicking on "[..]", scrolling the list until you see the directory you want, and then double-clicking on the directory.

24. Type **brochure** in the Filename text box and press ENTER.

The Save publication as dialog box looks like this:

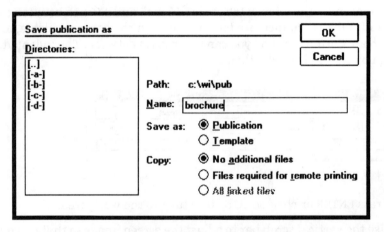

You are now ready to construct the middle column.

Constructing the Middle Column

You build the middle column in two separate phases. First, you construct the lower part of the middle column. The lower portion consists of the company name, copied from the cover, followed by the address and phone numbers, which you enter. Later, you add a block of text written in WordPerfect to the upper part of the column.

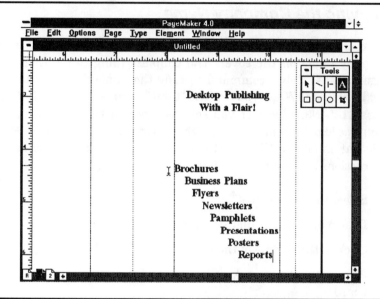

Figure 5-16. *Completed slogan and product list at "Actual size"*

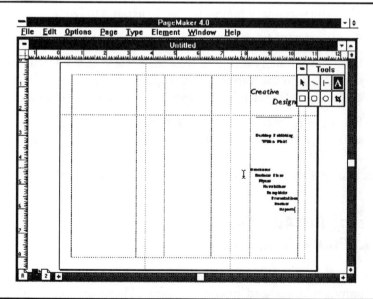

Figure 5-17. *First page of brochure with slogan and product list in right column*

Copying the Company Name

The company name in the middle column is the same size and style as the company name on the cover. The simplest thing to do, then, is to use PageMaker's "Copy" command to copy the name from the cover to the middle column. When you use the "Copy" command on the Edit menu or press CTRL-INS, whatever you selected goes on the Clipboard. Then, by using the "Paste" command from the Edit menu or pressing SHIFT-INS, the information on the Clipboard is copied to the center of the screen. The instructions to do that are as follows:

1. Select the pointer tool.

2. Drag a horizontal ruler guide down to 6.8 inches on the vertical ruler.

3. Click in the middle of the company name on the cover to select it.

4. Press CTRL-INS to make a copy of the company name onto the Clipboard.

5. Move the mouse pointer to 5.5 inches on the horizontal ruler and 6.5 inches on the vertical ruler.

6. Click the secondary mouse button to expand to "Actual size" view.

7. Press SHIFT-INS to insert the company name in the middle of the screen.

8. Drag the company name so that the bottom of the word "Designs" is just sitting on the horizontal ruler guide that you placed at 6.8 inches, and so the left text selection boxes are on the left column guide.

9. Place the pointer on one of the right text selection boxes (the black squares in the corners) and drag it to the right column guide.

Figure 5-18 shows the company name positioned in the middle column.

Adding the Address And Phone Numbers

The final step in creating the lower-middle column is entering the company's address and phone numbers. These are centered below the

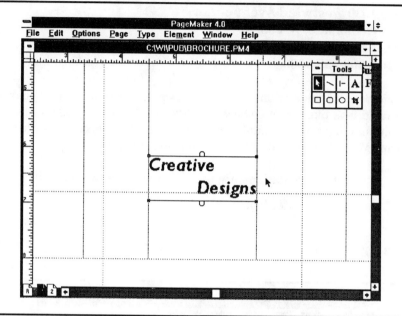

Figure 5-18.   *Company name in the middle column*

company name and use the default 12-point Times type. The instructions to do this are as follows:

1. Select the text tool.

2. Click the text tool to the right of the left column guide of the middle column at 7.1 inches on the vertical ruler.

3. Press CTRL-SHIFT-C to center the address and phone numbers.

4. Press CTRL-T and check that the default type specifications have not changed from "Times", "12" points, "Auto" Leading, and "Normal" Type style. Press ENTER.

5. Type the following address and phone numbers, pressing ENTER after each line, and type two spaces between the state and the ZIP code:

1900 Westwind Avenue
Oceanside, WA 98999
1-800-555-5000
1-206-555-5000

When you have entered the address and phone numbers, your screen should look like the one shown in Figure 5-19. You must now adjust the column guides on the middle column so that it can accept the block of text from WordPerfect that you will be placing there.

6. Click the secondary mouse button for a "Fit in window" view.

7. Select the pointer tool.

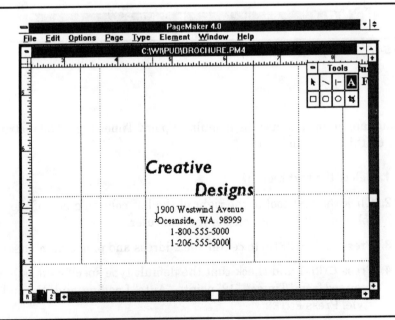

Figure 5-19.   *Middle column with company name and address entered*

8. Drag the left column guide of the middle column (between columns 2 and 3) from 4.5 to 4 inches on the horizontal ruler.

9. Drag the right column guide of the middle column (between columns 3 and 4) from 6.5 to 7 inches on the horizontal ruler.

10. Press CTRL-S to save the brochure.

You have now completed all of the direct entry work, and your screen should look like the one in Figure 5-20. This would be a good time to take a break. If you leave PageMaker, remember to check all your defaults when you return, including the landscape orientation of the target printer. When you are ready to resume, you can place the text you created in WordPerfect.

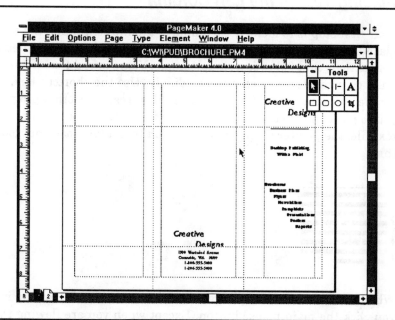

Figure 5-20. *Page 1 with middle and right columns filled in*

Placing Text on the First Page

Placing text is easy. You simply identify the file containing the text and the upper-left corner of the column in which you want it placed. PageMaker then flows the text into that column until it reaches the bottom margin, other text, or a graphic. If there is more text than the original column can hold, you can pick up and flow the excess into as many additional columns as necessary to complete the article or whatever you are placing.

In this brochure you initially place the text in the left column of the first page. Then you place a block of text in the middle column and place the remainder on the second page. In Chapter 7 you will learn how to flow multiple columns of text automatically with PageMaker's "Autoflow" feature.

Placing Text in the Left Column

Your first step is to identify the name of the file containing the text to be placed. Remember that the \WI\PUB directory that is specified in the instructions that follow is a sample name. Yours may differ. If it does, you must change the instructions accordingly. Use the shortcut key, CTRL-D, for the Place command. Place retrieves files created by other programs for you to place in the current publication. When PageMaker has retrieved a text file, the pointer changes to a *text icon* (not a text tool) that looks like this:

When you have a text icon, PageMaker flows text into the column in which you click the main mouse button. Except when you are flowing the text, you can still use the pointer to choose commands, scroll the window, and change pages even though it has become a text icon. The pointer again becomes the familiar arrow icon when you move it to the menu bar, the horizontal or vertical scroll bar, or to the page icons. The primary function here, however, is to place text in columns. The steps to identify the file and place the text in the left column are as follows:

1. Press CTRL-D to get the Place file dialog box.

2. Click on BROCH.WP5 in the Files list box if it is shown. Otherwise, press TAB to go to the text box and type **\wi\pub\broch.wp5** (BROCH.WP5 is the name given to the text file in WordPerfect); then press ENTER. The Place file dialog box looks like this:

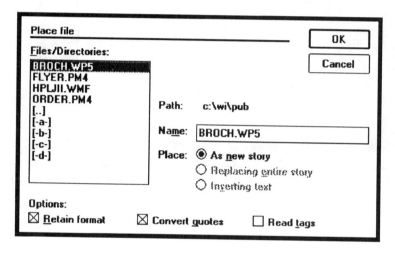

3. Move the text icon pointer to the left column guide of the left column at 2 inches on the vertical ruler. This is just above the horizontal ruler guide you placed at 2.15 inches.

4. Click the main mouse button.

Text flows into and fills the left column from the point you clicked the main mouse button. Your screen should look like the one shown in Figure 5-21. On the top and bottom of the text is a selection box with text handles—lines on either ends of the column of text with tiny boxes on their ends and a loop in the center like a window shade. The top loop is empty and the bottom loop has a downward-pointing triangle in it. The empty loop means that this is the beginning of the article. The triangle means that there is more text than could be placed in the left column. If you place all the text in the column, an empty loop appears at the bottom.

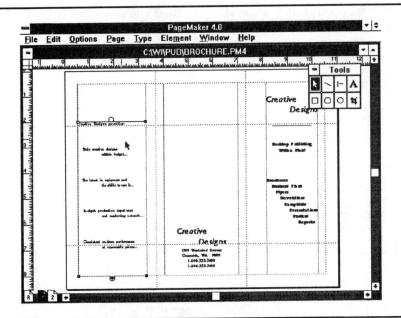

Figure 5-21.   *Page 1 showing the text placed in the left column*

The text handles work in several ways. If you click on the triangle in the bottom loop, your pointer once again turns into a text icon, and you can flow the remaining text into another column by clicking in that column. If you press and hold the main mouse button while pointing at either the top or bottom loop, the text handles work like window shades, moving up or down, showing or hiding text as they go. Finally, you can point on any of the four tiny boxes on the ends of the handles and drag the text inside or beyond the original column boundaries. In that case PageMaker reflows the text to fit the new line length. Here you use the window shade principle to define exactly how much text is to remain in the left column.

5. Point on the triangle in the loop of the lower handle, press and hold the main mouse button, and drag the handle up until you have only the title line at the top and four two-line pairs beneath it.

6. Release the main mouse button.

7. If your screen still does not look like Figure 5-21, it may be because the "Times" font in WordPerfect is not the same as the "Times" font in PageMaker. To correct this, select the text tool, click it in the text in column 1, press CTRL-A to "Select all" of the WordPerfect text, press CTRL-T for "Types specs...", change the typeface to "Times", (don't make any other changes), and click "OK".

The left column is complete if it looks like the one shown in Figure 5-21. You are now ready to work on the middle column.

Flowing Text into the Middle Column

For the middle column, you pick up the remaining text to be placed by clicking on the bottom loop of the text handle in the left column, again turning the pointer into a text icon. Then, by clicking near the top of the middle column, you flow the text down that column. Notice that it stops when it reaches the company name. Finally, using the window-shade effect, you "roll up" the text, leaving only the single block of text that you want in the middle column. The instructions to do this are as follows:

1. Click on the triangle in the bottom loop in the left column. The pointer becomes a text icon.

2. Move the text icon to the left column guide of the middle column at 1.5 inches on the vertical ruler and click.

Text should flow down the column, stopping just above the company name.

3. Drag the lower loop up until only a two-line paragraph remains.

4. Drag the remaining two-line paragraph so the bottom line is just sitting on the horizontal ruler guide at 2.15 inches. The bottom line in the middle column should be in line with the first line of text in the left column, as shown in Figure 5-22.

This completes the first page. Save the brochure, and then continue with page 2.

5. Press CTRL-S to save the brochure.

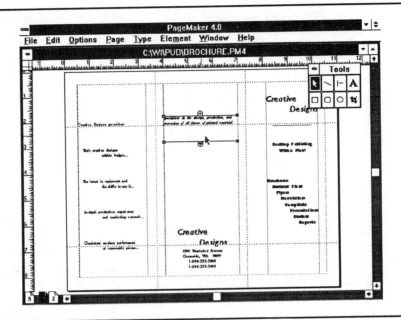

Figure 5-22. *Complete text of page 1*

Building Page Two

The second page is the inside of the brochure. As you fold back the cover (the right column of page 1) and then the inside flap (the left column of page 1), you will see the second page in its entirety. It consists of the remaining text that you created in WordPerfect. You simply flow it in column by column. When you are done, you will look at each column to make sure that it is aligned with the others.

Flowing Text onto Page Two

Flow the text, column by column from the left, filling each column until the bottom loop of the right column contains an empty loop. Use the following instructions to do that:

1. Click in the middle of the paragraph at the top of the middle column of page 1 to reselect it. (Saving the publication deselected it.)

2. Click on the lower loop in the text handle of that paragraph and again obtain a text icon.

3. Click on the page 2 icon.

4. Place the text icon on the left column guide of the left column and on the top margin of the page.

5. Click the main mouse button.

Text should flow in to fill the column as shown in Figure 5-23. There should be a bold heading and three paragraphs. Not all of the third paragraph may be visible until the text is adjusted. This column of text, as a whole, may need to be moved up and then the text handle pulled down so that the last paragraph can be completely seen. Had you originally

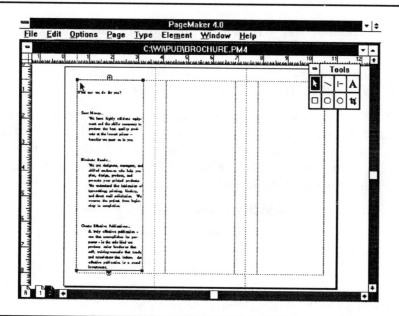

Figure 5-23.   *Second page with the left column as it is initially filled in*

placed the text icon above the top margin so that all the text fit in the column, the column guides that you set up for the left column would not be in effect because they do not extend above the top margin. Instead PageMaker would use some arbitrary lines as the default column guide.

6. Press and hold the main mouse button in the middle of the left column until you see a four-headed arrow icon. Then drag the text up until the dotted line in the vertical ruler, showing where the upper handle is, reads .2 inch.

7. Pull down the bottom handle until the rest of the third paragraph is visible.

In pulling down the bottom handle and displaying the third paragraph, the indent on either the last or second to the last line may be temporarily removed. If that happens, drag the handle up above the third paragraph (but not into the second paragraph), release the main mouse button, and then drag the handle down again. The third paragraph should then be correct and fully visible, as shown in Figure 5-24.

8. Click on the loop in the bottom handle of the left column, changing the pointer to a text icon.

9. Place the text icon against the left column guide and the top margin in the middle column, and click the main mouse button.

10. If you don't see a short line segment at the bottom of the fourth paragraph, drag the middle column up so that the top line of text in the middle column is roughly in line with the top line of text in the left column. (You will fine-tune it later.) Then pull the bottom handle down until the last short line of the fourth paragraph is visible.

11. Click on the loop at the bottom of the middle column.

12. Place the text icon in the left corner under the top margin in the right column and click.

This completes placing text on page 2, as shown in Figure 5-25. Now you want to align the three columns horizontally.

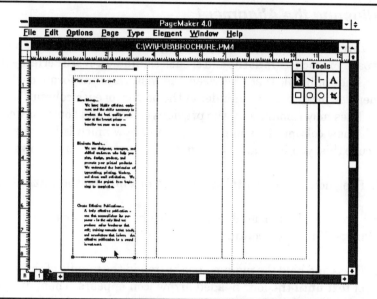

Figure 5-24. *Second page with the text in the left column adjusted to fit*

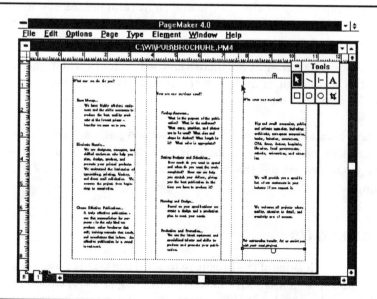

Figure 5-25. *Second page completely filled in with text*

Adjusting the Alignment

The three columns are probably not aligned because of the variable amount of space you picked up at the end of each column. In WordPerfect you placed four lines of blank space between the material that forms each column. When you pick up the remainder at the bottom of each column, some of the four lines may remain with the previous column and some may come over to the new column. It is impossible to tell how much is in either column. To cure this, you individually align the columns now, as follows:

1. Drag down a horizontal ruler guide to 1 inch on the vertical ruler.

This horizontal ruler guide should now be just under each of the three headings. If it is not, continue on.

2. Press and hold the main mouse button in the middle of the left column of text until the four-headed arrow icon appears. Then, drag the text up or down until the heading is just sitting on the horizontal ruler guide.

3. Similarly, adjust the middle and right columns. As you are adjusting the columns, make sure that the text stays aligned horizontally within the column.

4. Place the pointer at 5.2 inches on the horizontal ruler and 2 inches on the vertical ruler and click the secondary mouse button to go to the "Actual size" view.

Figure 5-26 shows the middle of the second page at actual size. Now, at actual size, see if the alignment is correct. If it is, go on to the cleanup phase. Otherwise, use the procedure just described in step 2 to adjust the alignment.

Cleaning Up

Examine both sides of the brochure to see if the text is properly aligned for a "balanced" and attractive look. If something is awry, click on it with the pointer tool and, while holding down the main mouse button, position the offending text in a better location. When you are done, save and print the

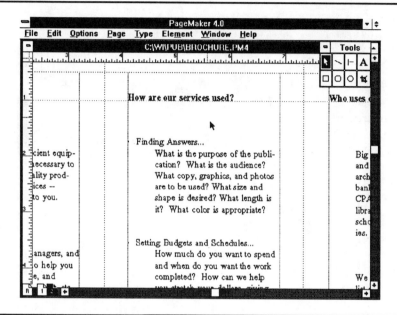

Figure 5-26.   *Middle of the second page at actual size*

brochure. The instructions that follow assume that the text in the left column of the first page is a little low. If that is not the case with your brochure, substitute for the left column of the first page the section you want to correct in your brochure in the following instructions.

1. Click on the page 1 icon.

2. If necessary, click the secondary mouse button to go to the "Fit in window" view.

3. To position the left column on the screen at actual size, place the pointer at 2.5 inches on the vertical ruler and 3.5 inches on the horizontal ruler; then press the secondary mouse button.

4. Drag the text in the left column up until the heading is just sitting on the horizontal ruler guide placed at 2.15 inches.

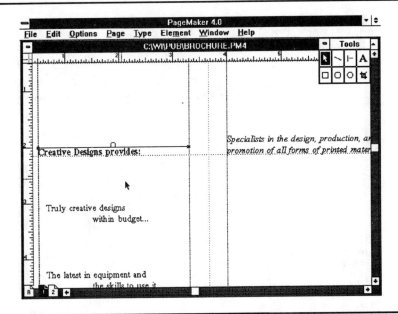

Figure 5-27.   *Close-up of the first page showing the alignment of the left column*

When you are satisfied that the left and middle columns of the first page are properly aligned (they should look like those shown in Figure 5-27) continue on to save and print the brochure as follows:

5. Press CTRL-S to save the file.

6. Press CTRL-P to bring up the Print dialog box.

7. After readying your printer and making any necessary changes to the Print dialog box, press ENTER to start printing.

Your printed brochure should look like the one shown in Figures 5-28 and Figure 5-29.

Creative Designs provides:

Specialists in the design, production, and promotion of all forms of printed material.

Creative Designs

· Truly creative designs
within budget...

**Desktop Publishing
With a Flair!**

· The latest in equipment and
the skills to use it...

**Brochures
Business Plans
Flyers
Newsletters
Pamphlets
Presentations
Posters
Reports**

· In-depth production experience
and marketing network...

Creative Designs

· Consistent on-time performance
at reasonable prices...

1900 Westwind Avenue
Oceanside, WA 98999
1-800-555-5000
1-206-555-5000

Figure 5-28. *First page of the printed brochure without the graphic*

What can we do for you?

· Save Money...
We have highly efficient equipment and the skills necessary to produce the best quality products at the lowest prices -- benefits we pass on to you.

· Eliminate Hassle...
We are designers, managers, and skilled craftsmen who help you plan, design, produce, and promote your printed products. We understand the intricacies of typesetting, printing, bindery, and direct mail solicitation. We oversee the project from beginning to completion.

· Create Effective Publications...
A truly effective publication - one that accomplishes its purposes - is the only kind we produce: sales brochures that sell; training manuals that teach; and newsletters that inform. An effective publication is a sound investment.

How are our services used?

· Finding Answers...
What is the purpose of the publication? What is the audience? What copy, graphics, and photos are to be used? What size and shape is desired? What length is it? What color is appropriate?

· Setting Budgets and Schedules...
How much do you want to spend and when do you want the work completed? How can we help you stretch your dollars, giving you the best publication in the time you have to produce it?

· Planning and Design...
Based on your specifications we create a design and a production plan to meet your needs.

· Production and Promotion...
We use the latest equipment and specialized talents and skills to produce and promote your publication.

Who uses our services?

Big and small companies, public and private agencies, including architects, aerospace companies, banks, bakeries, contractors, CPA firms, doctors, hospitals, libraries, local governments, schools, universities, and wineries.

We will provide you a specific list of our customers in your industry if you request it.

We welcome all projects where quality, attention to detail, and creativity are of concern.

For outstanding results, let us assist you with your next project.

Figure 5-29. *Second page of the printed brochure without the graphic*

Adding Options

The options consist of placing some vertical lines between columns and placing a graphic on the cover. Your sense may be that these clutter up the brochure, or you may have other design objections. Also, you may be unable to print the graphic with your laser printer, depending on the amount of memory in the printer (a LaserJet+, Series II, LaserJet III, or a LaserWriter will; a regular LaserJet may not). So, at your option, continue.

Placing Vertical Lines

The vertical lines or rules are drawn on the vertical ruler guides that mark the points where the brochure is folded. The rules serve two purposes: first, they assist in folding the brochure; second, when the brochure is opened, they help to visually separate the three columns. The instructions to draw the lines are as follows:

1. Click on the secondary mouse button to go to the "Fit in window" view.

2. Select the perpendicular-line tool.

3. Draw a line along the vertical ruler guide at 3.67 inches on the horizontal ruler from the top margin at 0.5 inch to the bottom margin at 8 inches.

4. Select the Line option of the Element menu and check that "Hairline" is still the chosen default.

5. As in step 3, draw a line along the vertical ruler guide at 7.33 inches on the horizontal ruler.

6. Click on the page 2 icon to go the second page.

7. If necessary, click on the secondary mouse button to return to the "Fit in window" view.

8. Draw two lines between the top and bottom margins along the vertical ruler guides at 3.67 and 7.33 inches on the horizontal ruler.

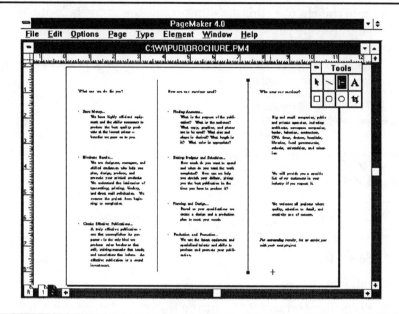

Figure 5-30. *Second page of brochure showing the vertical lines with guides turned off*

9. Select the Options menu and choose "Guides" to turn them off and allow you to see the lines you just drew.

Figure 5-30 shows the second page with vertical lines.

10. Select the Options menu and choose "Guides" to turn them back on again.

Placing a Graphic

To add some visual identification to the brochure, you add a line drawing of a Hewlett Packard LaserJet Series II printer to the cover. As discussed earlier in this chapter, this drawing (graphic) was created with Micrografx Designer. At this point, we need only retrieve the file and place it on the cover.

When you retrieve "draw type" files, the pointer changes to a draw icon (a pencil), as shown here:

The instructions to place the graphic are as follows:

1. Select the pointer tool.

2. Click on the page 1 icon to return there.

3. Place the pointer at 6.5 inches on the vertical ruler and 8 inches on the horizontal ruler. Click the secondary mouse button to go to "Actual size" view.

4. Drag the horizontal ruler guide that was placed earlier at 6.8 inches up to 6.5 inches on the vertical ruler.

5. Drag a new horizontal ruler guide down to 7.3 inches on the vertical ruler.

The space between the two horizontal ruler guides in the right column (shown in Figure 5-31) is where the graphic is placed.

6. Press CTRL-D to display the Place file dialog box.

7. Double-click on the file HPLJII.WMF in the list box if it is displayed, or type **\pm\pub\hpljii.wmf**. (You may have a different extension if you didn't use the Windows metafile format.)

The Place file dialog box looks like this:

Place file

OK

Cancel

Files/Directories:

BROCH.WP5
FLYER.PM4
HPLJII.WMF
ORDER.PM4
[..]
[-a-]
[-b-]
[-c-]
[-d-]

Path: c:\wi\pub

Name: HPLJII.WMF

Place: ⦿ As independent graphic
○ Replacing entire story
○ Inserting text

Options:

☒ Retain format   ☒ Convert quotes   ☐ Read tags

---

8. Place the draw icon in the corner of the left column guide of the right column and the horizontal ruler guide at 6.5 inches; then drag it diagonally to the right margin and the horizontal ruler guide at 7.3 inches.

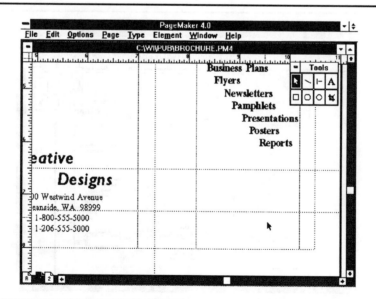

Figure 5-31.   *Lower-right corner of the cover*

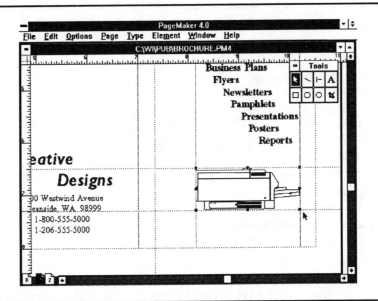

Figure 5-32.   *Lower part of the cover showing the graphic as it is first placed*

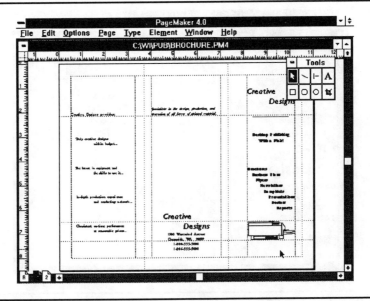

Figure 5-33.   *Final first page with graphic in "Fit in window" view*

As you can see in Figure 5-32, the graphic fits nicely in the spot set aside for it. Yours may do the same, or it may come in the wrong size or in the wrong position as a result of a positioning error. You can correct either condition.

If the position is incorrect, simply point in the middle of the graphic and drag it in the direction necessary for proper positioning. If the size is wrong, point on one of the tiny boxes in a corner and drag the box diagonally to either expand or contract the graphic to fit your requirements.

Figure 5-33 shows the final first page in the "Fit in window" view. This completes the brochure. All that remains is to save and print it.

9. Click the secondary mouse button to go to the "Fit in window" view.

10. Press CTRL-S to save the brochure.

11. Press CTRL-P to bring up the Print dialog box. Make any necessary changes, ready your printer, and press ENTER to start printing.

12. If you want to leave PageMaker at this point, press CTRL-Q, and then double-click on the Windows Control menu and click on "OK" to leave Windows.

Your final printed result should look like that shown in Figure 5-1—a professional-quality brochure. In Chapter 6 you generate a set of financial statements of equal quality.

6 Generating an Annual Report

The annual report discussed in this chapter is suitable for many organizations interested in communicating their financial performance and corporate progress to their shareholders or backers. It contains a formal set of financial reports, several graphs on the financial position over the past several years, and a narrative discussion about the company's performance over the past year and prospects for the new year. For the purposes of the example, the normal annual report of 15 to 20 pages has been truncated to 6 pages. (The finished 6 pages are shown in Figures 6-1 a-f.) In addition to these 6 pages, an annual report normally includes a table explaining changes in financial position, a set of notes on the financial statements, and a descriptive narrative and photographs about the company.

In this chapter you combine the three primary ingredients in an annual report—tabular financial data, graphical financial data, and narrative—with a simple but attractive design. You create the tabular and graphical financial data with Lotus 1-2-3 (Release 2.2 was used) and write the narrative in Microsoft Word. As in previous chapters, you may, of course, use other products that serve the same functions. You use PageMaker's master pages to create a master design for all but the first page. Then you place the tabular, graphical, and narrative information on the regular pages (the actual pages of the report), align and adjust them, and add some titles and lines. The result is an attractive professional-looking annual report.

If you use a word processor other than Mircosoft Word, read through the Word instructions and then duplicate them in your word processor. If you use a spreadsheet program other than Lotus 1-2-3 for the tabular data, you must forego PageMaker's 1-2-3 Text Filter. This converts the columns of a 1-2-3 (2.0 to 2.2) or Symphony worksheet to properly formatted columns separated by properly aligned tabs. You can also use Excel and copy an Excel worksheet or a section of it to the Clipboard and paste it on to a PageMaker publication. It will have tabs where you need them to preserve the columns. Also, if you save an Excel worksheet to a text file (use "File Save As" and click on "Options" and "Text") it will have the appropriate tabs. Otherwise, you must create an ASCII text file and then manually place tabs before each number (a very laborious job). Of course, you can use a word processor, either in column mode or with tabs, for the tabular data. PageMaker must be able to import the word processor's files and keep the tabs or columns intact. Test a sample before doing the entire set of tables. You may have problems when you enter the data and perform the arithmetic. Generally a spreadsheet is much easier in those areas. Also, PageMaker 4's Table Editor can be used for this purpose.

For the graphical data, you can use Symphony, Microsoft Chart, Chart-Master, or Excel in place of 1-2-3. The instructions here apply to Symphony as well as to 1-2-3.

Planning and Designing
The Annual Report

In previous chapters planning and design have been almost trivial. In this chapter both take on real significance. The quality of your publication and the ease with which you produce it depend on how well you have done the planning and design.

Preparing the Plan

Planning the publication of an annual report can be a sizable task. It involves coordinating the efforts of several people to create the narrative, tables, and graphs, all requiring top management approval. The report must be produced on a fixed schedule that puts it in the hands of shareholders just before the annual meeting.

Begin planning by identifying the components of the report, who will produce them, and who must approve them. Then develop a schedule by first determining the date by which the report must be in the hands of shareholders. Backing off from that date, plot all activities to determine

Micro Corporation of America
1990 Annual Report

Profile

Micro Corporation of America is observing its eleventh anniversary as a company providing microcomputer systems and related services worldwide. Incorporated in 1979, the company has been publicly owned since 1986.

MCA corporate headquarters is in Silicon Valley, California, the heartland of America's computer technology. The company's 487 employees serve clients from five regional offices in New York, Atlanta, Dallas, Chicago, and Los Angeles, plus two international offices in London, England, and Tokyo, Japan.

The company is organized into three operating groups.

MCA Systems is a leading supplier of microcomputer systems to small and medium sized businesses, which it also provides with other services and products.

MCA Government Systems serves local, state, and federal government agencies, developing state-of-the-art computer software and designing and integrating computer systems.

MCA Systems Services provides systems engineering and technical assistance, scientific support services, and training programs to a wide variety of clients.

MCA stock is traded over the counter, under the ticker symbol of MICA.

The company is an equal opportunity employer, M/F/H/V.

Figure 6-1a.   *The finished annual report (page 1)*

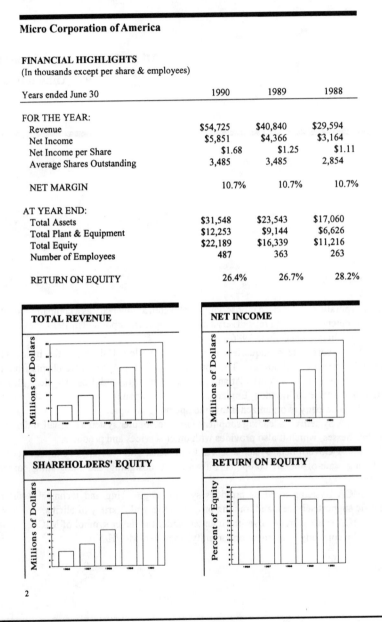

Micro Corporation of America

FINANCIAL HIGHLIGHTS
(In thousands except per share & employees)

Years ended June 30	1990	1989	1988
FOR THE YEAR:			
Revenue	$54,725	$40,840	$29,594
Net Income	$5,851	$4,366	$3,164
Net Income per Share	$1.68	$1.25	$1.11
Average Shares Outstanding	3,485	3,485	2,854
NET MARGIN	10.7%	10.7%	10.7%
AT YEAR END:			
Total Assets	$31,548	$23,543	$17,060
Total Plant & Equipment	$12,253	$9,144	$6,626
Total Equity	$22,189	$16,339	$11,216
Number of Employees	487	363	263
RETURN ON EQUITY	26.4%	26.7%	28.2%

TOTAL REVENUE

NET INCOME

SHAREHOLDERS' EQUITY

RETURN ON EQUITY

2

Figure 6-1b. *The finished annual report (page 2)*

Micro Corporation of America

To our shareholders:

Micro Corporation of America achieved record earnings for the fifth consecutive year in fiscal 1990, its eleventh year in business.

Net income for the year ended June 30, 1990, totaled $5,850,000, or $1.68 per share, representing a 34 percent increase from the prior year's record $4,366,000, or $1.25 per share. Fiscal 1990 revenue was $54,725,000, a 34 percent increase from $40,840,000 a year earlier.

Shareholders' equity increased 36 percent to $22,189,000, while the rate of return on average shareholder equity was an outstanding 26.4 percent. Bookings rose substantially, resulting in a 46 percent increase in the backlog, to $78,374,000.

We have continuously strengthened the company's balance sheet in the five years since fiscal 1986. Shareholders' equity has increased by over 400 percent, yet the return on equity has remained a very healthy 26 percent.

All Segments Growing

Continued success by MCA Systems, largest of the company's three operating groups, in obtaining large computer systems integration contracts should increase revenue profitably.

MCA Government Systems has identified large new segments of the markets they serve that offer potential for producing substantial additional revenue and earnings.

MCA Systems Services sees a growth opportunity in developing and marketing its capabilities for fabricating complex microcomputer software. The group also plans major efforts to market its technical support skills. Both of these efforts are aimed at contract opportunities developing in fiscal 1991.

New Director, Management Promotions

At the shareholders' meeting in October 1989, George E. Maynard, the retired chairman of Maynard Associates, Inc., was elected a director of the company, succeeding William J. Shallcross, who did not stand for reelection.

Roberto A. Martinez, president of MCA Systems Services since 1988, was elected a senior vice president of the company, and James R. Harrington, vice president-finance and chief financial officer since 1987, was named executive vice president and chief financial officer.

Looking Ahead to 1991

The company has the key ingredients for success in the markets into which it is moving, and I am optimistic about its future.

I expect fiscal 1991 to be an even better year than fiscal 1990. New products and services will be coming to market in addition to new contracts that will offer a firm foundation for growth in the new year. The men and women of Micro Corporation of America are committed to the long-term growth and success of the company.

Jennifer E. Evans
Chairman and President

3

Figure 6-1c. *The finished annual report (page 3)*

Micro Corporation of America

CONSOLIDATED STATEMENT OF OPERATIONS
(In thousands except per share data)

Years ended June 30	1990	1989	1988
REVENUE			
Net Sales	$54,725	$40,840	$29,594
COST OF SALES			
Cost of Goods Sold	14,776	11,027	7,990
Direct Costs	1,256	937	679
Total Cost of Sales	16,032	11,964	8,670
GROSS INCOME	$38,693	$28,876	$20,924
INDIRECT OPERATING COSTS			
Salaries & Wages	13,930	10,395	7,533
Payroll Taxes	1,811	1,351	979
Employee Benefits	1,478	1,103	799
Total Labor Expense	17,218	12,850	9,311
Advertising	3,095	2,310	1,674
Depreciation	1,935	1,444	1,046
Leases & Rentals	2,902	2,166	1,569
Taxes	1,548	1,155	837
Miscellaneous	1,161	866	628
Total Nonlabor Expense	10,641	7,941	5,754
Total Indirect Expense	27,859	20,790	15,065
NET OPERATING INCOME	$10,834	$8,085	$5,859
Other Income (Expense)	(2,476)	(1,848)	(1,339)
NET INCOME BEFORE TAXES	8,358	6,237	4,520
Provision for Income Taxes	2,507	1,871	1,356
NET INCOME	$5,851	$4,366	$3,164
NET INCOME PER SHARE	$1.68	$1.25	$1.11
AVERAGE SHARES OUTSTANDING	3,485	3,485	2,854

4

Figure 6-1d. *The finished annual report (page 4)*

Micro Corporation of America

CONSOLIDATED STATEMENT OF CONDITION
(In thousands)

Years ended June 30	1990	1989	1988
ASSETS			
Current Assets			
Cash and Equivalents	1,286	960	695
Net Accounts Receivable	7,483	5,584	4,047
Inventory	9,737	7,266	5,266
Total Current Assets	$18,506	$13,810	$10,008
Plant and Equipment			
Leasehold Improvements	5,678	4,237	3,071
Furniture & Equipment	10,897	8,132	5,893
Subtotal at Cost	16,575	12,369	8,963
Less Accum. Depreciation	(4,322)	(3,225)	(2,337)
Net Plant & Equipment	$12,253	$9,144	$6,626
Other Assets	789	589	427
TOTAL ASSETS	$31,548	$23,543	$17,060
LIABILITIES			
Current Liabilities			
Accounts Payable	3,683	2,749	1,992
Current Portion of Notes	487	363	263
Taxes Payable	2,378	1,775	1,286
Total Current Liabilities	$6,548	$4,887	$3,541
Net Long Term Notes	2,811	2,318	2,304
TOTAL LIABILITIES	$9,359	$7,204	$5,845
EQUITY			
Common Stock	697	697	571
Paid-in Capital	3,485	3,485	2,854
Retained Earnings	18,007	12,157	7,791
TOTAL EQUITY	$22,189	$16,339	$11,216
TOTAL LIABILITIES & EQUITY	$31,548	$23,543	$17,060

5

Figure 6-1e.   *The finished annual report (page 5)*

Micro Corporation of America

One Micro Way
Silicon Valley, CA 94123
(800) 555-1234 or
(415) 555-4321

Figure 6-1f.   *The finished annual report (top of page 6)*

when each event must occur, based on how long each will take. In scheduling the publication of an annual report you should be aware of all time-consuming steps, leave plenty of time for review and approval, and have all contributors committed to achieving the schedule.

Planning the budget is largely a matter of how fancy you want the report to be. On the low end you can simply reproduce what comes off your laser printer and have an attractive and low-cost annual report. At the other extreme you can incorporate a number of four-color photographs, print the report on special paper, and bind it in a glossy cover. Whichever way you choose, the budgeting is a significant aspect of planning.

Creating the Design

Designing the annual report requires four steps: determining the format and general content, identifying the constraints, designing the master page layout, and designing any custom aspects of the regular pages. Although the last two steps are more obviously design-related, they must be built on the foundation of the first two.

Annual reports are usually produced on 8 1/2 by 11-inch pages—a good format for production on a laser printer. These pages are printed double-sided and have facing pages. The annual report you build in this chapter uses this standard format.

The content of your annual report—the number and length of narrative articles, the number of photographs, the number of tables and graphs—is the primary constraint around which you must build a design. It is, of course, difficult to get this information early. Without it, though, you can only guess at the detail design (which is often what is done).

Other than the size and content, the constraints boil down to special requirements for color, typefaces, types of paper, and any special effects, such as cutting a patterned hole in a page. Annual reports are meant to reflect the pride that owners and managers have in an organization. As a result, they can be very elaborate and present a real challenge to the designer.

Designing the Master Pages   PageMaker's master page feature is very useful because it allows you to design a pair of facing pages that can be carried over to a number of regular pages. In the design presented here, three elements can be placed on the master pages and then repeated automatically on the regular pages: a 6-point line at the top of both pages, the company name just under the line, and the page number at the bottom of the page.

If this doesn't sound like much of an advantage, remember that each of these three elements appear on all 6 pages (or 15 to 20 pages in a real-world annual report), identically placed and spaced on each page. Further, should you want to change any of the elements, you need only change the master pages to make a change throughout the entire publication.

As with all PageMaker pages, you create the master pages by manipulating the image area within which the master design elements are placed. You create this area by setting the page setup margins and column guides. For this annual report, the image area is formed by a single column with 1/2-inch top, bottom, and outside margins. The inside margin is 2 inches, partly for binding purposes and partly as a design element. With the master design elements, this image area provides the master layout for the annual report.

Designing the Regular Pages   Your primary design task on the regular pages is to determine how to place the report's content within the master layout so that you have an easy-to-read, attractive publication. The content can be divided into three classes: tables, graphs, and narrative. Each of these must be separately designed into the annual report and yet must be consistent, or at least harmonious, with the rest of the publication.

One way to provide consistency among different components of a publication is to standardize a typeface and type size. For this annual report you use Times New Roman (Times) throughout: the company name and headings of the tables and narrative are 14-point bold; the bodies of both the tables and narrative are 12-point Roman (medium weight); and the headings on the graphs are 10-point bold.

This selection assumes that you are using the fonts that are included in the PageMaker 4 package. If that is not the case, use the fonts you have that are closest to these. For example, if you have Bitstream fonts, you can replace Times New Roman with Dutch and keep everything else the same. Of course, you must adjust the spacing. See Appendix B for more about fonts.

The second technique for getting a consistent look among the different components is to standardize the type and thickness of the lines you use. On the master page a 6-point line is specified to be the heading on each page. This line is also used as a heading for the four graphs. Similarly, a 1-point line is used as the secondary header line on all tables and graphs. Finally, a hairline is used on the tables to separate item categories.

A third technique, a consistent column width for both tables and narrative, is also used to give the annual report a harmonious look. For the early material, which should be easily read, the single 6-inch column is very effective for both the tables and narrative. For the notes and detail material in the back of the report, you would probably specify narrower columns.

The result of the design is a clean-looking and easy-to-read annual report. It also is not difficult to produce with PageMaker, Microsoft Word, and 1-2-3. Start out by looking at how the components are built in Word and 1-2-3.

Developing the Tables, Graphs, and Narrative

The discussion here on developing the components in 1-2-3 and Microsoft Word is brief and primarily limited to the constraints that PageMaker places on files brought over from these applications. If you are using different applications to create the material, you still may find it worthwhile to read this material because of the general instructions it contains on creating the components of the annual report.

Writing the Narrative With Microsoft Word

The narrative in the annual report consists of two segments: the Profile section on the cover and the letter to the shareholders on page 3. You could build these as either one or two files. Because both segments use a common typeface, size, and column width, you will combine them in one file and thereby gain a small savings in keystrokes.

Text created with Microsoft Word and placed by PageMaker can transmit to PageMaker all of its major formatting characteristics. This includes typeface, type style and size, all types of tabs, indents, and line spacing. All of the formatting that you need for the narrative in the annual report can be applied in Microsoft Word and transmitted to PageMaker.

Setting Defaults   The default settings required in Word are straightforward. You want your default character format to be 12-point Times with no other style. You want the paragraph formatting to include justified alignment and have a 14.4-point line spacing. These defaults serve for formatting the majority of the narrative—the body of the text. Each heading is made bold individually and changed to 14-point type size and a 16-point line spacing as each is entered. The headings still use the Times typeface.

Entering Text   Load Word or your word processor now and enter the narrative for the annual report shown in Figure 6-2. Start by setting the defaults previously discussed and then type the narrative itself.

As you can see, a heading (actually the word "Profile") is the first thing you type. You want to make this bold, 14 points in size, with a 16-point line spacing. Since you want to preserve the defaults, type the word, press ENTER, and then go back, highlight the word, and change its style, size, and line spacing. Then use the arrow keys to move to the next line where you again press ENTER for a blank line, and then begin typing the narrative. Treat each of the headings in this manner.

Other than the headings, there is nothing unusual about entering the narrative. Simply type the paragraphs shown in Figure 6-2. On the second

Profile ← 14-point Times-Bold, 16-point line spacing

← 12-point Times-Roman, 14.4-point line spacing

1 line {

Micro Corporation of America is observing its eleventh anniversary as a company providing microcomputer systems and related services worldwide. Incorporated in 1979, the company has been publicly owned since 1986.

MCA corporate headquarters is in Silicon Valley, California, the heartland of America's computer technology. The company's 487 employees serve clients from five regional offices in New York, Atlanta, Dallas, Chicago, and Los Angeles, plus two international offices in London, England, and Tokyo, Japan.

The company is organized into three operating groups.

MCA Systems is a leading supplier of microcomputer systems to small and medium sized businesses, which it also provides with other services and products.

MCA Government Systems serves local, state, and federal government agencies, developing state-of-the-art computer software and designing and integrating computer systems.

MCA Systems Services provides systems engineering and technical assistance, scientific support services, and training programs to a wide variety of clients.

MCA stock is traded over the counter, under the ticker symbol of MICA.

The company is an equal opportunity employer, M/F/H/V.

2 lines {

To our shareholders: ← 14-point Times-Bold, 16-point line spacing

← 12-point Times-Roman, 14.4-point line spacing

1 line {

Micro Corporation of America achieved record earnings for the fifth consecutive year in fiscal 1990, its eleventh year in business.

Net income for the year ended June 30, 1990, totaled $5,850,000, or $1.68 per share, representing a 34 percent increase from the prior year's record $4,366,000, or $1.25 per share. Fiscal 1990 revenue was $54,725,000, a 34 percent increase from $40,840,000 a year earlier.

Shareholders' equity increased 36 percent to $22,189,000, while the rate of return on average shareholder equity was an outstanding 26.4 percent. Bookings rose substantially, resulting in a 46 perceı increase in the backlog, to $78,374,000.

We have continuously strengthened the company's balance sheet in the five years since fiscal 1986. Shareholders' equity has increased by over 400 percent, yet the return on equity has remained a very healthy 26 percent.

Figure 6-2.   *The text to be entered with Microsoft Word (page 1)*

1 line {   14-point Times-Bold, 16-point line spacing

All Segments Growing   12-point Times-Roman, 14.4-point line spacing

Continued success by MCA Systems, largest of the company's three operating groups, in obtaining large computer systems integration contracts should increase revenue profitably.

MCA Government Systems has identified large new segments of the markets they serve that offer potential for producing substantial additional revenue and earnings.

MCA Systems Services sees a growth opportunity in developing and marketing its capabilities for fabricating complex microcomputer software. The group also plans major efforts to market its technical support skills. Both of these efforts are aimed at contract opportunities developing in fiscal 1991.

1 line {

New Director, Management Promotions

At the shareholders' meeting in October 1989, George E. Maynard, the retired chairman of Maynard Associates, Inc., was elected a director of the company, succeeding William J. Shallcross, who did not stand for reelection.

Roberto A. Martinez, president of MCA Systems Services since 1988, was elected a senior vice president of the company, and James R. Harrington, vice president-finance and chief financial officer since 1987, was named executive vice president and chief financial officer.

1 line {

Looking Ahead to 1991

The company has the key ingredients for success in the markets into which it is moving, and I am optimistic about its future.

I expect fiscal 1991 to be an even better year than fiscal 1990. New products and services will be coming to market in addition to new contracts that will offer a firm foundation for growth in the new year. The men and women of Micro Corporation of America are committed to the long-term growth and success of the company.

3 lines {

Jennifer E. Evans
Chairman and President

Figure 6-2.   *The text to be entered with Microsoft Word (page 2)*

and successive paragraphs of each section, press TAB to indent those paragraphs, using Word's default 0.5-inch tab settings. At the end of the document, just before the chairman's name and title, add three blank lines.

When you are done entering the narrative, save the file in \WI\PUB (or the directory you are using) with the name FINSTAT.DOC (for financial statement). Finally, you may wish to print the document with Word. You will find the results look very similar to the final product produced by PageMaker.

Producing the Tables And Graphs With Lotus 1-2-3

A major benefit of Lotus 1-2-3 is that you can produce both the tables and graphs in the same package. With this integration, you can be assured that the graphs reflect the numbers in the tables. Such a capability is valuable in an annual report.

Building the Tables   PageMaker's powerful 1-2-3 Text Filter converts the labels, numbers, and formulas of a 1-2-3 or Symphony worksheet into a properly aligned and formatted table in PageMaker. The left, right, and center alignment of labels and the fixed, scientific, currency, comma, general, percent, plus and minus, date, time, and text formats all convert properly. Most important, the columns of the worksheet are transferred to PageMaker as tabbed columns with appropriate left, right, or center alignment. Because of PageMaker's limit of 40 tab stops, a maximum of 40 columns can be imported. (If, however, a column is "hidden" in 1-2-3, it does not come across to PageMaker and is not counted as one of the 40 allowed.)

The 1-2-3 Text Filter places a worksheet in PageMaker with a default font of 10-point Courier. You can change this to another font that does not use fixed spacing. In this chapter the font is changed to 12-point Times. Also, the tab stops created by the 1-2-3 Text Filter are moved to provide slightly wider columns and overall alignment on the right margin. Both the tab stops and font can also be changed by changing the style sheet (named WKS) that the 1-2-3 Text Filter automatically creates and attaches to all worksheets brought into PageMaker. Style sheets will be discussed in the next chapter.

One additional characteristic of the 1-2-3 Text Filter does not affect the example presented in this chapter, but may affect other work you do with

1-2-3 and PageMaker: the 1-2-3 Text Filter places a hidden right parenthesis on all numbers. This allows the proper alignment of negative
currency-formatted numbers and negative comma-formatted numbers
with other number formats. The parenthesis is hidden by "Paper" coloring.
Of course, if a number is a negative currency-formatted number or a
negative comma-formatted number, the right parenthesis is made visible
by changing it to black coloring. Because of these hidden right parentheses,
you should not highlight the entire table and change its color. Doing so
would reveal the right parentheses; if that happens, the only way to hide
them again is on a one-by-one basis.

If you are using Symphony, note that all character formatting—such as
bold, italics, and underlining—is lost when you transfer the tables to
PageMaker.

There are three tables in the annual report: the Financial Highlights
table, which summarizes information from the other two tables, is shown
in Figure 6-3; the Consolidated Statement of Operations (income statement) is shown in Figure 6-4; and the Consolidated Statement of Condition
(balance sheet) is shown in Figure 6-5. Because the first table draws

	A	B	C	D
53	FINANCIAL HIGHLIGHTS			
	(In thousands except per share & employees)			
56	Years ended June 30	1990	1989	1988
	FOR THE YEAR:			
59	→Revenue	$54,725	$40,840	$29,594
	Net Income	$5,851	$4,366	$3,164
	Net Income per Share	$1.68	$1.25	$1.11
	Average Shares Outstanding	3,485	3,485	2,854
	NET MARGIN	10.7%	10.7%	10.7%
	AT YEAR END:			
67	→Total Assets	$31,548	$23,543	$17,060
	Total Plant & Equipment	$12,253	$9,144	$6,626
	Total Equity	$22,189	$16,339	$11,216
	Number of Employees	487	363	263
72	→RETURN ON EQUITY	26.4%	26.7%	28.2%

Figure 6-3.   *Financial Highlights table as it looks in 1-2-3*

	A	B	C	D
1	CONSOLIDATED STATEMENT OF OPERATIONS (In thousands except per share data)			
4	Years ended June 30	1990	1989	1988
	REVENUE Net Sales	$54,725	$40,840	$29,594
	COST OF SALES Cost of Goods Sold Direct Costs Total Cost of Sales	14,776 1,256 16,032	11,027 937 11,964	7,990 679 8,670
14	GROSS INCOME	$38,693	$28,876	$20,924
	INDIRECT OPERATING COSTS Salaries & Wages Payroll Taxes Employee Benefits Total Labor Expense	13,930 1,811 1,478 17,218	10,395 1,351 1,103 12,850	7,533 979 799 9,311
	Advertising Depreciation Leases & Rentals Taxes Miscellaneous Total Nonlabor Expense	3,095 1,935 2,902 1,548 1,161 10,641	2,310 1,444 2,166 1,155 866 7,941	1,674 1,046 1,569 837 628 5,754
29	Total Indirect Expense	27,859	20,790	15,065
	NET OPERATING INCOME	$10,834	$8,085	$5,859
	Other Income (Expense)	(2,476)	(1,848)	(1,339)
	NET INCOME BEFORE TAXES	8,358	6,237	4,520
	Provision for Income Taxes	2,507	1,871	1,356
39	NET INCOME	$5,851	$4,366	$3,164
	NET INCOME PER SHARE	$1.68	$1.25	$1.11
43	AVERAGE SHARES OUTSTANDING	3,485	3,485	2,854

Figure 6-4. *Consolidated Statement of Operations table as it looks in 1-2-3*

	H	I	J	K
1	CONSOLIDATED STATEMENT OF CONDITION (In thousands)			
4	Years ended June 30	1990	1989	1988
	ASSETS			
	Current Assets			
	Cash and Equivalents	1,286	960	695
	Net Accounts Receivable	7,483	5,584	4,047
	Inventory	9,737	7,266	5,266
11 →Total Current Assets	$18,506	$13,810	$10,008
	Plant and Equipment			
	Leasehold Improvements	5,678	4,237	3,071
	Furniture & Equipment	10,897	8,132	5,893
	Subtotal at Cost	16,575	12,369	8,963
	Less Accum. Depreciation	(4,322)	(3,225)	(2,337)
	Net Plant & Equipment	$12,253	$9,144	$6,626
	Other Assets	789	589	427
22	TOTAL ASSETS	$31,548	$23,543	$17,060
	LIABILITIES			
	Current Liabilities			
	Accounts Payable	3,683	2,749	1,992
	Current Portion of Notes	487	363	263
	Taxes Payable	2,378	1,775	1,286
	Total Current Liabilities	$6,548	$4,887	$3,541
	Net Long Term Notes	2,811	2,318	2,304
33	TOTAL LIABILITIES	$9,359	$7,204	$5,845
	EQUITY			
	Common Stock	697	697	571
	Paid-in Capital	3,485	3,485	2,854
	Retained Earnings	18,007	12,157	7,791
	TOTAL EQUITY	$22,189	$16,339	$11,216
43	TOTAL LIABILITIES & EQUITY	$31,548	$23,543	$17,060

Figure 6-5.   *Consolidated Statement of Condition table as it looks in 1-2-3*

information from the other two, it is worthwhile to build a single spreadsheet containing all three tables and the four graphs.

All three tables are built with four columns. The leftmost column, for the descriptions, is 30 characters wide. The other columns, for the numbers, are each 10 characters wide. The titles and line descriptions use standard left alignment, while the numbers use standard right alignment.

Most of the numbers are formatted with a comma format, called "punctuated" in Symphony, and no decimal places. Therefore, the global format should be set to that (/Worksheet Global Format , 0 and press ENTER). In the income statement and balance sheet, summary lines are formatted as currency, again with no decimal places. The net income per share is formatted as currency with two decimal places, and the two percentage lines in the Financial Highlights table are formatted as percentages with one decimal place.

Detail lines in the tables are indented three spaces at the first level, six spaces at the second level, and nine spaces at the third level (simulating tab stops every three characters). When these tables are brought over to PageMaker, the indents are translated to roughly one, two, and three characters.

PageMaker refers to the three tables as named ranges. The income statement is placed in the range A1 through D43 and is named INCSTAT. The instruction to create the named range for the income statement is as follows:

/Range Name Create incstat ENTER **a1.d43** ENTER

You must name the other two ranges in a similar manner. The balance sheet is placed in the range H1 through K43 and is called BALSHT. The Financial Highlights table is placed in the range A53 through D72 and is called FIHI. When you have finished building the worksheet, save it with the following information:

/File Save c:wi\pub\finstat ENTER

1-2-3 (2.0 through 2.2) automatically adds the extension .WK1 to the filename.

Using Figures 6-3, 6-4, and 6-5 and the information just given, build the 1-2-3 worksheet containing the three tables. Then you can use the information in the tables to build the graphs.

Building the Graphs   Text that is part of a graphic is seldom of as high a quality as text set as text, so you want to have as little text on the graphs as possible. For example, you can add the titles to the graphs in Page-Maker. Because you cannot produce a 1-2-3 graph without some markings on the Y-axis, you must live with that, even though they cannot be sized or positioned very well. To balance the Y-axis markings, you will add the years to the X-axis, because it is almost impossible to match the type size in PageMaker, and then the markings on the X- and Y-axes would be different.

The four graphs, shown in Figures 6-6 through 6-9, are produced from data in the Financial Highlights table, except that the progression of years is reversed and there are two additional years. Figure 6-10 shows the revised data used for the graphs. Note that most of the amounts have been divided by 1000 to produce figures in millions. This produces more meaningful summary figures for graphing. Also, the percent return on equity has been multiplied by 100 so that it can be printed on the Y-axis as a whole

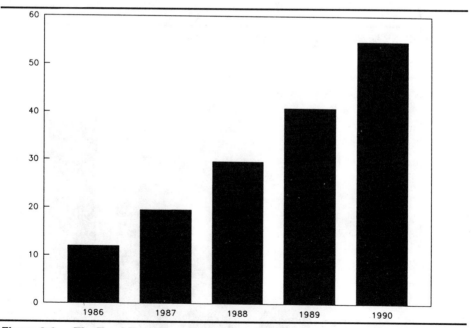

Figure 6-6.   *The Total Revenue graph produced by 1-2-3*

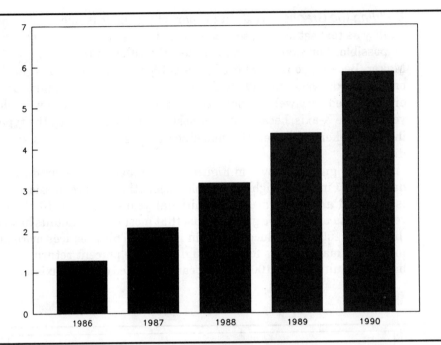

Figure 6-7.   *The Net Income graph produced by 1-2-3*

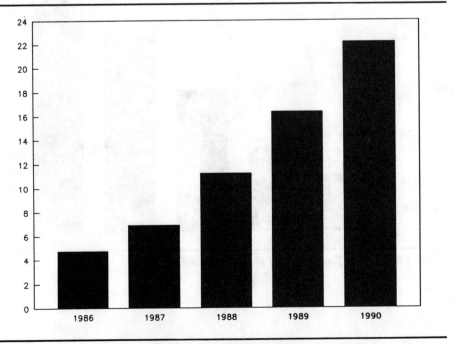

Figure 6-8.   *The Shareholders' Equity graph produced by 1-2-3*

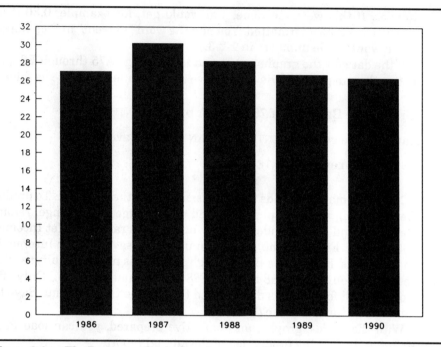

Figure 6-9. *The Return on Equity graph produced by 1-2-3*

	A	B	C	D	E	F
74	DATA FOR GRAPHING					
	Years ended June 30	1986	1987	1988	1989	1990
	FOR THE YEAR:					
77 →	Revenue in Millions	$11.9	$19.5	$29.6	$40.8	$54.7
	Net Income in Millions	$1.3	$2.1	$3.2	$4.4	$5.9
	Net Income per Share	$0.89	$1.10	$1.11	$1.25	$1.68
	AT YEAR END:					
83 →	Total Assets in Millions	$6.9	$11.2	$17.1	$23.5	$31.5
	Total Equity in Millions	$4.7	$6.9	$11.2	$16.3	$22.2
	Number of Employees	108	173	263	363	487
86 →	RETURN ON EQUITY (%)	27.0	30.2	28.2	26.7	26.4

Figure 6-10. *The data from which the graphs are produced*

number. If this were not done, you would get, for example, 0.30 if not formatted or 30% if formatted. You add the word "Percent" in PageMaker, so you want whole numbers in 1-2-3.

If the data for the graphs are stored in the range A75 through F88, the instructions to produce, view, and save the Revenue graph are as follows:

/Graph Type Bar **X b76.f 76** ENTER **A b79.f 79** ENTER

Name **C**reate **revenue** ENTER **V**iew ENTER ESC **S**ave ESC ESC

c:\wi\pub\revenue ENTER

1-2-3 automatically adds the extension .PIC to the filename. To produce the remaining three graphs, you need only change the A range, rename the graph, and save it under the new name. (The range for Net Income is B80 through F80, and the graph is named and saved under Income; for Shareholders' Equity it is B85 through F85 and is named Equity; and for Return on Equity it is B88 through F88 and is named Return.) Only after producing all four graphs do you need to **Q**uit the Graph menu. Save the entire worksheet with the /**F**ile **S**ave command.

With the tables, graphs, and narrative prepared, you can load Page-Maker and begin the production of the annual report.

Defining the Layout

Because the annual report is a six-page publication, creating a good working layout is more significant than it was in earlier chapters. Much of the weight of this falls on the master pages, where the master layout is established. Also, the defaults now affect more work and so are more important.

Setting the Defaults

Setting the defaults upon starting a new publication should almost be second nature to you by now. The pattern of going through the Target printer, Page setup, and Type specifications dialog boxes is virtually the same as in previous chapters. However, the annual report has only a single column on most pages, so there is no need to bring up the Column guides dialog box unless you have changed the startup default. Start with the Target printer dialog box.

Target Printer   There are no unusual settings necessary in the Target printer dialog box, although it is a good habit to check it. Load PageMaker now. Check that the printer is set to "Portrait" orientation and that the other settings in this dialog box are the way you want them with the following instructions:

1. Choose "Target printer..." from the File menu.

2. Double-click on the printer you want to use.

3. Click on the Portrait option button.

4. Make any other necessary changes to the dialog box.

5. Click on "OK" twice to close the dialog box and the list of printers.

6. Click on the Maximize button to maximize the application window.

Page Setup   The Page setup dialog box needs a little more attention. You must be sure that the Double-sided and Facing pages check boxes are turned on (an "X" appears in the box) and that the number of pages and margins are set. Do that with the following instructions:

1. Choose "New" from the File menu.

2. Type **6** in the Number of pages text box.

3. Click on the Tall option button to turn it on if it isn't already.

4. If they are not already checked, click on the Double-sided and Facing pages check boxes.

5. Drag across the "1" in the Inside margin text box.

6. Type **2** for the Inside margin and press TAB.

7. Type **.5** for the Outside margin and press TAB.

8. Type **.5** for the Top margin and press TAB.

9. Type **.5** for the Bottom margin.

Your dialog box should look like the one shown in Figure 6-11.

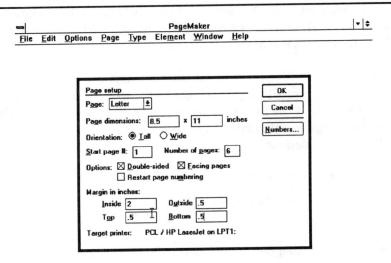

Figure 6-11.   *The Page setup dialog box*

10. Click on "OK" to close the dialog box.

Other Defaults   The other defaults consist of the type specifications, the use of rulers and their unit of measure, the default line width, the type alignment, and turning off the Toolbox. You may want to make some of these permanent defaults, not just defaults for a given publication. If so, you must set them *before* opening a new publication, immediately following the printer setup. Should you want to do that now, choose "Close" from the File menu, carry out the following instructions, and then go back and redo the page setup. Otherwise, just follow these instructions:

1. If necessary, choose "Rulers" from the Options menu to turn them on.

2. Choose "Preferences..." from the Edit menu.

3. Click on the downward-pointing arrow to the right of first the Measurement system text box and then the Vertical ruler text box, clicking on "Inches decimal" in each. Then click on "OK" to close the Preferences dialog box.

4. Choose "Toolbox" from the Window menu to turn it off.

5. Click on the publication window Maximize button to maximize it.

6. Choose "Type specs..." from the Type menu.

7. Click on the downward-pointing arrow to the right of the Font text box and then click on "Times".

8. Press TAB, and then type **14** in the Size text box.

9. Make sure "Auto" leading is selected.

10. Click the "Bold" check box to turn it on.

Your Type specifications dialog box should look like the one shown in Figure 6-12. Throughout the annual report, you will change the type specifications frequently, both for a particular use and as a default.

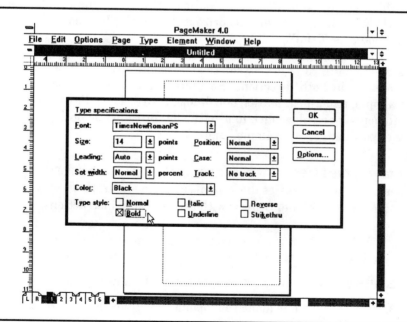

Figure 6-12.   *The initial Type specifications dialog box*

11. Click on "OK" to close the Type specifications dialog box.

12. Choose "Align left" from the "Alignment" option of the Type menu to turn it on.

13. Choose "6 pt" from the "Line" option of the Element menu to set it as the line width default.

Like the type specifications, the line width default will change several times while you build the annual report. The defaults now set represent the initial settings that you need to construct the master pages.

Constructing the Master Pages

As you saw in the design, each master page contains a heavy 6-point line at the top, the company name just under the line, and a page number in the lower-outside corner. The following paragraphs describe how to produce these elements.

In the instructions that follow you will often use specific ruler coordinates, such as "5 inches on the horizontal ruler." This is abbreviated as "5H." When both vertical and horizontal ruler coordinates are needed, they are noted as "5H/3V."

When two pages are displayed together on the screen, the zero point of the horizontal ruler is between the two pages. From that point the ruler's scales go in both directions. So there are two of each scale mark, for example, two 1-inch marks, one for each page. The following instructions tell you which ruler mark to use (the left or right) by noting it in front of the coordinates; for example, "right 5H/3V."

Drawing the Lines   The heavy line at the top of each page is the common design element that ties the annual report together. It is a very simple but important technique. Draw it with the following instructions:

1. Click on one of the master page icons (L or R) to bring them on the screen.

2. Press SHIFT-F3 to select the perpendicular-line tool.

3. Next, draw a line along the top margin of the left page from left 8H to left 2H.

The 6-point line is considerably wider than the margin guide. As a result, the line can sit above the guide or hang below it. In this case you want the line to hang below the guide.

4. Draw a line along the top margin of the right page from right 2H to right 8H.

Entering the Name   The second element on the master pages is the company name immediately below the line you just drew. You enter the name on the left page, copy it to the Clipboard, and then insert it on the right page. The instructions for this are as follows:

1. Drag down a horizontal ruler guide to 0.8V.

2. Place the pointer at left 6.5H and 1.5V.

3. Click the secondary mouse button to expand the view to "Actual size".

4. Press SHIFT-F4 to select the text tool.

5. Position the I-beam with the small middle crossbar sitting on the horizontal ruler guide at 0.8V to the right of the left margin and click the main mouse button.

6. Type **Micro Corporation of America**.

Your screen should look like that shown in Figure 6-13.

7. Drag across the company name to select it.

8. Press CTRL-INS to copy the company name to the Clipboard.

9. Use the horizontal scroll bar at the bottom to shift the screen to the right until right 2.5H is in the middle of your screen.

10. Position the I-beam with the small middle crossbar sitting on the horizontal ruler guide at 0.8V to the right of the left margin on the right page, and click the main mouse button.

11. Press SHIFT-INS to copy the company name back onto the publication.

When you press SHIFT-INS, you should see a second copy of the company name appear at the top of the right page.

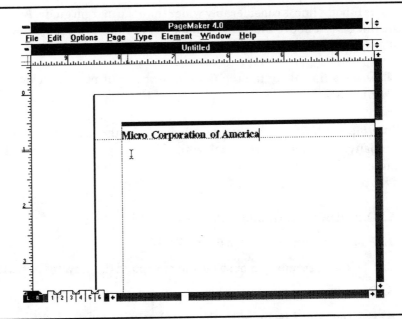

Figure 6-13. *The left master page with the line and name in place*

12. Drag across the company name on the right page or press SHIFT-HOME to highlight the name.

13. Press CTRL-SHIFT-R to right-align it.

14. Use the horizontal scroll bar to shift the screen to the right right 6.5H is in the middle of your screen.

The company name should be properly aligned on the right master page, as shown in Figure 6-14.

Adding the Page Number PageMaker can automatically number the pages of a document. If you enter CTRL-SHIFT-3 on the master pages where

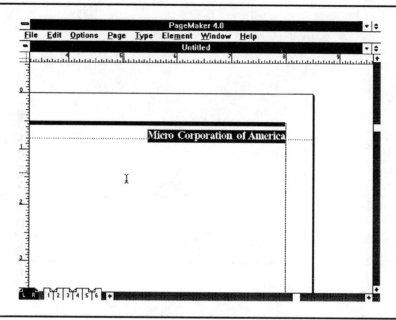

Figure 6-14.   *The right master page showing the company name properly aligned*

you want the page number to appear, PageMaker inserts the numbers on the regular pages. Use the following instructions to do that:

1. Click the secondary mouse button to go to "Fit in window" view.

2. Place the pointer at left 6.5H/9.5V.

3. Click the secondary mouse button to expand the view to "Actual size".

4. Place the small middle crossbar of the I-beam on the bottom margin at 10.5V, to the right of the left margin, and click the main mouse button.

5. Press CTRL-T to open the Type specifications dialog box.

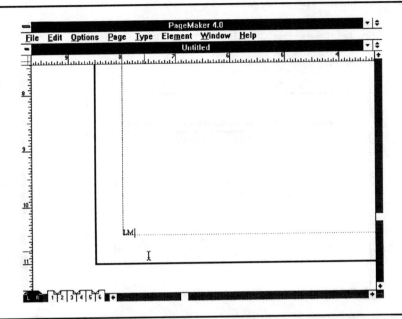

Figure 6-15. *The lower-left master page showing the page number placeholder*

6. Press TAB, type **10** in the Size text box, click on "Normal" for the Type style and on "OK" to close the dialog box.

7. Press CTRL-SHIFT-3 to place the page number on the master page.

The letters "LM" (for Left Master) should appear in the lower-left corner of your left master page, as shown in Figure 6-15. This is a *placeholder* for the page number on even-numbered pages.

8. Drag across the page number to select it.

9. Press CTRL-INS to copy the page number to the Clipboard.

10. Use the horizontal scroll bar to shift the screen to the right until right 2.5H is in the middle of your screen.

11. Position the I-beam with the small middle crossbar sitting on the bottom margin at 10.5V to the right of the left margin on the right page, and click the main mouse button.

12. Press SHIFT-INS to make a second copy of the page number back on the publication.

Now the placeholder for the page number should be RM for Right Master.

13. Drag across the page number on the right page to highlight it.

14. Press CTRL-SHIFT-R to right-align the page number on the right page.

15. Use the horizontal scroll bar to shift the screen to the right until right 6.5H is in the middle of your screen.

The placeholder for the page number should be properly aligned on the right master page, as shown in Figure 6-16.

16. Click the secondary mouse button to go to "Fit in window" view.

17. Press CTRL-S to open the Save dialog box.

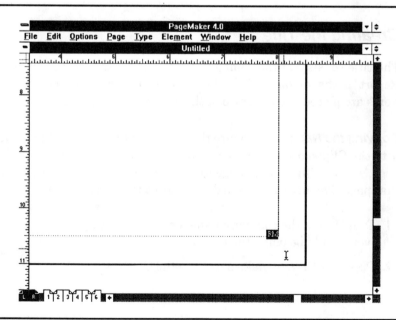

Figure 6-16. *The lower-right master page showing the page number placeholder*

18. Double-click on "[..]" in the "Directories" list box, scroll the list to \WI\PUB or the directory you are using, and double-click on that directory.

19. Type **finstat** for the filename, and press ENTER to complete saving the file.

Building the Title Page

Now that the master pages are complete, you can begin building the regular pages. Because the first page is the title page, you construct it differently than the others. To do that you must get rid of all the master page items. You then use the same design elements from the master pages—the company name and the 6-point line—but in different positions to create the title. Once the title is complete, you place the first segment of the narrative—the company profile—on the bottom of the title page.

Creating the Title

The title consists of the company name on top, the words "1990 Annual Report" in the middle, and the default 6-point line on the bottom. All three items are placed about a third of the way down the page.

Copying the Name   To ensure that the company name is the same, copy it to the Clipboard before leaving the master pages. Then go to the first page, get rid of the master page items, and recopy the company name onto that page. The instructions to do that are as follows:

1. Drag across the company name on the right master page to select it (you should be using the text tool).

2. Press CTRL-INS to make a copy on the Clipboard.

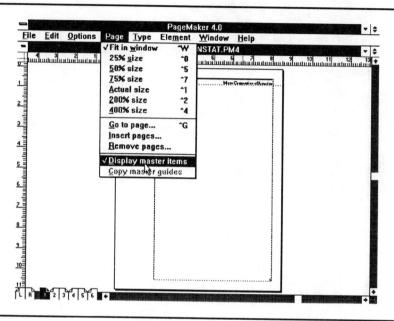

Figure 6-17. *The Page menu with "Display master items" highlighted*

3. Click on the page 1 icon to go to that page. Note that right master page items are displayed.

4. Choose "Display master items" from the Page menu to turn off the master items on page 1, as shown in Figure 6-17.

5. Drag a horizontal ruler guide down to 3V.

6. Position the I-beam with the small middle crossbar sitting on the horizontal ruler guide at 3V to the right of the left margin, and click the main mouse button.

7. Press SHIFT-INS to copy the company name onto the first page, as shown in Figure 6-18.

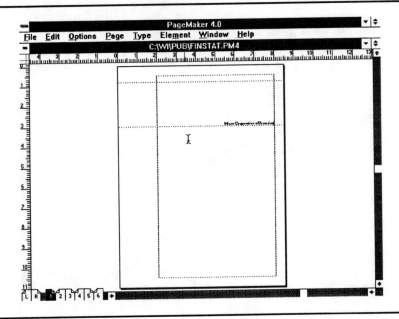

Figure 6-18. *Page 1 with the company name in place*

Adding the Second Title Line The second line of the title is placed immediately below the company name and is set in the default 14-point bold Times font. The instructions for adding the second line are as follows:

1. Using the pointer (F9), drag the horizontal ruler guide from 3V to 3.3V.

2. Place the pointer at 5H/4V.

3. Click the secondary mouse button to expand the view to "Actual size".

4. Press F9 to return to the text tool.

5. Place the middle crossbar of the I-beam on the horizontal ruler guide at 3.3 and click the main mouse button.

6. Press CTRL-SHIFT-R for right alignment.

7. Type **1990 Annual Report**.

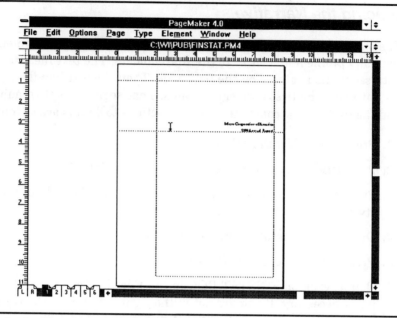

Figure 6-19. *Page 1 with the two title lines*

If your second line is not (for some reason) in 14-point bold Times, as shown in Figure 6-19, highlight the line and change the type specifications.

Drawing the Line The standard 6-point line is placed below the two title lines. The following instructions assume that the 6-point line is still the default.

1. Click the secondary mouse button to go to "Fit in window" view.

2. Press F9 to select the pointer.

3. Drag the horizontal ruler guide at 3.3V down to 4V.

4. Press SHIFT-F3 to select the perpendicular-line tool.

5. Draw a line across the horizontal ruler guide at 4V from the left to the right margin (from 2H to 8H). Let the line hang beneath the ruler guide.

Placing the Narrative

The narrative that you wrote in Microsoft Word had two main segments—a company profile and a letter to the shareholders. The text file containing both segments is placed on the first page. Then the text handle is pulled up until only the first segment remains. That segment is then adjusted, and the first page is complete. The instructions to do this are as follows:

1. Press F9 to select the pointer.

2. Press CTRL-T to open the Type specifications dialog box.

3. Press TAB, type **12** in the Size text box, click on "Normal" for the Type style, and then click on "OK".

4. Drag the horizontal ruler guide at 4 down to 6V.

5. Press CTRL-D to open the Place dialog box.

6. Double-click on FINSTAT.DOC in the Files list box, using the scroll bar if necessary. If you are not in the right directory, TAB over to the text box, type **c:\wi\pub\finstat.doc**, and press ENTER.

7. Click the text icon on the horizontal ruler guide at 6V and the left margin.

If you have not made any changes in the narrative, your page should look like that shown in Figure 6-20. The short line at the very bottom of the page is the "To our shareholders:" line from the second segment of the narrative. You need to drag the lower text handle above this line. When you have done that, your page should look like the one shown in Figure 6-21. You can then check this first segment.

8. Drag the lower loop of the text handle upward until it is above the bottom line, as shown in Figure 6-21.

9. Press SHIFT-F4 to select the text tool.

10. Drag the text tool across the word "Profile" in the heading. Press CTRL-T to open the Type specifications dialog box.

Check the settings against the formatting you applied in Word—Times, 14-point size, 16-point leading (line spacing in Word), and bold. If anything is not correct, fix it, and then click on "OK".

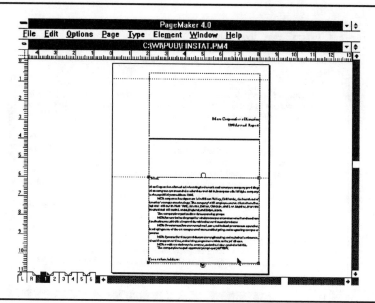

Figure 6-20. *Page 1 with the text as initially placed*

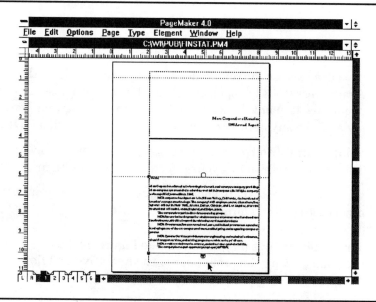

Figure 6-21. *Page 1 with the text adjusted*

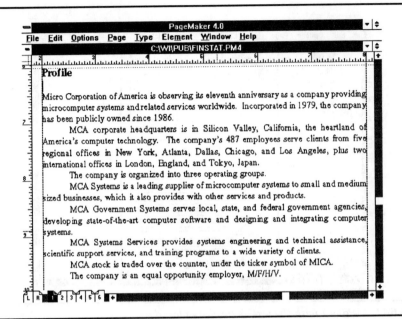

Figure 6-22. *Cover narrative on page 1*

11. Next drag across the remainder of the text displayed on the first page. Again press CTRL-T to open and check the type specifications. This text should be 12-point Times with 14.4-point leading and Normal type style. Make any necessary corrections, and then click on "OK".

12. Point on 5H/8V and press the secondary mouse button for "Actual size". The cover narrative fills your screen, as shown in Figure 6-22.

13. Check over the text. It should be justified, properly indented, and otherwise correctly formatted.

Your completed first page will look like Figure 6-23 when it is printed. Now you can pick up the remainder of the narrative and flow it onto the third page.

Micro Corporation of America

1990 Annual Report

Profile

Micro Corporation of America is observing its eleventh anniversary as a company providing microcomputer systems and related services worldwide. Incorporated in 1979, the company has been publicly owned since 1986.

MCA corporate headquarters is in Silicon Valley, California, the heartland of America's computer technology. The company's 487 employees serve clients from five regional offices in New York, Atlanta, Dallas, Chicago, and Los Angeles, plus two international offices in London, England, and Tokyo, Japan.

The company is organized into three operating groups.

MCA Systems is a leading supplier of microcomputer systems to small and medium sized businesses, which it also provides with other services and products.

MCA Government Systems serves local, state, and federal government agencies, developing state-of-the-art computer software and designing and integrating computer systems.

MCA Systems Services provides systems engineering and technical assistance, scientific support services, and training programs to a wide variety of clients.

MCA stock is traded over the counter, under the ticker symbol of MICA.

The company is an equal opportunity employer, M/F/H/V.

Figure 6-23.   *Page 1 as it is printed*

Forming the Letter to the Shareholders

The third page is entirely taken up with the letter to the shareholders—the second segment of the narrative. This letter is flowed onto the page and then aligned in rapid order.

Flowing the Text

Before leaving page 1, you pick up the text from the lower text handle, turn the pages, and flow the remaining narrative onto page 3. The instructions to do this are as follows:

1. Press F9 to select the pointer, and click the secondary mouse button to go to "Fit in window" view.
2. Click on the text to select it. The text handles should appear.
3. Click on the lower loop of the text handle. The text icon should appear.
4. Click on the icon for pages 2 and 3.
5. Place the text icon on the left margin and the ruler guide at 0.8 (below the company name and the line) of page 3, and click to flow the text down the page.

Aligning the Text

As shown in Figure 6-24, the letter should completely flow on to the page. The bottom loop in the text handle should be empty. All you need to do is center the text vertically, and then save the publication. Do that with these instructions:

1. Point the mouse in the center of the text on page 3, and press and hold the main mouse button. A four-headed arrow appears.
2. Drag the letter down, keeping it in the margins, until the upper marker in the vertical ruler is at 1.0, and then release the main mouse button.
3. Press CTRL-S to save the annual report.

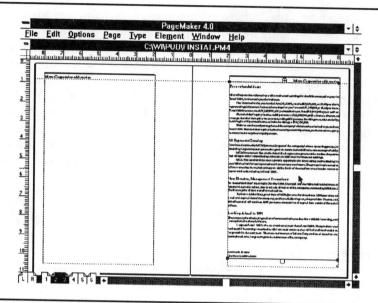

Figure 6-24. *Page 3 with the text as it is initially placed*

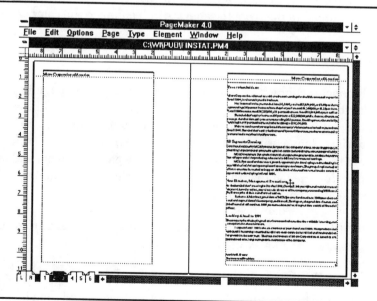

Figure 6-25. *Page 3 with the text in its final position*

The letter on page 3 exactly fits the page, as shown in Figure 6-25, or when printed in Figure 6-26. Actually the original letter was longer, so text was removed until the fit was achieved. Had you wanted to include more text, you could have reduced the text size and/or the leading in the rest of the letter. If you do change the leading, remember to change it on a paragraph-by-paragraph basis. If you select the entire letter and change the leading, you also change the leading of the three paragraph headings, making them hard to read.

With all of the narrative pages completed, you can now turn to tables and graphs, beginning with the Financial Highlights table and the graphs that go on page 2.

Assembling the Financial Highlights and Graphs

The second page is assembled from a combination of the Financial Highlights table and the four graphs. The table is placed at the top of the page, and the four graphs are arranged at the bottom. In addition, a number of lines are added to the page to separate and enhance the components.

Bringing in the Table

The Financial Highlights table is placed on the second page in a manner similar to the placing of other text, with one extra step. An additional dialog box, the 1-2-3 Text Filter dialog box, appears to enable you to select the appropriate range within the worksheet. When you have selected the range, a text icon, which you can flow onto the page in the normal manner, appears. You then adjust the tabs, change the font, and finally draw a line under the dates at the top of the table to set them off.

Placing the Table   Your first task is to retrieve the table from the disk. To do that, use the following instructions:

1. Press CTRL-D to open the Place dialog box.

2. Scroll the list box until FINSTAT.WK1 appears, and then double-click on FINSTAT.WK1.

Micro Corporation of America

To our shareholders:

Micro Corporation of America achieved record earnings for the fifth consecutive year in fiscal 1990, its eleventh year in business.

Net income for the year ended June 30, 1990, totaled $5,850,000, or $1.68 per share, representing a 34 percent increase from the prior year's record $4,366,000, or $1.25 per share. Fiscal 1990 revenue was $54,725,000, a 34 percent increase from $40,840,000 a year earlier.

Shareholders' equity increased 36 percent to $22,189,000, while the rate of return on average shareholder equity was an outstanding 26.4 percent. Bookings rose substantially, resulting in a 46 percent increase in the backlog, to $78,374,000.

We have continuously strengthened the company's balance sheet in the five years since fiscal 1986. Shareholders' equity has increased by over 400 percent, yet the return on equity has remained a very healthy 26 percent.

All Segments Growing

Continued success by MCA Systems, largest of the company's three operating groups, in obtaining large computer systems integration contracts should increase revenue profitably.

MCA Government Systems has identified large new segments of the markets they serve that offer potential for producing substantial additional revenue and earnings.

MCA Systems Services sees a growth opportunity in developing and marketing its capabilities for fabricating complex microcomputer software. The group also plans major efforts to market its technical support skills. Both of these efforts are aimed at contract opportunities developing in fiscal 1991.

New Director, Management Promotions

At the shareholders' meeting in October 1989, George E. Maynard, the retired chairman of Maynard Associates, Inc., was elected a director of the company, succeeding William J. Shallcross, who did not stand for reelection.

Roberto A. Martinez, president of MCA Systems Services since 1988, was elected a senior vice president of the company, and James R. Harrington, vice president-finance and chief financial officer since 1987, was named executive vice president and chief financial officer.

Looking Ahead to 1991

The company has the key ingredients for success in the markets into which it is moving, and I am optimistic about its future.

I expect fiscal 1991 to be an even better year than fiscal 1990. New products and services will be coming to market in addition to new contracts that will offer a firm foundation for growth in the new year. The men and women of Micro Corporation of America are committed to the long-term growth and success of the company.

Jennifer E. Evans
Chairman and President

3

Figure 6-26. *Page 3 as it is printed*

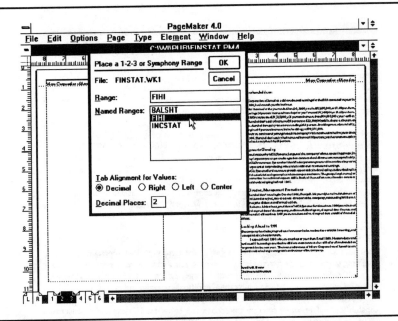

Figure 6-27. *The 1-2-3 Text Filter dialog box*

3. The 1-2-3 Text Filter dialog box appears with the named ranges in a list box, as shown in Figure 6-27.

4. Double-click on FIHI in the list box, and the text icon should appear.

5. Place the text icon on page 2 at the left margin and 1.2V; then click the main mouse button.

The table should flow onto the page just as it looked in 1-2-3, as shown in Figure 6-28.

Adjusting Tabs   The columns, as they come across from 1-2-3, are a little narrower than you want. It is difficult to adjust the widths perfectly in 1-2-3. It is easier to use PageMaker's Indents/tabs dialog box to move the tabs to where you want them.

In PageMaker you can use four different types of tabs: left-aligned tabs, center tabs, right-aligned tabs, and decimal tabs (the 1-2-3 Text Filter

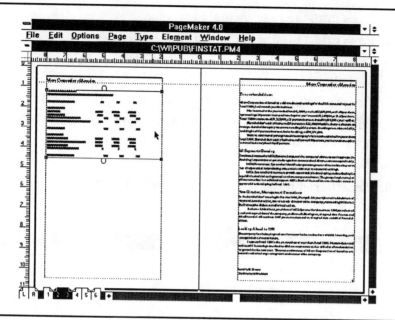

Figure 6-28. *Initial placement of the Financial Highlights table*

default). For the financial tables in the annual report, you want to use either right-aligned tabs or decimal tabs, and in either case you can adjust individual lines. With right-aligned tabs you have straight columns, as in 1-2-3 itself, with one exception: negative numbers in parentheses do not line up due to the right parenthesis. This must be adjusted by using decimal tabs for just the lines with negative numbers. If the entire table is formatted with decimal tabs, the negative numbers are properly aligned but the dollar per share numbers and percentages stick out to the right. This is probably acceptable or even desirable to indicate that these numbers are different from the numbers around them. Of course, you can also adjust the lines that stick out. In the annual report, you use decimal tabs without adjustment.

Move the tabs now with the following instructions:

1. Press SHIFT-F4 to select the text tool.

2. Drag across the entire table on page 2 to highlight it.

3. Press CTRL-1 to go to "Actual Size" view.

4. Press CTRL-I to open the Indents/tabs dialog box.

5. Click on the decimal tab button in the lower-right corner of the four tab buttons.

6. Place the leftmost tab stop by clicking 3.75 on the tab rule.

7. Click on the right-pointing arrow on the right of the tab ruler until you can see 6 on the ruler.

8. Place the center tab stop by clicking at 4.75.

9. Place the rightmost tab stop by clicking at 5.75. Your dialog box should look like the one shown here:

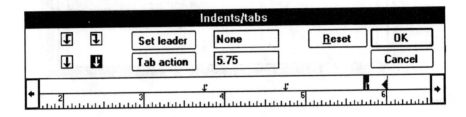

10. Click on "OK" to close the dialog box.

Changing the Font The default font that the 1-2-3 Text Filter applies is 10-point Courier. You change this to 12-point Times and make the heading bold with the following instructions:

1. Choose "Type specs" from the Type menu.

2. From the Type specifications dialog box select "Times" and "12" points, and click on "OK".

3. Press UP ARROW to get to the top of the table and drag across the heading "Financial Highlights."

4. Press CTRL-SHIFT-B to make the heading bold.

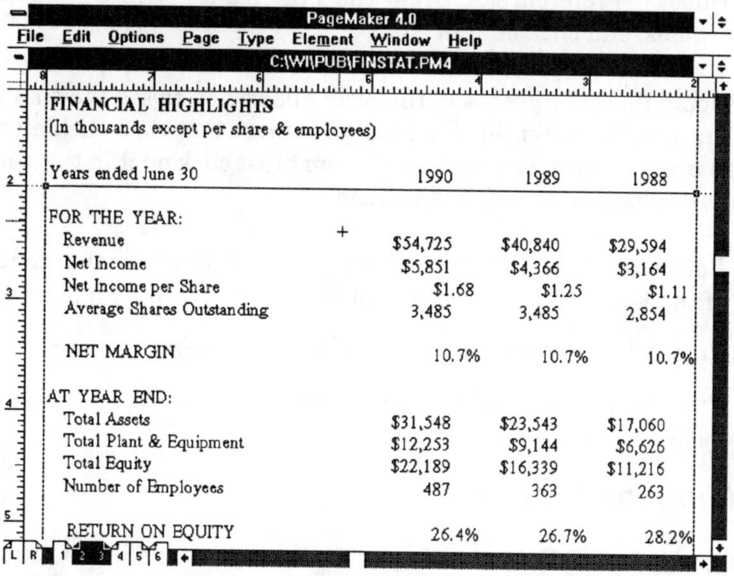

Figure 6-29. *The Financial Highlights table with the line in place*

Drawing the Line   To finish the Financial Highlights table, you place a line under the years to set them apart as shown in Figure 6-29. Do that now with the following instructions:

1. Drag a horizontal ruler guide down to 2V (it should be immediately under the row that begins "Years ended").

2. Press SHIFT-F3 to select the perpendicular-line tool.

3. Draw a line across the horizontal ruler guide at 2V—from the left to the right margin.

4. Choose "Preferences..." from the Edit menu, click on "Back" under Guides, and click on "OK".

Placing the ruler guides in the back allows you to see the smaller lines you draw and to select them without pressing CTRL when clicking on them. If you need to move a guide, though, you must click on it in the margins or you will select the drawn line instead.

5. Before deselecting the line, choose the "1 pt" line from the "Line" option of the Element menu. Your screen should look like Figure 6-29.

6. Press CTRL-W to return to "Fit in Window" view.

7. Press CTRL-S to save the publication.

Adding the Graphs

The graphs are built in four stages: first, a layout grid is constructed, and a number of lines are drawn; second, the 1-2-3 graphs are placed; third, the graphs are aligned on the grid; and fourth, the titles are added to each graph. Each stage is discussed in the paragraphs that follow.

Drawing the Lines   To set the graphs apart and give them a weight equal to the other components of the annual report, you draw a set of lines around them. To draw these lines accurately and to place the graphs accurately, you need to add an extensive network of horizontal and vertical ruler guides as well as dividing the page into two columns. Once this layout is complete, the lines can be drawn. The instructions to build the grid and draw the lines are as follows:

1. Press F9 to select the pointer.

2. Choose "Column guides ..." from the Options menu.

The Column guides dialog box that is displayed has a check box "Set left and right pages separately". Because you don't care about page 3, the easiest solution is to set both pages the same—that is, to leave the check box empty. If for some reason your dialog box comes up with the box checked, simply click on the box to turn it off. You get columns on page 3 as well as on page 2, but that doesn't matter. The column guides on page 3 do not affect the text that is already on the page.

3. Type **2** in the Number of columns text box, press TAB, type **.4** in the Space between columns text box, and press ENTER.

4. Drag down six horizontal ruler guides to 5.5, 6, 7.5, 8, 8.5, and 10 on the vertical ruler.

5. Drag over four vertical ruler guides to 7.5, 5.5, 4.3, and 2.3 on the left horizontal ruler.

When you have completed the layout grid for the graphs, your screen should look like the one shown in Figure 6-30.

6. Press SHIFT-F3 to select the perpendicular-line tool. Select the Options menu and make sure that both "Snap to rulers" and "Snap to guides" are on (checked).

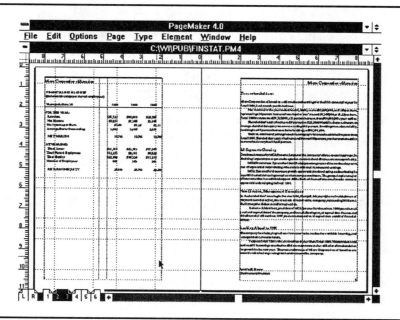

Figure 6-30. *The layout grid for the graphs on page 2*

7. Draw a line along the horizontal ruler guide at 5.5V from left 8H to left 5.2H.

8. Before deselecting the line you just drew, look at the "Line" option of the Element menu and make sure that the 6-point line is still chosen. If it isn't, click on it for the selected line; then switch to the pointer tool and again choose the 6-point line to reset the default. Switch back to the perpendicular-line tool.

9. Draw a line along the horizontal ruler guide at 5.5V from left 4.8H to left 2H.

10. Draw two lines along the horizontal ruler guide at 8V—one from left 8H to left 5.2H, and the second from left 4.8H to left 2H.

11. Press F9 to select the pointer.

12. Choose the "1 pt" line in the Line option of the Element menu.

13. Press F9 to reselect the perpendicular-line tool.

14. Draw two lines along the horizontal ruler guide at 6V—one from left 8H to left 5.2H and the second from 4.8H to left 2H.

15. Draw two lines along the horizontal ruler guide at 8.5V—one from left 8H to left 5.2H and the second from left 4.8H to left 2H.

16. Draw two lines along the vertical ruler guide at left 8H—one from 5.5V to 7.7V and the second from 8V to 10.2V.

17. Draw two lines along the vertical ruler guide at left 4.8H—one from 5.5V to 7.7V and the second from 8V to 10.2V.

18. Select the Options menu and choose "Guides" to turn them off so you can better see the lines you just drew. Figure 6-31 shows the results.

19. When you have finished admiring your work, again choose "Guides" from the Options menu to turn them back on.

20. Press CTRL-S to save the publication.

This might be a good time to take a break. If you leave PageMaker, remember to check the defaults and reset them as necessary when you return.

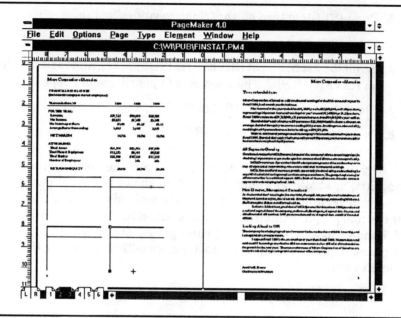

Figure 6-31.   *The completed lines for the graphs on page 2 with "Guides" turned off*

Placing the Graphs   You will add the four graphs to page 2 at precise points. Instead of simply clicking the main mouse button at a point and letting the graph fill the page (it would fill a much larger area than you want), you press and hold the main mouse button to drag the graph to the opposite corner of the area you want to fill. This sizes the graph on placement instead of making it a separate step. The points at which you place and then drag the graphs are not always on ruler guides (although the resulting graphs are). Therefore you must turn off the "Snap to guides" option. (Leave "Snap to rulers" on.) To place and size the graphs, use the following instructions:

1. Press F9 to select the pointer.

2. Place the pointer at left 5H/7.5V.

3. Click the secondary mouse button to expand to "Actual size" view.

4. Press CTRL-U to turn off the "Snap to guides" option.

5. Press CTRL-D to open the Place dialog box.

6. Scroll the list box until REVENUE.PIC appears, and then double-click on REVENUE.PIC. The draw icon (a pencil) should appear.

7. Place the draw icon at left 7.85H/6V.

8. Drag the draw icon to left 5.5H/7.65V.

As you are dragging the draw icon toward the opposite corner, a box appears, as shown in Figure 6-32, which shows you the dimensions that the graph occupies. When you release the main mouse button, you see that the actual graph is smaller and should sit on the horizontal ruler guide at 7.5 and be against the vertical ruler guides at 7.5 and 5.5, as shown in Figure 6-33. The box that appears in Figure 6-32 shows where the selection handles are.

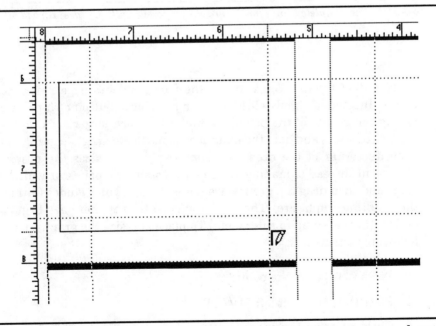

Figure 6-32. *The placement of the Revenue graph before the main mouse button is released*

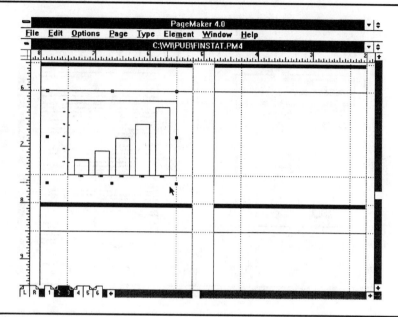

Figure 6-33. *The final placement of the Revenue graph after the main mouse button is released*

9. If the Revenue graph is not sitting on the horizontal ruler guides at 7.5V or is not against the vertical ruler guides at 7.5 and 5.5H, drag it into position.

10. Press CTRL-D to open the Place dialog box.

11. Scroll the list box until INCOME.PIC appears, and then double-click on INCOME.PIC. The draw icon should appear.

12. Place the draw icon at left 4.65H/6V.

13. Drag the draw icon to left 2.3H/7.65V.

14. If the Income graph is not sitting on the horizontal ruler guide at 7.5V or is not against the vertical ruler guides at 4.5 and 2.3H, drag it into position.

15. Use the vertical scroll bar to position the screen downward so that the lower pair of graph placeholders is visible.

16. Press CTRL-D and double-click on EQUITY.PIC. The draw icon should appear.

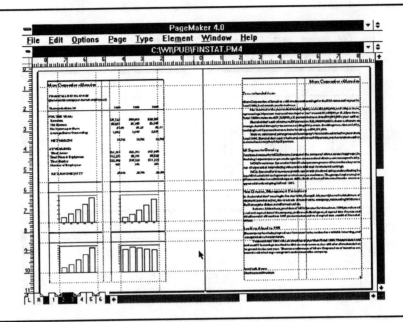

Figure 6-34.   *The four graphs in position after placement*

17. Place the draw icon at 7.85H/8.5V and drag it to 5.5H/10.15V.

18. Adjust the placement of the Equity graph as necessary.

19. Press CTRL-D, scroll the list box, and double-click on RETURN.PIC.

20. Place the draw icon at 4.65H/8.5V and drag it to 2.3H/10.15V.

21. Adjust the placement of the Return graph as necessary.

Figure 6-34 shows the four graphs as they should look after placement.

Adding the Titles   Your final task in building the graphs is to add titles
to each one. These titles are in 12-point bold Times and are placed between
the 6-point and 1-point lines above each graph. To add the titles, use the
following instructions:

1. Press CTRL-T to open the Type specifications dialog box.

2. Click on "Bold" for the "Type style".

3. Click on "OK" to close the Type specifications dialog box.

4. Press CAPS LOCK to turn it on.

5. Press SHIFT-F4 to select the text tool.

6. Click the text tool at left 7.9H/8.3V.

7. Type an em space (CTRL-SHIFT-M), and type **SHAREHOLDERS' EQUITY**.

8. Click at 4.7H/8.3V, type an em space, and type **RETURN ON EQUITY**.

9. Use the vertical scroll bar to position the screen upward so that the upper pair of graphs is visible.

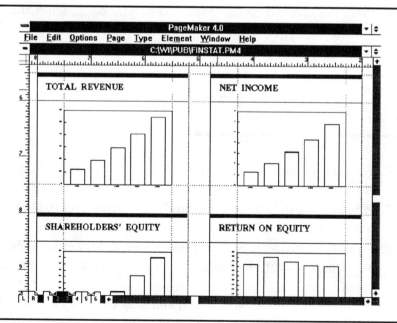

Figure 6-35.   *The primary titles on the graphs*

10. Click at 7.9H/5.8V, type an em space, and type **TOTAL REVENUE**.

11. Click at 4.7H/5.8V, type an em space, and type **NET INCOME**.

   Your screen should look like Figure 6-35.

12. Press F9 for the pointer and press CTRL-T to open the Type specifications dialog box.

13. Press TAB, type **10** in the Size text box, click on "Normal" for the Type style, and click on "OK" to close the dialog box.

14. Press F9 for the text tool, click at 7.9H/7.9V, press CAPS LOCK to turn it off, and type **Millions of Dollars**.

15. Drag over the words "Millions of Dollars," choose "130%" from the "Set width" option, and choose "Very Loose" from the "Track" option, both on the Type menu. Also press CTRL-SHIFT-C to center the words.

16. Press F9 to reselect the pointer. Click on the words "Millions of Dollars," and drag one of the right-hand text handles to 6.4H.

17. From the Element menu, choose "Text rotation...", select the second rotational step, 90-degrees to the left, as shown here. Then click on "OK".

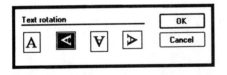

18. With the pointer, drag the rotated words "Millions of Dollars" so they span from 6V to 7.6V at 7.8H.

19. When the words "Million of Dollars" are in place, press CTRL-INSERT to copy them.

20. Press SHIFT-INSERT to paste a copy of the words back on the publication, and drag that copy to a similar position on the Net Income graph.

21. Press SHIFT-INSERT to paste a second copy of the words "Millions of Dollars" back on the publication, and drag that copy to a position on the Equity graph similar to the position on the Revenue graph.

22. Press SHIFT-F3 for the text tool, click at 4.7H/10.4V, and type **Percent of Equity**.

23. Drag over the words "Percent of Equity," choose "130%" from the "Set width" option, and choose "Very loose" from the "Track" option, both on the Type menu. Also press CTRL-SHIFT-C to center the words.

The purpose of changing the width and the tracking is to spread the words out to equal the height of the graph.

24. Press F9 to select the pointer. Click on the words "Percent of Equity" and drag one of the right-hand text handles to 3.4H.

25. From the Element menu, choose Text rotation...", select the second rotational step, 90-degrees to the left, and click on "OK".

26. With the pointer, drag the rotated words "Percent of Equity" so they span from 8.55V to 9.95V at 4.65H.

27. Press CTRL-S to save the annual report.

Figure 6-36 shows the completed titles on each of the four graphs, while Figure 6-37 shows page 2 as it looks when printed.

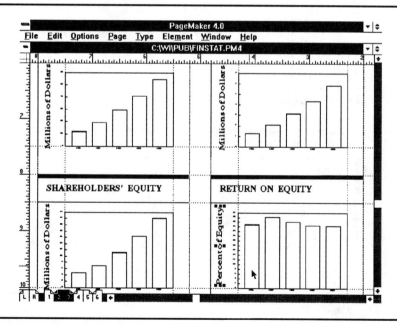

Figure 6-36. *The completed titles on the graphs*

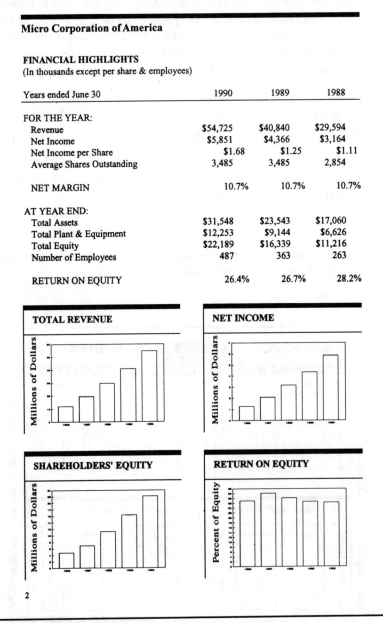

Micro Corporation of America

FINANCIAL HIGHLIGHTS
(In thousands except per share & employees)

Years ended June 30	1990	1989	1988
FOR THE YEAR:			
Revenue	$54,725	$40,840	$29,594
Net Income	$5,851	$4,366	$3,164
Net Income per Share	$1.68	$1.25	$1.11
Average Shares Outstanding	3,485	3,485	2,854
NET MARGIN	10.7%	10.7%	10.7%
AT YEAR END:			
Total Assets	$31,548	$23,543	$17,060
Total Plant & Equipment	$12,253	$9,144	$6,626
Total Equity	$22,189	$16,339	$11,216
Number of Employees	487	363	263
RETURN ON EQUITY	26.4%	26.7%	28.2%

TOTAL REVENUE

NET INCOME

SHAREHOLDERS' EQUITY

RETURN ON EQUITY

2

Figure 6-37. *Page 2 as it is printed*

Adding the Financial Statements

You place the Consolidated Statement of Operations (income statement) on page 4 and the Consolidated Statement of Condition (balance sheet) on page 5. You handle them exactly as you did the Financial Highlights table: you place the table, set the tab stops, make the heading bold, and add the lines.

Placing the Tables   Retrieving text files should be almost routine by now. Do it twice more with the following instructions:

1. Press CTRL-T to open the Type specifications dialog box.

2. Press TAB, type **12** in the Size text box, and assure that "Auto" is in the Leading text box and that "Normal" is checked for the Type style.

3. Click on "OK" to close the Type specifications dialog box.

4. Click on the icon for pages 4 and 5 to change pages.

5. Drag horizontal ruler guides down to 1.2V and 9.8V.

6. Press CTRL-D to open the Place dialog box.

7. Scroll the list box until FINSTAT.WK1 appears, and then double-click on FINSTAT.WK1. The 1-2-3 Text Filter dialog box appears.

8. Double-click on INCSTAT and the text icon appears.

9. Place the text icon on page 4 at the left margin and the horizontal ruler guide at 1.2V; then click the main mouse button.

10. Press CTRL-D and double-click on FINSTAT.WK1.

11. From the 1-2-3 Text Filter dialog box, double-click on BALSHT.

12. Click the text icon on page 5 at the left margin and the horizontal ruler guide at 1.2V.

13. Adjust the tables on both pages 4 and 5 until the top line is just under the horizontal ruler guide at 1.2V, as shown in Figure 6-38.

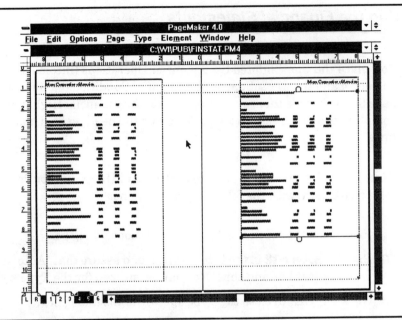

Figure 6-38. *Tables properly aligned on pages 4 and 5*

Changing the Font and Tabs The changes to be made to the tables on pages 4 and 5 are the same as the changes you made to the Financial Highlights table on page 2. Highlight the table, move the tabs, change the font, and make the heading bold by following these instructions:

1. Press SHIFT-F4 to select the text tool.

2. Drag across the entire table on page 4 to highlight it, and press CTRL-1 to go to "Actual size" view.

3. Press CTRL-I to open the Indents/tabs dialog box.

4. Click on the decimal tab button and click three tab stops at 3.75, 4.75, and 5.75 on the tab ruler. Your dialog box should look like this:

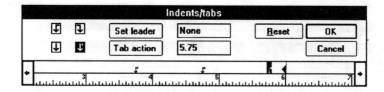

5. Click on "OK" to close the dialog box.

6. Choose "Type specs..." from the Type menu.

7. From the Type specifications dialog box, select "Times" for Font, press TAB, type **12** for Size, and click on "OK".

8. Press UP ARROW to go to the top of the table. If there is a blank line (because of extra tabs) between the first and second line, delete it by moving the insertion point to the unwanted line and pressing BACK-SPACE.

9. Drag across only the heading ("Consolidated Statement of Operations") on page 4, and press CTRL-SHIFT-B to make it bold.

10. Press CTRL-W to go to "Fit in window" view, drag across the entire table on page 5 to select it, and press CTRL-1 for "Actual size" view.

11. Press CTRL-I, click on the decimal tab button, click three tab stops at 3.75, 4.75, and 5.75, and click on "OK".

12. Press CTRL-T, select "Times", press TAB, type **12**, and click on "OK".

13. Press UP ARROW to go to the top of the table, and delete the blank line between the first and second lines, if it is present.

14. Drag across the heading ("Consolidated Statement of Condition") and press CTRL-SHIFT-B to make it bold.

15. Press CTRL-W to change to "Fit in window" view.

16. Press CTRL-S to save your work.

When you complete these steps, your pages 4 and 5 should look like those shown in Figure 6-39.

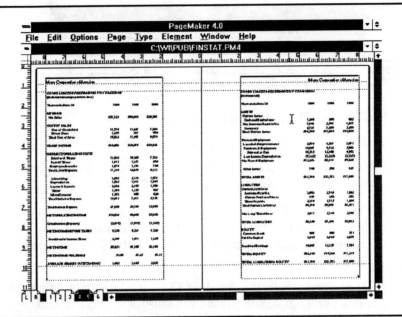

Figure 6-39. *The financial statements with the tabs adjusted*

Drawing Lines Your final task to complete the tables on pages 4 and 5 is to add a series of lines on each of them to emphasize or separate various segments. Like the Financial Highlights table, both of these have a 1-point line under the dates. In addition, though, a number of hairlines are added to the table itself. Add these lines by using the following instructions:

1. Press CTRL-U to turn the "Snap to guides" option back on.

2. Press SHIFT-F3 to select the perpendicular-line tool.

3. Drag a horizontal ruler guide down to 2V.

4. Draw a line across the table on page 4 on the horizontal ruler guide at 2V from left 8H to 2H.

```
─                            PageMaker 4.0                         ▼ ↕
File  Edit  Options  Page  Type  Element  Window  Help
─                       C:\WP\PUB\INSTAT.PM4                       ▼ ↕
```

Miscellaneous		1,161	866	628
Total Nonlabor Expense		10,641	7,941	5,754
Total Indirect Expense		27,859	20,790	15,065
NET OPERATING INCOME		$10,834	$8,085	$5,859
Other Income (Expense)		(2,476)	(1,848)	(1,339)
NET INCOME BEFORE TAXES		8,358	6,237	4,520
Provision for Income Taxes		2,507	1,871	1,356
NET INCOME		$5,851	$4,366	$3,164
NET INCOME PER SHARE		$1.68	$1.25	$1.11
AVERAGE SHARES OUTSTANDING		3,485	3,485	2,854

Figure 6-40. *The lines at the bottom of the Statement of Operations table*

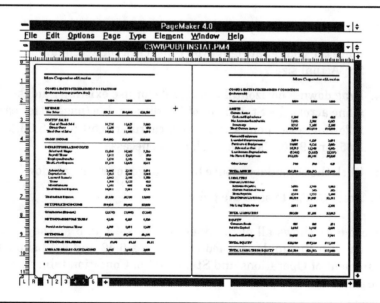

Figure 6-41. *Pages 4 and 5 with the completed lines ("Guides" turned off)*

5. Select the "Line" option of the Element menu and confirm that "1 pt" is chosen; if not, choose it now and for the next line.

6. Draw a similar line across the table on page 5 on the horizontal ruler guide at 2V from right 2H to 8H.

7. Press F9 to select the pointer.

8. Choose "Hairline" from the "Line" option of the Element menu.

9. Press F9 to reselect the perpendicular-line tool.

10. Place the pointer at left 5H/4V and click the secondary mouse button for "Actual size".

11. Drag down a horizontal ruler guide and draw a line across the Statement of Operations table (page 4) for each of the following five points on the vertical ruler: 2.65, 4.05, 7.45, 9.05, 9.85. Drag the existing ruler guide at 9.80 down to 9.90 and draw a line across it. Use the scroll bar as necessary.

Note that the last two lines produce a double line at the bottom of the Statement of Operations table, as shown in Figure 6-40.

12. Click the secondary mouse button to go to "Fit in window" view.

13. Place the pointer at right 5H/4V and click the secondary mouse button for "Actual size".

14. Drag down a horizontal ruler guide (or use existing guides) and draw a line across the Statement of Condition table (page 5) for each of the following seven points on the vertical ruler: 3.50, 5.60, 5.65, 7.85, 9.50, 9.85, and 9.90. Use the scroll bar as necessary.

15. Click the secondary mouse button to go to "Fit in window" view.

16. Press CTRL-S to save the publication.

Figure 6-41 shows all of the lines on pages 4 and 5 as they look on the screen with the guides turned off. Figures 6-42 and 6-43 show how the Statement of Operations and Statement of Condition tables look as they are printed.

Micro Corporation of America

CONSOLIDATED STATEMENT OF OPERATIONS
(In thousands except per share data)

Years ended June 30	1990	1989	1988
REVENUE			
Net Sales	$54,725	$40,840	$29,594
COST OF SALES			
Cost of Goods Sold	14,776	11,027	7,990
Direct Costs	1,256	937	679
Total Cost of Sales	16,032	11,964	8,670
GROSS INCOME	$38,693	$28,876	$20,924
INDIRECT OPERATING COSTS			
Salaries & Wages	13,930	10,395	7,533
Payroll Taxes	1,811	1,351	979
Employee Benefits	1,478	1,103	799
Total Labor Expense	17,218	12,850	9,311
Advertising	3,095	2,310	1,674
Depreciation	1,935	1,444	1,046
Leases & Rentals	2,902	2,166	1,569
Taxes	1,548	1,155	837
Miscellaneous	1,161	866	628
Total Nonlabor Expense	10,641	7,941	5,754
Total Indirect Expense	27,859	20,790	15,065
NET OPERATING INCOME	$10,834	$8,085	$5,859
Other Income (Expense)	(2,476)	(1,848)	(1,339)
NET INCOME BEFORE TAXES	8,358	6,237	4,520
Provision for Income Taxes	2,507	1,871	1,356
NET INCOME	$5,851	$4,366	$3,164
NET INCOME PER SHARE	$1.68	$1.25	$1.11
AVERAGE SHARES OUTSTANDING	3,485	3,485	2,854

Figure 6-42.   *The finished Statement of Operations table (page 4) as it is printed*

Micro Corporation of America

CONSOLIDATED STATEMENT OF CONDITION
(In thousands)

Years ended June 30	1990	1989	1988
ASSETS			
Current Assets			
Cash and Equivalents	1,286	960	695
Net Accounts Receivable	7,483	5,584	4,047
Inventory	9,737	7,266	5,266
Total Current Assets	$18,506	$13,810	$10,008
Plant and Equipment			
Leasehold Improvements	5,678	4,237	3,071
Furniture & Equipment	10,897	8,132	5,893
Subtotal at Cost	16,575	12,369	8,963
Less Accum. Depreciation	(4,322)	(3,225)	(2,337)
Net Plant & Equipment	$12,253	$9,144	$6,626
Other Assets	789	589	427
TOTAL ASSETS	$31,548	$23,543	$17,060
LIABILITIES			
Current Liabilities			
Accounts Payable	3,683	2,749	1,992
Current Portion of Notes	487	363	263
Taxes Payable	2,378	1,775	1,286
Total Current Liabilities	$6,548	$4,887	$3,541
Net Long Term Notes	2,811	2,318	2,304
TOTAL LIABILITIES	$9,359	$7,204	$5,845
EQUITY			
Common Stock	697	697	571
Paid-in Capital	3,485	3,485	2,854
Retained Earnings	18,007	12,157	7,791
TOTAL EQUITY	$22,189	$16,339	$11,216
TOTAL LIABILITIES & EQUITY	$31,548	$23,543	$17,060

5

Figure 6-43.   *The finished Statement of Condition table (page 5) as it is printed*

Finishing the Back Cover

The back cover of the annual report, page 6, has only the company's address and phone number in addition to the items from the master page. Use the following instructions to finish that page and the annual report:

1. Press F9 to select the pointer.

2. Click on the page 6 icon to turn the page.

3. Press CTRL-T to open the Type specifications dialog box.

4. Press TAB, type **14** in the Size text box, and click on "Bold" for the Type style.

5. Click on "OK" to close the Type specifications dialog box.

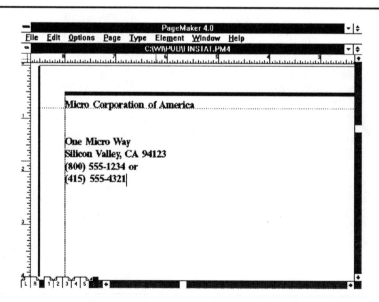

Figure 6-44. *The completed last page*

Micro Corporation of America

One Micro Way
Silicon Valley, CA 94123
(800) 555-1234 or
(415) 555-4321

6

Figure 6-45.   *The completed last page as it is printed*

6. Place the pointer at left 5.5H/2V, and click the secondary mouse button for "Actual size".

7. Press SHIFT-F4 to select the text tool.

8. Click at 1.5 to the right of the left margin to place the insertion point.

9. Type the following lines, pressing ENTER at the end of each line.

One Micro Way

Silicon Valley, CA 94123

(800) 555-1234 or

(415) 555-4321

When you are done, page 6 should look like Figure 6-44 on the screen and like Figure 6-45 when it is printed.

10. Press CTRL-S to save the publication.

11. Press CTRL-P to open the Print dialog box. Make any necessary changes, and press ENTER to print the annual report.

12. Choose "Close" from the System menu of both PageMaker and Windows to leave the environment.

The finished annual report is a very attractive piece. The newsletter in Chapter 7 is even nicer!

▌▌▌ *Advanced PageMaker Publications*

Part Three focuses on two applications to demonstrate PageMaker's more advanced functions. These two complex applications produce a newsletter in Chapter 7 and a catalog in Chapter 8. Because you are now familiar with the basics of PageMaker, the pace quickens in Part III. The emphasis is less on explaining the features and more on using them to create an application.

One of the primary uses of PageMaker has been to create newsletters. Consequently, no PageMaker book is complete without exploring this application in detail. The newsletter in Chapter 7 is modeled after an actual one that is produced with PageMaker. It demonstrates how to create a multipage newsletter with three or four columns per page, using graphics and text from multiple sources. In Chapter 7 you use the master layout pages in conjunction with custom pages to produce a dummy publication. The dummy is a base from which all issues of the newsletter are created. In many ways this is the most important chapter in the book: when you complete this chapter, you will be well versed in the essentials of using PageMaker to produce complex publications.

In Chapter 8 you will produce three pages of a catalog. Like the newsletter in Chapter 7, the catalog is modeled after one that is created with Page-Maker. This chapter demonstrates how to produce a multipage, two-column product catalog using the master page layout as a standard.

7 *Preparing a Newsletter*

In Chapter 7 you discover that creating a newsletter is a task well suited to PageMaker. You create a four-page newsletter that uses graphics, multiple fonts, multiple columns, varying line widths, automatic and customized leading, and other techniques to make attractive and readable copy.

An actual newsletter is used as the example in this chapter. It is *The Orator,* a quarterly that was published for the Churchill Club by Opinion Movers of Palo Alto, California. The *Orator* was created with the Macintosh version of PageMaker. You will see that the IBM version also works for this example. The names of most individuals and companies on the original newsletter have been changed, except for public figures and the editor, Rich Karlgaard, who has generously given ideas and advice for this chapter.

The newsletter articles are written by several individuals: the newsletter's regular staff and two contributing authors. For the purposes of this example, assume that the articles written by the staff were produced with Microsoft Word for Windows. One contributing author used Microsoft Word as the word processor; the other used WordPerfect. Part of your task in this chapter is to take text from these three word processors and integrate them into one newsletter.

The newsletter contains two graphics. When publishing the actual newsletter, Opinion Movers created a placeholder for the graphics in the newsletter and then gave the actual graphics to a commercial printer to place and print. In this chapter you create placeholders for both graphics. Then you create a computer file of the first graphic with a scanner and place it in the placeholder by using PageMaker. You do not create the second graphic.

You need not use all three word processors or the scanner. Simply read the explanation, noting the particulars about the text, and then use your own word processor (if it is supported by PageMaker). For the graphics you can substitute clip art if you want experience in placing and working with graphics. Or you can simply read the details and be satisfied with providing the space for the graphics to see how you work with text around the graphics in PageMaker. A disk that contains both the text and the graphic is available from the authors; you can order it by using the form in the front of this book.

Planning and Designing the Newsletter

As with all publications, planning and design are critical to the successful creation of a newsletter.

Planning the Newsletter

The planning stage for a newsletter may be extensive because the publisher may be coordinating the efforts of many individuals. Bringing all factors together against a deadline, and within budget, can be a challenge.

Essentially, the planning task consists of four steps:

1. Identifying what materials—graphics, articles, and artwork—are needed in the newsletter

2. Identifying who is responsible for each item

3. Determining when each item must be submitted in order to be included in the newsletter

4. Determining what the newsletter costs and what the cost elements are

You must do the planning in detail. For example, you must both identify what articles are needed and be able to state how many words long the text should be. If you need 500 words and get 1000, you're in as much trouble as if you received 100 words. You must plan for contingencies in any case. If a writer breaks her leg the day before a deadline, you must be able to "wing" it; that is, you must have plans to cover such an event, such as other writers or "filler" articles.

The Orator contains text from four sources: standard newsletter text, such as the masthead, which is present in all the newsletters; articles prepared for this particular issue by *The Orator* staff; a short article from one contributing author; and a longer article by a second contributing author. Figures 7-1 through 7-4 show the four pages.

The length of each article is closely planned and monitored by the staff to fit in the available space in the four-page newsletter. The planning closely ties in with the design of the newsletter.

Designing the Newsletter

A primary step in the task of designing the newsletter is to evaluate the newsletter for standard formatting, graphics, and text; that is, to determine which parts of the newsletter are the same from issue to issue. By isolating these standard parts and saving them separately, you can save yourself many hours of repetitive work.

One of the overall objectives of this chapter is to produce a dummy publication containing all recurring graphics, formatting, and text, and then to use that to create an issue of *The Orator*. To do this requires that you examine the makeup and layout of each page of the newsletter. If you examine the four pages in Figures 7-1 through 7-4, you can see some common design elements in each. For example, lines play an important design role.

Lines   Lines are frequently used to create highlights and points of interest, as well as to define areas of the newsletter. Most of the lines are hairline width and are used to define margins, columns, and boxes for short inserts. Other lines are wider, marking the heads of columns, separating categories of information, or emphasizing certain articles. In the actual *Orator,* the staff creates wider lines by drawing boxes and filling them with black shading. Then the commercial printer varies the lines by using different colors and shades. However, in this chapter you will create most of the wider lines by drawing actual lines rather than boxes, making them 6 and 12 points wide, in contrast to the hairline width of most of the lines. Some of the wider lines contain text. You create those by drawing boxes, filling them with solid shading and then using *reverse type*—white letters on a black background—to create the text.

Fonts   For the text you enter in this chapter, you use two typefaces and 14 fonts. The Times typeface is used for most of the text, and Sans is used in a few instances. The title of the newsletter is 48 points; the headlines, 16 points; the text, some of which is italic, is 6, 8, 10, and 12 points.

Printer Memory   When designing the fonts you use, you must keep printer memory in mind. Depending on the amount of memory in your printer, you may have to restrict the variations you use in fonts to conserve printer memory. If you use downloaded fonts, you may be surprised at the memory they require, particularly the larger point sizes. Boxes with shading, even "Paper" shading, can also account for high usage of printer memory. Each layer of boxes takes additional memory.

Printing the newsletter with all of the fonts and other style elements mentioned here on an HP LaserJet Series II with 2.5MB creates no problems. Printing on an HP LaserJet IIP with 512KB requires reducing the number of fonts to nine, reducing the largest font from 48 to 30 points, and reducing the headlines from 16 to 14 points.

Shading   Shading is used in several ways. First, it is used as a background for headlines of some smaller inserts. Second, it provides the background in the placeholders for the graphics. Third, for articles that span two columns, a box is drawn and filled with "Paper" shading to cover the column dividers. Page 3 of the newsletter contains examples of the first and last types of shading.

Leading   To fit some of the text within the given space, you must vary the leading (the spacing between the lines). PageMaker assumes 120 percent leading in its "Auto" leading option. If you are using 10-point type, the automatic leading is 12 points, or 10/12. In two cases you make this smaller to squeeze the text together slightly. Although you could also make the font size smaller (which would hurt the look of the newsletter), here you vary the leading.

Advertisement   One advertisement, for the printer who donates the printing for the newsletter, is included in *The Orator*. Because the ad spans

THE ORATOR
Volume 4, Issue 4-November 1990

SOUTH AFRICA'S BUTHELEZI TO ADDRESS CHURCHILL CLUB ON DECEMBER 4TH

The Churchill Club will sponsor its eighth and final event of 1990 on Thursday, December 4th, at the Santa Clara Marriott. The guest: Gatsha Buthelezi, Chief Minister of the Kwa-Zulu homeland in South Africa. The event starts at 6 P.M.

Chief Gatsha Buthelezi claims the support of South Africa's six million Zulus, the nation's largest ethnic group. Despite his moderate voice (or perhaps because of it), this makes him a powerful voice in this turmoiled region. Tom Lodge, a political-science professor at the University of Witswatersrand, says, "It is a dangerous situation to leave Buthelezi out of the equation." Chief Buthelezi himself asserts, "There can't be a successful negotiation without me."

Chief Buthelezi comes across to many white South Africans as comfortingly moderate. To them, he embodies the hope for the future. He speaks about whites' fears without fanning them. He says he doesn't want to overthrow white South Africa's values and aspirations. Rather, he says, he wants blacks to be able to share them.

A more serious difference is between Chief Buthelezi and the African National Congress, the broadly based antiapartheid organization that has recently espoused violence. The ANC (and its leader, the jailed Nelson Mandela) quietly supported Buthelezi in the 1970s, recognizing his ability to mobilize people from the rural areas. But in the 1980s the ANC became impatient with Buthelezi's pleas for peaceful change. The group now espouses violence as a necessary catalyst for change in South Africa.

The Orator is published quarterly by The Churchill Club. Subscriptions are guaranteed free of charge to all corporate and individual members. Printing of The Orator is donated by Pandick Press, San Francisco.

Editor: Richard Karlgaard
Historian: Michael Perkins
Cartoonist: Kurt Peterson

Ennui and the brush-Winston as the artist

Broadly speaking, human beings may be divided into three classes: those who are toiled to death, those who are worried to death, and those who are bored to death.

Churchill himself, of course, was by no means immune to these afflictions about which he wrote. But what was he to do about it?

Churchill typically sought surcease in a number of activities, including reading, fencing, swimming, riding, hunting, flying, polo, horse racing, gardening, and bricklaying. He was also a collector of butterflies and tropical fish and had a number of pets.

Further, Churchill was something of the big kid indulging in everything from toy trains, tin soldiers, and erector sets to

"The tired parts of the mind can be rested and strengthened, not merely by rest, but by using other parts"

building sandcastles and snowmen.

The common denominator in all this activity was change. As Churchill himself writes,

Continued on page 2

Figure 7-1. *Page 1 of the newsletter*

Change is the master key. A man can wear out a particular part of his mind by continually using it and tiring it. The tired parts of the mind can be rested and strengthened, not merely by rest, but by using other parts. It is only when new cells are called into activity, when new stars become lords of the ascendant, that relief, repose, refreshment are afforded.

At age 40 Churchill found himself out of political office for the first time in fifteen years and he needed to discover a new way to creatively fill up the hours.

Exercise, travel, solitude, light socializing, even golf (which he likened to chasing a pill around a cow pasture) did not suffice. It was then, with a friend's encouragement, that he took up painting.

Intensity, Relish and Audacity
Painting at once provided Churchill an opportunity to use his hands as well as a different part of his brain. The "muse of painting" had come to his rescue.

The nonprofit Churchill Club provides a nonpartisan forum for public discourse on timely issues, particularly those in which business and politics converge. The Club is named after Winston Churchill, whose character and career personify the democratic values of open discourse, diversity and freedom. Accordingly, Club membership is without regard to sex, lifestyle, legitimacy, sobriety, race, color, creed, physical or mental disposition, or origin.

When Churchill took up the brush, he did it with the same intensity, relish, and audacity as everything he undertook, and he was not discouraged by the results. Painting also proved to be the perfect diversion. In Painting as a Pastime he writes,

I know nothing which, without exhausting the body, more entirely absorbs the mind. Whatever the worries of the hour or the threats of the future, once the picture has begun to flow along, there is no room for them in the mental screen. They pass out into shadow and darkness. All one's mental light, such as it is, becomes concentrated on the task. Time stands respectfully aside.

Churchill chose to devote his painting to landscapes and still lifes in an impressionist style. His brilliant colors became a type of trademark: "I cannot pretend to be impartial about the colours," he wrote. "I rejoice with the brilliant ones and am genuinely sorry for the poor browns."

In search of beautiful scenes, Churchill took his easel with him wherever he traveled including the Middle East and North America. On a trip to Scotland he wrote to his wife, "In the afternoon I went out and painted a beautiful river in the afternoon light with crimson and golden hills in the background."

From the Riviera he writes of a villa that he painted "all in shimmering sunshine and violet shades."

There is something about a martini —a tingle remarkably pleasant

Thus began poet Ogden Nash in *A Drink with Something in It.*

The perfect dry martini contains gin, vermouth, and a twist of lemon. It must be very cold, but not contain ice or water, so keep your gin in the freezer and vermouth in the refrigerator. The especially discriminating may use Tanqueray gin and Noilly extra dry vermouth.

Polish a martini glass and put it in the freezer along with your jigger and stirring rod. The glass should be large, but light, with a feathered rim and a long stem to keep the martini cold. With a sharp knife, cut a generous twist from a ripe, fresh lemon. Be careful to separate the yellow peel from the white pulp, as the peel contains the lemon oil and the pulp would impart a bitter flavor to the martini.

Take the glass from the freezer. Twist the lemon peel to release its oil. Rub the oily surface around the inside of the glass and along its rim, then drop the twist in the glass. Take the gin from the freezer (or Stolichnaya vodka if you feel diffident about gin) and measure two jiggers into the glass. Take the vermouth from the refrigerator and measure a third of a jigger into the glass. Stir vigorously, but do not shake. Remove to a pleasant setting and enjoy.

by "Christopher Russell"

Antidote to Melancholy and Ennui
In the end, painting was to prove one of the chief antidotes to Winston's sometime melancholy and ennui. It also served to deepen Churchill's powers of observation, so much that he had come to see that "the whole world is open with all its treasures, even the simplest objects have their beauty."

Like the poet and artist William Blake, Churchill had learned not only to see with, but through the eye.

Contributed by
Michael Perkins
Club Historian

MY EARLY LIFE

It took me three tries to pass into Sandhurst. There were five subjects, of which Mathematics, Latin and English were obligatory, and I chose in addition French and Chemistry. In this hand I held only a pair of Kings--English and chemistry. Nothing less than three would open the jackpot. I had to find another useful card.

W.S. CHURCHILL

Figure 7-2. *Page 2 of the newsletter*

THE ORATOR   *Page 3*

Members Only

GOVERNOR DEUKMEJIAN INTRODUCES CHILDREN'S INITIATIVE AT 10-9-90 MEETING

Governor George Deukmejian proposed a $5 million program to bolster statewide child care and medical services at a joint meeting of the Churchill Club and Commonwealth Club on October 9, 1990.

Before 500 people at the San Jose Hyatt, the governor outlined a seven-point "children's initiative" that included a call for expanded drug abuse prevention programs and a crackdown on parents who evade payment of child support.

He also promised to hire more senior citizens to work in child care centers and offered to write legislation providing incentives for drug companies to produce vaccines for childhood diseases.

The Churchill Club thanks the Commonwealth Club for co-sponsoring this fine event.

COMING DECEMBER 4TH

"IMMIGRATION OUT OF CONTROL," COLORADO'S LAMM TELLS CLUB

Warning that the United States is at a crossroads, Colorado Governor Richard Lamm called for stronger border control measures during an address to the Churchill Club on October 16, 1990.

"The creativity and capital of this country, for all its genius, cannot keep pace with the demands put on it if we have to solve not only our own unemployment rate, but that of Mexico, Guatemala, and El Salvador," said the four-term governor.

CLUB MEMBERS IN THE NEWS

Board member Bill Reichert is now vp/marketing at The Learning Company, a Menlo Park-based educational software firm. Reichert's alma mater, New Venture Consultants, is the newest corporate member of the Club... John Sewell, former vice president and general manager of Kodak's largest division, joined the board of Redlake Corporation, a Morgan Hill company that manufactures and sells photo-instrumentation equipment. Redlake is also a Club corporate member... Bob Hansens of Business Solutions Consultants is forming the Silicon Valley Entrepreneur's Club. First meeting is scheduled for January 24th at the San Jose Hyatt. Call Bob at (408) 458-1303 for more information... Club chairman Tony Perkins has returned to Silicon Valley Bank as vice president of SVB's technology group. Also new with SVB are Club members Henry Kellog and Eric Jones.

T.J. Rodgers confirmed for late January

Semiconductor entrepreneur T.J. Rodgers will address the Churchill Club in late January.

Founder and CEO of Cypress Semiconductor, Rodgers has engineered one of Silicon Valley's brightest stories of late. Cypress went public last summer at a valuation of $270 million.

Invitations to a *Night with T.J. Rodgers* will be mailed in early January.

CLUB INFORMATION

Membership
Ken Bailey
Silver City Bank
(415) 555-1234

Speaker Information
Julia Conner
Pacific Research Capital
(415) 555-4321

Media Relations
Susan Casper
Ocean Products
(408) 555-9876

Former H&Q president Tom Volpe on February 19th

Tom Volpe, founder of Volpe Covington, a new investment banking firm that includes Arthur Rock and Warren Hellman as major investors, will address the Churchill Club on Thursday, February 19th.

Volpe has had a meteoric career in investment banking. After taking his AB and MBA from Harvard —with a one-year stopover at the London School of Economics—he began his career with White, Weld & Company, later moving to Blyth, Eastman, Dillon.

At age 30 Volpe joined Hambrecht & Quist as a general partner and opened the investment banking firm's New York Office. In 1984 he became president and CEO of H&Q.

Invitations to *A Night with Tom Volpe* will be mailed to all Club members in early January.

Pandick California, Inc.

The **Financial Printer**

(415) 543-4433

Offices in

San Francisco • Los Angeles • Newport Beach

Figure 7-3.   *Page 3 of the newsletter*

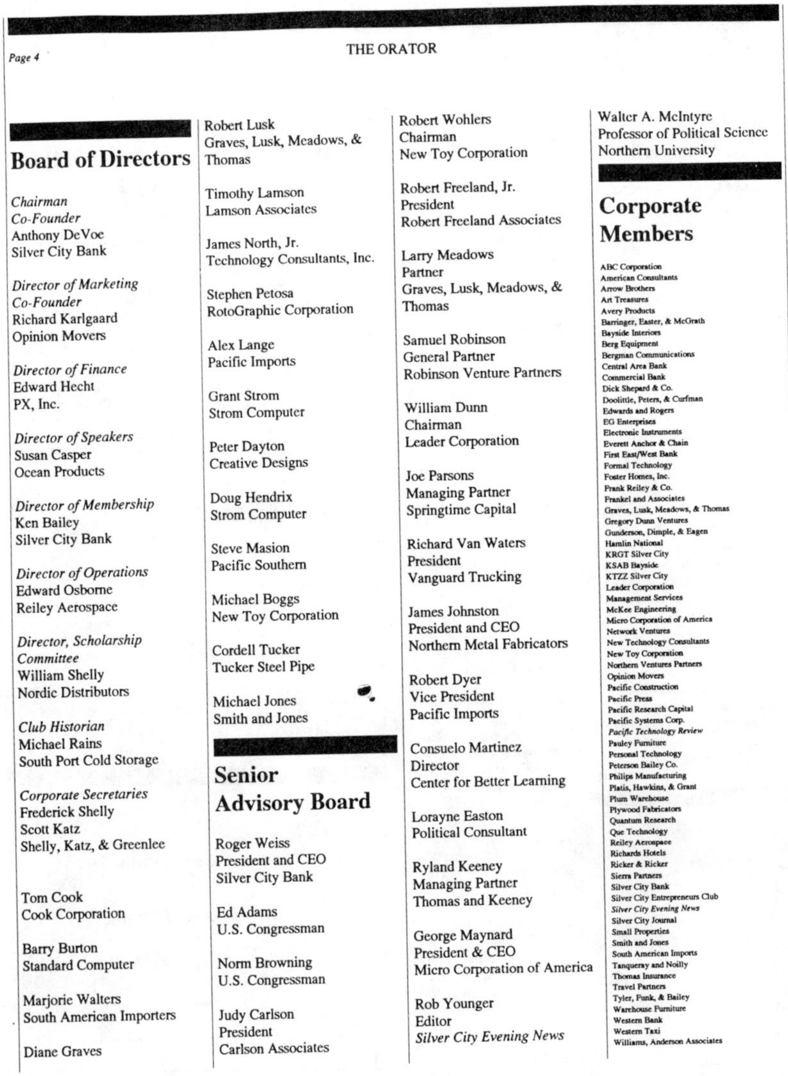

Board of Directors

Chairman
Co-Founder
Anthony DeVoe
Silver City Bank

Director of Marketing
Co-Founder
Richard Karlgaard
Opinion Movers

Director of Finance
Edward Hecht
PX, Inc.

Director of Speakers
Susan Casper
Ocean Products

Director of Membership
Ken Bailey
Silver City Bank

Director of Operations
Edward Osborne
Reiley Aerospace

Director, Scholarship
Committee
William Shelly
Nordic Distributors

Club Historian
Michael Rains
South Port Cold Storage

Corporate Secretaries
Frederick Shelly
Scott Katz
Shelly, Katz, & Greenlee

Tom Cook
Cook Corporation

Barry Burton
Standard Computer

Marjorie Walters
South American Importers

Diane Graves

Robert Lusk
Graves, Lusk, Meadows, &
Thomas

Timothy Lamson
Lamson Associates

James North, Jr.
Technology Consultants, Inc.

Stephen Petosa
RotoGraphic Corporation

Alex Lange
Pacific Imports

Grant Strom
Strom Computer

Peter Dayton
Creative Designs

Doug Hendrix
Strom Computer

Steve Masion
Pacific Southern

Michael Boggs
New Toy Corporation

Cordell Tucker
Tucker Steel Pipe

Michael Jones
Smith and Jones

Senior Advisory Board

Roger Weiss
President and CEO
Silver City Bank

Ed Adams
U.S. Congressman

Norm Browning
U.S. Congressman

Judy Carlson
President
Carlson Associates

Robert Wohlers
Chairman
New Toy Corporation

Robert Freeland, Jr.
President
Robert Freeland Associates

Larry Meadows
Partner
Graves, Lusk, Meadows, &
Thomas

Samuel Robinson
General Partner
Robinson Venture Partners

William Dunn
Chairman
Leader Corporation

Joe Parsons
Managing Partner
Springtime Capital

Richard Van Waters
President
Vanguard Trucking

James Johnston
President and CEO
Northern Metal Fabricators

Robert Dyer
Vice President
Pacific Imports

Consuelo Martinez
Director
Center for Better Learning

Lorayne Easton
Political Consultant

Ryland Keeney
Managing Partner
Thomas and Keeney

George Maynard
President & CEO
Micro Corporation of America

Rob Younger
Editor
Silver City Evening News

Walter A. McIntyre
Professor of Political Science
Northern University

Corporate Members

ABC Corporation
American Consultants
Arrow Brothers
Art Treasures
Avery Products
Barringer, Easter, & McGrath
Bayside Interiors
Berg Equipment
Bergman Communications
Central Area Bank
Commercial Bank
Dick Shepard & Co.
Doolittle, Peters, & Curfman
Edwards and Rogers
EG Enterprises
Electronic Instruments
Everett Anchor & Chain
First East/West Bank
Formal Technology
Foster Homes, Inc.
Frank Reiley & Co.
Frankel and Associates
Graves, Lusk, Meadows, & Thomas
Gregory Dunn Ventures
Gunderson, Dimple, & Eagen
Hamlin National
KRGT Silver City
KSAB Bayside
KTZZ Silver City
Leader Corporation
Management Services
McKee Engineering
Micro Corporation of America
Network Ventures
New Technology Consultants
New Toy Corporation
Northern Ventures Partners
Opinion Movers
Pacific Construction
Pacific Press
Pacific Research Capital
Pacific Systems Corp.
Pacific Technology Review
Pauley Furniture
Personal Technology
Peterson Bailey Co.
Philips Manufacturing
Platis, Hawkins, & Grant
Plum Warehouse
Plywood Fabricators
Quantum Research
Que Technology
Reiley Aerospace
Richards Hotels
Ricker & Ricker
Sierra Partners
Silver City Bank
Silver City Entrepreneurs Club
Silver City Evening News
Silver City Journal
Small Properties
Smith and Jones
South American Imports
Tanquery and Noilly
Thomas Insurance
Travel Partners
Tyler, Funk, & Bailey
Warehouse Furniture
Western Bank
Western Taxi
Williams, Anderson Associates

Figure 7-4. *Page 4 of the newsletter*

two columns, you create a box around the column guides and rules and fill the box with "Paper" to hide the dividing guides and rules. Then you type the text for the ad in PageMaker, varying the font sizes and style as you type. The advertisement is a standard part of the newsletter and is included in the dummy publication.

Graphics There are two graphics: a standard club logo of Winston Churchill that occurs in every publication and a sketch or cartoon that varies with each issue. You scan the Churchill graphic to create a computer-readable file that is then placed in the dummy publication. After doing this once, you need not repeat it with each issue.

You create a placeholder for the second graphic and assume that you give the illustration to the commercial printer to size and print. With an actual newsletter, you would probably produce the two graphics in the same way so that the "look" would be consistent.

If you do not have access to a scanner, you can substitute clip art for the Churchill graphic. That allows you to experiment with placing the graphic, even though it is not exactly right for the publication.

Layout The layout for the newsletter is measured in picas and points, which is the most accurate method for what you are doing. Picas and points are the standard units of measurement in the U.S. printing industry. There are approximately 6 picas per inch and 12 points per pica. Figure 7-5 shows the standard page layout with the primary measurements. You use 3 picas for the left and right margins, 2.5 picas for the top margin, 4 picas for the bottom margin, and 0.75 pica (9 points) to separate the columns. The standard page will have four columns, although the first page has three.

Creating Text and Graphics
For the Newsletter

Next you create the text and graphics for the newsletter. The text is created outside of PageMaker with word processors that can interface with Page-Maker. The Churchill graphic is produced by a scanner, which must be able to produce a file containing a computer image that is compatible with

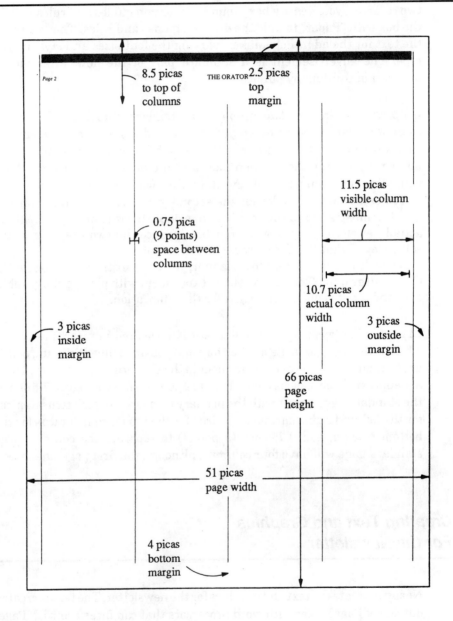

Figure 7-5. *Standard layout used in* The Orator

PageMaker. The second graphic is pasted on the newsletter before it is printed by a commercial printer, so you needn't concern yourself with it here.

Creating Text with The Word Processors

Three word processors are used to create the text that is integrated into the newsletter. You may not want to use all three, or you may have a different word processor that you normally use. In that case create the text files with your own word processor. The most heavily used word processor for this newsletter is Word for Windows.

Creating Text with Microsoft Word for Windows

Assume here that the staff of *The Orator* writes all their text using Microsoft Word for Windows as the word processor. This package was selected because it is Windows compatible and can transmit a full complement of typefaces, sizes, and styles to PageMaker, all of which the newsletter makes considerable use.

Two files are built with Word for Windows. One contains four items of standard text that appear in all issues of the newsletter. The other contains six specific articles that appear only in this one issue. You would normally create several files for this many articles.

Figure 7-6 contains the standard text that you enter with Word for Windows. It is the longest file and takes some time to enter. Be patient because you learn much about composing with PageMaker while using a file of this size.

Creating Styles with Word for Windows

In Word for Windows you can predefine styles and use them repeatedly to specify the fonts and other style elements you want. For the first file you create a set of styles for this newsletter. It has a separate style for each change in font. You can quickly apply these styles as you type and know that you have a consistent application of style. Both Word for Windows and PageMaker use these styles to format the text properly. To change a style in either Word for Windows or PageMaker, you simply change the definition of the style, and all of the text that uses that style instantly changes everywhere in the document.

The Orator is published quarterly by The Churchill Club. Subscriptions are guaranteed free of charge to all corporate and individual members. Printing of The Orator is donated by Pandick Press, San Francisco.

2 returns

Editor: Richard Karlgaard
Historian: Michael Perkins
Cartoonist: Kurt Peterson

10-point
Times
italics
style-BI

2 returns

The nonprofit Churchill Club provides a nonpartisan forum for public discourse on timely issues, particularly those in which business and politics converge. The Club is named after Winston Churchill, whose character and career personify the democratic values of open discourse, diversity and freedom. Accordingly, Club membership is without regard to sex, lifestyle, legitimacy, sobriety, race, color, creed, physical or mental disposition, or origin.

2 returns

CLUB INFORMATION

Membership
Ken Bailey
Silver City Bank
(415) 555-1234

Speaker Information   Italics
Julia Conner
Pacific Research Capital
(415) 555-4321

Media Relations
Susan Casper
Ocean Products
(408) 555-9876

10-point Sans
style-BN

2 returns

Board of Directors ← 16-point Times bold
style-HL

Chairman
Co-Founder
Anthony DeVoe
Silver City Bank

Director of Marketing
Co-Founder   Italics (BI)
Richard Karlgaard
Opinion Movers

10-point Times
style-BM

Director of Finance
Edward Hecht
PX, Inc.

Director of Speakers
Susan Casper
Ocean Products

Rest of file
(unless noted)

Figure 7-6. *STANDARD.DOC file created with Word for Windows (1 of 3)*

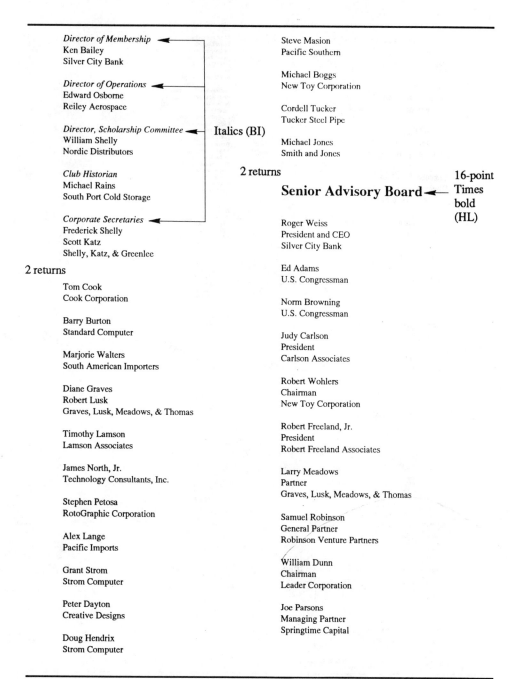

Director of Membership
Ken Bailey
Silver City Bank

Director of Operations
Edward Osborne
Reiley Aerospace

Director, Scholarship Committee   Italics (BI)
William Shelly
Nordic Distributors

Club Historian
Michael Rains
South Port Cold Storage

Corporate Secretaries
Frederick Shelly
Scott Katz
Shelly, Katz, & Greenlee

2 returns

Tom Cook
Cook Corporation

Barry Burton
Standard Computer

Marjorie Walters
South American Importers

Diane Graves
Robert Lusk
Graves, Lusk, Meadows, & Thomas

Timothy Lamson
Lamson Associates

James North, Jr.
Technology Consultants, Inc.

Stephen Petosa
RotoGraphic Corporation

Alex Lange
Pacific Imports

Grant Strom
Strom Computer

Peter Dayton
Creative Designs

Doug Hendrix
Strom Computer

Steve Masion
Pacific Southern

Michael Boggs
New Toy Corporation

Cordell Tucker
Tucker Steel Pipe

Michael Jones
Smith and Jones

2 returns

Senior Advisory Board   16-point Times bold (HL)

Roger Weiss
President and CEO
Silver City Bank

Ed Adams
U.S. Congressman

Norm Browning
U.S. Congressman

Judy Carlson
President
Carlson Associates

Robert Wohlers
Chairman
New Toy Corporation

Robert Freeland, Jr.
President
Robert Freeland Associates

Larry Meadows
Partner
Graves, Lusk, Meadows, & Thomas

Samuel Robinson
General Partner
Robinson Venture Partners

William Dunn
Chairman
Leader Corporation

Joe Parsons
Managing Partner
Springtime Capital

Figure 7-6. *STANDARD.DOC file created with Word for Windows (2 of 3)*

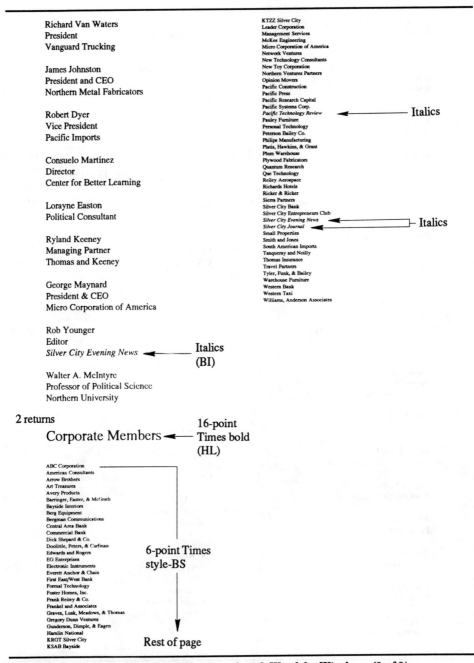

Richard Van Waters
President
Vanguard Trucking

James Johnston
President and CEO
Northern Metal Fabricators

Robert Dyer
Vice President
Pacific Imports

Consuelo Martinez
Director
Center for Better Learning

Lorayne Easton
Political Consultant

Ryland Keeney
Managing Partner
Thomas and Keeney

George Maynard
President & CEO
Micro Corporation of America

Rob Younger
Editor
Silver City Evening News ← Italics (BI)

Walter A. McIntyre
Professor of Political Science
Northern University

KTZZ Silver City
Leader Corporation
Management Services
McKee Engineering
Micro Corporation of America
Network Ventures
New Technology Consultants
New Toy Corporation
Northern Ventures Partners
Opinion Movers
Pacific Construction
Pacific Press
Pacific Research Capital
Pacific Systems Corp.
Pacific Technology Review ← Italics
Pauley Furniture
Personal Technology
Peterson Bailey Co.
Philips Manufacturing
Platis, Hawkins, & Grant
Plum Warehouse
Plywood Fabricators
Quantum Research
Que Technology
Reiley Aerospace
Richards Hotels
Ricker & Ricker
Sierra Partners
Silver City Bank
Silver City Entrepreneurs Club
Silver City Evening News ← Italics
Silver City Journal
Small Properties
Smith and Jones
South American Imports
Tanqueray and Noilly
Thomas Insurance
Travel Partners
Tyler, Funk, & Bailey
Warehouse Furniture
Western Bank
Western Taxi
Williams, Anderson Associates

2 returns

Corporate Members ← 16-point Times bold (HL)

ABC Corporation
American Consultants
Arrow Brothers
Art Treasures
Avery Products
Barringer, Easter, & McGrath
Bayside Interiors
Berg Equipment
Bergman Communications
Central Area Bank
Commercial Bank
Dick Shepard & Co.
Doolittle, Peters, & Curfman
Edwards and Rogers
EG Enterprises
Electronic Instruments
Everett Anchor & Chain
First East/West Bank
Formal Technology
Foster Homes, Inc.
Frank Reiley & Co.
Frankel and Associates
Graves, Lusk, Meadows, & Thomas
Gregory Dunn Ventures
Gunderson, Dimple, & Eagen
Hamlin National
KRGT Silver City
KSAB Bayside

6-point Times style-BS

Rest of page

Figure 7-6.   *STANDARD.DOC file created with Word for Windows (3 of 3)*

You define six styles for the newsletter. These are used to change the typeface between Times and Sans; or to change the size to 6, 10, 12, or 16 points; or to apply the italic style. Load Word for Windows and follow these steps to define a style:

1. Choose "Define Styles..." from the Format menu. The Define Style Name dialog box opens with the "Normal" style highlighted.

2. Type **BM,Body Medium**, click on "Options", press DEL to delete "Normal" in the "Based on" text box, click on "Character", select "Times" from the "Font" list box, press TAB, type **10** in the "Points" text box, click on "OK", and click on "Define".

Steps 1 and 2 produce the first style—Body Medium, or BM. In addition to being 10-point Times medium as you have set it, BM also assumes the defaults of "Left" alignment and "Auto" line spacing (click on "Paragraph" to assure yourself of that and then click on "OK".) This style was defined first because it is the standard upon which you base all of the other styles. In other words, all of the other styles are the Body Medium style with some modification. For example, BS, Body Small, is 6-point Body Medium—flush left, 6-point Times medium with "Auto" leading—and BI, Body Italic is italicized Body Medium—flush left, 10-point Times italic with "Auto" leading.

Basing a set of styles off of a single style is a very useful capability. It means that you can change the base style and change all of the derivatives as well. For example, all but one of the styles use the Times typeface. If you wanted to change all occurrences of Times to Palatino, all you would need to do is change the Body Medium style to Palatino, and all of the derivative styles change except those that were originally defined with a different typeface. Continue on now and define the rest of the styles.

3. Type **BL,Body Large**, click on the downward-pointing arrow to the right of the "Based On" text box, use the scroll bar to locate and click on "BM,Body Medium" to select it as the based-on style; click on "Character", press TAB, type **12** for the point size, click on "OK", and click "Define". Body Large is defined as the same as Body Medium, but at 12 points in size instead of 10.

4. Type **BS,Body Small**, select "BM,Body Medium" as the based-on style, change the character size to 6, both as just described, and click on "Define".

5. Repeat step 3 for BI,Body Italic, which is defined as Body Medium with italic; BN,Body Sans, which is Body Medium with Sans; and HL, Heading Large, which is Body Medium with 16-point bold type.

When you have entered all of the styles, your dialog box should look like this:

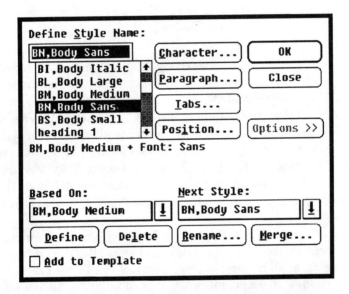

6. Click on "OK" to close the Define Style Name dialog box.

Applying Styles with Word for Windows   Use Figure 7-6 to type the first file. Input the column independently, using the styles indicated. The file itself is one continuous column. Use a single line between sections and paragraphs unless directed otherwise. For example, "2 returns" means to press ENTER twice.

Follow these steps to enter the text:

1. If the ruler and the style ribbon are not turned on, choose them from the View menu.

2. Click on the downward-pointing arrow to the right of the "Style" text box on the right of the ruler. Use the scroll bar and click on "BI, Body Italic" style to apply it. Then type the first three paragraphs in Figure 7-6, and press ENTER at the end.

3. Press CTRL-S, type **BN,Body Sans**, and press ENTER to apply that style. Then type **CLUB INFORMATION** and the following text that uses the Sans typeface, as shown in Figure 7-6. Before typing the first line of each section—for example, **Membership**—press CTRL-I to make the line italic. At the end of the line and before pressing ENTER, press CTRL-SPACEBAR to return to Roman or nonitalicized type.

4. Choose "Styles..." from the Format menu, double-click on "HL,Heading Large" to apply it, and type **Board of Directors**.

5. Type the remaining text applying the HL, BM, BI, and BS styles as indicated. Use any of the three techniques demonstrated in the previous steps to apply the styles.

6. When you have entered the text, save the file under the name \WI\PUB\STANDARD.DOC.

The second file produced with Word for Windows contains the six articles that appear in this single issue. Figure 7-7 shows these articles. Follow these steps to enter the text:

7. Open a new document, choose "Define Styles..." from the Format menu, click on "Options" and then "Merge", select "STANDARD.DOC", and press ENTER. The STANDARD.DOC styles are transferred to the new document. Click on "OK" or press ENTER to close the Define Styles dialog box.

8. Type the articles, applying the various styles as shown in Figure 7-7 and using any of the methods described in the discussion of the STANDARD.DOC document.

9. When you complete typing the new document, save it in the \WI\PUB directory with the name VOL4ISS4.DOC (for Volume 4, Issue 4).

You create the next file with Microsoft Word 5.

SOUTH AFRICA'S BUTHELEZI TO ADDRESS CHURCHILL CLUB ON DECEMBER 4TH

16-point
Times Bold (HL)

The Churchill Club will sponsor its eighth and final event of 1986 on Thursday, December 4th, at the Santa Clara Marriott. The guest: Gatsha Buthelezi, Chief Minister of the Kwa-Zulu homeland in South Africa. The event starts at 6 P.M.

Chief Gatsha Buthelezi claims the support of South Africa's six million Zulus, the nation's largest ethnic group. Despite his moderate voice (or perhaps because of it), this makes him a powerful voice in this turmoiled region. Tom Lodge, a political-science professor at the University of Witswatersrand, says, "It is a dangerous situation to leave Buthelezi out of the equation." Chief Buthelezi himself asserts, "There can't be a successful negotiation without me."

12-point
Times (BL)

Chief Buthelezi comes across to many white South Africans as comfortingly moderate. To them, he embodies the hope for the future. He speaks about whites' fears without fanning them. He says he doesn't want to overthrow white South Africa's values and aspirations. Rather, he says, he wants blacks to be able to share them.

A more serious difference is between Chief Buthelezi and the African National Congress, the broadly based antiapartheid organization that has recently espoused violence. The ANC (and its leader, the jailed Nelson Mandela) quietly supported Buthelezi in the 1970s, recognizing his ability to mobilize people from the rural areas. But in the 1980s the ANC became impatient with Buthelezi's pleas for peaceful change. The group now espouses violence as a necessary catalyst for change in South Africa.

2 returns

Members Only ◄──── 16-point Times Bold (HL)

GOVERNOR DEUKMEJIAN INTRODUCES CHILDREN'S INITIATIVE AT 10-9-86 MEETING ◄

Governor George Deukmejian proposed a $5 million program to bolster statewide child care and medical services at a joint meeting of the Churchill Club and Commonwealth Club on October 9, 1986.

Before 500 people at the San Jose Hyatt, the governor outlined a seven-point "children's initiative" that included a call for expanded drug abuse prevention programs and a crackdown on parents who evade payment of child support.

He also promised to hire more senior citizens to work in child care centers and offered to write legislation providing incentives for drug companies to produce vaccines for childhood diseases.

The Churchill Club thanks the Commonwealth Club for co-sponsoring this fine event.

Italic
(BI)

2 returns

"IMMIGRATION OUT OF CONTROL," COLORADO'S LAMM TELLS CLUB ◄

10-point
Times
(BM)

Warning that the United States is at a crossroads, Colorado Governor Richard Lamm called for stronger border control measures during an address to the Churchill Club on October 16, 1986.

"The creativity and capital of this country, for all its genius, cannot keep pace with the demands put on it if we have to solve not only our own unemployment rate, but that of Mexico, Guatemala, and El Salvador," said the four-term governor.

Figure 7-7. *VOL4ISS4.DOC file created with Word for Windows (1 of 2)*

CLUB MEMBERS IN THE NEWS

Board member Bill Reichert is now vp/marketing at The Learning Company, a Menlo Park-based educational software firm. Reichert's alma mater, New Venture Consultants, is the newest corporate member of the Club... John Sewell, former vice president and general manager of Kodak's largest division, joined the board of Redlake Corporation, a Morgan Hill company that manufactures and sells photo-instrumentation equipment. Redlake is also a Club corporate member... Bob Hansens of Business Solutions Consultants is forming the Silicon Valley Entrepreneur's Club. First meeting is scheduled for January 24th at the San Jose Hyatt. Call Bob at (408) 458-1303 for more information... Club chairman Tony Perkins has returned to Silicon Valley Bank as vice president of SVB's technology group. Also new with SVB are Club members Henry Kellog and Eric Jones.

2 returns

T.J. Rodgers confirmed for late January ◄— 16-pt Times Bold (HL)

Semiconductor entrepreneur T.J. Rodgers will address the Churchill Club in late January.
Founder and CEO of Cypress Semiconductor, Rodgers has engineered one of Silicon Valley's brightest stories of late. Cypress went public last summer at a valuation of $270 million.
Invitations to a *Night with T.J. Rodgers* will be mailed in early January.

10-pt Times (BM)

2 returns

Former H&Q president Tom Volpe on February 19th ◄—

Tom Volpe, founder of Volpe Covington, a new investment banking firm that includes Arthur Rock and Warren Hellman as major investors, will address the Churchill Club on Thursday, February 19th.
Volpe has had a meteoric career in investment banking. After taking his AB and MBA from Harvard --with a one-year stopover at the London School of Economics--he began his career with White, Weld & Company, later moving to Blyth, Eastman, Dillon.
At age 30 Volpe joined Hambrecht & Quist as a general partner and opened the investment banking firm's New York Office. In 1984 he became president and CEO of H&Q.
Invitations to *A Night with Tom Volpe* will be mailed to all Club members in early January.

Figure 7-7. *VOL4ISS4.DOC file created with Word for Windows (2 of 2)*

Creating a File with Microsoft Word 5 One contributing author, Christopher Russell (a pen name), uses Microsoft Word 5 as his word processor. The Word file is very short, as shown in Figure 7-8.

Within this article you will use three different fonts, all with the Times typefaces: 16-point bold for the headline, 10-point Roman for the text, and 10-point italic in two places. With Microsoft Word 5.0 or 5.5, you can easily apply all of these styles and then transfer them to PageMaker.

Start Word (or your word processing program) and type the short article, adding the formatting as shown in Figure 7-8. You may want to use the same styles as you used in the first two files if you are using the same word processing program. When you are done, save the file in the \WI\PUB directory with the name MARTINI.DOC.

There is something about a martini ◄┐
                                        ├─16-point Times Bold (HL)
  --a tingle remarkably pleasant ◄┘

Thus began poet Ogden Nash in *A Drink with Something in It.* ◄──── Italics (BI)

The perfect dry martini contains gin, vermouth, and a twist of lemon. It must be very cold, but not
contain ice or water, so keep your gin in the freezer and vermouth in the refrigerator. The especially
discriminating may use Tanqueray gin and Noilly extra dry vermouth.
  Polish a martini glass and put it in the freezer along with your jigger and stirring rod. The
glass should be large, but light, with a feathered rim and a long stem to keep the martini cold. With a
sharp knife, cut a generous twist from a ripe, fresh lemon. Be careful to separate the yellow peel from
the white pulp, as the peel contains the lemon oil and the pulp would impart a bitter flavor to the
martini.
  Take the glass from the freezer. Twist the lemon peel to release its oil. Rub the oily surface
around the inside of the glass and along its rim, then drop the twist in the glass. Take the gin from the
freezer (or Stolichnaya vodka if you feel diffident about gin) and measure two jiggers into the glass.
Take the vermouth from the refrigerator and measure a third of a jigger into the glass. Stir vigorously,
but do not shake. Remove to a pleasant setting and enjoy.

10-point
Times
(BH)

Italics (BI) ──►*by "Christopher Russell"*

Figure 7-8. *MARTINI.DOC file created with Microsoft Word 5*

The last file is entered with WordPerfect.

Creating a File with WordPerfect The second contributing author, Michael Perkins, uses WordPerfect. His article is one in an ongoing series about Winston Churchill, so the file is appropriately named CHURCHIL.WP. The text is primarily 10-point Times, as shown in Figure 7-9, and the

16-point Times Bold——►**Ennui and the brush-Winston as the artist**

Italics ——— *Broadly speaking, human beings may be divided into three classes: those who are toiled to death, those who are worried to death, and those who are bored to death.*

Churchill himself, of course, was by no means immune to these afflictions about which he wrote. But what was he to do about it?

Churchill typically sought surcease in a number of activities, including reading, fencing, swimming, riding, hunting, flying, polo, horse racing, gardening, and brick-laying. He was also a collector of butterflies and tropical fish and had a number of pets.

Further, Churchill was something of the big kid indulging in everything from toy trains, tin soldiers, and erector sets to building sandcastles and snowmen.

The common denominator in all this activity was change. As Churchill himself writes,

Italics ——— *Change is the master key. A man can wear out a particular part of his mind by continually using it and tiring it. The tired parts of the mind can be rested and strengthened, not merely by rest, but by using other parts. It is only when new cells are called into activity, when new stars become lords of the ascendant, that relief, repose, refreshment are afforded.*

At age 40 Churchill found himself out of political office for the first time in fifteen years and he needed to discover a new way to creatively fill up the hours.

Exercise, travel, solitude, light socializing, even golf (which he likened to chasing a pill around a cow pasture) did not suffice. It was then, with a friend's encouragement, that he took up painting.

Italics ——— *Intensity, Relish and Audacity*
Painting at once provided Churchill an opportunity to use his hands as well as a different part of his brain. The "muse of painting" had come to his rescue.

When Churchill took up the brush, he did it with the same intensity, relish, and audacity as everything he undertook, and he was not discouraged by the results. Painting also proved to be the perfect diversion. In Painting as a Pastime he writes,

Italics——— *I know nothing which, without exhausting the body, more entirely absorbs the mind. Whatever the worries of the hour or the threats of the future, once the picture has begun to flow along, there is no room for them in the mental screen. They pass out into shadow and darkness. All one's mental light, such as it is, becomes concentrated on the task. Time stands respectfully aside.*

Churchill chose to devote his painting to landscapes and still lifes in an impressionist style. His brilliant colors became a type of trademark: "I cannot pretend to be impartial about the colours," he wrote. "I rejoice with the brilliant ones and am genuinely sorry for the poor browns."

In search of beautiful scenes, Churchill took his easel with him wherever he traveled including the Middle East and North America. On a trip to Scotland he wrote to his wife, "In the afternoon I went out and painted a beautiful river in the afternoon light with crimson and golden hills in the background."

From the Riviera he writes of a villa that he painted "all in shimmering sunshine and violet shades."

Figure 7-9. CHURCHIL.WP *file created with WordPerfect (1 of 2)*

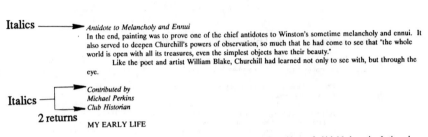

Italics ———→ *Antidote to Melancholy and Ennui*
In the end, painting was to prove one of the chief antidotes to Winston's sometime melancholy and ennui. It also served to deepen Churchill's powers of observation, so much that he had come to see that "the whole world is open with all its treasures, even the simplest objects have their beauty."

Like the poet and artist William Blake, Churchill had learned not only to see with, but through the eye.

Italics ———→ *Contributed by*
Michael Perkins
Club Historian

2 returns

MY EARLY LIFE

It took me three tries to pass into Sandhurst. There were five subjects, of which Mathematics, Latin and English were obligatory, and I chose in addition French and Chemistry. In this hand I held only a pair of Kings--English and chemistry. Nothing less than three would open the jackpot. I had to find another useful card.

W.S. CHURCHILL

Figure 7-9. *CHURCHIL.WP file created with WordPerfect (2 of 2)*

headline is 16-point Times. The Churchill quotes are in italics. The majority of the formatting that you apply in WordPerfect 5.1 is transferred to PageMaker. This includes typefaces, sizes, styles, tabs, and indents. Therefore, type the Churchill articles now, applying the formatting shown in Figure 7-9. When you are done, save the file in the \WI\PUB directory with the name CHURCHIL.WP.

You now have the four text files ready to be integrated into PageMaker. This is a good time to take a break. When you return, you will create the graphics for the newsletter.

Using Graphics Within the Newsletter

You have several options for using graphics within PageMaker. You can create a graphic with one of the painting or drawing programs, such as Windows Paint or Micrografx Designer; you can create a graphic file by scanning a photo or line drawing with a scanner; or you can take the graphic to a commercial printer to photographically place and size it on the newsletter before it is printed.

Opinion Movers lets the commercial printer handle the graphic for *The Orator*. Figure 7-10 shows the camera-ready artwork of Winston Churchill that is submitted to the printer along with the newsletter master copy.

Figure 7-10.   *WSCHURCH.TIF scanned art*

If you have a scanner, the Churchill drawing in Figure 7-10 is reproduced in Appendix C and can be removed for use here. If you do not have a scanner but wish to try placing a graphic, substitute a clip art graphic for the actual graphic in this book. For example, you might use the PEOPLE.PIC drawings in Micrografx's Clip Art Collection. If you do not want to handle the graphics right now, simply follow the instructions for building the newsletter, including saving a spot for the graphics. You still get the experience of working around the graphics, which is valuable in itself.

Scanning Graphics for PageMaker   If you have a scanner and want to produce the newsletter with a scanned drawing, follow these instructions:

1. Remove Appendix C from the book.
2. Start your scanner and load its driver software.
3. Scan the logo.
4. Crop the resulting screen image so that only the logo is left.
5. Using the path and name \WI\PUB\WSCHURCH.TIF, save the file.

Creating Clip Art for the Newsletter   If you want to place some graphics within the newsletter and do not have access to a scanner, you can substitute some clip art for the actual graphics.

You can bring clip art directly into PageMaker; you simply need to use the filename for the piece of clip art instead of WSCHURCH.TIF in the instructions later in this chapter. You may need to crop the resulting image or do some custom sizing, but that will be obvious if it is necessary.

Now that you have created the text and graphics, you can begin to build the newsletter. The first thing you do is to set defaults within PageMaker.

Setting Defaults

Some of the defaults you set become permanent within your PageMaker system and are present on loading the program (unless you change them again), while others are set for the current publication only. The timing of default selection determines the extent to which they are permanent. You change many of these as you create individual parts of the newsletter, but the overall defaults govern many aspects of the tasks you are doing.

Startup Defaults

When you set defaults with no publications on the desktop or before opening or initiating a publication, the defaults become permanent to the PageMaker system. This means that they are present each time you start PageMaker.

In the following paragraphs you set as startup defaults the target printer and preferences for measurement—not necessarily because you want them to be PageMaker system defaults, but because they affect the page setup, which is normally your first step in creating a new publication. For example, before you set up the margins, you want to specify what scale is used—inches? centimeters? picas?

If you are using PageMaker, close any active publications so you have no publications open for the next few steps. If you are not currently using PageMaker, load it now.

Establishing the Target Printer   Follow these steps to establish your printer:

1. Choose "Target printer..." from the File menu.

2. When the dialog box is displayed, double-click on the target printer you want to use for the newsletter. If you do not see it, use the scroll bar to find it.

3. Verify that the settings for your printer are correct, and include letter-size paper and portrait orientation. If one or more are not set, click on the appropriate check box to choose it.

4. When all settings are as you want them, click on "OK" for both the Settings and Target printers dialog boxes

Setting Page Preferences   In this newsletter you use picas and points for the scale on the rulers. Set that default in this way:

1. Choose "Preferences..." from the Edit menu.

2. Select "Picas" from both the Measurement system option box and the Vertical ruler option box.

3. Click on "Back" under Guides so lines and boxes are more easily moved, and click on "OK" to close the dialog box.

Once you have established the startup defaults, you can establish the publication defaults.

Publication Defaults

The publication defaults are effective for the current publication only. They are set after a publication has been initiated within PageMaker. In this case your first step is to create a new publication and establish the page setup options.

Establishing Margins The margins for the newsletter are extremely important. With multiple columns, each additional character of space matters when you are trying to fit text within the given area. In addition, if you make your margins too small, the outer edges of your text may not print. (Printers have an outer limit beyond which they do not print.) You set the inside and outside margins to 3 picas, the top margin to 2.5 picas, and the bottom margin to 4 picas.

To set the margin specifications, follow these steps:

1. Choose "New..." from the File menu.

2. Verify that the options checked in the Page setup dialog box are "Letter": 51 by 66 picas, "Tall", "Double- sided", and "Facing pages".

3. If not already highlighted, drag across the "Number of pages" option and type **4**.

4. Drag across the "Inside" margin and then set it and the "Outside" margin at 3 picas, the "Top" margin at 2.5, and the "Bottom" margin at 4, as shown in Figure 7-11. Press TAB to go from one to the other.

5. Press ENTER to complete the dialog box.

Your screen should show the page outline with the dotted margin guides within it.

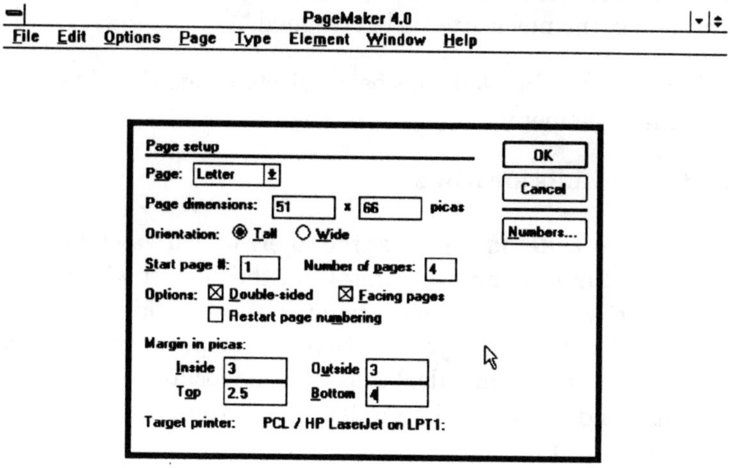

PageMaker 4.0

File Edit Options Page Type Element Window Help

Page setup

Page: Letter

Page dimensions: 51 x 66 picas

Orientation: ⦿ Tall ◯ Wide

Start page #: 1   Number of pages: 4

Options: ☒ Double-sided ☒ Facing pages
☐ Restart page numbering

Margin in picas:
Inside 3   Outside 3
Top 2.5   Bottom 4

Target printer: PCL / HP LaserJet on LPT1:

OK   Cancel   Numbers...

Figure 7-11.   *The Page setup dialog box*

Setting Line Widths   Most of the lines within the newsletter are hairline width. Set that as the publication default.

Establishing Type Specifications   The first file to place within the newsletter is the Microsoft Word STANDARD.DOC file. Most of its text is 10-point Times, normal style. Set the default type specifications to be consistent:

1. Press CTRL-T for the Type specifications dialog box.

2. Select "Times" for the Font, press TAB, and type **10** for the Size. Verify that "Normal" is set for Type style, Position, Case, and Width, and that "Auto" is set for Leading.

3. When you finish, click on "OK" to complete the dialog box.

Another default that you want to establish is the text alignment. Most of the text in the newsletter is left-aligned.

4. Verify that "Align left" has been selected from the "Alignment" option of the Type menu.

Your type defaults are now set.

Setting Other Options   You use the rulers in two ways while building the newsletter. First, when switching from the "Fit in window" view to the "Actual size" view, you place the pointer before making the switch so that you can control the image you get. Second, you place different forms of text (articles, headings, and titles) that must be located in specific spots. The horizontal and vertical ruler guides, which you pull from the rulers, are essential for that task.

In addition, you want access on the screen to the horizontal and vertical scroll bars, the magnetic properties of the "Snap to guides" option and, at least at first, the Toolbox. You use the shortcut keys to access the Toolbox for most of the chapter. Also, the "Guides" option lets you see the non-printed margin, column, and ruler guides on the screen.

1. Verify that "Snap to rulers", "Guides", and "Snap to guides" are checked on the Options menu. If any are not, choose them now. Also, verify that the Toolbox is displayed. If it is not, turn it on in the Window menu.

You can see the horizontal ruler across the top of the page and the vertical ruler on the left side of the page, as well as the Toolbox. The ruler should be in picas and show that the page is 66 picas long by 51 picas wide.

2. Maximize both the application and document windows to access the maximum working area.

Important Techniques Used
In This Chapter

Throughout the chapter you repeatedly use techniques for working with text and graphics. These techniques are not explained each time they are used; rather, they are described here. If you need to review a technique, you can scan this section of the chapter to refresh your memory.

Switching Between the "Actual size" And "Fit in window" Views

To place the text, graphics, and lines exactly, you must switch between the "Actual size" and "Fit in window" views many times. You will find that this is an extremely efficient way to place and then verify lines, text, and graphics. There are two steps. First, when you are in "Fit in window" view and want the "Actual size" view, position your pointer on what you want to appear in the middle of the screen and then press the secondary mouse button. To help you place the pointer, you often are given the horizontal and vertical ruler coordinates like this: 6H/2.5V, which should be read "6 picas on the horizontal ruler and 2.5 picas on the vertical ruler." Second, when you are in "Actual size" and want a "Fit in window" view, press the secondary mouse button. The secondary mouse button acts as a switch between the two views.

Try it out now for a quick test:

1. Place your pointer at 6H/6V and press the secondary mouse button for an "Actual size" view.

2. Return to the "Fit in window" view by pressing the secondary mouse button.

You can also return to the "Fit in window" by pressing CTRL-W. Since the precision placement is not needed when returning to the "Fit in window" view as it is when going to "Actual size," CTRL-W is often the preferred approach. For the rest of the book, only the statement "return to the 'Fit in window' view" is used, and you can decide whether to use the secondary mouse button or CTRL-W.

Concepts of Layers

With PageMaker, you build publications in layers. For instance, entered text is one layer. When you place a graphic on top of the text, that becomes a second layer. If you build a box or draw a line, you add another layer. You can see the top layer and, if it is transparent, what lies beneath it. You manipulate the layers, and consequently what appears, by filling boxes with shading and by sending the layers either to the front or the back of the layer stack. For example, if you type text and then draw a box around it without a fill pattern or screen, you can still see the text because the box is empty. However, if you fill it with shading, you cannot see the text until you send the box to the back of the stack. Then the text is on top and the shaded box appears in the background.

The Toolbox Tools

The Toolbox contains four tools that you need—the pointer tool, the text tool, the perpendicular-line tool, and the square-corner tool. You switch from one to another to perform various tasks. Although you start with the Toolbox, you soon want to remove its image from the screen so that you can see all of the horizontal ruler. After you hide it, you use shortcut keys to access the tools, for example, SHIFT-F4 for the text tool. You are reminded at the time which keys to use—though you will soon memorize them. Remember the F9 is a toggle between the pointer and the last tool you use. For example, if you are using the text tool and want to use the pointer, press F9. If you then want to return to the text tool, press F9 again.

Selecting Text and Graphics

Every time you want to do something with text or graphics within Page-Maker, you must first select it—that is, highlight it or form a selection box around it. Depending on what you want to do, you first choose the correct tool and then select the text or graphics.

Selecting Text   You can select text with either the text tool or the pointer tool, depending on what you want to do. For example, if you want to move an entire block of text from one spot on the page to another, you use the pointer tool. However, if you want to change the type specification for the text, you highlight it with the text tool.

If you are selecting text with the pointer tool, simply place the pointer on the text and click the main mouse button. The text is enclosed in a selection box.

If you are selecting text with the text tool, you must first drag over the text with the I-beam to highlight it. Then you specify what you want done with the text.

If you repeatedly try to select some text and cannot, or can only select something else, the "something else" is getting in the way. For example, if the block of text is not on the top layer, you may have to bring it to the front in order to work with it. You can see the various selection areas by choosing "Select all" from the Edit menu. It allows you to see whether the "something else" is on the top layer or whether you are not placing the pointer in the correct spot. If the text you want was created on the master page and you are currently trying to select it on a regular page, you must return to the master to select it.

Selecting Lines or Graphics If you have just created a line or box, it may still be selected if you have not deselected it by clicking the main mouse button somewhere else. You can tell by the tiny boxes that appear around the item. If the item has been deselected, you must select the graphic or line with the pointer tool.

To select an item, you place the tip of the pointer on the line or graphic and click the main mouse button. The selected item is displayed with two tiny boxes on either end if it is a line or with eight tiny boxes around it if it is a box or a graphic.

To select a line or graphic, you may have to work around other items that get in the way. You may have a column or margin guide, for instance, that is repeatedly selected instead of the line you want. To select a line that lies over or near it, you may have to press the CTRL key while you are clicking on the desired line to get around the guides. If that doesn't work, try "Lock guides" on the Option menu, or as a final means you may have to move the guide to get at the one you want. Alternatively, as mentioned earlier, you may use the "Bring to front" command to bring the graphic to the front in order to select it, or use the "Send to back" command if text or other graphics are interfering with the selection.

Deselecting Selected Text or Graphics To deselect anything, simply click your pointer on something else—it can be on other text you want to select or on the Pasteboard. You can select an item after it has been deselected by following the rules just outlined.

Moving Text or Graphics

Moving text or graphics is a three-step process: (1) Select the item with the pointer tool; (2) press and hold the main mouse button until the pointer becomes a four-arrow icon; and (3) drag the item wherever you want it on the screen.

Copying Text or Graphics

Copying text or graphics with the pointer tool is a five-step process: (1) highlight or select the item with the pointer tool; (2) copy it by pressing CTRL-INS; (3) find the page where you want the item inserted; (4) press SHIFT-INS to paste the copy back on the screen; and (5) press the main mouse button with the pointer tool and drag the item where you want it.

If you want multiple copies, you can continue with step 3 because the copy remains available to you until you cut or copy something else.

Copying text with the text tool is done when you want to copy and then insert the text into another text block. In this case you click the insertion point to indicate where the text is to be placed before pressing SHIFT-INS.

Setting Up a Dummy Publication

PageMaker's ability to create a dummy publication saves you an enormous amount of time by providing a standard framework within which you can build all the issues of a newsletter. Essentially, you create a newsletter with all the standard and recurring portions; then you load that publication and customize it for the specific issue you are building.

The newsletter has two recurring page formats, as shown in Figure 7-12. The first page has three columns, a title, and a standard graphic between two columns. The three remaining newsletter pages contain four columns with a smaller title and page numbers. Because the last three pages have the same basic layout, you can use PageMaker's master page facility to create them.

Master pages allow you to set up a standard look for the newsletter and replicate that throughout the publication. You create a standard grid, or layout, and then format it only once rather than for each page that is the same.

Constructing master pages is appropriate for pages 2 through 4. The first page is unique to the newsletter, although it appears the same for all issues. You can build a "custom" page for it. Pages 2 through 4, although identical per the master page layout, have features unique to one particu-

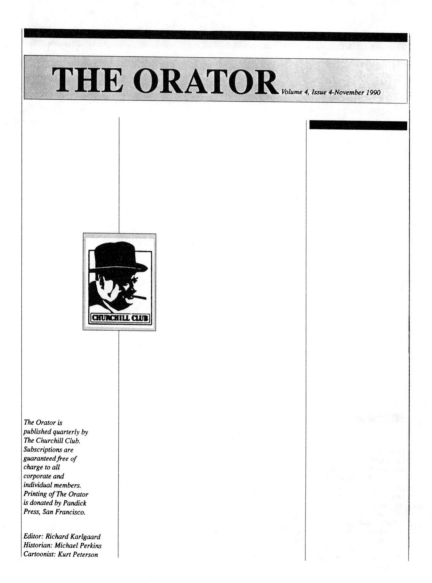

The Orator is
published quarterly by
The Churchill Club.
Subscriptions are
guaranteed free of
charge to all
corporate and
individual members.
Printing of The Orator
is donated by Pandick
Press, San Francisco.

Editor: Richard Karlgaard
Historian: Michael Perkins
Cartoonist: Kurt Peterson

Figure 7-12. *The complete dummy publication (1 of 4)*

The nonprofit Churchill Club provides a nonpartisan forum for public discourse on timely issues, particularly those in which business and politics converge. The Club is named after Winston Churchill, whose character and career personify the democratic values of open discourse, diversity and freedom. Accordingly, Club membership is without regard to sex, lifestyle, legitimacy, sobriety, race, color, creed, physical or mental disposition, or origin.

Figure 7-12.   *The complete dummy publication (2 of 4)*

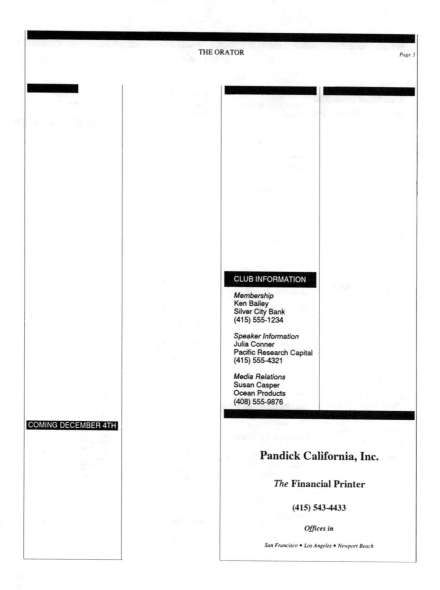

THE ORATOR   *Page 3*

CLUB INFORMATION

Membership
Ken Bailey
Silver City Bank
(415) 555-1234

Speaker Information
Julia Conner
Pacific Research Capital
(415) 555-4321

Media Relations
Susan Casper
Ocean Products
(408) 555-9876

COMING DECEMBER 4TH

Pandick California, Inc.

The **Financial Printer**

(415) 543-4433

Offices in

San Francisco • Los Angeles • Newport Beach

Figure 7-12.   *The complete dummy publication (3 of 4)*

Board of Directors

Chairman
Co-Founder
Anthony DeVoe
Silver City Bank

Director of Marketing
Co-Founder
Richard Karlgaard
Opinion Movers

Director of Finance
Edward Hecht
PX, Inc.

Director of Speakers
Susan Casper
Ocean Products

Director of Membership
Ken Bailey
Silver City Bank

Director of Operations
Edward Osborne
Reiley Aerospace

Director, Scholarship
Committee
William Shelly
Nordic Distributors

Club Historian
Michael Rains
South Port Cold Storage

Corporate Secretaries
Frederick Shelly
Scott Katz
Shelly, Katz, & Greenlee

Tom Cook
Cook Corporation

Barry Burton
Standard Computer

Marjorie Walters
South American Importers

Diane Graves

Robert Lusk
Graves, Lusk, Meadows, &
Thomas

Timothy Lamson
Lamson Associates

James North, Jr.
Technology Consultants, Inc.

Stephen Petosa
RotoGraphic Corporation

Alex Lange
Pacific Imports

Grant Strom
Strom Computer

Peter Dayton
Creative Designs

Doug Hendrix
Strom Computer

Steve Masion
Pacific Southern

Michael Boggs
New Toy Corporation

Cordell Tucker
Tucker Steel Pipe

Michael Jones
Smith and Jones

Senior Advisory Board

Roger Weiss
President and CEO
Silver City Bank

Ed Adams
U.S. Congressman

Norm Browning
U.S. Congressman

Judy Carlson
President
Carlson Associates

Robert Wohlers
Chairman
New Toy Corporation

Robert Freeland, Jr.
President
Robert Freeland Associates

Larry Meadows
Partner
Graves, Lusk, Meadows, &
Thomas

Samuel Robinson
General Partner
Robinson Venture Partners

William Dunn
Chairman
Leader Corporation

Joe Parsons
Managing Partner
Springtime Capital

Richard Van Waters
President
Vanguard Trucking

James Johnston
President and CEO
Northern Metal Fabricators

Robert Dyer
Vice President
Pacific Imports

Consuelo Martinez
Director
Center for Better Learning

Lorayne Easton
Political Consultant

Ryland Keeney
Managing Partner
Thomas and Keeney

George Maynard
President & CEO
Micro Corporation of America

Rob Younger
Editor
Silver City Evening News

Walter A. McIntyre
Professor of Political Science
Northern University

Corporate Members

ABC Corporation
American Consultants
Arrow Brothers
Art Treasures
Avery Products
Barringer, Easter, & McGrath
Bayside Interiors
Berg Equipment
Bergman Communications
Central Area Bank
Commercial Bank
Dick Shepard & Co.
Doolittle, Peters, & Curfman
Edwards and Rogers
EG Enterprises
Electronic Instruments
Everett Anchor & Chain
First East/West Bank
Formal Technology
Foster Homes, Inc.
Frank Reiley & Co.
Frankel and Associates
Graves, Lusk, Meadows, & Thomas
Gregory Dunn Ventures
Gunderson, Dimple, & Eagen
Hamlin National
KRGT Silver City
KSAB Bayside
KTZZ Silver City
Leader Corporation
Management Services
McKee Engineering
Micro Corporation of America
Network Ventures
New Technology Consultants
New Toy Corporation
Northern Ventures Partners
Opinion Movers
Pacific Construction
Pacific Press
Pacific Research Capital
Pacific Systems Corp.
Pacific Technology Review
Pauley Furniture
Personal Technology
Peterson Bailey Co.
Philips Manufacturing
Platis, Hawkins, & Grant
Plum Warehouse
Plywood Fabricators
Quantum Research
Que Technology
Reiley Aerospace
Richards Hotels
Ricker & Ricker
Sierra Partners
Silver City Bank
Silver City Entrepreneurs Club
Silver City Evening News
Silver City Journal
Small Properties
Smith and Jones
South American Imports
Tanqueray and Noilly
Thomas Insurance
Travel Partners
Tyler, Funk, & Bailey
Warehouse Furniture
Western Bank
Western Taxi
Williams, Anderson Associates

Figure 7-12. *The complete dummy publication (4 of 4)*

lar page but constant from issue to issue. For example, an ad for the printer of *The Orator* always appears in the same spot on page 3. The unique features are developed on individual page layouts that are copies of the master pages. Together, the customized page 1 and individualized master pages make up the dummy publication.

The first step is to construct the master pages.

Constructing Master Pages

You have several tasks to complete when you build the master pages. First, reset the zero point. There is a zero point on both the horizontal and vertical rulers; you reset this so you can accurately measure the positions on a page. Second, install several horizontal ruler guides to help you place the headings and the top of the text. Third, type in the name of the newsletter. Fourth, add the four columns with minimal space between them. Next, draw in lines along the left and right margins and between the column guides. In doing this you draw one line and then copy it to the other places so that you can be sure the lines are all exactly the same length. Finally, place an automatic page number on the pages.

Setting Up the Zero Point and Ruler Guides   After bringing up the image of the left and right master pages, you reset the zero point. You want the point to be at the intersection of the top and left margins. Then, to position the title correctly, you place four horizontal ruler guides.

When you have facing pages on the screen, the zero point on the horizontal ruler is initially in the center, and the ruler marks go in both directions. Therefore, you have two 6s, two 2.5s, and so forth on the horizontal ruler. To clarify which marks you are using, the instructions state "left" or "right" for the side of the horizontal ruler currently being used—for example, "left 6H" or "right 42.5H."

Follow these steps to set the zero point and horizontal ruler guides:

1. Click the Master page icons (L,R). Two facing pages appear on your screen.

2. Place your pointer at left 42H/6V, and press the secondary mouse button for an "Actual size" view.

3. Place the pointer in the intersection of the horizontal and vertical rulers (below the document window Control menu), and drag the zero

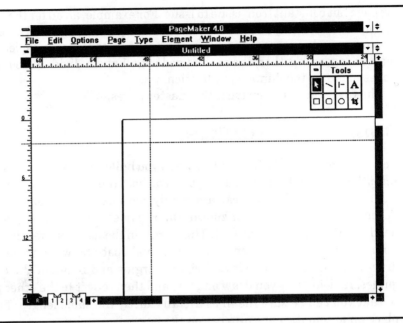

Figure 7-13. *Resetting the zero point on the left master page*

point to the intersection of the left and top margins (not the top of the page) of the left master page, as shown in Figure 7-13.

4. Drag two horizontal ruler guides down to 2.5 and 6 picas on the vertical ruler.

5. Return to the "Fit in window" view.

Entering the Design Line and the Title Now draw the 12-point line along the top margin so that the title can be placed with it in sight.

1. Using the perpendicular-line tool (SHIFT-F3), draw a line on the top margin of the left master page from the left to the right margin.

2. While the line is still selected, choose "12pt" from the "Line" option of the Element menu.

Before you deselect the line, verify that it is correctly drawn in an "Actual size" view. Then draw an identical line on the top margin of the right master page. Before you can place the line accurately, you must hide the Toolbox. From now on you use the shortcut keys to get the tools you need.

3. While the line is selected, place your pointer at 12H/6V, press the secondary mouse button, and verify that the line is between the left and right margins and that it hangs down from the top margin. Use the horizontal scroll bar to adjust the screen.

4. Hide the Toolbox by choosing "Toolbox" from the Window menu or double-clicking on its Control menu.

5. Return to the "Fit in window" view by pressing the secondary mouse button and, using the perpendicular-line tool, draw a second line on the top margin of the right master page.

6. While the line is selected, choose "12pt" from the "Line" option.

You may have to use the "Actual size" view to place it perfectly. Do this by placing your pointer between the left and right master pages and clicking the secondary mouse button. Your screen should look like the one shown in Figure 7-14. You can scroll back and forth with the horizontal

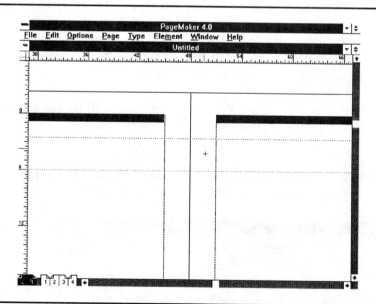

Figure 7-14.   *Two 12-point lines on the master pages*

scroll bar to see the whole top line. The line should be placed exactly between the left and right margins and should hang down from the top margin.

7. When you are satisfied with the line placement, return to the "Fit in window" view.

Now you can type the heading on the left master page and then copy it to the right master page.

8. With the text tool (SHIFT-F4), place the pointer at 18H/6V and click the secondary mouse button. Then place the pointer at 1H/2.5V and click the main mouse button.

9. Press CTRL-T for the Type specifications dialog box, press TAB, type **8** for Size, and click on "Italic" for Type style. Click on "OK" when you are done.

10. Type **Page**, insert a space, and then press CTRL-SHIFT-3 to place PageMaker's automatic page numbering character.

When you press CTRL-SHIFT-3 all at the same time on a master page you are telling PageMaker that you want the automatic page counter to locate its results at that location. The letters "LM" appear where you pressed CTRL-SHIFT-3 on the master page. On the regular pages, however, the actual page number appears. Next you type the title.

11. Press TAB and CTRL-T. Press TAB again, type **10** for the Size, click on "Normal" for the Type style, and press ENTER.

12. Press CAPS LOCK and type **THE ORATOR**.

13. Press CTRL-I to open the Indents/tabs dialog box. Select the centering tab (lower-left box), and click at 22.5 on the ruler, as shown here:

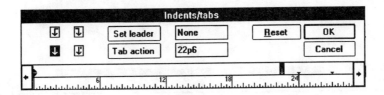

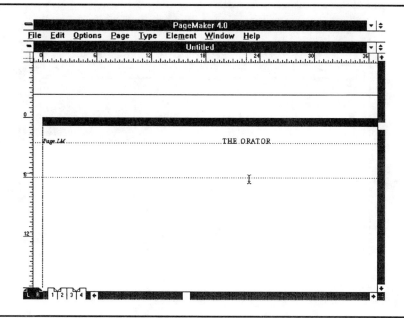

Figure 7-15.   *"The Orator" in the middle of the left master page*

14. Click on "OK." When your screen is redisplayed you see that the page number is left-aligned and that "THE ORATOR" is centered, as shown in Figure 7-15.

To reproduce the title and page number on the right master pages, proceed as follows:

15. Return to the "Fit in window" view.

16. Place the pointer at 78H/6V and click the secondary mouse button. Then place the pointer at 76H/2.5V and click the main mouse button. The insertion point disappears.

17. Press CTRL-SHIFT-R to right-align the title, press TAB, type **THE ORA-TOR**, and press TAB again.

18. Press CAPS LOCK to turn it off. Then press CTRL-T, press TAB, type **8**, and click on "Italic" and "OK".

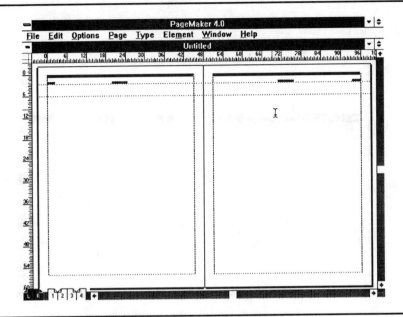

Figure 7-16.   *Titles and page numbers placed on master pages*

19. Type **Page**, press SPACEBAR, and press CTRL-SHIFT-3.

20. Press CTRL-I to open the Indents/tabs dialog box. Select the centering tab, click at 22.5 (or *22p6*) on the ruler and click on "OK."

21. Return to the "Fit in window" view.

Figure 7-16 shows the titles and page numbers correctly placed on the master pages. Next you set up the columns and draw the column dividers.

Setting Up Columns   Except for the first page, the newsletter pages contain four columns. Spacing between the columns is 0.75 pica, or 9 points (because there are 12 points per pica). This can be typed as either **.75** or as **0p9**, for 0 picas and 9 points. After you have built the columns, you draw a line down the center of the first set of column guides to separate the columns, and along the left margin. Then you copy these lines to the other column guides and margins on both pages.

If the original line is too short or too long, delete it by pressing DEL while it is still selected and draw another line. If the line is not centered between the column guides or is too high or too low, reposition it by selecting it with the pointer tool and pressing the main mouse button until the four-arrow icon allows you to move it exactly where you want it.

To set up the columns and column dividers, follow these steps:

1. Choose "Column guides..." from the Options menu.

2. Type **4**, press TAB, type **.75** or **0p9**, and press ENTER to specify four columns and the dividing space between them.

3. Turn off "Snap to guides" by pressing CTRL-U and turn off "Snap to rulers" by pressing CTRL-SHIFT-Y.

4. Select the perpendicular-line tool by pressing SHIFT-F3.

5. Draw a vertical line down between the leftmost set of column guides from the horizontal ruler guide at 11H/6V to the bottom margin.

6. While the line is selected, verify in the "Actual size" view that the top and bottom of the line are exactly on the horizontal ruler guides and in the center between the column guides.

7. If the line is incorrectly placed, select the pointer tool (F9) and drag the line so that it is correctly placed.

Figure 7-17 shows the "Actual size" view of the top of the column. Notice how the line is in the center of the column guides and against the horizontal ruler guide.

8. While the line is selected, copy it by pressing CTRL-INS.

9. Arrange your screen so that the first, second, and third sets of column guides are visible on the screen; then select the pointer (F9) and press SHIFT-INS.

A copy of the line is inserted on the screen. If you are in the "Actual size" view, the top of the line is off the screen. You can move it with the pointer tool by dragging it down (or up, if you are looking at the bottom). You may have to drag it several times to pull the top of the line within the image area.

10. Drag the line down and over to the second set of column guides, and place it between them with the top of the line against the horizontal ruler guide.

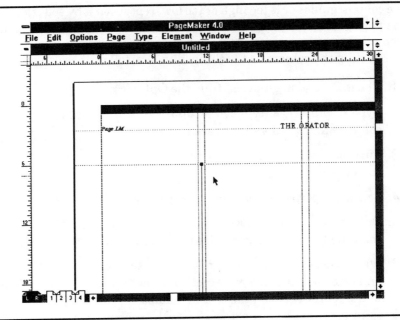

Figure 7-17. *View of the top of the columns with the new dividing line*

Until you delete something else, you can access the copied line by pressing SHIFT-INS. You needn't copy it again and again. If you must delete a line and start again, you must select the original line with the pointer tool (possibly by also pressing CTRL) and copy it again.

11. In the same way, install the column dividers for the rest of the columns on both the left and right master pages (three on each page).

It is sometimes difficult to exactly center the column dividers between the two column guides. Your ability to do this may depend on the resolution of your mouse. If you are having trouble, make sure that "Snap to rulers" and "Snap to guides" are turned off (not checked) in the Options menu. Having done that and after trying several times, give up if you cannot exactly center the line—just do the best you can.

The final task in setting up the master pages is to draw the lines on the left and right margins, from the top to the bottom margins. You draw them slightly outside of the left and right margin guides.

12. Restore the "Snap to rulers" by pressing CTRL-SHIFT-Y.

13. In the "Fit in window" view and with the perpendicular-line tool (SHIFT-F3), draw a vertical line from the top margin (0V) to the bottom margin (59.5V) along the left margin guide of the left master page.

14. In the "Actual size" view, verify that it is the proper length and accurately placed. If not, either delete it and start again or drag it to a better location.

15. With the pointer tool (F9), in the "Actual size" view, reselect (press CTRL if necessary) and drag the line to left .25H (1/4 pica, or 3 points, is the smallest mark in the "Actual size" view.) See Figure 7-18.

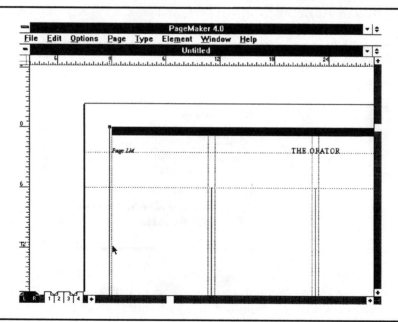

Figure 7-18.   *The "Actual size" view of line outside margin*

16. When it is acceptable, and before it is deselected, copy it by pressing CTRL-INS.

17. Place copies next to the right margin on the left master page and next to the left and right margins on the right master page. Do this by pressing SHIFT-INS and dragging the line to each site. Place the lines 1/4 pica outside of the margin guides (at 45.25, 50.75, and 96.25). You will find that it is easier to both place and verify in the "Actual size" view.

18. Return to the "Fit in window" view.

Saving the Dummy Publication The final step in setting up a master page is to save it on disk.

1. Choose "Save as..." from the File menu.

2. When the Save publication as dialog box is displayed, select the directory you want to use (C:\WI\PUB here), press TAB, and type the filename **dummy** as shown here, and press ENTER.

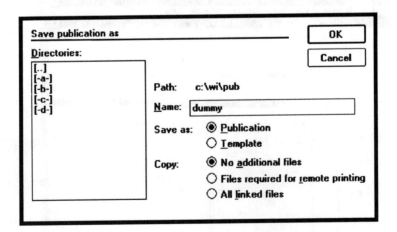

For now, save this as a publication. When you are done with the dummy, you will save it as a template. Saving a publication as a template causes PageMaker to open a copy when you next use it, instead of the original.

You have now created the master pages for pages 2 through 4 of the newsletter, and they will be of enormous benefit to you. Next you must customize page 1. Then you individualize a copy of the master pages for the dummy pages 2 through 4.

Customizing Page 1

Page 1 does not use the elements of the master pages that you use for the other three pages. However, you create a custom page for the dummy publication to set the standard for page 1 in all future issues.

Page 1 contains some fancy design elements that you'll have fun creating. As you saw in Figure 7-12, the title is contained in a box with a shaded background. After you build the three columns on the page, you place a second box for the Churchill club logo between columns 1 and 2.

First, you place the ruler guides.

Placing Horizontal and Vertical Guides   When you bring up page 1 on the screen, you can see that it echoes the master page format with four columns. Because you cannot change the master format except on the master pages, you must cancel the master format for page 1 and construct a new one specifically for it. Even after you cancel the master format, the unprintable lines remain. You delete these by temporarily specifying that the page has only one column.

To cancel the master page format and to install the guides, follow these instructions:

1. Click on the page 1 icon.
2. Choose "Display master items" from the Page menu to turn off the display of these items.
3. Choose "Column guides..." from the Options menu, type **1**, and press ENTER.
4. Move the zero point to the intersection of the left and top margins, at 51H/0V.
5. Press SHIFT-INS to bring in a copy of the outside line created on the master pages. In the "Actual size" view, position the line at left 0.25H/0V.
6. Press SHIFT-INS again to bring in a second outside line. Position it at right 45.25H/0V.
7. Move the horizontal ruler guide at 2.5V to 3V and the one at 6V to 5.5V.

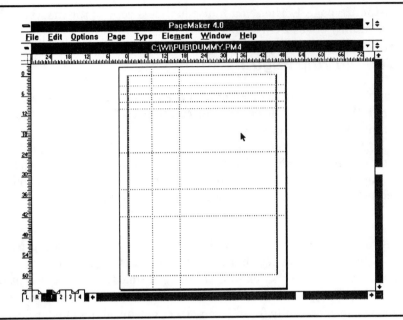

Figure 7-19. *Ruler guides installed on page 1*

8. Drag five new horizontal ruler guides to 8, 10, 23, 34, and 42 picas on the vertical ruler. Use the vertical scroll bar to adjust the view.

9. Drag two vertical guides to right 7 and 15.5 picas on the horizontal ruler.

10. Return to the "Fit in window" view.

Your screen should look like the one shown in Figure 7-19.

Entering the Title Before entering the title, you must draw the line on the top of the page, because placing the title depends to some extent on that. You then center-align, change the type style, and type the title. After you have ensured that the title is placed correctly, you build a box around it, filling the box with 10% shading and sending it to the back so that the title can be seen.

Follow these instructions for creating the title:

1. Restore "Snap to guides" by pressing CTRL-U. (Both the "Snap to guides" and "Snap to rulers" should be turned on.)

2. Using the perpendicular-line tool (SHIFT-F3), draw a line along the top margin from the left to the right margin.

3. Choose "12pt" from the "Line" option.

4. Select the text tool (SHIFT-F4), place it at 18H/6V, and click the secondary mouse button for an "Actual size" view.

5. Place the tool at 2H/5.5V, and click the main mouse button to position the insertion point.

6. Center the text by pressing CTRL-SHIFT-C.

7. Press CTRL-T for the Type specifications dialog box, press TAB, and type **48** in the Size text box. Then click on "Bold" in the Type style text box to turn it on, and click on "OK" to close the dialog box.

8. Press CAPS LOCK.

9. Type **THE ORATOR**.

Without breaking the line, you can enter the type specifications for the rest of the title information. (When developing the dummy for an actual newsletter, you would not specify an actual volume or issue, as you do here. Instead, you might type **Volume 0, Issue 0**, creating a placeholder for the numbers, which would be entered later when you customize the dummy for a specific newsletter.)

10. Press CAPS LOCK to release it.

11. Press CTRL-T for the Type specifications dialog box, press TAB, and type **10** for Size. Then click on "Bold" to turn it off, click on "Italic" to turn it on, and click on "OK" to close the dialog box.

12. Insert a space, type **Volume 4, Issue 4**, press CTRL-SHIFT-= for an em dash, and then type **November 1990**.

13. Using the pointer tool (F9), select the title text and drag it so that the center bars of the H, E, and R are on the horizontal ruler guide at 5.5V. Keep the right end of the text selection box on the right margin at 45H.

Your screen should look like that shown in Figure 7-20.

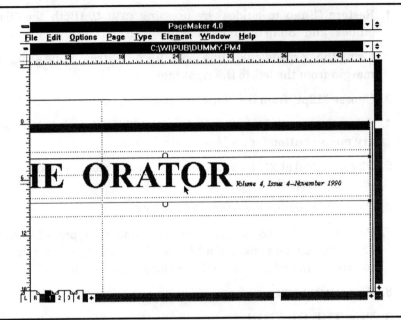

Figure 7-20. *Title as entered, before a box surrounds it*

Now you are ready to draw the box around the title. To do this you use the square-corner tool and drag the box from the left margin above the title to the right margin below the title. Then you fill the box with shading and send it to the back.

14. If necessary, adjust the screen so that you can see the left margin and as much of the title as possible in "Actual size" view.

15. Select the square-corner tool (SHIFT-F5) and place it at 0H/3V.

16. Drag the box to 45H/8V and release the main mouse button.

17. If the box is not correctly placed on the margin and guides, drag it with the pointer tool (F9) until you are satisfied with its placement.

18. With the box still selected, select "10%" from the Fill option of the Element menu.

19. Send the box to the back by pressing CTRL-B.

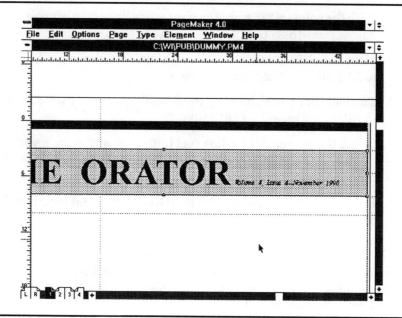

Figure 7-21. *Title with shaded box behind it*

Your screen should look like that shown in Figure 7-21.

Now you can set up the columns for page 1.

Setting Up Columns for Page 1 Page 1 has three columns. They use the same separation space as the master pages, 0.75 pica (9 points). After PageMaker places the column guides on your page, you move them so that the center column is the widest. It contains the lead article for all issues. Then you draw the column divider lines, using the copy function to replicate them.

Follow these steps to set up the columns:

1. Return to the "Fit in window" view.

2. Choose "Column guides..." from the Options menu and type **3**. Ensure that the column separation of 0p9 pica has carried over from the master pages, and click on "OK".

3. With the pointer (F9), move the right guide line of the left pair of column guides from 15.25 to 11.5 picas on the horizontal ruler.

4. Move the right guide line of the right pair of column guides from 30.5 to 33.5 picas on the horizontal ruler.

5. Turn off "Snap to guides" by pressing CTRL-U, and turn off the "Snap to rulers" by pressing CTRL-SHIFT-Y.

6. Select the perpendicular-line tool (SHIFT-F3) and draw a vertical line down the center of the left column guides, from 10V to the bottom margin.

7. Before the line is deselected, verify its position and length in "Actual size" view.

If the line is too short or too long, delete it with the DEL key and draw another. If the line is the correct length but is placed too close to one of the guide lines or is too high or too low, reposition it by dragging it to the correct place with the pointer tool.

8. When the line is correct, copy it by pressing CTRL-INS.

9. Adjust the screen so that the top of the right set of column guides is visible in the "Actual size" view.

10. Press SHIFT-INS and drag the line between the right set of column guides.

11. Verify the line placement and correct it if necessary.

12. Return to the "Fit in window" view.

Next the Churchill logo is added to page 1.

Installing Graphic Placeholders and Design Lines   Two design elements on page 1 need to be handled in the dummy. First, all issues have a silhouette of Winston Churchill between the first and second columns, as shown in Figure 7-12. You draw a box to mark its position, over which the actual graphic is placed—either by you or by a commercial printer. Second, a 12-point line always marks the top of the third column, the secondary article for the newsletter. First draw the line and make it 12 points wide.

Follow these steps to draw the line:

1. Restore "Snap to guides" by pressing CTRL-U and "Snap to rulers" by pressing CTRL-Y.

2. Select the perpendicular-line tool (SHIFT-F3).

3. Place it at 34H/10V and press the secondary mouse button for the "Actual size" view.

4. Draw a line from the left column guide of column 3 to the right margin (33.5H to 45H), over the horizontal ruler guide at 10V. (It should not touch either the solid column divider or the outer right line.)

5. Choose "12pt" from the "Line" option.

You should now have a 12-point line. If you want to reposition the line, drag it to where you want it. Next build the graphic placeholder.

6. Return to the "Fit in window" view.

7. Select the square-corner tool (SHIFT-F5).

8. Draw a box from 7H/23V to 15.5H/34V. (It covers the box created by the horizontal and vertical ruler guides.)

9. Choose "10%" from the "Fill" option.

Your screen will look like that shown in Figure 7-22.

Now you want to get rid of the two vertical ruler guides that you are finished with. You keep the horizontal ruler guides.

10. With the pointer (F9), remove the two vertical ruler guides by dragging them off the page.

Placing the Scanned Graphic   While you are on page 1, you can now place the Churchill graphic on the placeholder. Because of the layers that you are working with (currently two—the column dividers and the shaded box), you must manipulate the graphic a bit. First, place the file WSCHURCH.TIF on page 1 to the side of the placeholder. Then draw a smaller box by tracing over part of the graphic and filling the box with white. Drag the white box over to the placeholder and then drag the actual

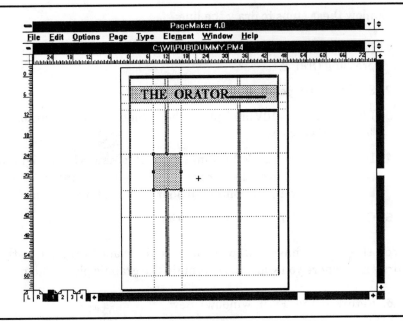

Figure 7-22. *Page 1 with the graphic placeholder*

graphic. Because you can see through the graphic to the shaded place-holder, the white box is necessary to maintain the contrast of the graphic to the shaded background.

Follow these steps to install the graphic:

1. Return to the "Fit in window" view, if you are not there.

2. Place your pointer at 16H/30V, and press the secondary mouse button for an "Actual size" view.

3. Press CTRL-D and double-click the filename WSCHURCH.TIF (the name may differ if you are using clip art instead of the scanned Churchill graphic).

4. Place the icon at 24H/24V, to the side of the placeholder.

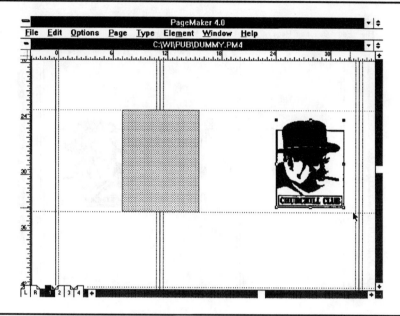

Figure 7-23.   *The graphic placed next to placeholder*

5. Drag the icon so that the right edge is at 31.5H and the bottom edge is at 33.5V. Then release the main mouse button.

6. Your graphic should look like that shown in Figure 7-23.

7. Using the square-corner tool (SHIFT-F5), draw a box on top of the graphic on the border lines, from 24H/25V to 31.5H/33.5V.

8. Choose "Paper" from the "Fill" option.

9. With the pointer tool (F9), select the box and drag it over the placeholder so that it looks like Figure 7-24. The horizontal alignment should be at 7.5 and 15, and the vertical alignment should be at 25 and 33.5.

10. Choose "None" from the "Line" option.

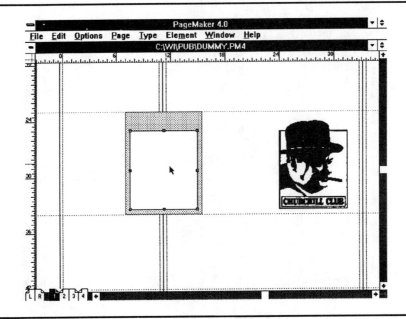

Figure 7-24.   *The white box placed over graphic placeholder*

11. Click on the graphic to select it, and drag it over the white box on the placeholder.

The resulting graphic should look like that shown in Figure 7-25.

12. Return to the "Fit in window" view.

13. Save the file by pressing CTRL-S.

Next, you flow the standard text through the dummy publication.

Flowing the Standard Text

The standard text, now contained in the Word for Windows file STAN-DARD.DOC, is part of every issue. From issue to issue, some of the text is always placed in the same location, such as the general information about

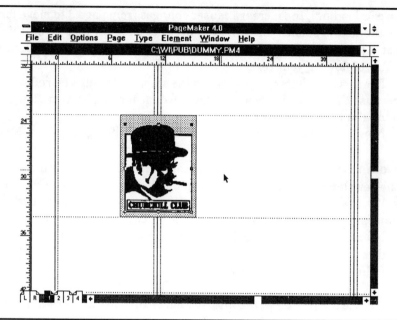

Figure 7-25.   *The completed club logo*

The Orator found on page 1. Other text is placed around the issue-specific articles and may vary in location from one issue to the next, such as the "Club Information" article. You still flow all the standard information into the dummy publication, realizing that since you are preparing a specific issue, some of the standard text may have to be moved in other issues.

Pointers on Flowing Text   When you name the file you want to place, in this case the STANDARD.DOC file, the pointer becomes the text icon, which is used to flow the text. You place the icon, flow as much text at a time as you want, manipulate the text, and then flow the next batch. Correctly deciding how much text to flow can save you much time. You want to flow all the text in a file if you don't know how long it is or if it requires much editing. This is because PageMaker treats the file as one long, continuous string of characters. Some types of editing changes reverberate throughout the file. For example, if on page 3 you increase the size of the space required for an article (perhaps through a change in type size or leading), the increase causes changes from page 3 to move forward as the text is pushed forward. You may have to flow text several times to get it just right. Careful editing of text in the word processor reduces the effort of flowing your text.

For this newsletter you are saved the steps of flowing and reflowing text because this preliminary work has been done for you. You can flow the text a bit at a time.

Now you can place some standard text on each page.

Flowing Page 1   The first page contains some general information about the newsletter, plus the names of primary individuals working on it. Figure 7-12 shows that the first part of the information is narrower than the three names. You achieve this effect by creating two text blocks, squeezing one to half a column width, and then flowing the second block at normal column width.

Follow these steps to place the first page:

1. Place the pointer at the intersection of 10H/48V and press the secondary mouse button.

You are looking at the lower-left corner of page 1. Adjust the screen so that you can see both the horizontal ruler guide at 42 picas and the bottom margin.

2. Press CTRL-D to enter the name of the file to place.

3. Double-click on STANDARD.DOC. Use the horizontal scroll bar to find the filename if necessary.

4. Place the text icon against the left margin at 42V, and click the main mouse button.

Your screen should look like that shown in Figure 7-26.

5. Place the pointer on one of the tiny boxes on the right end of the top text handle and drag it toward the center of the column, squeezing the box until you reach 7.75 picas on the horizontal ruler.

Some of the text disappears because the column is now narrower.

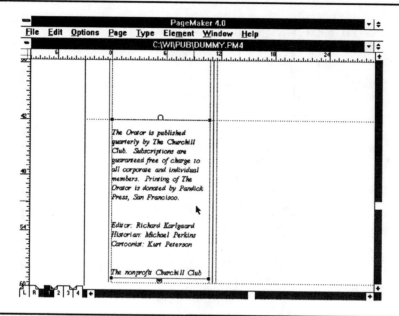

Figure 7-26. *Flowing the first segment of the standard text*

6. Drag the bottom handle up until only the first paragraph is displayed.

7. Click on the bottom handle for the text icon.

8. Place the icon against the left margin at 54V, and click the main mouse button.

9. If necessary, again "roll up the handle" so only the three names appear.

10. Arrange both text blocks so that the names rest on the bottom margin and the top of the upper text block is on 44V, as shown in Figure 7-27. You do this by clicking on each of the text blocks to select them and then dragging them to their respective locations. You may want to use the text tool (SHIFT-F4) to insert carriage returns to get better line endings.

11. Return to the "Fit in window" view.

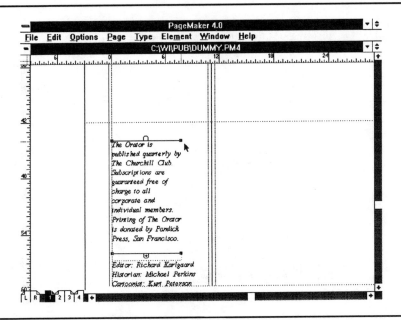

Figure 7-27.   *Standard text on page 1*

12. Select the bottom text block, and then click the bottom handle for the text icon.

You can handle page 2 in much the same way.

Flowing Standard Text on Page 2   Page 2 contains a paragraph that briefly explains the function and background of the Churchill Club, sponsors of *The Orator*. You place it on the page much as you did with page 1. Above the text is a 12-point line across two thirds of the column.

Notice that the horizontal ruler's zero point is still placed on the right page's top and left margins. This results in a split ruler—pages 2 and 3 have common ruler scales such that 30 picas may be found on either page. Assume, if you are working on page 2, that the measurements given are for the left side of the zero point. That is reversed when you work on page 3, of course.

Follow these steps for page 2:

1. Click the page 2 icon.

2. Drag a horizontal ruler guide to 42V.

3. Place the text icon in the first column of page 2 on the new guide and the left margin; then click the main mouse button.

4. Place the pointer in the middle of the new text block, and press the secondary mouse button for the "Actual size" view (at about 46H/50V).

5. Adjust the text handle until one full paragraph shows.

6. Drag the text block so that the bottom line rests on the bottom margin.

7. Using the perpendicular-line tool (SHIFT-F3), draw a line above the text at 42V from the left margin to 45H, as shown in Figure 7-28.

8. Select "12pt" from the "Line" option.

9. Select the text block with the pointer tool (F9), and click the bottom handle for the text icon.

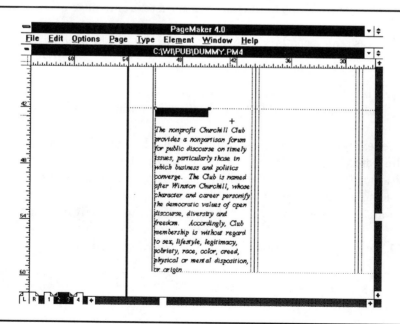

Figure 7-28. *Page 2 standard text placed on the bottom margin*

Page 2 is completed. In certain issues you may want to move this standard text elsewhere on the page, but you will usually find it here. Page 3 is next.

Flowing Standard Text on Page 3   The third page contains a small block of text entitled "Club Information," which you must treat slightly differently. First, you want to squeeze the text vertically, rather than horizontally as you did on the first page. To do this you change the leading from "Auto" to "11" points, which for this text is one point less than the default. As you recall, the leading is the space between the lines. You are reducing this space.

In addition, you have a design element in the title—a black bar with white letters. To achieve this reversed effect, you draw a box around the title of the block, fill it with "Solid" shading, and then send it to the back layer. The letters of the title are reversed and stand out against the background. (Your printer may not be able to print reverse type. If that is the case, substitute black lettering in a 10% shaded box.)

Remember that since you are working on page 3, you use the horizontal ruler to the right of the zero point.

Follow these steps to flow the standard text onto page 3:

1. Press the secondary mouse button for the "Fit in window" view.

2. Drag a horizontal ruler guide to 27V.

3. Place the text icon on the third column, on the new guide and the left column guide (23H/27V); then click the main mouse button.

The text flows into the third column. About halfway down the text you see the words "Board of Directors," or perhaps just a thicker line, which is the title for the next segment of the standard text. You can verify this by placing the pointer next to the title, pressing the secondary mouse button for an "Actual size" view, and then returning to the "Fit in window" view.

4. Drag the bottom text handle up above the heading, as shown here:

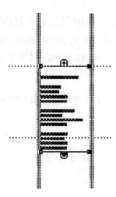

Now you can change the leading for the text block.

5. Place the pointer in the text block at 26H/36V, and press the secondary mouse button to get the "Actual size" view.

6. Select the text tool (SHIFT-F4) and highlight the whole text block.

7. Open the Type specifications dialog box by pressing CTRL-T.

8. Drag the text tool across "Auto" in the "Leading" text box.

9. Type **11** and press ENTER.

The text is now shorter on the screen.

10. With the pointer (F9), drag the text block until the bottom telephone number rests on the horizontal ruler guide at 42V and is slightly in from the left column guide, at about 24H. The title appears to be roughly centered between the two column guides, as shown in Figure 7-29, and should be slightly below the horizontal ruler guide at 27V.

Now you reverse the title, build a box around it, fill the box with shading, and send it to the back.

11. With the text tool (SHIFT-F4), drag across the heading "CLUB INFOR-MATION." Then, from the "Type style" option of the type menu, select "Reverse". The words "CLUB INFORMATION" disappear—they have become white on a white background.

12. Verify that the "Snap to guides" option is on, and drag a horizontal ruler guide down to 28.75V.

13. Select the square-corner tool (SHIFT-F5) and place it on the left column guide and horizontal ruler guide, above the title text, at about 23H/27V.

14. Drag a box diagonally until it rests on the right column guide and the new horizontal ruler guide at 33.5H/28.75V.

15. Choose "Solid" from the Shades menu.

16. Send it to the back by pressing CTRL-B.

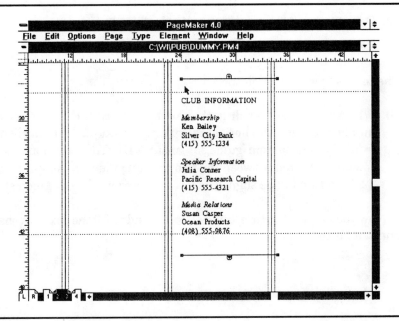

Figure 7-29. *Placing the standard text on page 3*

When you have completed building and filling the box, the text on page 3 should look like this:

17. Return to the "Fit in window" view.

18. With the pointer tool (F9), select the page 3 text and then click the bottom handle for the text icon.

The last page contains the remaining text of STANDARD.DOC.

Flowing Standard Text on Page 4   Page 4 contains solely standard text. It lists officers, members of the Board of Directors and Senior Advisory Board, and, finally, Corporate Members. You flow the text over the entire page, using PageMaker's Autoflow feature. You then adjust the text to better fit the page. In addition to flowing the text, you insert some design elements in the form of lines to separate the categories. Figure 7-30 shows the completed page 4 as it is printed.

Follow these steps to flow text on page 4.

1. Select "Autoflow" from the Options menu, and click the Page 4 icon.

2. Place the text icon (note that it has changed to indicate autoflow) in the first column, at the left margin and 7V, below the horizontal ruler

Page 4   THE ORATOR

Board of Directors

Chairman
Co-Founder
Anthony DeVoe
Silver City Bank

Director of Marketing
Co-Founder
Richard Karlgaard
Opinion Movers

Director of Finance
Edward Hecht
PX, Inc.

Director of Speakers
Susan Casper
Ocean Products

Director of Membership
Ken Bailey
Silver City Bank

Director of Operations
Edward Osborne
Reiley Aerospace

Director, Scholarship
Committee
William Shelly
Nordic Distributors

Club Historian
Michael Rains
South Port Cold Storage

Corporate Secretaries
Frederick Shelly
Scott Katz
Shelly, Katz, & Greenlee

Tom Cook
Cook Corporation

Barry Burton
Standard Computer

Marjorie Walters
South American Importers

Diane Graves

Robert Lusk
Graves, Lusk, Meadows, &
Thomas

Timothy Lamson
Lamson Associates

James North, Jr.
Technology Consultants, Inc.

Stephen Petosa
RotoGraphic Corporation

Alex Lange
Pacific Imports

Grant Strom
Strom Computer

Peter Dayton
Creative Designs

Doug Hendrix
Strom Computer

Steve Masion
Pacific Southern

Michael Boggs
New Toy Corporation

Cordell Tucker
Tucker Steel Pipe

Michael Jones
Smith and Jones

Senior Advisory Board

Roger Weiss
President and CEO
Silver City Bank

Ed Adams
U.S. Congressman

Norm Browning
U.S. Congressman

Judy Carlson
President
Carlson Associates

Robert Wohlers
Chairman
New Toy Corporation

Robert Freeland, Jr.
President
Robert Freeland Associates

Larry Meadows
Partner
Graves, Lusk, Meadows, &
Thomas

Samuel Robinson
General Partner
Robinson Venture Partners

William Dunn
Chairman
Leader Corporation

Joe Parsons
Managing Partner
Springtime Capital

Richard Van Waters
President
Vanguard Trucking

James Johnston
President and CEO
Northern Metal Fabricators

Robert Dyer
Vice President
Pacific Imports

Consuelo Martinez
Director
Center for Better Learning

Lorayne Easton
Political Consultant

Ryland Keeney
Managing Partner
Thomas and Keeney

George Maynard
President & CEO
Micro Corporation of America

Rob Younger
Editor
Silver City Evening News

Walter A. McIntyre
Professor of Political Science
Northern University

Corporate Members

ABC Corporation
American Consultants
Arrow Brothers
Art Treasures
Avery Products
Barringer, Easter, & McGrath
Bayside Interiors
Berg Equipment
Bergman Communications
Central Area Bank
Commercial Bank
Dick Shepard & Co.
Doolittle, Peters, & Curfman
Edwards and Rogers
EG Enterprises
Electronic Instruments
Everett Anchor & Chain
First East/West Bank
Formal Technology
Foster Homes, Inc.
Frank Reiley & Co.
Frankel and Associates
Graves, Lusk, Meadows, & Thomas
Gregory Dunn Ventures
Gunderson, Dimple, & Eagen
Hamlin National
KRGT Silver City
KSAB Bayside
KTZZ Silver City
Leader Corporation
Management Services
McKee Engineering
Micro Corporation of America
Network Ventures
New Technology Consultants
New Toy Corporation
Northern Ventures Partners
Opinion Movers
Pacific Construction
Pacific Press
Pacific Research Capital
Pacific Systems Corp.
Pacific Technology Review
Pauley Furniture
Personal Technology
Peterson Bailey Co.
Philips Manufacturing
Platis, Hawkins, & Grant
Plum Warehouse
Plywood Fabricators
Quantum Research
Que Technology
Reiley Aerospace
Richards Hotels
Ricker & Ricker
Sierra Partners
Silver City Bank
Silver City Entrepreneurs Club
Silver City Evening News
Silver City Journal
Small Properties
Smith and Jones
South American Imports
Tanqueray and Noilly
Thomas Insurance
Travel Partners
Tyler, Funk, & Bailey
Warehouse Furniture
Western Bank
Western Taxi
Williams, Anderson Associates

Figure 7-30.   *Printout of final of page 4*

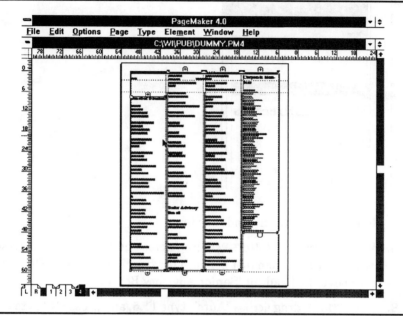

Figure 7-31.   *Page 4 as it is autoflowed*

guide at 6V, and click the main mouse button. The remaining text will fill the page, as shown in Figure 7-31.

3. Select the perpendicular-line tool (SHIFT-F3) and draw a line across the top of column 1, on the horizontal ruler guide at 6V.

4. Choose "12pt" from the "Line" option.

5. Place the pointer at 35H/10V, and click the secondary mouse button for an "Actual size" view.

6. With the pointer tool (F9), drag a horizontal ruler guide down to 8.5 on the vertical ruler. Then select and drag the text in the first column until the heading is sitting on the new ruler you placed, as shown in the following illustration:

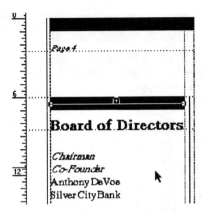

7. Return to the "Fit in window" view.

8. With the text tool (SHIFT-F4), drag across and highlight the first and second columns from just beneath the heading "Board of Directors" to just above the heading "Senior Advisory Board."

9. Press CTRL-T, drag across "Auto", type **11.5**, and press ENTER to change the leading.

10. Beginning just after the heading "Senior Advisory Board," drag across the remainder of column two, column three, and possibly the very top of column four, stopping just before the heading "Corporate Members." All of the "Senior Advisory Board" section is now highlighted.

11. Press CTRL-T, drag across "Auto", type **11.5**, and press ENTER.

12. In a similar fashion, highlight the remainder of the text beneath the headline "Corporate Members" and change its leading to 7.5 points.

13. With the pointer (F9), point on 36H/48V and press the secondary mouse button to go to the "Actual size" view.

14. Click on the first column and adjust the bottom text handle until "Diane Graves" is the last item in the column.

15. In "Fit in Window" view, click on the second column and drag the text down until it is just under the horizontal ruler guide at 6V.

16. Pull the bottom text handle up until it reaches the lower margin. "Carlson Associates" should be the last line in the column.

17. Similarly, drag down and adjust the bottom of columns three and four so that they line up like this:

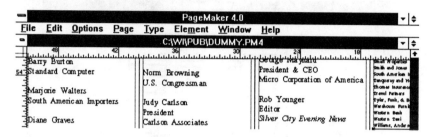

18. In the "Fit in window" view, press the secondary mouse button at 32H/44V.

19. Drag a horizontal ruler guide down to 41V and, with the perpendicular-line tool (SHIFT-F3), draw a line across the second column on the new horizontal ruler guide.

20. Choose "12pt" from the "Line" option.

21. Remove the horizontal ruler guide.

22. With the text tool (SHIFT-F4), place the insertion point just to the left of the "A" in "Advisory." Press BACKSPACE and ENTER to move "Advisory" down to the second line.

23. In the "Fit in window" view, press the secondary mouse button at 18H/14V.

24. With the pointer tool (F9), drag the horizontal ruler guide at 8.5V down to 9V and, with the perpendicular-line tool (SHIFT-F3), draw a line across the fourth column on the new horizontal ruler guide.

25. Choose "12pt" from the "Line" option.

26. Remove the horizontal ruler guide.

27. With the text tool (SHIFT-F4), place the insertion point just to the left of the "M" in "Members." Press BACKSPACE and ENTER to move "Members" down to the next line.

28. Return to the "Fit in Window" view and save your work by pressing CTRL-S.

Figure 7-32 shows what the finished page 4 now looks like.

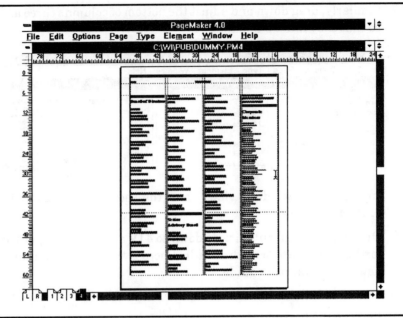

Figure 7-32.   *The completed page 4*

Finishing the Dummy

You need to include several other items in the dummy publication. First, you must place an advertisement on page 3. Second, you need a graphic placeholder on page 3. Finally, you must place some design lines.

Placing an Advertisement   The advertisement spans two columns. You draw a small narrow box over the column dividers, fill it with "Paper" shading, and then type in the text. Each line of the ad varies in type size, so you must specify the type size for each line. For some you use the shorthand method of pressing F3 to decrease the type size to the next smaller size. Also, the text must be centered.

Follow these steps to complete the advertisement:

1. Click on the Page 3 icon.

2. Place your pointer at right 30H/48V and press the secondary mouse button for an "Actual size" view.

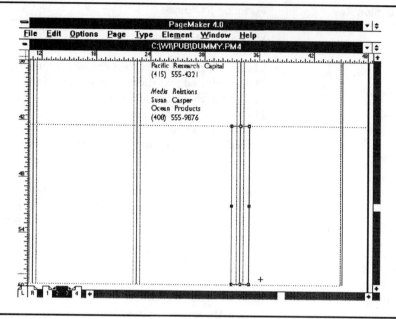

Figure 7-33.   *Box around the column dividers*

3. Drag the horizontal ruler guide from 42V to 42.5V.

4. Using the square-corner tool (SHIFT-F5), draw a box around the column guides, from 33H/42.5V to the bottom margin guides at 35H/59.5V. The box should encompass the column guides, as shown in Figure 7-33.

5. Choose "Paper" from the "Fill" option while the box is selected.

6. Choose "None" from the "Line" option.

7. Using the perpendicular-line tool (SHIFT-F3), draw a line at 42.5V from the left column guide in column 3 to the right margin guide.

8. Choose "12pt" from the "Line" option.

9. Draw another line across the bottom margin connecting the two existing vertical lines, so that a solid line appears on the bottom three sides of the box.

10. Select the text tool (SHIFT-F4) and click it in the box at 24H/47V.

Function Key	Function Perfomed
F1	Opens the help index
F2	(None)
F3	Makes selected text the next smaller standard point size
F4	Makes selected text the next larger standard point size
F5	Makes selected text normal style
F6	Makes selected text bold style
F7	Makes selected text italic style
F8	Makes selected text underlined style
F9	Toggles between the pointer and the tool last used
F10	Opens the menu
F11	Goes to the previous page in the publication
F12	Goes to the next page in the publication
SHIFT-F1	Pointer becomes a question mark for context-sensitive help
SHIFT-F2	Selects the diagonal-line tool
SHIFT-F3	Selects the perpendicular-line tool
SHIFT-F4	Selects the text tool
SHIFT-F5	Selects the square-corner tool
SHIFT-F6	Selects the rounded-corner tool
SHIFT-F7	Selects the oval or circle tool
SHIFT-F8	Selects the cropping tool

Table 7-1. *Function Key Assignments*

11. Press CTRL-SHIFT-C to center the text.

12. Press CTRL-T for the Type specifications dialog box, press TAB, type **16** in the Size text box, click on "Bold", and click "OK".

13. Type **Pandick California, Inc.**, and press ENTER twice.

The line wraps around, but you will straighten it out in a moment.

The next set of instructions uses the function keys to change the size and style of type. If you can remember them, these keys can save you time over using the menu or the regular keyboard equivalents. Table 7-1 provides a list of functions assigned to each function key. Appendix F provides a complete alphabetical list of all keyboard commands as well as all the menu options.

14. Press F3 to choose the next smaller type size, 14 points. Press F5 to turn off bold and F7 to turn on italics.

15. Type **The**, press F5 to turn off italics, press F6 to turn on bold, insert a space, type **Financial Printer**, and press ENTER twice.

16. Press F3 for 12 points.

17. Type **(415) 543-4433** and press ENTER twice.

18. Press CTRL-T, press TAB, type **10** for Size, click on "Bold" to turn it off, click on "Italic" to turn it on, and click on "OK" to close the dialog box.

19. Type **Offices in** and press ENTER twice.

The list of offices contains a bullet between each of the cities. You get a bullet by pressing SHIFT-CTRL-8 simultaneously.

20. Press F3 twice for a type size of 8 points.

21. Type **San Francisco**, press SPACEBAR, press SHIFT-CTRL-8, press SPACEBAR, type **Los Angeles**, press SPACEBAR, press SHIFT-CTRL-8, press SPACEBAR, type **Newport Beach**, and press ENTER.

Now straighten the text by selecting it with the pointer tool and stretching the selection box across the fourth column. The text is rearranged as you intended.

22. Select the pointer (F9) and click on the text you just typed.

23. Drag the tiny box on one of the right ends of the text handles to the right margin, as shown in Figure 7-34.

24. Return to the "Fit in window" view.

25. Press CTRL-S to save the newsletter.

Next you build a placeholder for the graphic that is always placed on page 3.

Building a Graphic Placeholder   The graphic placeholder contains a graphic that varies with each issue. Follow these steps to establish the placeholder:

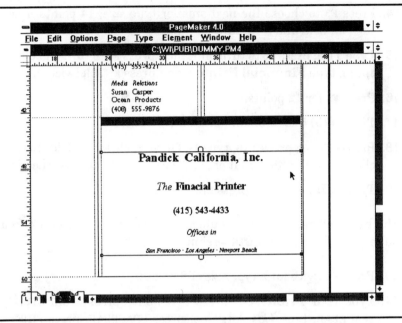

Figure 7-34. *The finished ad on page 3*

1. Drag the horizontal ruler guide at 42.5V to 44V.

2. Place the pointer at 3H/51V, and press the secondary mouse button for an "Actual size" view.

3. Click the text tool (SHIFT-F4) at 0.5H/45V.

4. Press CTRL-SHIFT-C to center the text.

5. Press CTRL-T, select "Sans" from the Font option box, click on "Reverse" for Type style, and click on "OK". (When you type reverse type you cannot see what you are typing until you build a box around it and fill it with solid fill.) Click on "OK" to "Set color to Paper?".

6. Type **COMING DECEMBER 4TH.**

7. With the square-corner tool (SHIFT-F5), build a box from the left margin guide at 0H/44V to the left column guide at 10.75H/45V.

8. Choose "Solid" from the "Fill" option.

9. Send the box to the back by pressing CTRL-B.

10. If necessary, use the pointer (F9) to adjust "COMING DECEMBER 4TH" so that it is centered vertically in the box. If needed, turn off "Snap to rulers" and "Snap to guides". Once you have centered the text, turn "Snap to guides" and "Snap to rulers" back on.

11. With the perpendicular-line tool (SHIFT- F3), draw a line connecting the line at left 0.25H to the column divider at 11H, along the bottom margin at 59.5H.

Your screen should look like the one shown in Figure 7-35.

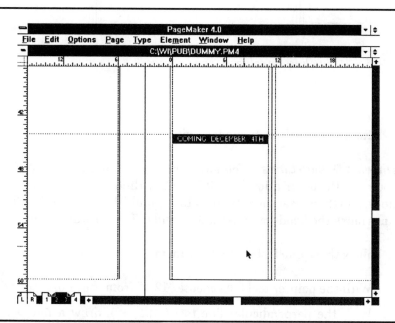

Figure 7-35. *Graphic placeholder with title*

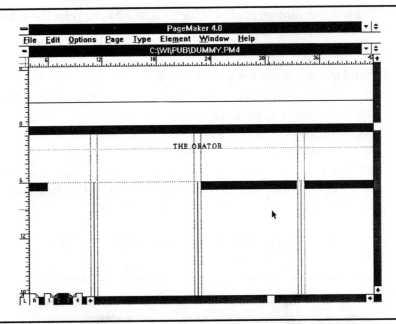

Figure 7-36. *Design lines on columns 3 and 4, page 3*

12. Return to the "Fit in window" view.

Drawing Design Lines You must draw three lines on page 3. To do this you reset the publication default from "Hairline" to "12pt", draw the three lines, and then reset the default to its original "Hairline" setting. The three lines mark the heads of columns 1, 3, and 4. The lines are shown in Figure 7-36.

Follow these quick steps to draw them:

1. With the pointer tool (F9), choose "12pt" from the "Line" option.

2. With the perpendicular-line tool (SHIFT-F3), draw a line across the horizontal ruler guide on page 3 at 6V in the left column, for about half of the column width, from the left margin to right 6H.

3. Place the pointer at right 24H/6V, and press the secondary mouse button for an "Actual size" view.

4. In the third column, draw a line from the left column guide at about 23H to the right column guide at 33.5H on the horizontal ruler guide at 6V.

5. In the fourth column, draw a line from the left column guide at 34.25H to the right margin on the horizontal ruler at 6V.

6. With the pointer (F9), choose "Hairline" from the "Line" option.

The results are shown in Figure 7-36. The first and most exacting part of building the newsletter is over. Now you must save and print your work.

7. Return to the "Fit in window" view.

Saving and Printing
The Dummy Publication

This completes construction of the dummy publication. You must now save it as a template, knowing that you will be saving yourself all this work each time you publish another issue of your newsletter.

1. From the File menu, choose "Save as...", click on "Template", and click on "OK".

Also print the file so that you can see exactly how the pages look at this point. After correcting any problems that you may have with the dummy, it should look like Figure 7-12.

2. Print the file by pressing CTRL-P and then clicking "OK" on the Print dialog box.

Now you're ready to begin constructing Volume 4, Issue 4, of *The Orator*.

Constructing a Specific Issue Of the Newsletter

Constructing a specific issue of any newsletter is really a trial-and-error process. First you place graphics on the dummy publication, and then you flow one text file, page by page, line by line, adjusting and enhancing it until the page is the way you want it to appear. Then you go on to the next page. After you finish with one file, you then go to the next and flow it, until all the text files are flowed.

You must have a good idea how long the articles are and how much space you have in each column of the newsletter. Space depends to a great extent on the number of columns, the type sizes, and the special graphics and design elements you use. You will not know exactly what length articles you can work with until you have experimented with PageMaker.

When you are dealing with unknown newsletter capacities and article lengths, it is important first to flow the higher priority articles in total. Then you will know what space you have left, telling you what text you have to cut or add in order to complete the newsletter.

Creating Page 1 of the Newsletter

You will build Issue 4 of *The Orator* page by page. First, you flow the lead article from the VOL4ISS4.DOC file, followed by the first part of the CHURCHIL.WP file. You can mix files in this way, flowing one before you have finished with another when you know the length of the files and have edited them. You insert several design elements, such as an emphasized quote from the Churchill article. You finish the page by filling in "Continued on page 2" at the end of column 3. When you are finished and it is printed, your page should look like that shown in Figure 7-37.

Handling the Lead Article   The lead article in this newsletter exactly fits in the middle column on page 1. With the text wrap feature in PageMaker, flowing the text around the graphic is completely automatic. You switch between the "Fit in window" and "Actual size" views to place the text and verify its placement.

THE ORATOR

Volume 4, Issue 4-November 1990

SOUTH AFRICA'S BUTHELEZI TO ADDRESS CHURCHILL CLUB ON DECEMBER 4TH

The Churchill Club will sponsor its eighth and final event of 1990 on Thursday, December 4th, at the Santa Clara Marriott. The guest: Gatsha Buthelezi, Chief Minister of the Kwa-Zulu homeland in South Africa. The event starts at 6 P.M.

Chief Gatsha Buthelezi claims the support of South Africa's six million Zulus, the nation's largest ethnic group. Despite his moderate voice (or perhaps because of it), this makes him a powerful voice in this turmoiled region. Tom Lodge, a political-science professor at the University of Witswatersrand, says, "It is a dangerous situation to leave Buthelezi out of the equation." Chief Buthelezi himself asserts, "There can't be a successful negotiation without me."

Chief Buthelezi comes across to many white South Africans as comfortingly moderate. To them, he embodies the hope for the future. He speaks about whites' fears without fanning them. He says he doesn't want to overthrow white South Africa's values and aspirations. Rather, he says, he wants blacks to be able to share them.

A more serious difference is between Chief Buthelezi and the African National Congress, the broadly based antiapartheid organization that has recently espoused violence. The ANC (and its leader, the jailed Nelson Mandela) quietly supported Buthelezi in the 1970s, recognizing his ability to mobilize people from the rural areas. But in the 1980s the ANC became impatient with Buthelezi's pleas for peaceful change. The group now espouses violence as a necessary catalyst for change in South Africa.

The Orator is published quarterly by The Churchill Club. Subscriptions are guaranteed free of charge to all corporate and individual members. Printing of The Orator is donated by Pandick Press, San Francisco.

Editor: Richard Karlgaard
Historian: Michael Perkins
Cartoonist: Kurt Peterson

Ennui and the brush-Winston as the artist

Broadly speaking, human beings may be divided into three classes: those who are toiled to death, those who are worried to death, and those who are bored to death.

Churchill himself, of course, was by no means immune to these afflictions about which he wrote. But what was he to do about it?

Churchill typically sought surcease in a number of activities, including reading, fencing, swimming, riding, hunting, flying, polo, horse racing, gardening, and brick-laying. He was also a collector of butterflies and tropical fish and had a number of pets.

Further, Churchill was something of the big kid indulging in everything from toy trains, tin soldiers, and erector sets to

> **"The tired parts of the mind can be rested and strengthened, not merely by rest, but by using other parts"**

building sandcastles and snowmen.

The common denominator in all this activity was change. As Churchill himself writes,

Continued on page 2

Figure 7-37. *Printout of completed page 1*

Follow these steps to complete the lead article:

1. Select "Save as..." from the File menu and type **nov90nl** in the Name text box. This ensures that the dummy is preserved.

2. Click on the page 1 icon.

3. In the "Actual Size" view, click on the outer box around The Churchill Club logo.

4. Select "Text wrap..." from the Element menu, and then click on the middle wrap option ("All sides icon") to flow text around the graphic. The far right text flow option automatically highlights, as does the 1-pica default separation, as shown here:

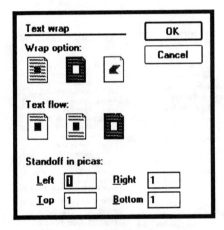

5. Click on "OK", and a border appears around the graphic.

6. Return to the "Fit in window" view and select "Autoflow" from the Options menu to turn it off.

7. Press CTRL-D for the Place dialog box, and double-click on VOL4ISS4.DOC. The pointer becomes a text icon.

8. Place the text icon on top of column 2 (11.5H/10V), and click the main mouse button to flow the text.

The text flows around the graphic and continues to the bottom of the column. Your screen should look like Figure 7-38.

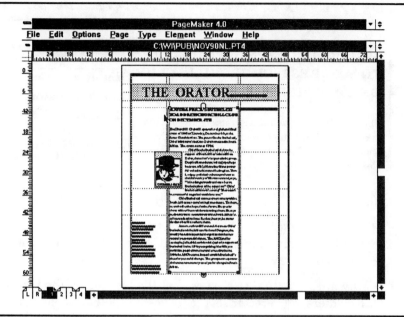

Figure 7-38.   *Leading article placed on page 1*

Placing the Second Article on Page 1   The second article is several columns long, and only the first part fits on page 1. In addition, you must emphasize a quote from the article by specifying a different type font and setting it off between lines.

Follow these steps to complete page 1:

1. Press CTRL-D for the Place dialog box.

2. Double-click the filename CHURCHIL.WP. The pointer becomes the text icon.

3. Place the icon in the top of the third column at 33.5H/12V and then click on it.

4. In the "Actual size" view, look at the placement and drag the text block so that it is aligned properly below the 12-point line, as shown here:

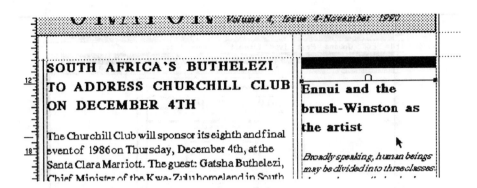

5. In the "Fit in window" view, verify that you have a horizontal ruler guide at 42V.

6. Select the text in column 3, and pull the handle up to the horizontal ruler guide at 42V.

7. Verify in the "Actual size" view that the last line of the text block is "tin soldiers, and erector sets to". Click on the Pasteboard to deselect the block.

8. Choose "None" (the top leftmost) text wrap icon from the text wrap dialog box, reached from the Element menu.

9. Using the perpendicular-line tool (SHIFT-F3), draw a line in the third column from the left column guide to the right margin guide, on the horizontal ruler guide at 42V.

10. Choose "6pt" from the "Line" option.

11. Select the text tool (SHIFT-F4) and click on it in the third column at 43.5V, below the new line.

12. Press CTRL-SHIFT-L for left-align.

13. Press CTRL-T for the Type specifications dialog box, select "Sans" in the Font text box, press TAB, type **12** for Size, and click on "OK".

14. Type **" The tired parts of the mind can be rested and strengthened, not merely by rest, but by using other parts"** (include the quotation marks).

15. With the pointer (F9), drag a horizontal ruler guide just below the newly typed text (to 50V).

16. Using the perpendicular-line tool (SHIFT-F3), draw a line from the left column guide to the right margin guide along the horizontal guide at 50V.

17. Choose "6pt" from the "Line" option.

18. With the pointer (F9), select the newly typed quote and center it between the lines. The top should be at about 43.25V, as shown here:

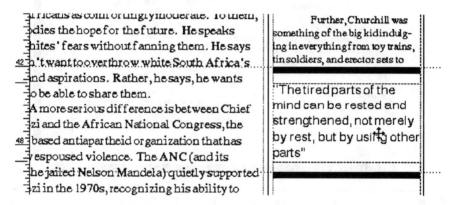

19. With the pointer (F9), select the text block above the new insert and click on the bottom handle of the text block.

20. Place the text icon just below the new line at 51V and click it.

21. Look at the text in the "Actual size" view, and drag it to a better location if necessary. The last line should end with the word "writes."

22. Pull the handle up or down so that your screen looks like that shown in Figure 7-39.

Your final task in the third column is to type a continuation note.

23. Using the text tool (SHIFT-F4), place your pointer in the third column at 58V and click on it.

24. Press CTRL-SHIFT-R to right-align the next text.

25. Press CTRL-T for the Type specifications dialog box, ensure that "Times" is selected for Font, press TAB, type **8** for Size, click on "Italic" for the Type style, and click on "OK".

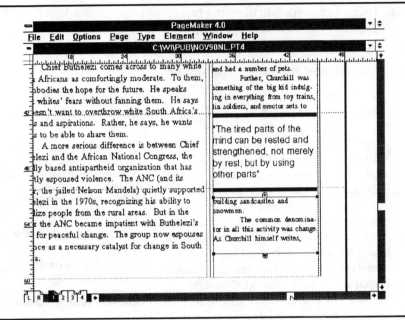

Figure 7-39. *Bottom of column 3 on page 1*

26. Type **Continued on page 2**.

27. If the line is not placed correctly, switch to the pointer tool (F9), click on it, and drag it to where you want.

28. Return to the "Fit in window" view.

Your screen should look like that shown in Figure 7-40.

Saving and Printing Page 1 This is a good time to save and print your work, using the following instructions:

1. Press CTRL-S to save the newsletter.

2. Press CTRL-P for the Print dialog box.

3. Drag across the "to" text box and type **1**.

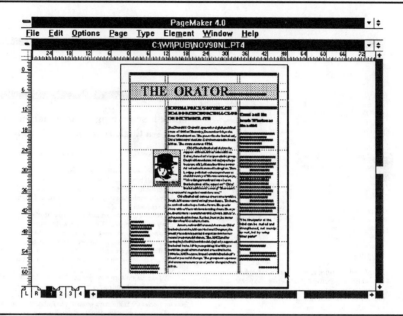

Figure 7-40.   *The completed page 1*

4. Click on "OK."

Your printed copy should look like Figure 7-37. Now you can work on page 2.

Creating Page 2
of the Newsletter

Page 2 is somewhat more complex, with three files placed within it, as seen in Figure 7-41. First, you prepare page 2 for the text, building a box to hold the MARTINI.DOC file and placing some design element lines. You handle the rest of the text, column by column, and flow the remaining CHURCHIL.WP file into the first three columns. Then you place the MARTINI.DOC file into a box that spans columns 2 and 3. Finally, you place the next segment of the VOL4ISS4.DOC file.

Change is the master key. A man can wear out a particular part of his mind by continually using it and tiring it. The tired parts of the mind can be rested and strengthened, not merely by rest, but by using other parts. It is only when new cells are called into activity, when new stars become lords of the ascendant, that relief, repose, refreshment are afforded.

At age 40 Churchill found himself out of political office for the first time in fifteen years and he needed to discover a new way to creatively fill up the hours.

Exercise, travel, solitude, light socializing, even golf (which he likened to chasing a pill around a cow pasture) did not suffice. It was then, with a friend's encouragement, that he took up painting.

Intensity, Relish and Audacity
Painting at once provided Churchill an opportunity to use his hands as well as a different part of his brain. The "muse of painting" had come to his rescue.

The nonprofit Churchill Club provides a nonpartisan forum for public discourse on timely issues, particularly those in which business and politics converge. The Club is named after Winston Churchill, whose character and career personify the democratic values of open discourse, diversity and freedom. Accordingly, Club membership is without regard to sex, lifestyle, legitimacy, sobriety, race, color, creed, physical or mental disposition, or origin.

When Churchill took up the brush, he did it with the same intensity, relish, and audacity as everything he undertook, and he was not discouraged by the results. Painting also proved to be the perfect diversion. In Painting as a Pastime he writes,

I know nothing which, without exhausting the body, more entirely absorbs the mind. Whatever the worries of the hour or the threats of the future, once the picture has begun to flow along, there is no room for them in the mental screen. They pass out into shadow and darkness. All one's mental light, such as it is, becomes concentrated on the task. Time stands respectfully aside.

Churchill chose to devote his painting to landscapes and still lifes in an impressionist style. His brilliant colors became a type of trademark: "I cannot pretend to be impartial about the colours," he wrote. "I rejoice with the brilliant ones and am genuinely sorry for the poor browns."

In search of beautiful scenes, Churchill took his easel with him wherever he traveled including the Middle East and North America. On a trip to Scotland he wrote to his wife, "In the afternoon I went out and painted a beautiful river in the afternoon light with crimson and golden hills in the background."

From the Riviera he writes of a villa that he painted "all in shimmering sunshine and violet shades."

There is something about a martini —a tingle remarkably pleasant

Thus began poet Ogden Nash in *A Drink with Something in It.*

The perfect dry martini contains gin, vermouth, and a twist of lemon. It must be very cold, but not contain ice or water, so keep your gin in the freezer and vermouth in the refrigerator. The especially discriminating may use Tanqueray gin and Noilly extra dry vermouth.

Polish a martini glass and put it in the freezer along with your jigger and stirring rod. The glass should be large, but light, with a feathered rim and a long stem to keep the martini cold. With a sharp knife, cut a generous twist from a ripe, fresh lemon. Be careful to separate the yellow peel from the white pulp, as the peel contains the lemon oil and the pulp would impart a bitter flavor to the martini.

Take the glass from the freezer. Twist the lemon peel to release its oil. Rub the oily surface around the inside of the glass and along its rim, then drop the twist in the glass. Take the gin from the freezer (or Stolichnaya vodka if you feel diffident about gin) and measure two jiggers into the glass. Take the vermouth from the refrigerator and measure a third of a jigger into the glass. Stir vigorously, but do not shake. Remove to a pleasant setting and enjoy.

by "Christopher Russell"

Antidote to Melancholy and Ennui
In the end, painting was to prove one of the chief antidotes to Winston's sometime melancholy and ennui. It also served to deepen Churchill's powers of observation, so much that he had come to see that "the whole world is open with all its treasures, even the simplest objects have their beauty."

Like the poet and artist William Blake, Churchill had learned not only to see with, but through the eye.

Contributed by
Michael Perkins
Club Historian

MY EARLY LIFE

It took me three tries to pass into Sandhurst. There were five subjects, of which Mathematics, Latin and English were obligatory, and I chose in addition French and Chemistry. In this hand I held only a pair of Kings--English and chemistry. Nothing less than three would open the jackpot. I had to find another useful card.

W.S. CHURCHILL

Figure 7-41. *Printout of completed page 2*

Preparing Page 2   You have several tasks to prepare page 2 before flowing the text. You must reset the zero point so that it is located where the top and left margins meet. You must drag another horizontal ruler guide to mark the location of the bottom of a box. Then you draw the box that spans columns 3 and 4 and holds the MARTINI.DOC text. You fill the box with "Paper" to cover the column guides and line. Then you draw a line to mark the bottom of the box. You also draw a 12-point line on the top of the two columns to highlight the insert.

Follow these steps to prepare the page:

1. Click the page 2 icon and return to the "Fit in window" view, if you are not already there.

2. Reset the zero point by placing the pointer where the horizontal and vertical rulers meet and dragging the zero point to the top and left margins on page 2. (Make sure that the horizontal zero point is on the margin, not the line outside the margin. You may want to go to the "Actual size" view to verify this.)

3. Using the pointer tool (F9), drag the horizontal ruler guide at 44H to 37.5V.

4. Using the square corner tool (SHIFT-F5), draw a box from 33H/6V to 35H/37.5V. The lines of the box should just enclose the column guides between columns 3 and 4.

5. Choose "None" from the "Line" option.

6. Choose "Paper" from the "Fill" option.

7. Using the perpendicular-line tool (SHIFT-F3), draw a line across the bottom of the box over the horizontal ruler guide from the left column guide in column 3 to the right margin guide in column 4 (from about 23H/37.5V to 45H).

8. Draw another line at the head of the columns over the horizontal ruler guide at 6V, from the left column guide to the right margin guide (23H/6V to 45H).

9. Choose "12pt" from the "Line" option.

Now you can flow the MARTINI.DOC file.

Placing the MARTINI.DOC File The text is placed on top of the box you just created. It fits perfectly.

Follow these steps to place the Microsoft Word file:

1. If you are in the "Actual size" view, return to the "Fit in window" view.

2. Press CTRL-D to specify the filename to place.

3. In the Place dialog box, double-click on the filename MARTINI.DOC. You may need to use the horizontal scroll bars to find it. The pointer becomes the familiar text icon.

4. To force the text to span columns, place the icon at 23H/8V, next to the left column guide under the line marking the top of columns 3 and 4, and drag the pointer to 45H/37.5V. Then release the main mouse button.

The lower loop of the selection box is empty, indicating that the entire file has been placed.

5. Place the pointer in the middle of the text, at about 32H/18V, and click the secondary mouse button for an "Actual size" view.

6. Examine the text and make any necessary adjustments.

Your screen should look like that shown in Figure 7-42.

7. Return to the "Fit in window" view.

8. Look at the vertical placement of the martini article, and adjust it if necessary so that an equal amount of space is above and below the text.

Next, you will finish placing the CHURCHIL.WP file.

Completing the WordPerfect File Page 1 contains the first part of the CHURCHIL.WP file. To continue placing it, simply click on the text handle at the bottom of the text on page 1 to get the text icon. Then you can automatically flow the text into the first three columns of page 2.

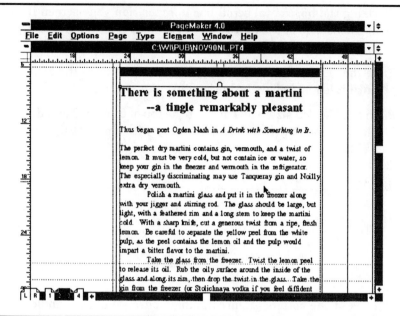

Figure 7-42.   *The martini article*

Follow these steps to flow the rest of the file:

1. Click on the page 1 icon.

2. To reselect the CHURCHIL.WP file, click on the last paragraph of text in column 3 (above the continuation note).

3. Click on the bottom handle for the text icon, click on the page 2 icon, and select "Autoflow" from the Options menu.

4. On page 2, place the text icon at 0H/6V at the top of column 1, and click the main mouse button.

5. In the "Actual size" view, look at the top of the text in the first column and ensure that it is just below the horizontal ruler guide at 6V.

6. Using the horizontal scroll bar to reposition your screen image, look at the bottom of the flowed text in column 1, and, if necessary, drag it up so that the last line reads "rescue."

7. In the "Fit in window" view, pull down the text in the second column until it is just below the horizontal ruler guide at 6V.

8. In the "Actual size" view, look at the top of column 2 and drag the text block so that the first line is lined up with the first line in column 1, like this:

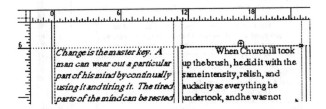

9. Look at the bottom of the column and drag the text handle up so that the last line reads, "and violet shades."

10. Return to the "Fit in window" view and pull down the text in the third column until the top is at 38.5V.

11. In the "Actual size" view, examine the top of the column and adjust its position if necessary.

12. Drag up the bottom handle so that the three lines of the author's identification are the last lines showing.

The author's name should be centered.

13. With the text tool (SHIFT-F4), highlight the three lines of the author's identification.

14. Press CTRL-SHIFT-C to center it.

Figure 7-43 shows the results.

15. Return to the "Fit in window" view and, with the pointer (F9) pull down the text in the fourth column, so that the top line ("MY EARLY LIFE") is just beneath the horizontal ruler guide at 37.5.

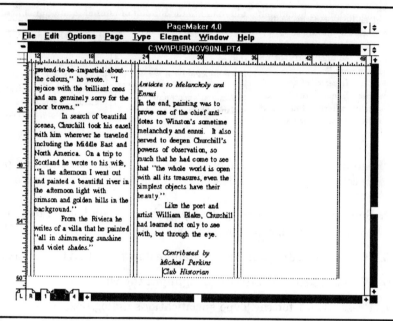

Figure 7-43.   *The last three lines of column 3 centered*

Your final task on page 2 is to enhance the text segment in column 4.

Enhancing Column 4   Column 4 contains a short insert, a sort of filler article, that quotes Winston Churchill. It is the last article on the CHUR-CHILL.WP file. You emphasize the insert by building a box around the title and Churchill's name, filling it with shading, sending it to the back, and reversing the type. You did this before for the "Club Information section" on page 3.

Follow these steps to build the insert:

1. Drag a horizontal ruler guide to 38.5V.

2. Place the pointer at 32H/48V, and click the secondary mouse button for an "Actual size" view.

3. Drag the text block so that the title is placed in the middle between the horizontal ruler guides, at 37.5 and 38.5, like this:

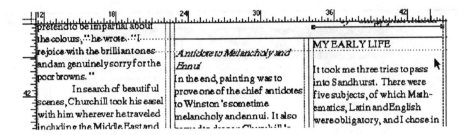

Keep in mind that you are building a box around the title and position it to account for the box, as described in the following instructions:

4. Squeeze the text block by dragging the right end of the text selection box from 45H to 43.5H and the left end from 34.25H to 35.75H.

5. If necessary, drag the bottom handle down until all text is displayed.

6. With the text tool (SHIFT-F4), highlight the whole text block.

7. Press CTRL-T for the Type specifications dialog box, select "Sans" for Font, press TAB, type **10** for Size, click on "Normal" for Type style, and click on "OK".

8. Highlight the title.

9. Center it by pressing CTRL-SHIFT-C. Also, reverse the title by selecting "Reverse" from the "Type style" option of the Type menu.

10. Highlight Churchill's name.

11. Center it by pressing CTRL-SHIFT-C. Also, reverse Churchill's name by selecting "Reverse" from the "Type style" option of the Type menu.

12. Using the square-corner tool (SHIFT-F5), draw a box around the title, from the right column guide on the left of the column to the right margin guide (from 34.25H/37.5V to 45H/38.5V).

13. Shade the box by choosing "Solid" from the "Fill" option.

14. Copy the box by pressing CTRL-INS.

15. Send the box to the back by pressing CTRL-B.

The box and type then look like this:

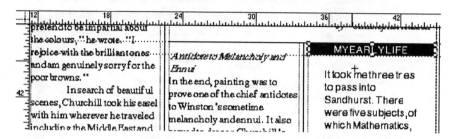

The bottom line needs to be moved down. You do this by adding space before the start of the paragraph of text and before the second to the last paragraph.

16. With the text tool (SHIFT-F4), click on the first line of the paragraph of text (beginning "It took me three tries"). Press CTRL-M to open the Paragraph specifications dialog box. Drag across the "Before" text box and type **.5** or **0p6** to add 1/2 pica or 6 points of space before the paragraph. Click on "OK".

17. Click just below the last line in the text paragraph ("useful card.") Press CTRL-M, drag across the "Before" text box, and type **.5** or **0p6** to add 1/2 pica or 6 points before the second to the last paragraph (the blank line before Churchill's name). Click on "OK".

18. Select the pointer tool (F9), and press SHIFT-INS for the copy of the box.

19. Drag the box down over Churchill's name so that it rests on the bottom margin.

20. Press CTRL-B to send the box to the back.

The screen should look like that shown in Figure 7-44.

21. Return to the "Fit in window" view.

22. Save the file by pressing CTRL-S.

Finally, print page 2 to see how it compares to Figure 7-41.

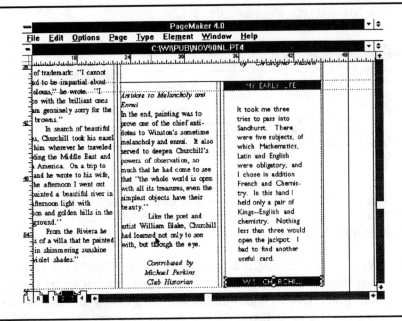

Figure 7-44.   *The insert with highlighted title and name*

23. Press CTRL-P for the Print dialog box.

24. Drag the Page range From text box and type **2**.

25. Drag the "to" text box, type **2**, and click on "OK".

Only page 3 remains to be completed.

Completing Page 3 of the Newsletter   You prepare page 3 by drawing some design element lines and then flowing the rest of the VOL4ISS4.DOC file. The file contains five more articles that flow one after the other.

Flowing the First Column   The first column consists of a heading, one article, and a graphic with a reversed title, as shown in Figure 7-45.

THE ORATOR

Members Only

GOVERNOR DEUKMEJIAN INTRODUCES CHILDREN'S INITIATIVE AT 10-9-90 MEETING

Governor George Deukmejian proposed a $5 million program to bolster statewide child care and medical services at a joint meeting of the Churchill Club and Commonwealth Club on October 9, 1990.

Before 500 people at the San Jose Hyatt, the governor outlined a seven-point "children's initiative" that included a call for expanded drug abuse prevention programs and a crackdown on parents who evade payment of child support.

He also promised to hire more senior citizens to work in child care centers and offered to write legislation providing incentives for drug companies to produce vaccines for childhood diseases.

The Churchill Club thanks the Commonwealth Club for co-sponsoring this fine event.

COMING DECEMBER 4TH

"IMMIGRATION OUT OF CONTROL," COLORADO'S LAMM TELLS CLUB

Warning that the United States is at a crossroads, Colorado Governor Richard Lamm called for stronger border control measures during an address to the Churchill Club on October 16, 1990.

"The creativity and capital of this country, for all its genius, cannot keep pace with the demands put on it if we have to solve not only our own unemployment rate, but that of Mexico, Guatemala, and El Salvador," said the four-term governor.

CLUB MEMBERS IN THE NEWS

Board member Bill Reichert is now vp/marketing at The Learning Company, a Menlo Park-based educational software firm. Reichert's alma mater, New Venture Consultants, is the newest corporate member of the Club... John Sewell, former vice president and general manager of Kodak's largest division, joined the board of Redlake Corporation, a Morgan Hill company that manufactures and sells photo-instrumentation equipment. Redlake is also a Club corporate member... Bob Hansens of Business Solutions Consultants is forming the Silicon Valley Entrepreneur's Club. First meeting is scheduled for January 24th at the San Jose Hyatt. Call Bob at (408) 458-1303 for more information... Club chairman Tony Perkins has returned to Silicon Valley Bank as vice president of SVB's technology group. Also new with SVB are Club members Henry Kellog and Eric Jones.

T.J. Rodgers confirmed for late January

Semiconductor entrepreneur T.J. Rodgers will address the Churchill Club in late January.

Founder and CEO of Cypress Semiconductor, Rodgers has engineered one of Silicon Valley's brightest stories of late. Cypress went public last summer at a valuation of $270 million.

Invitations to a *Night with T.J. Rodgers* will be mailed in early January.

CLUB INFORMATION

Membership
Ken Bailey
Silver City Bank
(415) 555-1234

Speaker Information
Julia Conner
Pacific Research Capital
(415) 555-4321

Media Relations
Susan Casper
Ocean Products
(408) 555-9876

Former H&Q president Tom Volpe on February 19th

Tom Volpe, founder of Volpe Covington, a new investment banking firm that includes Arthur Rock and Warren Hellman as major investors, will address the Churchill Club on Thursday, February 19th.

Volpe has had a meteoric career in investment banking. After taking his AB and MBA from Harvard —with a one-year stopover at the London School of Economics—he began his career with White, Weld & Company, later moving to Blyth, Eastman, Dillon.

At age 30 Volpe joined Hambrecht & Quist as a general partner and opened the investment banking firm's New York Office. In 1984 he became president and CEO of H&Q.

Invitations to a *Night with Tom Volpe* will be mailed to all Club members in early January.

Pandick California, Inc.

The Financial Printer

(415) 543-4433

Offices in

San Francisco • Los Angeles • Newport Beach

Figure 7-45.   *Printout of completed page 3*

Follow these steps to flow the text:

1. Reset the zero point to the top and left margins on page 3.

2. Verify that "Snap to guides" is on and that "Autoflow" is off, both from the Options menu.

3. Click the page 1 icon and then the lead article in the middle column so the article is enclosed in a selection box.

4. Click the bottom handle of the selection box.

5. Click the page 3 icon.

6. Place the text icon at the top of the first column of page 3 just under the line at 7V, and click the main mouse button.

7. In the "Actual size" view, look at the top of the text block and, if necessary, drag it so that the heading is just under the line at the head of the column, as shown in Figure 7-46.

The text block will have flowed until it encountered the graphic box. You want the text to end in the fourth paragraph, with the words "fine event."

8. Using the horizontal scroll bar, peruse the column in the "Actual size" view until you reach the bottom of the flowed text.

9. Drag the text handle up (or down) until it ends after the fourth paragraph. You may have to move the whole text block up closer to the top line.

The next column is very straightforward, except that you must change the leading to get all of the two articles to fit in the column. In this column the text begins at the same level as the top of the design line, on the horizontal ruler guide.

10. Click on the bottom text handle for the text icon and return to the "Fit in window" view.

11. Place the icon at the top of column 2 and click the main mouse button.

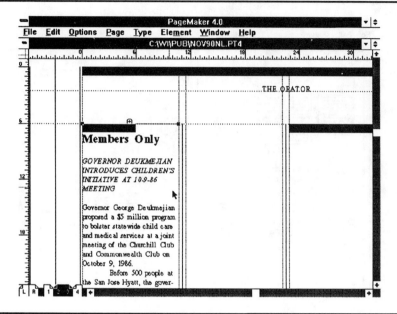

Figure 7-46.   *Column 1, page 3, headline aligned*

12. In "Actual size" view, look at the bottom of the column. Pull the text handle down and drag the text block higher in the column until the text "Eric Jones." is the last line in column 2.

You can see that to fit all text in column 2, you must drag the lower text handle almost off the page, as shown in Figure 7-47.

13. In the "Fit in window" view and with the text tool (SHIFT-F4), highlight the whole column of text (including the headlines).

14. Choose "Leading" from the Type menu, click on "Other", type **11.5**, and click on "OK".

The text shrinks so that it can be contained in the one column. Now you need to adjust the position of the text block.

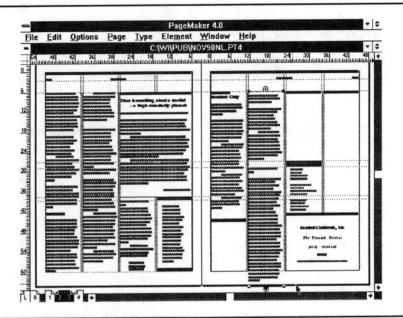

Figure 7-47. *Column 2, page 3, before leading is reduced*

15. Place your pointer at 18H/54V and press the secondary mouse button for an "Actual size" view.

16. With the pointer tool (F9), click somewhere in column 2 to get the selection box.

17. Drag the handle up so that the headline of the next article does not appear in column 2.

18. Return to the "Fit in window" view, place the pointer at 18H/12V, and press the secondary mouse button for an "Actual size" view of the top of column 2.

19. Drag a new horizontal ruler guide down to 8.5V.

20. Drag the text block in column 2 so that the title spans from the horizontal guide at 6V to the new horizontal guide at 8.5V. Then drag

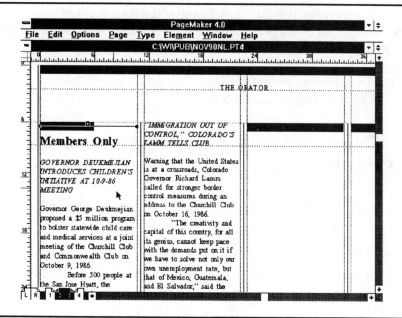

Figure 7-48.   *Headlines for columns 1 and 2 aligned*

the article in column 1 down so that it sits on the new horizontal guide at 8.5, as shown in Figure 7-48.

21. Scroll the window down until you can see the second heading, "CLUB MEMBERS IN THE NEWS." With the text tool (SHIFT-F4), click the insertion point to the left of the letter "I" in "IN" and press BACKSPACE followed by ENTER to split the lines at a better place.

22. When the positioning is as you want it, click on the bottom handle with the pointer (F9) for the text icon.

Flowing the next two columns is much easier.

Completing the Placement of the Text   The last two columns each contain one article that fits in the space available. You flow the text, verify that it is correctly positioned at the top of the column, drag the text handle down to get all of the text in the article, and then flow the next column. Follow these steps to finish this task:

1. Place the text icon at the top of column 3, under the heavy line, and click the main mouse button.

2. In "Actual size" view, look at the top of the column and adjust it so the first line of the headline sits on the horizontal ruler guide at 8.5V.

3. Drag the text handle down so that all the text in the article appears in column 3. The last line ends "mailed in early January."

4. With the pointer tool (F9), click on the bottom text handle to get the text icon.

5. Place the icon at the head of column 4 and click the main mouse button.

6. In the "Actual size" view, line up the headline in column 4 with the one in column 3, as shown in Figure 7-49.

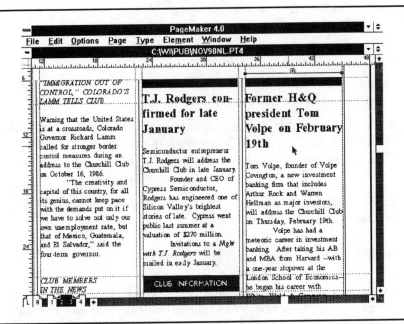

Figure 7-49.   *Headlines for columns 3 and 4 aligned*

7. In the "Fit in window" view, drag down the handle so that all text appears. (An empty handle appears.)

8. Verify the results with the "Actual size" view.

9. With the text tool (SHIFT-F4), highlight the body of text in column 3. Press CTRL-T and type **11.5** in the leading text box of the Type specs dialog box.

10. Similarly, highlight the body of text in column 4 and change its leading to 11.5.

11. With the text tool (SHIFT-F4), click the insertion point to the left of the "c" in "confirmed" in the column 3 headline. Press BACKSPACE and ENTER to move "confirmed" to the next line. In a like manner, move the word "late" to the next line.

12. Move the word "Tom" in column 4 down to the next line. Your final screen should look like Figure 7-50.

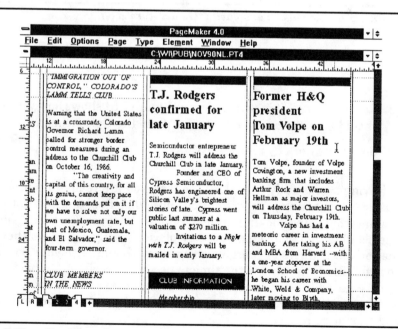

Figure 7-50. *Headlines for columns 3 and 4 with proper line breaks*

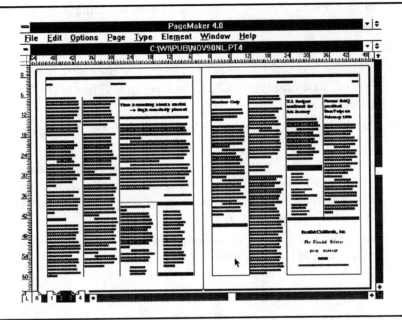

Figure 7-51. *Finished pages 2 and 3 with "Guides" turned off*

13. Return to the "Fit in window" view. Figure 7-51 shows how your screen should look if you turn off "Guides" from the Options menu.

14. Save your work by pressing CTRL-S.

Having successfully flowed all the text, you are ready to complete the final step—perusing your publication and adding final touches. You should examine the typing, looking for misspellings and typos. Look at the inserts, lines, and design elements. Are they placed exactly right? Do they meet the column dividers or margins where they should? Are your boxes long enough? Too long? This is the time to be very critical and to perfect your work. Final editing is often a repetitive process of examining the newsletter on the screen, printing it, examining the printout, correcting any errors, and reprinting it.

Using the Story Editor

In looking through your newsletter, you find several references to 1986 that should be 1990. Also, you might be unsure about several spellings. To handle both of these problems you use PageMaker 4's story editor.

The story editor provides a means of doing heavy editing on stories placed in a PageMaker publication, similar to what you might do in a word processing package. In this case you want to use the search and replace feature and the spelling checker. Follow these instructions:

1. Click on the page 1 icon and then click with the pointer (F9) on the article in column 2—the Buthelezi address.

2. From the Edit menu, choose "Edit story". The story window opens. Press the Maximize button to enlarge the window, as illustrated in Figure 7-52.

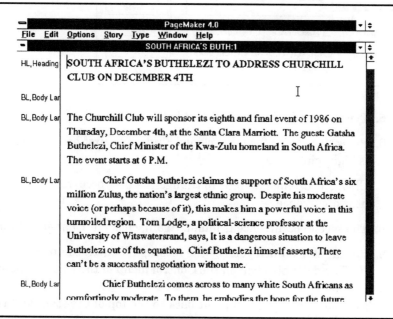

Figure 7-52.   *Lead story in the story window*

The story window provides a view different than the normal PageMaker layout view. Your original layout has not changed, you are just looking at it differently. The story window has a different set of menus. You use some of the menu options in editing the newsletter, but you should look the menus over in more detail on your own. The left column in Figure 7-52 displays the style names. You can turn these off with the Options menu. Also, with the Options menu you can turn on the display of hidden characters such as carriage returns (paragraph marks) and tabs. Do that next, and then search and replace 1986 using the "Change" option.

3. From the Options menu, choose "Display ¶". You see where your paragraph and tab characters are.

4. From the Edit menu, choose "Change...". The Change dialog box opens, as shown here:

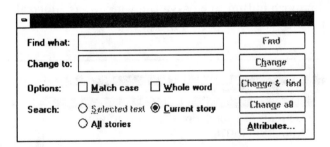

5. Type **86** in the "Find what" text box.

6. Press TAB, type **90**, and click on "Find". The first occurrence in line 1 is highlighted.

7. Click on "Change & find" to change the first occurrence and find the next occurrence.

8. The second occurrence is found. Again, click on "Change & find."

9. Repeat step 8 until you see the message "Search complete!". Click on "OK" and double-click on the Control menu of the Change dialog box.

Next, move the insertion point back to the top of the story and run the spelling checker.

10. Click the insertion point in front of "South" in the title.

11. Choose "Spelling..." from the Edit menu and click on "Start".

12. The first word that comes up is "Buthelezi." Click on "Ignore".

13. Complete the checking of the spelling, clicking on "Ignore" or making changes as necessary.

14. When you are done checking the spelling, double-click on the Control menu of the Spelling dialog box.

You are now ready to return the corrected story to the layout view.

15. From the Story menu, choose "Close story". You are returned to the layout view.

Once you are satisfied with its content, you need only print the final newsletter. But first you should save your work again.

16. Press CTRL-S to save the file.

17. Press CTRL-P for the Print dialog box.

18. Click on "All" to print pages 1 to 4. Click on "OK".

This concludes the newsletter project. It has been challenging and time-consuming, as you would expect with a task of this size. You can use many of the techniques you have used here with your own newsletters or similar work.

Chapter 8 presents you with another challenge, that of creating a catalog. You will continue to advance your skills in that chapter.

8 *Building A Catalog*

In this chapter you will create two regular pages and a title page of a catalog, as shown in Figures 8-1 through 8-3. Catalogs are usually built around a repetitive layout within which changing contents are placed. Therefore, the emphasis of the chapter is in building the master pages. The two regular catalog pages are constructed as an example of how the bulk of the catalog is built. Additionally, a title page is prepared to give you a further opportunity to use and place graphics. A complete catalog, of course, would have many pages with a number of different layouts.

The catalog that served as a model for this chapter is one published by MacPherson's wholesale art supply store in Emeryville, California. Mac-Pherson's built the catalog using PageMaker on the Macintosh. Doing this saved them considerable money and time compared with the previous method of typesetting and manual layout.

The creators of the MacPherson catalog construct it by pulling together and organizing the literature of a number of different vendors. They scan the artwork and photographs from the vendor's literature to convert it to computer-readable form, and they type the text into a word processor to give it a consistent format and font.

In this chapter you follow a similar procedure. You scan the artwork for these two pages and enter the text into Microsoft Word. If you do not have a scanner, use one of the compatible graphics programs (PC Paintbrush, Windows Paint, CorelDRAW, or Micrografx Designer) to prepare a graphic, or use commercially available clip art instead of a scanned image. Then follow the instructions for placing the graphic, changing the filename as necessary.

If you use a word processing program other than Microsoft Word, read through the Microsoft Word instructions and then duplicate them in your word processor.

Planning and Designing the Catalog

The planning and design of a catalog are essential to a successful publication, as you have seen in the other publications in this book.

Planning the Catalog

Planning a catalog primarily involves determining what will be included—which products from which vendors. Once you have determined that, you must consider how to get the latest literature, how to organize it, and who will scan the art and enter the text. Depending on the size of the catalog, this may be a one-person job, or many people may be involved. Of course, the larger the catalog and the more people involved, the more planning must be done.

Printing a catalog, like most desktop-published items, can vary from simply reproducing what comes off the laser printer to having the catalog commercially printed and bound. MacPherson took the latter approach, using a beautiful, multicolored cover and simple black-and-white printing of the regular pages.

Planning the schedule for the catalog largely depends on whether the catalog is aimed at a particular buying season, like Christmas, or has some other deadline. Obviously, if there is a deadline, the schedule takes on greater significance. Similarly, when planning the budget you must consider the size of the publication and how fancy the printing and binding will be. Also, distributing the catalog by mail can be a very large part of the budget and can dictate the weight and thus the size of the catalog.

Designing the Catalog

In designing the catalog you strive to create an attractive and functional layout that can be used for most of the content. Placing large numbers of

Wholesale Art Supplies

Graphic Arts, Drafting, and Engineering

1327 Park Avenue

Emeryville, CA 94608

(415) 428-9011

Figure 8-1.   *Title page of the catalog*

MacPherson

Watercolor Paint Sets

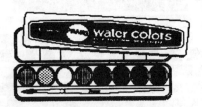

016

08

10308

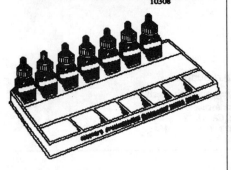

Prang Watercolor Sets (American Crayon)
Oval-8 Set contains 8 oval semi-moist half pan colors
with No. 7 brush. No. 16 Set contains 16 semi-moist
half pan colors, a No. 1 and 4 brush. Oval 16 Set
contains the same colors and brushes as No. 16 Set,
except with oval half pans. No. 8 Set contains 8 semi-
moist half pan colors with No. 7 brush. (Qty = Each)

Order No.	Item
AC16	Prang Watercolor Set
AC16-OVL	Prang Watercolor Set
AC8	Prang Watercolor Set
AC8-OVL	Prang Watercolor Set

Artista Watercolor Sets (Binney & Smith)
No. 080 set contains 8 oval half pans and a No. 7 brush.
No. 08 contains 8 half pans and a No. 7 brush. No. 016
contains 16 half pans and a No. 7 brush. (Qty = Each)

Order No.	Item
BS016	W/C Half Pan Set
BS08	W/C Half Pan Set
BS080	W/C Oval Pan Set

Gouache Sets (Caran D'Ache)
Highly concentrated light-resistant watercolors for
opaque painting. The No. 10308 Set contains 7 pans of
assorted colors and one tube of white. (Qty = Each)

Order No.	Item
CD10308	Pan Set 8 Colors with Brush
CD20313	Tube Set 13 Colors with Brush

Licolette Gouache Sets (Loew-Cornell)
Set 500-12 contains 10 opaque colors, white, and black.
Set 500-24 contains 22 opaque colors, white, and black.
(Qty = Each)

Order No.	Item
LK500-12	Licolette Gouache Set/12 Colors
LK500-24	Licolette Gouache Set/24 Colors

Radiant Concentrated Sets (Dr. Ph. Martin)
Each set is comprised of 14 colors to cover the entire
range as listed in groups, corresponding to the open-
stock radiant colors. DRA Set is all "A" colors. DRB
Set is all "B" colors. DRC Set is all "C" colors.
DRDST is all "D" colors. 1/2 oz. bottle size. (Qty =
Each)

Order No.	Item
DRA	Radiant CNC Set/14 All A
DRB	Radiant CNC Set/14 All B
DRC	Radiant CNC Set/14 All C
DRDST	Radiant CNC Set/14 All D

2

Figure 8-2. *Page 2 of the catalog*

MacPherson

Watercolor Paint Sets

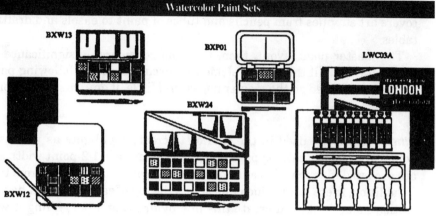

The Bijou No. 3 (Winsor & Newton)
The ideal companion for the traveling watercolorist.
Made of strong die-cast metal finished in black enamel
and packed in an attractive carrying case. Contains 18
semi-moist pans of Artists' Water Color and a sable
brush in a metal holder with protective cap. Size 2" x
5". (Qty = Each)

Order No.	Item
WNBXW12	No. 3 Bijou

The Bijou No. 2 (Winsor & Newton)
Same as Bijou No. 3, but contains 12 colors. Size 2" x
3-1/4". (Qty = Each)

Order No.	Item
WNBXW11	No. 2 Bijou

Sketchers Pocket Box (Winsor & Newton)
A compact white plastic box containing 12 square pans
of transparent watercolor and a pocket sable brush with a
protective cap. Size 4" x 2" x 1/2". (Qty = Each)

Order No.	Item
WNBXW13	W/C Pocket Box

Sketchers Box #24 (Winsor & Newton)
A black plastic box containing 24 square pans of
economical watercolor and a Series 33 sable brush.
Refill pans not available. Size 8-1/2" x 4-1/2" x 1/4".
(Qty = Each)

Order No.	Item
WNBXW24	W/C Set - 24 Colors

London Water Color Set #3A (Winsor & Newton)
Contains 10 London Water Colors in 7.5 ml. tubes.
Includes a watercolor brush, a six well/six slant tile
plastic palette, color chart and painting techniques
leaflet. (Qty = Each)

Order No.	Item
WNBXLW03A	London W/C Set #3A

London Water Color Set #4 (Winsor & Newton)
Contains 12 London Water colors in 7.5 ml. tubes in an
aluminum box with white enameled palette/lid, two
water color brushes, a color chart and a painting techniques leaflet. (Qty = Each)

Order No.	Item
WNBXLW04	London W/C Set #4

Page Water Color Sets (Winsor & Newton)
This range represents excellent value in inexpensive
water color sets for young artists. Colorfully designed
boxes make these sets ideal as gifts. Each set comes
with a brush and all are shrink-wrapped for protection
except #01 (Qty = Each)

Order No.	Item
WNBXP01	6 Pan Water Color Set
WNBXP05	12 Pan Water Color Set
WNBXP10	20 Pan Water Color Set
WNBXP15	30 Pan Water Color Set
WNBXP20	40 Pan Water Color Set
WNBXP25	50 Pan Water Color Set
WNBXP30	60 Pan Water Color Set
WNBXP35	78 Pan Water Color Set

Figure 8-3. *Page 3 of the catalog*

graphics and text blocks quickly is important, which precludes undue customization of individual pages. At the same time the design must accommodate a wide variety of items. For instance, MacPherson's catalog covers art supplies from pencils and tubes of paint to easels and drafting tables.

The master page layout, then, takes on considerable significance for most catalogs. All the design elements (discussed in the following paragraphs) are placed on the master pages, and little, if any, customization is done.

Lines   Lines are used in the catalog to create highlights as well as to define areas of the catalog page. Most of the lines are 1/2-point width and are used to define margins and columns or to separate graphics from text. In addition, there is a 1/4-inch line across the top of each page that has the section name in it. You create this line by drawing a box, filling it with shading, and using reverse type.

Fonts   The catalog uses only the Times typeface in four fonts. The company name on the inside of each catalog page is 18 points and bold; the page number and section name are 12 points and bold; and the text is 10 points, with headings in bold and the body in medium weight. The section name at the top of each page is in reverse type (white letters on a black background). Not all printers can provide reverse type. If your printer cannot, use black type in a 10% shaded box.

Memory Space   As you design the catalog, keep printer memory in mind. Depending on the printer you have, you may have to restrict the number of graphics and fonts you use. The pages described in this chapter can be printed on a 512KB HP LaserJet IIP. This printer prints only half a page of graphics at 300 dots per inch (dpi) before running out of memory. Also, if you are using downloaded fonts, remember that the larger point sizes take considerable memory space. Boxes with shading (even "Paper" shading), such as the shaded box at the top of the catalog cover, also account for high usage of printer memory.

Shading   Shading is used in the catalog as a background for the section name in the box across the top of each page. "Solid" fill is applied. You could choose to shade your graphics or even some of the text. Just remember the memory ramifications.

Leading In the example pages produced in this chapter, only "Auto" leading is used. PageMaker assumes 120% leading in its default "Auto" leading setting. The 10-point type used in the catalog text has 12 points of leading with the "Auto" option, which is expressed as 10/12. You may want to vary the leading on pages you produce to squeeze additional text onto a page or to expand text to fill a page.

Graphics Four separate graphics are used in the catalog. One, the title for the catalog, is produced directly with Micrografx Designer. The other three, two sets of products and the logo, are scanned and produce TIFF files.

Layout The layout for the catalog is in decimal inches, often the easiest system with which to work. You will use a standard 8 1/2 by 11-inch format, with a 1-inch inside margin and 0.75-inch top, outside, and bottom margins which are PageMaker defaults. The wider inside margin is for binding purposes. The regular pages have two columns with 0.25-inch spacing between the columns, although the first page has only one column.

The next step is to create the text and graphics.

Creating Text and Graphics for the Catalog

You create the catalog text and graphics outside of PageMaker with graphics and word processing packages that can interface with it. As mentioned earlier, the catalog text is produced with Microsoft Word. The graphics come from various sources: a company name graphic created in Micrografx Designer, and the company logo and catalog product drawings created from scanned art. You can use your own word processor (if it works with PageMaker) and your own means of producing graphics if you wish.

If you are using another word processor, check to see if it is covered in this book and read about any restrictions you may have with it.

Another alternative for both the text and graphics is to purchase the companion disk for this book and use the files on that disk. See the offer at the front of this book.

If you do not have a scanner or Micrografx Designer, you can use clip art or any of the several painting and drawing programs supported by PageMaker. It is recommended that you do create or use some graphics because it allows you to experiment with placing graphics, even if they aren't exactly right for the publication. However, if you elect to avoid the graphics part altogether and just establish the placeholders in PageMaker, you will still gain valuable experience.

Creating Text
With Microsoft Word

You build only one file with Microsoft Word. In a full catalog you normally create several files and might use more than one word processor. Figure 8-4 contains the text that you enter with Microsoft Word.

The text consists of several paragraphs, each describing a product. Fortunately, with Microsoft Word you can transfer to PageMaker the typeface, type sizes, bold, and italics—everything you need in the catalog. This considerably reduces the work in PageMaker.

Load Microsoft Word or the word processing program you want to use. Place two tabs at 1.25 and 1.75 inches, respectively. Set your default formatting to 10-point Times, aligned-left, with "Auto" leading or line spacing. If you wish you can create a style sheet with two styles: a body medium (BM) that is 10-point Times, aligned-left, with "Auto" leading; and a heading medium (HM) that is body medium with bold.

Type the text shown in Figure 8-4. The heading or first line of each product description is bold or HM style. All the remaining text and numbers use the default formatting or BM style. Place two tabs between "Order No." and "Item" and one tab between the actual number and the description. Leave two blank lines between products.

When you complete typing the file, save it in the \WI\PUB directory with the filename CATALOG.DOC. If you are using a different directory for the PageMaker files created in this book, change the pathname to correspond to what you are using.

Prang Watercolor Sets (American Crayon)
Oval-8 Set contains 8 oval semi-moist half pan colors with No. 7 brush. No. 16 Set contains 16 semi-moist half pan colors, a No. 1 and 4 brush. Oval 16 Set contains the same colors and brushes as No. 16 Set, except with oval half pans. No. 8 Set contains 8 semi-moist half pan colors with No. 7 brush. (Qty = Each)

Order No.	Item
AC16	Prang Watercolor Set
AC16-OVL	Prang Watercolor Set
AC8	Prang Watercolor Set
AC8-OVL	Prang Watercolor Set

Artista Watercolor Sets (Binney & Smith)
No. 080 set contains 8 oval half pans and a No. 7 brush. No. 08 contains 8 half pans and a No. 7 brush. No. 016 contains 16 half pans and a No. 7 brush. (Qty = Each)

Order No.	Item
BS016	W/C Half Pan Set
BS08	W/C Half Pan Set
BS080	W/C Oval Pan Set

Gouache Sets (Caran D'Ache)
Highly concentrated light-resistant watercolors for opaque painting. The No. 10308 Set contains 7 pans of assorted colors and one tube of white. (Qty = Each)

Order No.	Item
CD10308	Pan Set 8 Colors with Brush
CD20313	Tube Set 13 Colors with Brush

Licolette Gouache Sets (Loew-Cornell)
Set 500-12 contains 10 opaque colors, white, and black. Set 500-24 contains 22 opaque colors, white, and black. (Qty = Each)

Order No.	Item
LK500-12	Licolette Gouache Set/12 Colors
LK500-24	Licolette Gouache Set/24 Colors

Radiant Concentrated Sets (Dr. Ph. Martin)
Each set is comprised of 14 colors to cover the entire range as listed in groups, corresponding to the open-stock radiant colors. DRA Set is all "A" colors. DRB Set is all "B" colors. DRC Set is all "C" colors. DRDST is all "D" colors. 1/2 oz. bottle size. (Qty = Each)

Order No.	Item
DRA	Radiant CNC Set/14 All A
DRB	Radiant CNC Set/14 All B
DRC	Radiant CNC Set/14 All C
DRDST	Radiant CNC Set/14 All D

The Bijou No. 3 (Winsor & Newton)
The ideal companion for the traveling watercolorist. Made of strong die-cast metal finished in black enamel and packed in an attractive carrying case. Contains 18 semi-moist pans of Artists' Water Color and a sable brush in a metal holder with protective cap. Size 2" x 5". (Qty = Each)

Order No.	Item
WNBXW12	No. 3 Bijou

Figure 8-4.   *Text created with Microsoft Word (1 of 2)*

The Bijou No. 2 (Winsor & Newton)
Same as Bijou No. 3, but contains 12 colors. Size 2" x 3-1/4". (Qty = Each)
Order No.   Item
WNBXW11   No. 2 Bijou

Sketchers Pocket Box (Winsor & Newton)
A compact white plastic box containing 12 square pans of transparent watercolor and a pocket sable
brush with a protective cap. Size 4" x 2" x 1/2". (Qty = Each)
Order No.   Item
WNBXW13   W/C Pocket Box

Sketchers Box #24 (Winsor & Newton)
A black plastic box containing 24 square pans of economical watercolor and a Series 33 sable brush.
Refill pans not available. Size 8-1/2" x 4-1/2" x 1/4". (Qty = Each)
Order No.   Item
WNBXW24   W/C Set - 24 Colors

London Water Color Set #3A (Winsor & Newton)
Contains 10 London Water Colors in 7.5 ml. tubes. Includes a watercolor brush, a six well/six slant tile
plastic palette, color chart and painting techniques leaflet. (Qty = Each)
Order No.   Item
WNBXLW03A   London W/C Set #3A

London Water Color Set #4 (Winsor & Newton)
Contains 12 London Water colors in 7.5 ml. tubes in an aluminum box with white enameled palette/lid,
two water color brushes, a color chart and a painting techniques leaflet. (Qty = Each)
Order No.   Item
WNBXLW04   London W/C Set #4

Page Water Color Sets (Winsor & Newton)
This range represents excellent value in inexpensive water color sets for young artists. Colorfully
designed boxes make these sets ideal as gifts. Each set comes with a brush and all are shrink-wrapped
for protection except #01 (Qty = Each)
Order No.   Item
WNBXP01   6 Pan Water Color Set
WNBXP05   12 Pan Water Color Set
WNBXP10   20 Pan Water Color Set
WNBXP15   30 Pan Water Color Set
WNBXP20   40 Pan Water Color Set
WNBXP25   50 Pan Water Color Set
WNBXP30   60 Pan Water Color Set
WNBXP35   78 Pan Water Color Set

Figure 8-4.   *Text created with Microsoft Word (2 of 2)*

Using Graphics in the Catalog

You have several options for using graphics within PageMaker. You can
create a graphic using one of the painting or drawing programs, such as

PC Paintbrush, Windows Paint, Micrografx Designer, or CorelDRAW. You can create a graphic file by scanning a photo or line drawing with a scanner. Or you can have a commercial printer photographically place and size the graphic in the catalog before it is printed.

MacPherson chose to scan the graphics for their catalog, as is done in this chapter. If you have a scanner, the graphics are reproduced in Appendix C and can be removed from the book for use here. If you do not have a scanner and wish to learn to place a graphic, draw a quick substitute or use clip art.

Creating the Title Page Name
With Micrografx Designer

The title page contains a stylized company name, as shown in Figure 8-5. You produce this in Micrografx Designer and then load it in PageMaker.

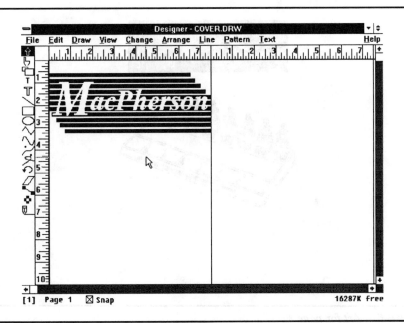

Figure 8-5. *Company name graphic created in Micrografx Designer*

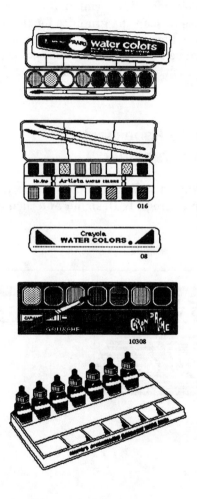

Figure 8-6. *Art for page 2*

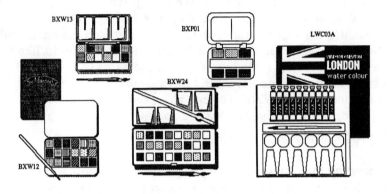

Figure 8-7.   *Art for page 3 and the logo*

Load Micrografx Designer or the graphics program you want to use. Set the typeface to Times bold italic. The first letter is 135-point, and the remaining letters are 95-point. Initially type **MacPherson** in black type.

After you type the name, draw 11 lines that are 3/16 (0.19) inch wide with 1/16 (0.06) inch between them and stepped from left to right by 1/4 inch. The first line is 6.5 inches long, the next is 6.75, and so on to 7.5 inches. There are three lines at 7.5 inches and then the lines begin to get smaller. The first of the smaller lines is only 1/8 inch to cover the foot of the "M".

After completing the lines, select the name, reverse it or color it white, and bring it to the top or front layer. In Designer, this is done by selecting "Color..." from the Text menu and choosing "White" from the "Color" option box. Then select "Move to front" from the Arrange menu.

Finally, arrange the name on the lines, and then the name and lines on the page, as shown in Figure 8-5. When your drawing looks like Figure 8-5, save it in the \WI\PUB directory with the name COVER.DWR, and then export the graphic as a Windows metafile to the \WI\PUB directory with the name COVER.WMF. You can also print the graphic if you wish.

Next you scan the catalog art to get the product pictures and the company logo.

Scanning the Catalog Art   If you have a scanner and want to produce the catalog with scanned graphics, turn on your scanner and load its driver software. Set your resolution to "300x300", brightness and contrast to "Normal" or "Automatic", mode to "Drawing", and file type to "TIFF". These options and their settings differ among scanners and their driver software, so set yours as close to these as possible. Also, if you are using a flatbed scanner instead of a hand-held scanner, define the smallest area of the page possible to just scan the object you want. This keeps your scanned files as small as possible.

You have three pieces of art to scan: one for page 2 of the catalog, as shown in Figure 8-6, and the art for page 3 and the MacPherson logo shown in Figure 8-7. All three pieces of art are contained in Appendix D. Remove Appendix D from the book now and scan each piece. Save the scanned images in the \WI\PUB directory with the names PAGE2.TIF, PAGE3.TIF, and LOGO.TIF.

Now that you have created the text and graphics for the catalog, you can begin to build the catalog. The first thing you do is set defaults within PageMaker.

Setting Defaults

As was the case in other chapters, your first task within PageMaker is to set the defaults. For the catalog you change both startup defaults (those that remain from one PageMaker session to another) and publication defaults (those that are unique to a publication).

Startup Defaults

The startup defaults you set are the target printer and preferences for measurement. This is done to assure that the page setup (a publication default) is correctly initiated.

If you are using PageMaker, close any active publication so that you have no publications open for the next few steps. If PageMaker is not active, load it now.

Establishing the Target Printer Establish your target printer with the following steps:

1. Choose "Target printer..." from the File menu.

2. When the dialog box is displayed, double-click on the printer you want to use for the catalog.

3. Verify that the settings are the way you want them. Most importantly, set Orientation to "Portrait" and DPI Resolution to "300" for laser printers. Make the necessary changes and click on "OK" for both the Setup and Target printer dialog boxes.

Setting Preferences For the catalog you use decimal inches for units of measurement. Verify that the scale is set for that in this way:

1. Choose "Preferences..." from the Edit menu.

2. Select "Inches decimal" from the Measurement system and Vertical ruler list boxes, click on "Back" under Guides, and then click on "OK".

With the startup defaults set, you can establish the publication defaults.

Publication Defaults

The publication defaults consist of the page setup, the line and type specifications, and the selection of several options you want—all very routine procedures by now.

Page Setup   For the first time in this book, you use the standard margins with which PageMaker is shipped. Therefore, unless you have changed the startup defaults in the page setup (by setting the page setup without a publication), the only default you need to change is the number of pages. Do this and check the other page settings with the following instructions:

1. Choose "New..." from the File menu.

2. Verify that the Page text box is set to "Letter", Orientation is set to "Tall", and Double-sided and Facing pages are checked.

3. Type **3** in the Number of pages text box.

4. Verify that the following margins are set: "1" for Inside, and "0.75" for Outside, Top, and Bottom, as shown in Figure 8-8.

5. Press ENTER to complete the dialog box.

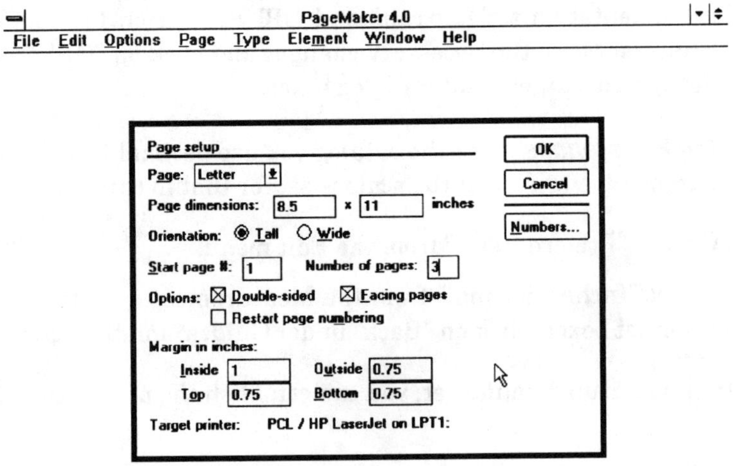

Figure 8-8.   *The Page setup dialog box*

6. If your application and/or document windows are not maximized, click on one or both Maximize buttons so they are.

Setting the Lines and Shades Defaults   All the lines within the catalog are 1/2 point in width. The only use of shading is the "Solid" fill in the box at the top of the page. Set these as defaults in this way:

1. Choose ".5 pt" from the "Line" option of the Element menu.

2. Choose "Solid" from the "Fill" option of the Element menu.

Establishing Type Specifications   The text in the catalog is 10-point Times. Even though Microsoft Word determines the font, set the default to 10-point Times so that any last-minute editing you do is correct. Set the type specifications accordingly.

1. Press CTRL-T for the Type specifications dialog box.

2. Verify that "Times" is the default Font, press TAB, type **10**, and verify that "Auto" leading and "Normal" Type style, Position, and Case are all set.

3. Click on "OK" to complete the dialog box.

All of the text in the body of the catalog is left-aligned, so set that now.

4. Verify that "Align left" is checked in the "Alignment" option of the Type menu.

This completes setting the type defaults.

Setting Other Options   The other options to choose or verify are "Rulers", "Snap to rulers", and "Snap to guides", and not using the "Toolbox." Follow these steps to make those choices.

1. Verify that "Rulers", "Guides", "Snap to rulers", and "Snap to guides" are checked on the Options menu.

2. If any are not, choose them.

3. If "Toolbox" is checked on the Window menu, click on it to turn it off.

Horizontal and vertical rulers should be on the screen, and the Toolbox should disappear.

Important Techniques Used in This Chapter

Several techniques for working with text and graphics are repeatedly used in this chapter. These techniques are described in this section.

Switching Between the "Actual size" And "Fit in window" Views

To accurately place the text, graphics, and lines, you must switch between the "Actual size" and "Fit in window" views many times. Quickly switching between these two views of a page is an extremely efficient way to place and then verify your work. Use the secondary mouse button to make this switch. If you are in the "Fit in window" view and want "Actual size", position your pointer on what you want to appear in the middle of the screen and press the secondary mouse button. To help you place the pointer, you are given the horizontal and vertical ruler coordinates in the format 6H/2.5V, which you should read as "6 inches on the horizontal ruler and 2.5 inches on the vertical ruler." When you are in "Actual size" and want the "Fit in window" view, simply press the secondary mouse button or press CTRL-W. To simplify this, when you must go from the "Actual size" view to "Fit in window", the instruction is "Return to the 'Fit in window' view".

The Toolbox

The Toolbox obscures a corner of your work area when you are using facing pages. For this reason you have turned it off. To select the necessary tools, you must use shortcut keys, such as SHIFT-F4 for the text tool. The instructions in this chapter tell you which keys to use, but you will soon memorize them.

Selecting Text and Graphics

Every time you want to do something with your text or graphics within PageMaker, you must first choose the correct tool, and then select the text or graphics—that is, highlight it or put a selection box around it. Finally, you carry out the task.

Selecting Text   You can select text with either the text tool or the pointer tool, depending on what you want to do. If you want to move a block of text from one spot on the page to another, you use the pointer. However, if you want to change the type specifications for text, you highlight it with the text tool.

To select text with the pointer tool, simply place the pointer on the text and click the main mouse button. The text then is enclosed in a selection box. To select text with the text tool, you must first drag over the text with the I-beam. It is then highlighted, and you can specify what you want done with the text.

Selecting Lines or Graphics   If you have just created a line or box, it may still be selected if you have not deselected it by clicking the main mouse button on something else. You can tell if it is still selected by the tiny boxes that appear on or around the item. If the item has been deselected, you can select a graphic or line again with the pointer tool.

Place the tip of the pointer on the line or graphic and click the main mouse button. The item selected is displayed with tiny boxes around or on the ends of it.

To select a line or graphic, you may have to work around other items that get in the way. A column or margin guide, for instance, may get selected instead of the line you want. To select a line that lies over or near a guide line, you may have to move the guide line to get at the line you want. Choosing "Lock guides" from the Options menu or pressing CTRL while clicking can help you select a line that is on a ruler guide. Alternatively, you can use the "Send to back" feature when other items are preventing you from selecting something.

Deselecting Selected Text or Graphics   To deselect anything, simply click your pointer on something else—either on other text or graphics that you want to select or on the Pasteboard.

Moving and Copying Text or Graphics Moving text or graphics is a three-step process: (1) select the item with the pointer tool; (2) while pointing on the line, press and hold the main mouse button until the pointer becomes a four-headed arrow; and (3) drag the item wherever you want it on the screen.

Copying text or graphics adds three more steps: (1) select the text or graphics as in step 1 in the previous list; (2) copy it by pressing CTRL-INS; (3) find the area or page where you want the item inserted; (4) press SHIFT-INS to get the copy back on the publication; (5) while pointing on the new copy, press and hold the main mouse button until the pointer becomes a four-headed arrow; and (6) drag the item wherever you want it on the screen.

If you want multiple copies, press SHIFT-INS again (assuming that you have not copied or deleted anything else in the meantime) because the copy remains on the Clipboard until you delete or copy something else.

Use the text tool to copy text and then insert it into another text block. In this case you click the insertion point to indicate where the text is to be placed before pressing SHIFT-INS.

Constructing the Master Pages

The master pages, as shown in Figure 8-9, contain five design elements common to both facing pages: (1) a 1/4-inch-wide box at the top of each page filled with "Solid" fill; (2) the company name just above the box on the inside of the page; (3) a logo also just above the box on the outside of the page; (4) a 1/2-point line across the bottom margin; and (5) a page number in the lower-outside corner of each page. There is also a vertical 1/2-point line of varying length down the middle of each page and a 1/2-point line across the right page. You must first produce the common elements and then add the unique lines.

Producing the Common Master Page Elements

To produce each of the common master page elements, follow the instructions given in the following paragraphs.

MacPherson

RM

Figure 8-9. *Master pages layout with common design elements*

Building the Boxes   The boxes at the top of each page, along with the logo and company name, tie the catalog together. Build the boxes using these instructions:

1. Click on one of the master page icons (L or R) to bring them on the screen.

The master pages are displayed as two facing pages on the screen. Notice on the horizontal ruler that the zero point is between the two pages. From that point the ruler's scales go in both directions, so there are two of each scale mark. You are told which ruler mark to use—the left or the right—by the word in front of the coordinates, for example, "right 5H/3V" unless it is obvious.

2. Drag a horizontal ruler guide down to 1V.

3. Press SHIFT-F5 to select the square-corner tool.

4. Place the crossbar at left 7.75H/.75V (the intersection of the top and left margins) and drag it to left 1H/1V (the intersection of the right margin and the new horizontal ruler guide).

5. Place the crossbar at right 1H/.75V and drag it to right 7.75H/1V.

Two filled boxes should appear, as shown in Figure 8-10.

Entering the Name   The second common element on the master pages is the company name immediately above the box that you just drew on the inside of each page. You enter the name on the left page, position it correctly on the page, copy it to the Clipboard, and then paste it on the right page. The instructions for this are as follows:

1. Place the pointer at left 1H/1V and click the secondary mouse button for the "Actual size" view.

2. By using the pointer tool (F9), drag the horizontal ruler guide at 1V up to 0.7V.

3. Press SHIFT-F4 to select the text tool.

4. Click the main mouse button at left 3H/0.6V.

5. Press CTRL-T for the Type specifications dialog box.

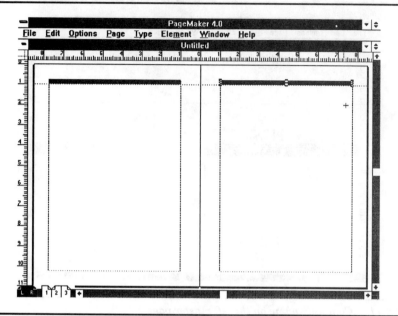

Figure 8-10.   *Two filled boxes at the top of the master pages*

6. Press TAB and type **18** in the Size list box. Click on "Bold" for Type style, and then click on "OK".

7. Type **MacPherson**.

8. Press F9 to select the pointer.

9. Click on the company name and drag it so that it sits on the horizontal ruler guide at 0.7V and the selection box spans from 3H to the right margin at left 1H, as shown in Figure 8-11. (You may need to be in the "Fit in window" view to do this.)

10. Press CTRL-INS to copy the name to the Clipboard.

11. Press SHIFT-INS to copy the name back on the publication.

12. Drag the second copy over to the right page so that it sits on the line at 0.7V and is aligned against the left margin at right 1H, as shown in Figure 8-12.

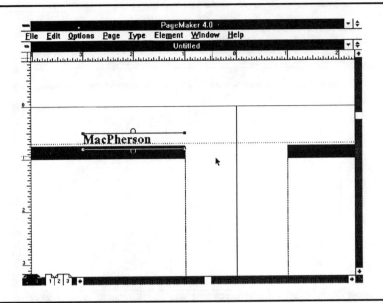

Figure 8-11.   *Company name on the left master page*

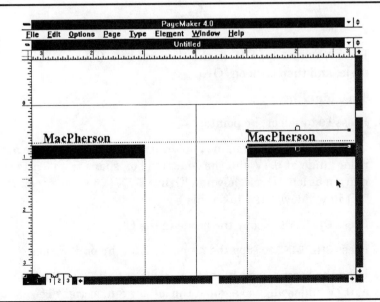

Figure 8-12.   *Company name on both master pages*

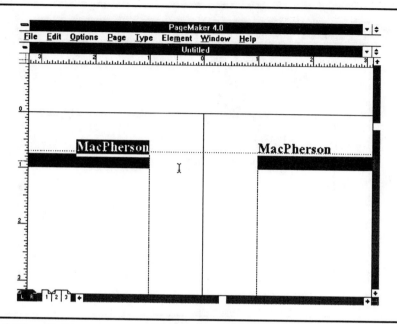

Figure 8-13.   *Right master page with the company name properly aligned*

13. Press SHIFT-F4 to select the text tool.

14. Drag across the company name on the left page to highlight the name.

15. Press CTRL-SHIFT-R to right-align the name.

When both company names are properly aligned, your screen should look like that shown in Figure 8-13.

Placing the Logo   You place the company logo just above the box on the outside of the page, even with the company name as shown in Figure 8-14. Do this with the following instructions:

1. Press F9 to select the pointer.

2. Return to the "Fit in window" view.

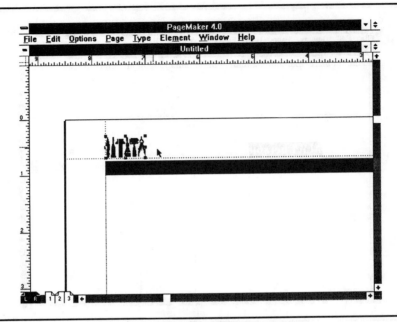

Figure 8-14.   *Logo in final position on the left master page*

3. Place the pointer at left 6H and 1V, and click the secondary mouse button for the "Actual size" view.

4. Drag a vertical ruler guide over to left 7.75H (on the left margin).

5. Press CTRL-D to open the Place dialog box.

6. Open the \WI\PUB directory, and scroll the list box until LOGO.TIF appears. Double-click on it, and the TIFF icon appears.

7. Place the TIFF icon on the left master page at left 7.75H/0.3V and drag it to left 7H/0.7V.

8. Adjust the logo until it is placed as shown in Figure 8-14.

9. Press CTRL-INS to copy the logo to the Clipboard.

10. Click the secondary mouse button for the "Fit in window" view.

11. Press SHIFT-INS to paste the logo back on the publication.

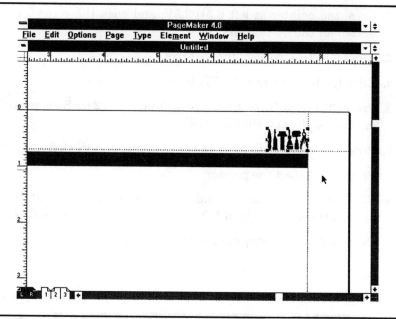

Figure 8-15.   *Logo aligned on the right master page*

12. Drag the second copy over to the upper-right corner of the right page.

13. Place the pointer at right 5.5H/1V, and click the secondary mouse button for the "Actual size" view.

14. Drag a vertical ruler guide over to right 7.75H (the right margin).

15. Drag the logo on the right page so that it sits on the line at 0.7V and is aligned against the right margin at right 7.75H, as shown in Figure 8-15.

Adding the Page Number   When you place a CTRL-SHIFT-3 code on the master pages where you want a page number to appear, PageMaker automatically inserts the correct page number on the regular pages. Do that with the following instructions:

1. Return to the "Fit in window" view.

2. Place the pointer at left 6.5H/9.5V, and click the secondary mouse button for the "Actual size" view.

3. Press SHIFT-F4 to select the text tool.

4. Click the text tool at left 7.7H/10.4V.

5. Press CTRL-T for "Type specs", press TAB, type **12** for Size, select "Bold" for Type style, and click on "OK".

6. Press CTRL-SHIFT-3 to place the page number on the left master page.

7. Press F9 to select the pointer.

8. Click on the page number and drag it so that the top is at 10.3V and against the left margin at left 7.75H, as shown in Figure 8-16.

9. Press CTRL-INS to copy the page number to the Clipboard.

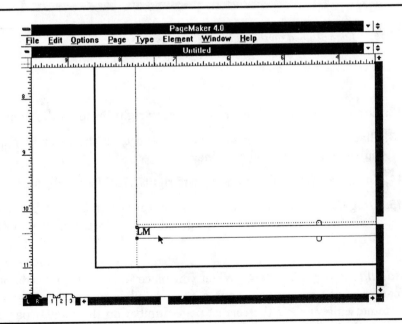

Figure 8-16.   *The page number in the lower-left corner of the left master page*

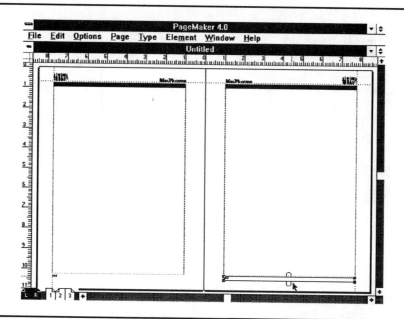

Figure 8-17. *Page number on the right page as it is originally placed*

10. Return to the "Fit in window" view.

11. Press SHIFT-INS to insert a copy of the page number on the page.

12. Drag the second page number to the right master page, below the lower margin, as shown in Figure 8-17.

13. Press SHIFT-F4 to select the text tool.

14. Drag across the page number on the right page to highlight it.

15. Press CTRL-SHIFT-R to right-align the page number on the right page.

16. Place the I-beam at right 6.5H/9.5V, and click the secondary mouse button for the "Actual size" view.

17. Press F9 to select the pointer.

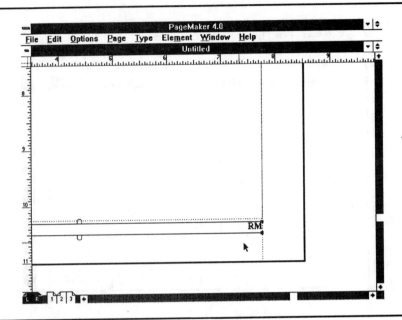

Figure 8-18. *Page number in the lower-right corner of the right master page*

18. Click on the page number and align it so that the top is at 10.3V and the right side is against the margin at right 7.75H, as illustrated in Figure 8-18.

19. Return to the "Fit in Window" view.

Drawing the Lines

Your next step is to add two lines to the left page and three to the right page. This provides two different basic layouts and the opportunity to vary the layout with a little customization. This layout is based on a two-column page. On the left, you have two vertical columns with a line separating them. On the right, the top part of the page is left open across both columns so that a graphic can span the page. The lower part of the page reverts to the two-column approach. It is therefore necessary to have a horizontal line in the middle of the right page as well as a vertical line down the lower

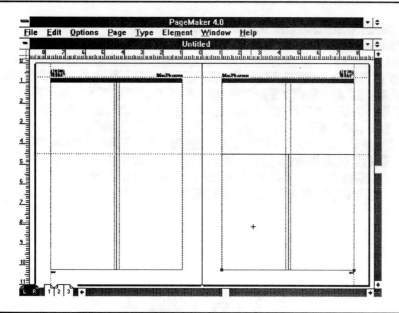

Figure 8-19.   *The Completed master pages*

part of the page. Both pages have a line across the bottom margin. When you have completed the final line, your master pages should look like those shown in Figure 8-19.

The instructions for drawing these lines are as follows:

1. Choose "Column guides..." from the Options menu.

2. Type **2** for the number of columns, press TAB, type **.25** for the space between columns, and press ENTER.

3. Press SHIFT-F3 to select the perpendicular-line tool.

4. Press CTRL-U to turn "Snap to guides" off.

5. Draw a vertical line from left 4.4H/1V down to 10.25V.

6. Drag a horizontal ruler guide down to 4.5V.

7. Draw a vertical line from right 4.4H/4.5V down to 10.25V.

Wholesale Art Supplies

Graphic Arts, Drafting, and Engineering

1327 Park Avenue

Emeryville, CA 94608

(415) 428-9011

Figure 8-20.   *Final printout of the title page*

8. Press CTRL-U to turn "Snap to guides" back on.

9. Draw a horizontal line from right 1H/4.5V over to right 7.75H.

10. Draw a horizontal line from left 7.75H/10.25V over to left 1H.

11. Draw a horizontal line from right 1H/10.25V over to right 7.75H. Your master pages should look like those shown in Figure 8-19.

12. Press CTRL-S to open the Save as dialog box.

13. Type **catalog** for the filename, and press ENTER to complete saving the file.

This would be a good time for a break. If you leave PageMaker, remember to check the defaults on reentering.

Building the Title Page

The title page is composed of three parts: the graphic title from Micrografx Designer, the company logo from the scanner, and a typed address (as shown in Figure 8-20). Most of the work is in preparing the graphics, so assembling it is simple and quick.

Bringing in the Graphic
From PC Paintbrush

First, bring in the company name graphic from Designer, and size it as shown in Figure 8-21.

Follow these instructions to place the company name:

1. Click the page 1 icon.

2. Choose "Display master items" from the Page menu in order to turn the options off.

3. Choose "Column guides..." from the Options menu, specify 1 column, and press ENTER to get rid of the column guides.

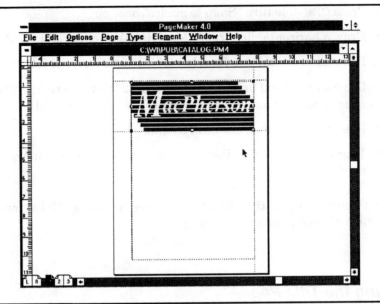

Figure 8-21. *Screen with the company title in place*

4. With the pointer tool (F9), move the horizontal ruler guide from 4.5V to 3.4V.

5. Press CTRL-D for the "Place" option.

6. When the Place dialog box is displayed, choose the filename COVER.WMF. You may have to use the horizontal scroll bar to find it.

7. Place the icon in the upper-left corner at right 1H/0.75V and drag it to right 7.75H/3.4V.

Your screen should look like that shown in Figure 8-21.

Placing the Company Logo

Next place the company logo.

1. Drag two horizontal ruler guides to 4.7V and 6.5V.

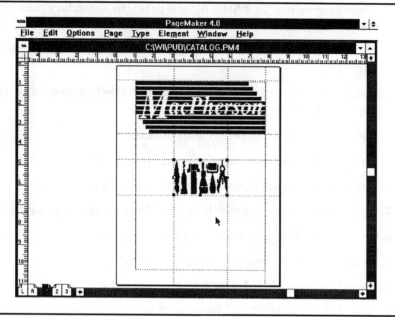

Figure 8-22. *Title page with logo placed*

2. Drag two vertical ruler guides to 3H and 5.8H.

3. Press CTRL-D for the "Place" option.

4. When the Place dialog box is displayed, click on the filename LOGO.TIF. You may have to use the horizontal scroll bar to find it.

5. Place the TIFF icon at 3H/4.7V and drag the selection box to 5.75H/6.5V.

6. Adjust the logo's position on the page until it looks like Figure 8-22.

Next, you type in the address.

Entering the Company Address

The last step in creating the title page is to enter the company address. You use the text tool and type in several lines in varying type sizes.
   Follow these instructions to enter the address:

1. Place your pointer at 4.5H/8.5V and press the secondary mouse button for an "Actual size" view.

2. Select the text tool (SHIFT-F4) and click the main mouse button at 4H/8.5V.

3. Press CTRL-T for the Type specifications dialog box, press TAB, type **14** for Size, and click on "OK".

4. Press CTRL-SHIFT-C to center the address.

5. Type **Wholesale Art Supplies** and press ENTER.

6. Press F3 for the next smaller type size (12 points).

7. Type **Graphic Arts, Drafting, and Engineering** and press ENTER.

8. Press F3 for the next smaller type size (11 points).

9. Type **1327 Park Avenue** and press ENTER.

10. Type **Emeryville, CA 94608** and press ENTER.

11. Type **(415) 428-9011** and press ENTER.

Your screen should look like that shown in Figure 8-23.

12. Return to the "Fit in window" view.

13. Press CTRL-S to save the catalog.

You have now completed the title page. The printed version of it can be seen in Figure 8-20. Now you can create the detail catalog pages.

Constructing the Detail Catalog Pages

A catalog would normally have many detail pages. To see how to build a catalog, you build two of the detail pages here. These detail pages, pages 2 and 3 of your publication, mirror the master pages; that is, all the elements of the master pages remain unchanged.

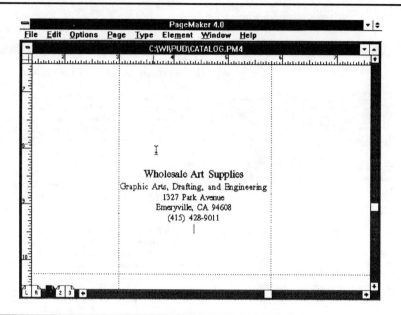

Figure 8-23.   *The screen image with address*

Assembling Page 2

You place three items on page 2, as shown in Figure 8-24: the art for the products being described, the text of the description, and the title of the current section of the catalog. The following paragraphs describe how each item is built.

Placing the Art   Earlier you scanned the art for page 2 and then saved it in a file called PAGE2.TIF. Your task here is to place and size that art so that it fits the layout for page 2. The instructions to do that are as follows:

1. Press F9 to select the pointer.

2. Click on the page 2 icon.

3. From the Options menu, verify that "Snap to guides" is on.

MacPherson

Watercolor Paint Sets

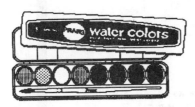

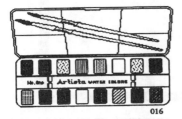

016

08

10308

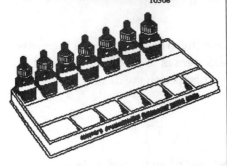

Prang Watercolor Sets (American Crayon)
Oval-8 Set contains 8 oval semi-moist half pan colors
with No. 7 brush. No. 16 Set contains 16 semi-moist
half pan colors, a No. 1 and 4 brush. Oval 16 Set
contains the same colors and brushes as No. 16 Set,
except with oval half pans. No. 8 Set contains 8 semi-
moist half pan colors with No. 7 brush. (Qty = Each)

Order No.	Item
AC16	Prang Watercolor Set
AC16-OVL	Prang Watercolor Set
AC8	Prang Watercolor Set
AC8-OVL	Prang Watercolor Set

Artista Watercolor Sets (Binney & Smith)
No. 080 set contains 8 oval half pans and a No. 7 brush.
No. 08 contains 8 half pans and a No. 7 brush. No. 016
contains 16 half pans and a No. 7 brush. (Qty = Each)

Order No.	Item
BS016	W/C Half Pan Set
BS08	W/C Half Pan Set
BS080	W/C Oval Pan Set

Gouache Sets (Caran D'Ache)
Highly concentrated light-resistant watercolors for
opaque painting. The No. 10308 Set contains 7 pans of
assorted colors and one tube of white. (Qty = Each)

Order No.	Item
CD10308	Pan Set 8 Colors with Brush
CD20313	Tube Set 13 Colors with Brush

Licolette Gouache Sets (Loew-Cornell)
Set 500-12 contains 10 opaque colors, white, and black.
Set 500-24 contains 22 opaque colors, white, and black.
(Qty = Each)

Order No.	Item
LK500-12	Licolette Gouache Set/12 Colors
LK500-24	Licolette Gouache Set/24 Colors

Radiant Concentrated Sets (Dr. Ph. Martin)
Each set is comprised of 14 colors to cover the entire
range as listed in groups, corresponding to the open-
stock radiant colors. DRA Set is all "A" colors. DRB
Set is all "B" colors. DRC Set is all "C" colors.
DRDST is all "D" colors. 1/2 oz. bottle size. (Qty =
Each)

Order No.	Item
DRA	Radiant CNC Set/14 All A
DRB	Radiant CNC Set/14 All B
DRC	Radiant CNC Set/14 All C
DRDST	Radiant CNC Set/14 All D

2

Figure 8-24. *Final page 2 printout*

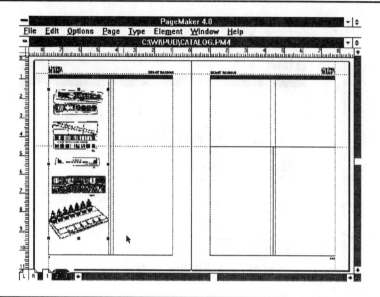

Figure 8-25. *Art in place on page 2*

4. Press CTRL-D to open the Place dialog box.

5. Scroll the list box until PAGE2.TIF appears. Double-click on PAGE2.TIF, and the TIFF icon appears.

6. Place the TIFF icon on page 2 at left 7.75H (left margin)/1.5V and drag it to left 4.5H (right column guide)/9.5V.

Your screen should look like that shown in Figure 8-25.

7. Place the pointer at left 6.5H/2.5V and click the secondary mouse button for the "Actual size" view.

8. Look at the placement of the art and compare it to Figure 8-26. Adjust it as necessary by using the pointer tool to drag the graphic block up or down on the page.

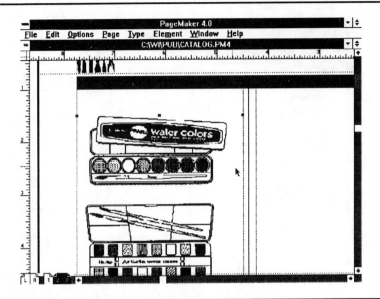

Figure 8-26.   *Detail of art on page 2*

Adding the Text   The text for both pages 2 and 3 was created using Microsoft Word and was saved in a file named CATALOG.DOC. You place the first part of that file here and then place the balance on page 3. The instructions to place the text on page 2 are as follows:

1. Return to the "Fit in window" view.

2. Drag a horizontal ruler guide down to 1.2V.

3. Press CTRL-D to open the Place dialog box.

4. Double-click on CATALOG.DOC., and the text icon appears.

5. Place the text icon on page 2 at left 4.25H/1.2V, and click the main mouse button.

6. Place the pointer at left 4.2H/2.5V, and click the secondary mouse button for the "Actual size" view.

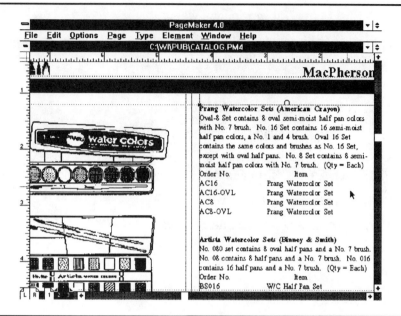

Figure 8-27. *Upper part of text on page 2*

7. If the upper part of your text is not aligned as shown in Figure 8-27, adjust it as necessary by dragging it with the pointer.

8. Use the vertical scroll bar to position the screen so that you can see the lower part of the text on page 2. Your screen should look like that shown in Figure 8-28.

9. If the lower part of your text is not aligned as shown in Figure 8-28, adjust it as necessary. Drag the handle down so that the fourth item under "Order No." (DRDST) shows on the screen.

Inserting the Title Your final task on page 2 is to add the section name in the box at the top of the page. You type the name in the box after setting the font to bold 12-point Times reverse type, and then you center it in all four directions. The instructions for this are as follows:

1. Return to the "Fit in window" view.

2. Place the pointer at left 4.4H/2V and click the secondary mouse button for the "Actual size" view.

3. Press SHIFT-F4 to select the text tool.

4. Click the text tool at left 4.4H/0.9V.

5. Press CTRL-T to open the Type specifications dialog box.

6. Press TAB, type **12** for Size, and click on "Bold", "Reverse", and "OK". Also, click on "OK" in answer to the question "Set color to paper?".

7. Type **Watercolor Paint Sets**.

8. Press CTRL-SHIFT-C to center the section name.

The text moves to the right, seemingly off center. You adjust this shortly.

9. Press F9 to select the pointer.

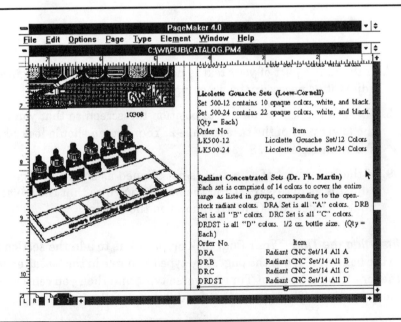

Figure 8-28. *Page 2 catalog items after tabs have been set*

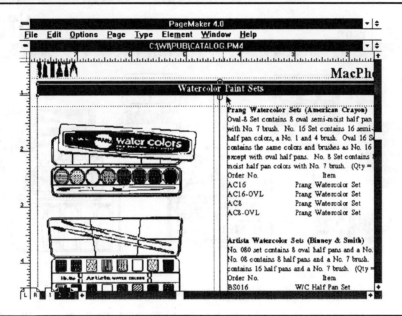

Figure 8-29.   *Text in the lower part of page 2*

10. Click on the section name to form the selection box around it.

11. With the pointer, center the section name both horizontally and vertically in the box, as shown in Figure 8-29.

12. Press CTRL-INS to copy the section name for use on page 3.

13. Press CTRL-S to save the catalog.

You have now completed page 2. When it is printed it should look like Figure 8-24.

Assembling Page 3

Page 3 is shown in Figure 8-30. The steps to assemble it are very similar to those for page 2, except that you do them in a different order. Because the section name is on the Clipboard, you place it first before it gets written

MacPherson

Watercolor Paint Sets

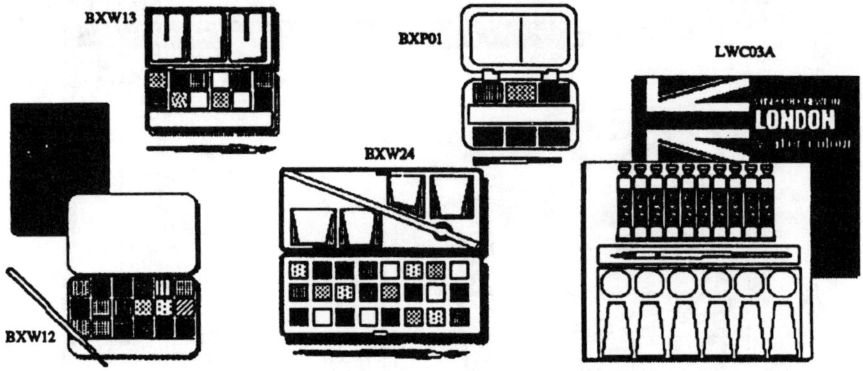

BXW13

BXP01

LWC03A

LONDON

BXW24

BXW12

The Bijou No. 3 (Winsor & Newton)
The ideal companion for the traveling watercolorist.
Made of strong die-cast metal finished in black enamel
and packed in an attractive carrying case. Contains 18
semi-moist pans of Artists' Water Color and a sable
brush in a metal holder with protective cap. Size 2" x
5". (Qty = Each)

Order No.	Item
WNBXW12	No. 3 Bijou

The Bijou No. 2 (Winsor & Newton)
Same as Bijou No. 3, but contains 12 colors. Size 2" x
3-1/4". (Qty = Each)

Order No.	Item
WNBXW11	No. 2 Bijou

Sketchers Pocket Box (Winsor & Newton)
A compact white plastic box containing 12 square pans
of transparent watercolor and a pocket sable brush with a
protective cap. Size 4" x 2" x 1/2". (Qty = Each)

Order No.	Item
WNBXW13	W/C Pocket Box

Sketchers Box #24 (Winsor & Newton)
A black plastic box containing 24 square pans of
economical watercolor and a Series 33 sable brush.
Refill pans not available. Size 8-1/2" x 4-1/2" x 1/4".
(Qty = Each)

Order No.	Item
WNBXW24	W/C Set - 24 Colors

London Water Color Set #3A (Winsor & Newton)
Contains 10 London Water Colors in 7.5 ml. tubes.
Includes a watercolor brush, a six well/six slant tile
plastic palette, color chart and painting techniques
leaflet. (Qty = Each)

Order No.	Item
WNBXLW03A	London W/C Set #3A

London Water Color Set #4 (Winsor & Newton)
Contains 12 London Water colors in 7.5 ml. tubes in an
aluminum box with white enameled palette/lid, two
water color brushes, a color chart and a painting techniques leaflet. (Qty = Each)

Order No.	Item
WNBXLW04	London W/C Set #4

Page Water Color Sets (Winsor & Newton)
This range represents excellent value in inexpensive
water color sets for young artists. Colorfully designed
boxes make these sets ideal as gifts. Each set comes
with a brush and all are shrink-wrapped for protection
except #01 (Qty = Each)

Order No.	Item
WNBXP01	6 Pan Water Color Set
WNBXP05	12 Pan Water Color Set
WNBXP10	20 Pan Water Color Set
WNBXP15	30 Pan Water Color Set
WNBXP20	40 Pan Water Color Set
WNBXP25	50 Pan Water Color Set
WNBXP30	60 Pan Water Color Set
WNBXP35	78 Pan Water Color Set

3

Figure 8-30. *Final printout of page 3*

over. Also, having done page 2, you will find page 3 a little easier. Use the following instructions to assemble page 3:

1. Return to the "Fit in window" view.

2. Press SHIFT-INS to paste the section name back onto the page.

3. Drag the section name into the box at the top of the right page.

4. Place the pointer at right 4.4H/2V, and click the secondary mouse button for the "Actual size" view.

5. Position the section name so that it is centered both vertically and horizontally in the box, as shown in Figure 8-31.

6. Return to the "Fit in window" view.

7. Click on the text on page 2, and then click on the loop in the handle at the bottom of the page. A text icon appears.

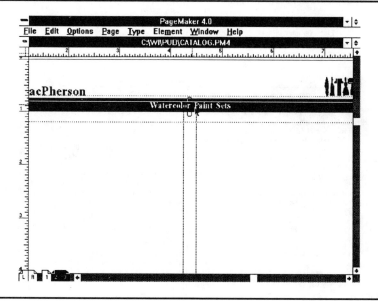

Figure 8-31. *Section name centered on page 3*

8. Place the text icon at right 1H/4.2V (above the line at 4.5V) and click the main mouse button.

9. Click on the loop in the handle at the bottom of the page.

10. Place the text icon at right 4.5H/4.4V and click the main mouse button.

11. Drag a horizontal ruler guide down to 4.7V.

12. Place the pointer at right 4.4H/6V, and click the secondary mouse button for the "Actual size" view.

13. Align both columns of text on page 3 so that the top line of the text is sitting on the new horizontal ruler guide at 4.7V, as illustrated in Figure 8-32.

14. Return to the "Fit in window" view.

15. Drag a horizontal ruler guide down to 4.2V.

16. Press CTRL-D to open the Place dialog box.

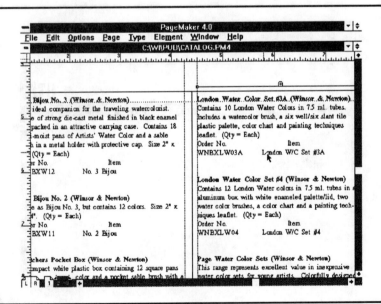

Figure 8-32.   *Text properly aligned on page 3*

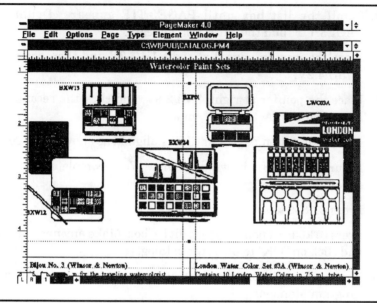

Figure 8-33.   *Art properly aligned on page 3*

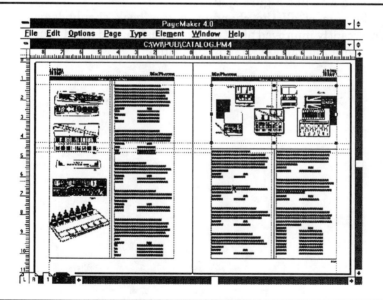

Figure 8-34.   *Completed pages 2 and 3*

17. Scroll the list box until PAGE3.TIF appears. Double-click on PAGE3.TIF, and the TIFF icon appears.

18. Place the icon on page 3 at right 1H/1.2V and then drag it to right 7.75H/4.2V.

19. Place the pointer at right 4.4H/2.8V, and click the secondary mouse button for the "Actual size" view.

20. Adjust the art on page 3 until it is aligned as shown in Figure 8-33.

21. Return to the "Fit in window" view. Your completed pages 2 and 3 should look like Figure 8-34.

22. Press CTRL-S to save the catalog.

23. Press CTRL-P to open the Print dialog box. Make any necessary changes and click on "OK" to print the catalog.

24. Choose "Close" from the Control menus of both PageMaker and the Program Manager.

This completes the construction of the sample catalog. Your printed page 3 should look like Figure 8-30.

The sum of all the chapters in this book should leave you with a significantly improved ability to plan, design, and build your own publications with PageMaker. Happy publishing!

IV Appendixes

A   INSTALLING WINDOWS AND PAGEMAKER

Windows and PageMaker can operate with many combinations of computers, disks, displays, and printers. Providing installation instructions would be a complex process were it not for the installation programs that come with both Windows and PageMaker. These programs do most of the work for you; you have only to determine what equipment you have and then run these programs, answering the questions they ask.

This appendix describes what equipment you need, how to determine what equipment you have, and how to start and use both the Windows and PageMaker installation programs. In addition, it discusses how you prepare to store the data you create with PageMaker, how to copy the Windows and PageMaker disks, and how to leave Windows and PageMaker.

This appendix is written for Windows 3 and PageMaker 4. While most of what is said here also applies to other versions of either product, you need to be on the lookout for differences.

What Equipment Do You Need?

Windows and PageMaker run on IBM PC/AT or PS/2 or compatible computers with an Intel 80286, 80386, or 80486 microprocessor. Windows 3 can run in three modes, and each mode has unique hardware requirements. You should use the most capable mode you can with the hardware you have available. The three modes and their requirements are as follows:

■ *386 enhanced mode* requires an Intel 80386 or higher processor and 2MB (megabyte, or millions of characters) or more of memory: 640KB (kilobyte, or thousands of characters) of *conventional memory,* and at least 1024KB of *extended memory* (see the discussion on memory later in this appendix). Windows 386 enhanced mode makes use of the 80386's virtual memory capability to use the disk as additional memory. Also, 386 enhanced mode allows you to run multiple non-Windows applications at one time (called *multitasking*), as well as multitask Windows applications. The most capable of the operating modes, 386 enhanced mode is recommended if possible.

■ *Standard mode* requires an Intel 80286 or higher processor and 1MB or more of memory: 640KB of conventional memory and at least 256KB of extended memory. Standard mode allows you to use extended memory and switch among non-Windows applications as well as multitask Windows applications. Standard mode is the normal operating mode.

■ *Real mode* requires an Intel 8086, 8088, or higher processor and 640KB of conventional memory. Real mode allows you to use the least amount of memory and provides the most compatibility with previous versions of Windows.

PageMaker requires more than the minimum hardware required for standard mode, so it is recommended that standard mode be the minimum operating environment.

Other system requirements for Windows and PageMaker are:

Memory   While Windows can run in either 1 or 2MB, Page-Maker requires at least 2MB and realistically should have 3 or 4MB. The more memory you have, the better PageMaker runs.

Disk   Windows and PageMaker require a hard disk and a floppy disk. You can use any kind of floppy disk— 5 1/4- or 3 1/2-inch, 360KB to 1.44MB (although if you have only 360KB floppies, you must order a special set of PageMaker installation disks for an additional charge). For Windows 3 you need at least 6MB of free hard-disk space; for PageMaker you need at least 4MB additional space and 6MB if you install all PageMaker options. You also should leave 2MB of disk space to swap sections of memory. To be comfortable you should have 15MB for Windows and Page-Maker.

Display

Windows and PageMaker require a graphics display and display adapter. It is recommended that you use an 8514/A, VGA, or Hercules adapter and display over EGA due to their higher resolution. Many other displays are supported by Windows and PageMaker.

Printer

While a printer is not necessary for Windows and PageMaker to run, you cannot print without one. Windows and PageMaker can use almost any printer. To get the most benefit from PageMaker, you should have either a PostScript printer such as an Apple LaserWriter II or an HP LaserJet II compatible printer with at least 1MB of memory.

Operating System

Windows 3 and PageMaker 4 require MS DOS or PC DOS versions 3.1 and above.

Mouse

A mouse is required for PageMaker and is very strongly recommended for Windows. You can use either a Microsoft mouse or any compatible pointing device.

Network

Windows and PageMaker run on the major local area networks including 3Com 3+ and EtherSeries, AT&T Starlan, IBM PC Network, IBM Token Ring Network, Novell NetWare, and Ungermann-Bass/One. It is strongly recommended, though, that each node have its own PageMaker application files, because only one node can use PageMaker application files stored on a server, and the speed of PageMaker on a server is unacceptable.

Math Coprocessor

A math coprocessor speeds up some functions in PageMaker, but it is not required. The type of coprocessor you need depends on the type and speed of processor you have: a 20 MHZ 80386 processor requires a 20 MHZ 80387 coprocessor, a 12 MHZ 80286 processor requires a 12 MHZ 80287 coprocessor, and so on.

Other   To use the Windows communications software, you need a Hayes-compatible modem.

What Equipment Do You Have?

When you install Windows and PageMaker, you must tell the installation programs which of your hard disk drives you want to install Windows and PageMaker on and what kind of display and printer you have, and you must answer several related questions. You must determine the answers to these questions, shown on Table A-1, before running the Setup program.

If you can answer the questions in Table A-1 without further information, do so and skip to "Preparing to Store Data." If you need further information, read the following sections. If you still cannot fill in the blanks, you may need to talk to the dealer from whom you purchased your computer, or call Microsoft Product Support (206-454-2030) or Aldus Technical Support (206-628-2320).

As you install Windows and PageMaker, suggested answers are provided by the installation programs for many of the questions. If you think you know the answers, you might try the installation and see if the installation programs agree with you. The very worst that can happen is that Windows and PageMaker will not run and you will have to redo the installation.

Memory

Windows and PageMaker can use three kinds of memory: conventional memory, extended memory, and expanded memory.

■ *Conventional memory,* which is in all machines, is the first 640KB of memory and is sometimes called *base memory.* DOS permanently uses some of this memory as do most memory-resident utilities you load. All applications, including Windows, also need some conventional memory.

1. How much memory do you have by type:
   Conventional memory: _____
   Extended memory: _____
   Expanded memory: _____
2. On which disk drive and directory will Windows be installed? _____
3. On which disk drive and directory will PageMaker be installed? _____
4. What kind of computer and processor are you using? _____
5. What is the layout of your keyboard (U.S. or foreign)? _____
6. What kind of display adapter do you have? _____
7. What kind of printer do you have? _____
8. To which computer port is your printer attached? _____
9. What fonts are available for your printer? _____
10. In which country are you using Windows and PageMaker? _____
11. What version of DOS are you using? _____
12. What kind of network are you connected to? _____
13. What kind of mouse are you using? _____
14. Do you know the contents of your CONFIG.SYS? _____
15. Do you know the contents of your AUTOEXEC.BAT? _____

Table A-1. *Microsoft Windows 3 and PageMaker 4 Installation Questions*

■ *Extended memory* is available on 80286, 80386, and 80486 computers. All memory beyond 640KB can be extended memory on these computers. An extended memory manager, such as Windows HIMEM.SYS, is needed to manage extended memory so two programs do not try to use the same extended memory at the same time. Some applications, such as standard and 386 enhanced mode Windows, can use extended memory directly with equal ease and speed as it uses conventional memory.

■ *Expanded memory* is available on most computers through an expansion memory board or, in some cases, on the motherboard. Memory beyond 640KB can be expanded memory, but an expanded memory manager is required. Expanded memory is indirectly accessed through a small amount of memory between 640KB and 1MB. Due to this and a heavy reliance on its management software, expanded memory is slower and more cumbersome to use than extended memory. There are several versions of expanded memory. The most recent is Lotus-Intel-Microsoft Expanded Memory Specifications (LIM EMS) 4.0.

You need to determine how much of each type of memory you have. This is normally done with a utility program that comes with your memory expansion board or with your computer. For Windows 3 and PageMaker, you should configure your memory to all extended memory beyond 640KB, or ask your dealer to do it. If you need expanded memory for another program, use the least possible amount, and configure the rest as extended memory. You should have at least 2MB extended memory to run Page-Maker.

Disk Drives

Windows and PageMaker require a hard disk to store your programs and data. If you have only one hard disk drive, it is your logical choice. If you have multiple hard disk drives, you should choose the one with the most room on it. The easiest way to find out how much space is left on your hard disk is to type **dir**. You can change disk drives by typing the drive letter followed by a colon (**c:**, for example). To comfortably run Windows and PageMaker, you need 12MB of disk space and you should have at least 2MB to store data files. All of this space can be either in one disk drive or spread over two or more. From a space-management standpoint it is probably easier if it is in one drive, although there might be some slight gain in efficiency if you place the programs on one drive and the data on another.

Disk Directories

Since a hard disk can store so much information, they should be divided into *directories*. Directories are artificial areas of unspecified size that contain files or subdirectories. With directories and subdirectories you can create a tree structure consisting of several levels. The highest level is called the *root directory*. Every hard disk has a root directory. Figure A-1 shows several of the many directory/subdirectory schemes that you can use to contain your Windows programs, PageMaker programs, and PageMaker data. The directory scheme used in this book is labeled Scheme A in Figure A-1. It is not necessary to use this scheme; just remember to change the

Directory Scheme A

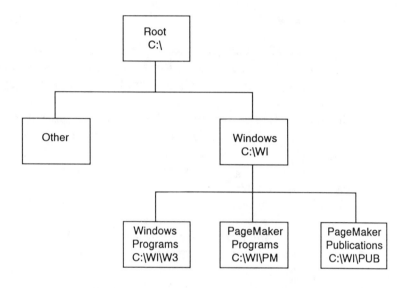

Directory Scheme B

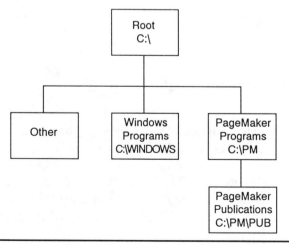

Figure A-1.   *Directory schemes*

instructions in this book for storing data if you elect to use some other scheme.

Displays

The choice of display is really a choice based on your *display adapter*—the card or module in your computer to which your display is connected. The installation program tries to determine what your display adapter is and lists its name as an option. You can accept that option or you can change to another. It is very likely that the display adapter found by the installation program is the correct one for your computer. Unless you are very certain you want to use a different display adapter, accept the option highlighted by the installation program; you can always come back and change it later.

You have four primary choices and a number of variations for display adapters. The four primary choices are a color graphics adapter (CGA), Hercules or monochrome graphics adapter (MGA), enhanced graphics adapter (EGA), and video graphics array (VGA). Most computers have a display adapter compatible with one of these. If the option highlighted by the installation program does not work, you cannot find a recognizable alternative in the list of options presented by the installation program, and none of the primary choices seems to work, look at the manuals that came with your computer. If you still cannot determine which adapter is right for your computer, contact either your computer dealer or Microsoft Customer Support.

Printers

The installation program for Windows presents over 150 printer models from which you can choose. With so many choices it is very likely that you can find your printer on the list. If you cannot find your printer, check your printer's manual to see if it emulates another printer. Some good bets are Apple LaserWriter II, HP LaserJet Plus, IBM Graphics Printer, or IBM Proprinter. If you cannot find a printer your printer emulates, select either "Generic/Text Only" or "Unlisted Printer" to use temporarily, and contact

Microsoft. They can probably send you a disk with the program or a driver for your printer.

You need to tell Windows to which port on your computer your printer is connected. There are two kinds of ports, serial and parallel, each with a unique type of cable. If you have a choice, use parallel; it is both faster and simpler. Parallel ports are labeled LPT1, LPT2, and LPT3. Serial ports are labeled COM1 through COM4. If you do not know which port to use, first try LPT1, then COM1, LPT2, and finally COM2. One of these four ports probably is the one you need.

Changing CONFIG.SYS

CONFIG.SYS is a file that, if present, is automatically referenced when you start your computer. It contains a series of parameters that tell DOS how to structure itself and what utility programs to load.

Of special importance to Windows are two parameters in CONFIG.SYS that tell the operating system how many files can be open at any one time and how many buffers to set up to hold file data. Windows and PageMaker require a minimum of 20 files and recommend 30 files be open at once, and you must have 10 or 20 buffers. Both files and buffers take up conventional memory (each file takes 48 bytes and each buffer 528 bytes). You therefore must consider how many to specify.

In addition to the file and buffer parameters, you must load one or more Windows utility programs with the CONFIG.SYS file. In all cases you should load the disk-caching utility SMARTDRV.SYS, which significantly speeds up getting information from the disk. Also, if you use SMARTDRV.SYS you can set your buffers to 10 and save conventional memory. If you are using an 80286 or above and have more than 640KB of memory, you need the extended memory manager HIMEM.SYS. If you need to run a program in expanded memory, you can use the utility program EMM386.SYS to convert extended memory into expanded memory on 80386 computers. If you are using an EGA display adapter and want to run a non-Windows application with Windows in real or standard mode, you should load the EGA.SYS utility.

You must have a CONFIG.SYS file and it should contain the following statements (where *path*\ is the path to your Windows directory— \WI\W3\ in this book).

FILES=30 (or some number greater than 20)

BUFFERS=10 (or 20 without SMARTDRV.SYS)

DEVICE=*path*\\HIMEM.SYS (if you have extended memory)

DEVICE=*path*\\SMARTDRV.SYS (must come after HIMEM.SYS)

SMARTDRV.SYS has two parameters after it that specify the normal cache size and the minimum cache size. For example, a CONFIG.SYS statement might be

DEVICE=SMARTDRV.SYS 1024 256

where the normal cache size is 1024 and the minimum cache size is 256. When Windows starts in standard or 386 enhanced mode and SMARTDRV.SYS is using extended memory, it reduces SMARTDRV.SYS to the minimum value.

When you run Windows Setup to install Windows, you are asked if you want Setup to check and add to or correct your CONFIG.SYS file. If you answer yes, all the above statements are added or adjusted as necessary to produce the correct CONFIG.SYS file for your system.

Changing AUTOEXEC.BAT

AUTOEXEC.BAT is a special *batch file* that is run immediately after the CONFIG.SYS file whenever you start your computer. A batch file contains a series of normal DOS commands that are run when you execute the file that contains them. You normally use an AUTOEXEC.BAT file to establish the default path with a DOS PATH command, to configure the DOS prompt with a PROMPT command, and to run various memory-resident or other programs that you want to run when you start your system.

For Windows and PageMaker you should include both the Windows and PageMaker directories in your PATH statement, and if you plan to do most of your work under Windows, you may want to load Windows from your AUTOEXEC.BAT file. Windows and PageMaker occasionally write a temporary file that is later erased. Sometimes, due to a power interruption or similar incident, these files do not get erased. It is, therefore, a good idea to place these temporary files in their own directory. You can do that with the AUTOEXEC.BAT file.

Your AUTOEXEC.BAT file might contain the following statements (without the parenthetical comments):

PROMPT PG (makes your DOS prompt C:\>)

Path C:\WI\W3; C:\WI\PM; C:\DOS (sets your default path)

SET TEMP=C:\TEMP

WIN (loads Windows)

These statements assume that Windows is in the C:\WI\W3 directory, PageMaker is in the C:\WI\PM directory, DOS is in the C:\DOS directory, and you have created a directory C:\TEMP to store temporary files.

The Windows Setup program asks you if you want to modify your AUTOEXEC.BAT file. If you answer yes, your Windows directory is added to your path statement, and WIN is added to the end of AUTOEXEC.BAT to load Windows.

Preparing to Store Data

When you use PageMaker, you create things that you want to come back and use again at a later time. To preserve this data you store it in files on a disk. The files are preserved when you turn the computer off. The programs that comprise Windows and PageMaker are also stored in files on a disk.

With a hard-disk-based system, you also have a floppy disk drive. Therefore, you can store the data on either floppy or hard disks. From the standpoint of both speed and ease of use, it is best to store data and programs on your hard disk. Since hard disks store so much information, they should be divided into directories, which are arbitrarily named areas that you establish for particular purposes. To prepare to store the data you create with PageMaker, you should create one or more directories.

Creating Directories
On a Hard Disk

To store the program files on a hard disk, the Windows and PageMaker installation programs automatically create directories for you or use directories you create or already have. The default name for the Windows directory is \WINDOWS, and for PageMaker it is \PM4, but you can name them anything you like and still use the installation program to create them.

If you want to use existing Windows and PageMaker directories, you can do so without concern. If you want to create your own directories to hold the Windows and PageMaker program files, use the following instructions. They show how to create the directories in Scheme A of Figure A-1 that are used in this book. Your computer should be turned on and you should be at an operating system prompt such as C> or C:\>.

1. Type **cd** and press ENTER to make sure you are in the root directory.

2. Type **md\wi** and press ENTER to create a directory named WI. (If you want to create a directory with a name different than WI, replace WI with the name you want to use in this and following instructions.)

3. Type **cd\wi** and press ENTER to change to the new WI directory.

4. Type **md w3**, press ENTER, type **md pm**, press ENTER, type **md pub**, and press ENTER to create three subdirectories under the \WI directory to hold Windows and PageMaker programs and the PageMaker publication files you create in this book.

If you want to use a scheme or name your directories something other than that shown in Scheme A, replace Scheme A and the names with the scheme and names you want to use. A directory name can be from one to eight characters long and can include all the letters, numbers, and special characters on your keyboard *except* the following:

" / \ [ ] : | > + = ; , * ?

You may want to create one or two other directories to hold other data files. To do so use separate data directories, rather than using the Windows or PageMaker program directories, for two reasons. First, when you get an update to Windows or PageMaker you remove the old program files and replace them with new ones. The easiest way to do this is to delete the entire contents of the directory. If there are data files you want to keep, you can't delete the entire contents of the directory. Second, if you want to do some file maintenance with DOS, the number of program files make looking for data files more difficult than if they had their own directory.

5. Type **md**, enter the directory name you want to use, and press ENTER for each directory you want to create. For example, type **md data** and press ENTER to create a sudirectory named DATA under the \WI directory.

You are going to want to create a directory to hold temporary files created by PageMaker. Do that with these instructions:

6. Type **cd** to return to the root directory.

7. Type **md\temp** to create a new directory named TEMP under the root directory.

Copying Your Disks

To protect the original floppy disks that contain the Windows and Page-Maker programs from being destroyed, you need to make a copy or *backup* of these disks before installing the programs (the Microsoft and Aldus licenses allow you to make one copy for this and only this purpose). The number of disks you have depends on whether you are using 5 1/4-inch or 3 1/2-inch disks. You need to make a copy of each of them, so you need the same number of new or reusable disks to use for the copy as there are original disks.

You can copy floppy disks in several ways. Since you need only a single floppy drive to run Windows and PageMaker, the following instructions use one floppy drive to copy the original disks. You can use a different method of copying if you prefer.

Caution The DISKCOPY command used here permanently removes *all* information on the disk. When reusing a disk, make sure you do not want any information that may be on it.

1. Count the number of disks that came with both Windows and Page-Maker and note their type: 5 1/4-inch 360KB, 5 1/4-inch 1.2MB, 3 1/2-inch 720KB, or 3 1/2-inch 1.44MB; 360 and 720KB disks are labeled DSDD (double-sided, double-density) and the 1.2 and 1.44MB disks are labeled DSHD (double-sided, high-density). Obtain and have handy that same number and type of new or reusable disks. Remember, on reusable disks you must be willing to get rid of any information on them.

2. If necessary, turn on your computer. You should have already installed DOS on your hard drive and have a basic understanding of entering commands from your keyboard, of the size capacity of your disk drives, and of how they are labeled (A, B, C, and so on).

3. You should be at the DOS prompt (for example C> or C:\>) and in the root directory. If you have been using your computer and/or do not know which directory you are in, type **cd** to return to the root directory.

4. Insert the first PageMaker or Windows disk to be copied in the floppy disk drive that is the same size as the disk that came with Windows and PageMaker (3 1/2- or 5 1/4-inch). It is assumed for the remainder of this appendix that this is drive A. If you are using a different drive, replace A (a, a:, or A:) with your drive letter in the instructions that follow.

5. At the DOS prompt, type **diskcopy a: a:** and press ENTER. The message "Insert SOURCE diskette in drive A:" appears. The SOURCE disk is the PageMaker or Windows disk being copied. Since it is already in the drive, press ENTER to confirm it.

6. When you see the message "Insert TARGET diskette in drive A:," insert the first new or reusable disk to which you wish to copy. If the disk is a new, unformatted disk, you see a message "Formatting while copying" telling you that the disk is also being formatted.

7. Soon you again see "Insert SOURCE diskette in drive A:." You must remove the first new or reusable disk and reinsert the first PageMaker or Windows disk. Then you see "Insert TARGET diskette in drive A:" telling you to remove the first PageMaker or Windows disk and reinsert the first new or reusable disk. This step is repeated a couple of times.

Remember that SOURCE refers to the disk *from* which you are copying and is the original PageMaker or Windows disk, and TARGET refers to the disk *to* which you are copying and is the new or reusable disk that holds the backup copy. The disk copy process takes several passes, so you must insert and remove each of the disks several times.

8. After several passes, you get a message "Copy another diskette (Y/N)?." Type **y** and press ENTER.

9. Once again you see the message "Insert SOURCE diskette in drive A:." Remove the disk from drive A that is now the copy of the first PageMaker or Windows disk, label it similar to the original disk, insert the second PageMaker or Windows original disk in drive A, and press ENTER.

10. Repeat steps 6 through 9 until you have copied all of the disks that came with your Windows and PageMaker packages.

11. When you have copied the necessary number of disks, type **n** in response to "Copy another diskette (Y/N)?," and press ENTER. You return to the DOS prompt. Remove the last copy disk from drive A.

When you have completed copying all disks, protect the new disks to prevent them from being written on or infected with a virus. To protect a 3 1/2-inch floppy disk, first turn it on its back so you can see the metal hub in the center. Then, with the metal end away from you, slide the small black plastic rectangle in the lower-right corner toward you or toward the outer edge of the disk. This leaves a hole you can see through. A 5 1/4-inch disk is protected by placing an adhesive tab over the notch on the upper right, looking at the disk from the front. Once a disk is protected, it cannot be written on until you reverse the protection process.

Place your original PageMaker disks in a safe location and use the copies you made for the installation process that follows. Use the original disks only to make additional copies.

Running the Installation Programs

Running the Windows and PageMaker installation or Setup program is very simple. As a matter of fact, you do it with only a few instructions (assuming your computer is turned on and you are at a DOS prompt—C> or C:\>).

1. Place the Windows Setup disk in drive A or any other floppy disk drive you have and close the door.

2. Type **a:** and press ENTER to make drive A current (if you are using a different drive, type that drive letter in place of A).

3. Type **setup** and press ENTER to start the Setup program.

4. Follow the instructions on the screen.

If you created the directories recommended above, you must type **c:\wi\w3** when asked for the directory in which to install Windows.

Check the list of system components against the table you prepared earlier. If there are discrepancies, check your table, and then use UP ARROW or DOWN ARROW to move the highlight to the item that is wrong, press ENTER, and select the alternative you want from the options presented.

You can install as many printers as you have available, but the first one you choose is the default, the one automatically used unless you tell Setup otherwise. When you have selected a printer (placed the mouse pointer on its name and pressed the left mouse button, or pressed ALT-L and used DOWN ARROW to move the highlight to it), you then click on the Install button or press ALT-I, click on "Configure" or press ALT-C, click on the computer port to use (LPT1, COM1, and so on) or press DOWN ARROW to move the highlight to it, and click on "OK" or press ENTER to complete installing the first printer. Repeat the process for each printer you want to install. Be sure to configure each printer by specifying the port to use. On some printers, laser printers in particular, you also must set them up. To do that, choose "Setup" from the Configure window (click on "Setup" or press ALT-S). When you are done installing all the printers you have, click on "OK" or press ENTER.

Near the end of running Setup you are asked if you want to search your hard disk for applications to run under Windows. At this time you do not want to do this because you have not installed PageMaker yet, so click on "Cancel" or press ESC.

With the answers in the equipment table and only minimal use of your intuition, you should be able to successfully install Windows. If you have problems, press the F1 function key for help screens about what you are doing at the moment.

5. When you have successfully completed installing Windows, reboot your computer and start Windows. If you allowed the installation program to modify your AUTOEXEC.BAT file, Windows automatically is started when you reboot. Otherwise you must change to your Windows directory (type **cd\wi\w3** and press ENTER if you are using the directories in this book), and manually start Windows by typing **win** and pressing ENTER.

Installing PageMaker

The PageMaker installation program must run under Windows—Windows must be running for PageMaker Setup to run. Given that, use these instructions to install PageMaker:

1. Place the PageMaker Disk 1 in drive A or any other floppy disk drive you have and close the door.

2. Move the mouse pointer until it is on the word "File" on the left side of the second bar from the top of the screen (the menu bar). Press and release the left mouse button to click on and open the File menu.

3. Move the mouse pointer to and click on the "Run" option of the File menu to choose that option.

4. Type **a:\aldsetup** and press ENTER to start the PageMaker Setup program.

You are presented with a list of PageMaker options you can choose to install. The default is to install the first three, so you need to identify the ones *not* selected that you *do* want, and those *selected* that you do *not* want installed. You need 3 to 4MB of hard disk space to install PageMaker itself (the first option) and at least 6MB to install all the options. The options and their content are as follows:

Option	Content
PageMaker 4.0	The PageMaker and Setup programs, the spelling and hyphenation dictionaries, the Table Editor, which is used to bring tables into PageMaker, and the ReadMe and Help files.
Tutorial	The files used with the *Getting Started* lessons.
Filters	The files used by PageMaker to convert word processing and graphic files so they can be placed in a PageMaker publication.
PostScript Templates	A set of PageMaker publication files that contain layout grids and templates for creating PostScript publications.
PCL Templates	A set of PageMaker publication files that contain layout grids and templates for creating HP PCL (Hewlett Packard LaserJet Printer Control Language) publications.

5. If you want to install an item that is not selected (selected items are in a colored or shaded band), press and hold CTRL while clicking on the item. If you want to *not* install an item that is selected, also press and hold CTRL while clicking on the item. In other words, pressing and holding CTRL and clicking is a toggle; if you change your mind, simply do it again and for the opposite effect. When you have identified the options you want to install, click on "OK."

6. Enter the directory you want to use to store PageMaker. The default is C:\PM4. If you want to use the directory scheme used in this book (Scheme A), type **c:\wi\pm** and press ENTER. Otherwise enter your directory name or accept the default and press ENTER.

7. Next you are asked to personalize your copy of PageMaker. Do that by typing your name, company name, and your serial number. Your serial number is on the bottom of the box PageMaker came in.

8. If you indicated that you wanted to install filters (and you should if you are going to use word processing and graphic programs outside of PageMaker to prepare text and graphics for placement in PageMaker as this book discusses), then you are next asked to select the filters you want to install. To select a filter, press and hold CTRL while clicking on the filters to install. When you have selected all of the filters you want

(for the various word processing programs you use), click on "OK." The Setup program will tell you the remaining disk space on your hard drive and the amount of space needed as you deselect or select options.

9. If you indicated that you wanted to install either PostScript or PCL templates (they are not used in this book but you might find them handy for starting publications of your own) then you are next asked to select the templates you want to install. To select a template, press and hold CTRL while clicking on the templates to install. When you have selected all of the templates you want, click on "OK."

10. Finally you see the message "Copying and decompressing" and a file name. This indicates you are done answering questions and the setup program is busy doing what it says. From here on you only need to follow the instructions on the screen.

Starting Windows and PageMaker

If you allowed the installation program to completely modify your AUTO-EXEC.BAT file, Windows automatically loads every time you reboot your computer. If you did not let the installation program modify your AUTO-EXEC.BAT file, you must change your path to include the Windows directory and then load Windows. Use these instructions if you did not modify your AUTOEXEC.BAT file (you should be at a DOS prompt):

1. Type **c:**, press ENTER, type **cd**, and press ENTER to make sure you are on hard disk drive C and in the root directory. If Windows is installed on a drive other than C, use the drive letter for the drive on which it is installed in place of C.

2. Type **path c:\wi\w3;c:\wi\pm;c:\dos;c:** and press ENTER to establish the path to use for running Windows and PageMaker.

If your Windows directory path is something other than \WI\W3 or if your PageMaker path is something other than C:\WI\PM, use your directory names in place of \WI\W3 and \WI\PM. If your DOS directory is something other than \DOS, use that directory name in place of \DOS.

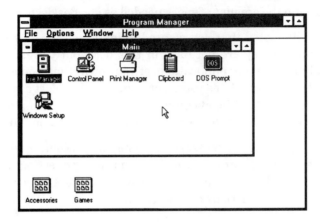

Figure A-2.   *Windows initial screen*

3. Type **win** and press ENTER to load Windows.

When Windows is loaded, your initial screen looks like Figure A-2.

The initial screen shows the Main group of Windows system applications under the Program Manager. Your first task is to identify the application programs, such as PageMaker, that you want to run under Windows.

4. Double-click (click twice in rapid succession) on the Windows Setup icon in the Main group window (or use the arrow keys to move the highlight to the Windows Setup icon and press ENTER).

5. Click on "Options" at the top of the Windows Setup window or press ALT-O. The Options menu opens.

6. Click on "Set Up Applications" or type **s** to choose "Set Up Applications" from the menu.

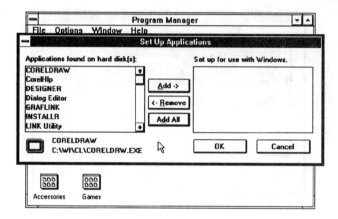

Figure A-3.   *The Set Up Applications window*

7. Click on "OK" or press ENTER to search all drives for applications to run under Windows. The search begins, and a thermometer bar is displayed to tell you how far along you are.

When the search is complete, you get a window with a list on the left and an empty box on the right, as shown in Figure A-3. You select the applications you want to run under Windows from the list on the left. You could choose "Add All", but that is not recommended because you would probably add more programs you don't want to use under Windows than programs you do. You therefore need to look down the list and select only those programs you are sure you want to run under Windows; be sure to include PageMaker. Non-Windows applications, such as Lotus 1-2-3 (2.2 and down and 3.1) and WordPerfect, can run under Windows 3, so you may want to include some of these applications. This is especially true if you can use 386 enhanced mode, because with 386 enhanced mode you can run multiple non-Windows applications and switch among them.

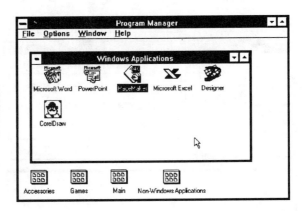

Figure A-4. *The Windows Applications window*

8. Click on the programs you want in the list on the left, clicking on the downward-pointing arrow on the right side of the list to scan it. From the keyboard, press DOWN ARROW to move the selection box to the programs you want to run under Windows and press SPACEBAR to select them.

9. When you have selected all of the programs you want to run under Windows, click on "Add" or press ALT-A. The programs appear in the box on the right.

10. When the process is complete, click on "OK" or press ENTER to close the Set Up Applications window. The Windows Setup window reappears.

11. Move the mouse pointer to the small horizontal bar in the upper-left corner of the Windows Setup window (the Control menu) and press the left mouse button twice in rapid succession (double-click). From the keyboard press ALT-SPACEBAR to open the Windows Setup Control

menu. Click on "Close" or type **C** to close the window. The Main group window reappears.

To load PageMaker you must close the Main group window and open the Windows Applications group window.

12. Again, double-click on the small horizontal bar in the upper-left corner of the Main group window, or press ALT- SPACEBAR and then RIGHT ARROW to open the Main group's Control menu in the upper-left corner of the Main group window. Type **C** to close the window.

13. Double-click on the Windows Applications icon at the bottom of the window, or press CTRL-F6 to move the highlight to the Windows Applications icon and press ENTER. The Windows Applications window opens, as shown Figure A-4.

14. Double-click on the PageMaker icon or press LEFT ARROW or RIGHT ARROW to move the highlight to it and press ENTER. PageMaker is loaded, as shown in Figure A-5.

Figure A-5.   *PageMaker as it is originally loaded*

Leaving PageMaker and Windows

When you wish to leave PageMaker and return to the DOS prompt, do so with these instructions:

1. Double-click on the bar in the upper-left corner of the PageMaker window (not the publication window), or press ALT-SPACEBAR and type **C**. You leave PageMaker and return to Windows.

2. Double-click on the bar in the upper-left corner of the Program Manager window (not the Windows Applications window), or press ALT-SPACEBAR and type **C**.

3. When asked if you want to end your Windows session, click on "OK" or press ENTER. Leave the default Save Changes dialog box checked to save the way you left the Windows screen. You are returned to DOS.

B On Fonts and Laser Printers

Laser printers and the type fonts they use are two major components of desktop publishing. In this book it is assumed that the reader is using a Hewlett-Packard (HP) LaserJet Series II or compatible printer with 2MB of add-on memory (2.5MB total memory) and the Adobe Times New Roman and Gill Sans typefaces. There are, of course, a number of alternatives for both printers and fonts. This appendix takes a brief look at some of these alternatives to see how they relate to desktop publishing.

The HP LaserJet Series II is the industry standard for laser printers and is emulated by the vast majority of new laser printers. The original HP LaserJet and, to a lesser extent, the HP LaserJet Plus were more limited in their ability to print the combined text and graphics that are the hallmark of desktop publishing.

The Times New Roman and Gill Sans typefaces are used in this book because they are adequate for building the products described and they are included with the Adobe Type Manager (ATM) in the PageMaker 4 package. Times New Roman and Gill Sans are similar to Times Roman and Helvetica, which are the industry standards for serif and sans serif fonts (see the discussion in Chapter 1), but numerous other options are available.

Alternative Laser Printers

A number of printers are compatible with the HP LaserJet Series II, including the HP LaserJet III. Many of these have all of the capabilities of the HP LaserJet Series II, and some offer significant advantages such as the LaserJet III's resolution enhancement technology (discussed later).

A major alternative to the HP LaserJet Series II comes not from different hardware but from a software product called a *page description language* (PDL) that runs in a printer. The most common PDL is PostScript by Adobe Systems, and its most common implementation is the Apple LaserWriter IINT and LaserWriter IINTX printers.

Other printer manufacturers, such as NEC, QMS, and Texas Instruments, produce laser printers that run PostScript, but the hallmark of PostScript implementation is the Apple LaserWriter IINT. The paragraphs that follow further explore the Apple LaserWriter IINT and PostScript and then briefly discuss the HP LaserJet Series II and compatible printers.

Apple LaserWriter and PostScript

Using a PDL (PostScript in particular), leaves to the printer the task of how to produce an image on a page. The computer and its applications, such as PageMaker, need only to describe the procedures and parameters necessary for PostScript to calculate where to place the image.

There are some obvious benefits to this. First, work is transferred to the printer, freeing the computer for other tasks. Second, less information is transferred from the computer to the printer, saving time. And third, storing the print image as a PostScript file on disk takes much less space than storing a conventional print image.

A less obvious benefit has to do with how PostScript works with fonts. PostScript uses fonts that are in *outline form*—a series of instructions that trace a particular character. In contrast, the fonts used on an HP LaserJet Series II are in *bit-mapped form*—a series of dots that produce a character of a particular size and weight. The outline form allows PostScript to scale a given character in the printer from very small to very large, to rotate a character, and to compress or squeeze a character. This saves time in communicating with the printer and saves memory in the printer. (Although an additional PostScript font does take additional memory in the printer, it is less than an additional bit-mapped font.)

Finally, a number of devices use PostScript, including several professional imagesetting devices. This means that you can build a publication in PageMaker, print it on the Apple LaserWriter IINT for proofing purposes, and then print the final copy on, say, a Linotronic 100P or 300P to get full typeset quality. The highest resolution on a standard Apple LaserWriter IINT or HP LaserJet Series II is 300 dpi (dots per inch); on most imagesetters it is 1200 dpi, and on some it is higher.

The Apple LaserWriter IINT and IINTX operate with an IBM PC/AT, PS/2, or compatible computer; you do not need a Macintosh. The "engine" that powers it, the inner mechanism which is built by Cannon, is the same as the HP LaserJet Series II. HP and Apple add their own controllers— electronic circuit boards that tell the mechanical parts what to do. Apple's controller includes PostScript.

The Apple LaserWriter IINT includes 11 Adobe PostScript typefaces with 35 fonts: Avant Garde, Bookman, Courier, Helvetica, Helvetica Narrow, New Century Schoolbook, Palatino, and Times each in medium weight (Roman), italic, bold, and bold italic. Additionally, there are Symbol and Zapf Dingbats in medium weight, and Zapf Chancery in medium italic.

The Apple LaserWriter IINT has 2MB of memory. Since the fonts take up so little memory on the LaserWriter, you have more memory remaining than you would using the same fonts on a bit-mapped printer such as an HP LaserJet Series II. Both Apple LaserWriters use a serial interface with IBM-compatible computers and a toner cartridge interchangeable with the HP LaserJet.

The Apple LaserWriter IINTX is considerably faster than the NT, can emulate an HP LaserJet, and can be directly connected to a disk drive for fonts. It also has a considerably higher price.

Apple recently announced two new members of the LaserWriter family. The first, the Personal LaserWriter SC, replaces the LaserWriter IISC. The Personal LaserWriter SC does not include PostScript, uses bit-mapped QuickDraw fonts, and costs less than half the price of the LaserWriter IINT. Both the Personal LaserWriter SC and the other new printer, the Personal LaserWriter NT, are half the speed (4 pages per minute) of the earlier Apple laser printers. The Personal LaserWriter NT uses PostScript like the LaserWriter IINT and IINTX (both of which are still on the market) but it is a new version of PostScript that is both faster and more memory efficient. The Personal LaserWriter NT costs about two-thirds what a LaserWriter IINT costs.

PostScript Alternatives

Most alternative PostScript printers have similar capabilities to the Apple LaserWriter IINT, sometimes with an added feature or two, and often a slightly lower price.

Two examples of alternative PostScript printers are the QMS PS-810 and the NEC SilentWriter LC890. Both of these printers have full Adobe PostScript, the same 35 Adobe PostScript fonts, 300 dpi resolution, and 8-page-per-minute print speed like the LaserWriter IINT. The QMS PS-810 uses the same Cannon SX printer engine as the LaserWriter IINT. Unlike the Apple LaserWriter IINT, both the QMS PS-810 and the NEC LC890 have HP LaserJet Plus emulation and a parallel port for connection to IBM PC-compatible computers. Also, the QMS printer has slightly faster processing speed and HP plotter emulation. The NEC printer has two 250-sheet paper trays that you can alternate, whereas both the Apple and QMS printers have a single 200-sheet tray. The NEC printer, however, uses a different technology for producing the image on the page that does not provide the clarity available on either the Apple or QMS printers. Also, the NEC is ranked lower in reliability than either the Apple or QMS printers, while the QMS is ranked equal to or slightly above the Apple. Both the QMS and NEC printers are priced lower than the Apple printer.

PostScript on a LaserJet   There are three means to implement Post-Script on an HP LaserJet Series II or compatible printer: adding a PostScript controller such as QMS's JetScript board, adding a PostScript cartridge such as Pacific Data Products' PacificPage, and using PostScript emulation software such as GoScript Plus from LaserGo. All three of these alternatives include the standard 35 fonts and reasonable implementations of the PostScript functionality. There are, however, significant differences in both speed and price. The controller is the most expensive and the fastest, the emulation software is the opposite by a large margin, and the cartridge is in the middle.

The QMS JetScript controller board is a full implementation of Adobe's PostScript including the standard 35 resident typefaces. JetScript, which is endorsed by HP, uses two plug-in cards, one that plugs into an IBM XT, AT, or compatible computer and the other that plugs into the Series II. A Series II with JetScript does everything an Apple LaserWriter IINT does, only faster. The cost of a stripped Series II with the JetScript board is about the same as the LaserWriter IINT.

Pacific Data's PacificPage and LaserGo's GoScript Plus both provide the standard 35 fonts and allow you to print as if you had a PostScript printer. The software is excruciatingly slow and is not cheap enough to make it worthwhile (it costs about two-thirds the cost of the cartridge, while the cartridge is one-third the cost of the controller board).

Non-PostScript Printers

In the class of non-PostScript laser printers, two new entries are of interest: the Hewlett Packard (HP) LaserJet III and the LaserMaster 1000.

The HP LaserJet III costs about the same as the HP LaserJet Series II and less than half what the Apple LaserWriter IINT costs. It uses the same Cannon SX 300 DPI engine, has 14 fonts, 8 of which (Times and Univers in Roman, bold, italic, and bold-italic) are scalable from 4 points up, rotatable, and can be outlined, shadowed, or reversed just like PostScript fonts. The LaserJet III also has a resolution-enhancement technology that varies the size and placement of the dots forming the image to smooth curves and fill in white space, thus reducing the "jaggies." The LaserJet III has the same rated speed (8 pages per minute) as the LaserJet Series II and the LaserWriter IINT and is considerably faster in terms of throughput (time from initiating the print command to getting the printed page). Options for the HP LaserJet III include an AppleTalk port and a plug-in cartridge that contains PostScript with the standard 35 fonts.

One other class of laser printer uses a PDL other than PostScript to place an image on a page but is PostScript compatible. Outstanding in this group is LaserMaster Corporation, which produces both controller boards and printers that are not only much faster than PostScript printers but also have several times the resolution of even the LaserJet III. The LaserMaster 1000 is a printer that provides a resolution of 1000 dpi, 135 built-in fonts, and throughput speeds several times faster than the LaserWriter IINTX, even though it uses the same Cannon SX engine. The LaserMaster 1000 costs slightly more than a LaserWriter IINTX, but that is about half what a 1200 dpi commercial imagesetter costs. The LaserMaster controllers work with any HP LaserJet, Apple LaserWriter, or Cannon Laser printer to increase their resolution to 800 dpi and supply 135 fonts. A LaserMaster controller and an HP LaserJet III costs about the same as a LaserMaster 1000. Both the printer and the controllers provide all of the features of PostScript and are fully PostScript compatible. In other words, any program, such as PageMaker, that can print with a PostScript printer can print with a LaserMaster printer or controller.

Font Alternatives

Fonts come in three classes: resident fonts built into the printer, cartridge fonts that are plugged into the printer, and soft fonts that are downloaded from floppy or hard disks through the computer to the printer.

Resident fonts are the most readily available but also the most limited as to typeface and size. HP LaserJet offered only Courier. The HP LaserJet Series II added the Line Printer font and Bold Courier, and the LaserJet III added scalable Times and Univers in four styles each, as well as more Courier styles. Other printers have different resident fonts (the Apple LaserWriter's resident fonts were discussed earlier). For the HP or non-PostScript world, however, you need fonts in addition to those that are resident for almost all desktop publishing applications. That means you must consider purchasing cartridge fonts and/or soft fonts separately.

Cartridge Fonts

The HP LaserJet family and many other laser printers provide slots for plug-in font cartridges. (The Apple LaserWriter does not.) Font cartridges are read-only memory (ROM) chips in a plug-in plastic cartridge with fonts stored on them. HP offers many cartridges, from the original A cartridge that has bold and italic Courier plus a landscape line printer, to the Z cartridge that has 8 to 14-point Times Roman and Helvetica. Companies such as Pacific Data offer many more cartridges like the PostScript cartridge previously described, a cartridge that incorporates all 25 of HP's cartridges in one cartridge, and an HP plotter emulator in a cartridge.

Cartridges have two major advantages. First, they do not have to be downloaded and therefore are immediately available. Second, they do not take memory. With the exception of PostScript cartridges, the major disadvantage is no one cartridge provides enough different fonts to do desktop publishing. As more fonts get stored in a cartridge and the use of two-cartridge slots increases, cartridges are becoming more viable. HP has a catalog called *LaserJet Printer Family Font Catalog* (publication number 5954-7324) that lists the cartridges and soft fonts that HP sells. Ask HP or your dealer for it.

Soft Fonts

Soft fonts provide the greatest variety of typefaces and sizes. They also take up valuable room in your printer's memory that you might otherwise fill with text and graphics. You quickly develop a love/hate relationship with soft fonts.

HP also sells soft fonts and lists them in the font catalog mentioned under cartridge fonts. HP's soft fonts come in two symbol sets: USASCII, which is the basic set of characters used in the United States, and Roman-8, which adds the Roman extension for many European languages. If you do not need the Roman extension most of the time, it is better to use the USASCII set because it takes less printer memory.

Prominent among soft font vendors are Adobe Systems, Inc. (producers of PostScript) and Bitstream, Inc. Both have large libraries of soft fonts for both HP LaserJet-compatible printers and PostScript printers.

Both Adobe and Bitstream have developed products (Adobe Type Manager and Bitstream FaceLift, respectively) for HP LaserJet-compatible printers that make use of one of PostScript's main features: from a library of outline fonts stored on your hard disk, they generate, on demand, bit-mapped fonts that can be scaled to any size for both the screen and the printer. This has several benefits. First, from one outline font you can get a large variety of type sizes from very small to very large. Second, the amount of disk space used by the fonts is greatly reduced. Third, you truly see a "what-you-see-is-what-you-get" screen image. Both of these products include the software to do the scaling and printer driving as well as several initial fonts. You can then buy additional fonts, and you can buy Bitstream fonts for use with Adobe Type Manager (ATM) and Adobe fonts for use with Bitstream FaceLift. Both ATM and FaceLift also work with PostScript printers, providing high resolution screen fonts for the PostScript printer fonts. PageMaker 4 includes ATM with Times New Roman and Gill Sans typefaces.

ATM Versus PostScript   A common question is "Now that Aldus is packaging ATM with PageMaker, why would anyone need PostScript or a PostScript printer?" The answer lies in a combination of what you are going to produce with PageMaker and the equipment you have available or want to buy.

Both ATM and PostScript are means of generating fonts from outlines for printing. PostScript does this in the printer at the time of printing, while ATM does it in the computer at the time characters are produced. Both ATM and PostScript fonts are generated with each use, so they do not require a lot of disk space. ATM adds screen fonts.

ATM is a program on disk that takes Type 1 font outlines and converts them to bit-mapped fonts for both screen and printer. PostScript is a program that permanently resides in the memory of a printer and converts type outlines (which can also be Type 1 font outlines) that are either stored in the printer or downloaded from the computer to bit-mapped fonts in the printer. Depending on the printer, varying numbers of typefaces are included, and additional downloaded font outlines can be purchased from many sources, including Adobe and Bitstream.

ATM and PostScript have several aspects of comparison. For the sake of this discussion, compare ATM with downloadable fonts used on an HP LaserJet Series II with 2.5MB to the resident PostScript fonts and system in an Apple LaserWriter IINT (the HP LaserJet III is such a significant improvement that it virtually negates many of the arguments for Post-Script printers).

You can quickly set aside some aspects. The hardware is the same—both printers are based on the same Cannon engine. The quality of the print is arguably the same (those who are extremely fussy might argue that the PostScript system is better). If you use ATM in either case, the screen fonts are the same.

A major reason for PostScript is that it provides a means of producing a document on a laser printer at 300 dots per inch that you can also take to an imagesetter and produce at 1200 or 2400 dots per inch without changing the document. Also, PostScript's resident fonts do not require downloading, and you have a large selection of fonts without taking up room on your hard drive. The negative side of PostScript is that the system costs approximately twice as much as ATM.

Either ATM with the LaserJet family or ATM with a PostScript printer gives you tremendous flexibility in specifying any size, any slant, and any rotation of a given typeface as you create a document. Also, printing time is virtually the same because in both cases the font must be constructed as you are printing. When you use a font in a document, ATM builds a screen font from the outlines stored on disk. When you print the document, the same outlines are used. Therefore, in both cases you get a true "what-you-see-is-what-you-get" screen image.

ATM basically gives you an excellent system at a moderate cost. ATM is a major improvement over the earlier fixed-size fonts that came from

HP and other sources, including Bitstream Fontware that came with PageMaker 3. Like PostScript, ATM uses a library of outline fonts from which it builds the bit-mapped fonts that you need. Thanks to the competition between Bitstream and Adobe, this library is now quite large.

The net result is that each user must determine if the ability to go to imagesetters and the other benefits of PostScript are worth its cost. ATM with a low-cost LaserJet printer is a very attractive alternative, especially since ATM is included with PageMaker. With LaserJet III it is almost unbeatable.

The addresses and phone numbers of the vendors mentioned in this appendix and elsewhere in this book are listed in Appendix E.

C Scanner Graphic For Chapter 7

Remove this page and scan the image of the Churchill Club's logo.

D *Scanner Graphics For Chapter 8*

To use the illustrations that appear in Chapter 8 in your own work, cut the following pages along the broken line and scan them into your machine.

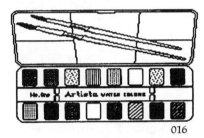

016

Cut along the dotted line.
Align in scanner on opposite edge.

08

10308

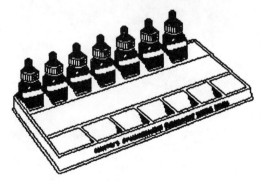

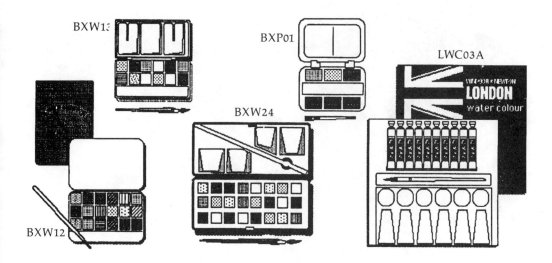

BXW13

BXP01

LWC03A

BXW24

BXW12

Cut along the dotted line.
Align in scanner on opposite edge.

E Vendor Addresses And Phone Numbers

Software Vendors

Computer-Aided Design

AutoCAD
AutoDesk, Inc.
2320 Marinship Way
Sausalito, CA 94965
(415) 331-0356

Generic CADD
Generic Software, Inc.
11911 North Creek Parkway S.
Bothell, WA 98011
(800) 228-3601 or (206) 487-2233

Desktop Publishing

PageMaker
Aldus Corporation
411 First Avenue South
Seattle, WA 98104-2871
(800) 333-2538 or (206) 622-5500

Graphics

CorelDRAW
Corel Systems Corporation
1600 Carling Avenue
Ottawa, Ontario, Canada K1Z 8R7
(613) 728-8200

Micrografx Designer
Micrografx, Inc.
1303 Arapaho
Richardson, TX 75081
(800) 733-DRAW or (214) 234-1769

PC Paintbrush and
Publisher's Paintbrush
ZSoft Corporation
450 Franklin Road, Suite 100
Marietta, GA 30067
(404) 428-0008

Windows Paint
Microsoft Corporation
One Microsoft Way
Redmond, WA 98052-6399
(800) 426-9400 or (206) 882-8080

Word Processing

Ami, Ami Professional
Samna Corporation
5600 Glenridge Drive
Atlanta, GA 30342-1334
(800) 831-9679

Word, Word for Windows
Microsoft Corporation
One Microsoft Way
Redmond, WA 98052-6399
(800) 426-9400 or (206) 882-8080

WordPerfect
WordPerfect Corporation
1555 North Technology Way
Orem, UT 84057
(800) 321-3280 or (801) 225-5000

Hardware Vendors

Printers

LaserJet Series II, LaserJet III
Hewlett-Packard Company
Boise Printer Division
P.O. Box 15
Boise, ID 83707-0015
(800) 752-0900 or (208) 323-6000

LaserMaster 1000, LaserMaster Series III
LaserMaster Corporation
7156 Shady Oak Road
Eden Prairie, MN 55344
(612) 944-9330

LaserWriter IINT, LaserWriter IINTX
Apple Computer, Inc.
20525 Mariani Avenue
Cupertino, CA 95014
(408) 996-1010

JetScript, PS-810
QMS, Inc.
One Magnum Pass
P.O. Box 81250
Mobile, AL 36618
(800) 631-2692 or (205) 633-4300

Scanners

Scanman Plus
Logitech, Inc.
6505 Kaiser Drive
Fremont, CA 94555
(800) 231-7717 or (415) 792-8500

PC Scan, PC Scan Plus
Dest Corporation
1201 Cadillac Court
Milpitas, CA 95035
(408) 946-7100

ScanJet
Hewlett-Packard Company
Business Computing Systems
10520 Ridgeview Court
Cupertino, CA 95014
(800) 752-0900

MS 300A
MicroTek Labs Inc.
16901 S, Western Avenue
Gardena, California 90247
(800) 654-4160

Mice

Logitech Mouse
Logitech, Inc.
6505 Kaiser Drive
Fremont, CA 94555
(800) 231-7717 or (415) 795-8500

Microsoft Mouse
Microsoft Corporation
One Microsoft Way
Redmond, WA 98052-6399
(800) 426-9400 or (206) 882-8080

Mouse Systems Mouse
Mouse Systems Corporation
2600 San Tomas Expressway
Santa Clara, CA 95051
(408) 988-0211

Other Vendors

Fonts

Type Library, Type Manager
Adobe Systems, Inc.
1585 Charleston Road
P.O. Box 7900
Mountain View, CA 94039-7900
(800) 833-6687 or (415) 961-4400

FaceLift, FontWare
Bitstream Inc.
215 First Street
Cambridge, MA 02142-1270
(800) 522-3668 or (617) 497-6222

HP Cartridges and Soft Fonts
Hewlett-Packard Company
Boise Printer Division
P.O. Box 15
Boise, ID 83707-0015
(800) 752-0900

PacificPage PostScript Cartridge
Pacific Data Products
9125 Rehco Road
San Diego, CA 92121
(619) 552-0880

Clip Art

Clip Art Collection
Micrografx, Inc.
1303 Arapaho
Richardson, TX 75081
(800) 733-DRAW or (214) 234-1769

Diagraph
Computer Support Corporation
2215 Midway Road
Carrollton, TX 75006
(214) 661-8960

ClickArt
T/Maker Company
1390 Villa Street
Mountain View, CA 94041-9908
(415) 962-0195

F Menu Options And Keyboard Commands

This appendix provides a complete listing of each of the menu options and keyboard commands in addition to the tools in the Toolbox and some of the special characters PageMaker can produce. In all applicable cases the key combination or keyboard shortcut is shown and a brief description is provided.

This appendix is meant to be a quick reference when you need to look something up quickly. Toward that end, the menu options also appear on a tear-out command card at the back of the book.

Menu Options

In PageMaker, options can be chosen in two ways: by selecting the menu and choosing the option with the mouse or the keyboard, or by pressing the shortcut keys. The following table lists, in alphabetical order, the alternate methods of choosing each PageMaker menu option.

Option	Menu	Shortcut Key	Description
25% size	Page	CTRL-0	Changes display size to 25% of actual
50% size	Page	CTRL-5	Changes display size to 50% of actual
75% size	Page	CTRL-7	Changes display size to 75% of actual
200% size	Page	CTRL-2	Changes display size to 200% of actual
400% size	Page	CTRL-4	Changes display size to 400% of actual
About PageMaker...[1]	Help		Provides version and registration data
Actual size	Page	CTRL-1	Changes display size to actual size
Align center	Type	CTRL-SHIFT-C	Aligns text at center
Align left	Type	CTRL-SHIFT-L	Aligns text on left
Align right	Type	CTRL-SHIFT-R	Aligns text on right
Alignment	Type		Sets how text is aligned
Auto leading	Type	CTRL-SHIFT-A	Applies 120% leading to text
Autoflow	Options		Toggles[2] flowing entire story
Bold	Type	F6 or CTRL-SHIFT-B	Sets bold type style
Book...	File		Groups several PageMaker publications
Bring to front	Element	CTRL-F	Moves text/graphics layer to top
Change...	Edit	CTRL-9	Searches for and replaces text, fonts, styles
Clear	Edit	DEL	Deletes selection—not to Clipboard
Close	File		Closes current publication
Close story	Story	CTRL-SHIFT-E	Closes current story window
Color palette	Windows	CTRL-K	Toggles display of color palette
Column guides...	Options		Sets up columns and their spacing
Commands...	Help		Provides help on menu commands

Option	Menu	Shortcut Key	Description
Copy	Edit	CTRL-C or CTRL-INS	Copies selection to Clipboard
Copy master guides	Page		Copies guide lines from master pages
Create index...	Options		Creates an index from a set of entries
Create TOC...	Options		Creates a table of contents
Cut	Edit	CTRL-X or SHIFT-DEL	Deletes selection to Clipboard
Define colors...	Element		Creates colors to apply to text or graphics
Define styles...	Type	CTRL-3	Defines paragraph styles
Display	Options		Toggles display of special characters in story view
Display master items	Page		Toggles display of master page items
Display style names	Options		Toggles display of style names in story view
Edit story / layout	Edit	CTRL-E	Toggles between layout view and story view
Exit	File	CTRL-Q	Leaves PageMaker
Export...	File		Saves text in word processing file
Fill	Element		Sets fill density and pattern
Find...	Edit	CTRL-8	Searches for text, fonts, or styles in story view
Find next...	Edit	CTRL-SHIFT-9	Searches for next occurrence in story view
Fit in window	Page	CTRL-W	Changes display size to fit in window
Font	Type		Sets typeface
Force justify	Type	CTRL-SHIFT-F	Spreads text evenly between margins
Go to page...	Page	CTRL-G	Displays another page
Guides	Options	CTRL-J	Toggles display of guide lines
Hyphenation...	Type	CTRL-H	Determines if and how words are hyphenated
Image control...	Element		Sets contrast, etc., of graphic

Option	Menu	Shortcut Key	Description
Import...	Story		Imports text in story view
Indents/tabs...	Type	CTRL-I	Sets indent and tab positions
Index...	Help	F1	Opens the help index
Index entry...	Options	CTRL-;	Creates an index entry
Insert pages...	Page		Adds one or more pages
Italic	Type	F7 or CTRL-SHIFT-I	Sets italic type style
Justify	Type	CTRL-SHIFT-J	Aligns text on both left and right
Leading	Type		Sets amount of space between lines
Line	Element		Sets line width and style
Link info...	Element		Supplies information on file links
Link options...	Element		Determines how linked items are stored and updated
Links...	File	CTRL-SHIFT-D	Manages links with text or graphics files
Lock guides	Options		Locks guide lines in place
New...	File	CTRL-N	Creates new publication
New story	Story		Creates new, untitled story window
No track	Type	CTRL-SHIFT-Q	Turns off any kerning
Normal style	Type	F5 or CTRL-SHIFT-SPACEBAR	Sets normal type style
Normal width	Type	CTRL-SHIFT-X	Sets normal character width
Open...	File	CTRL-O	Opens existing publication
Page setup...	File		Sets margins and other page options
Paragraph...	Type	CTRL-M	Sets paragraph specifications
Paste	Edit	INS or SHIFT-INS or CTRL-V	Inserts contents of Clipboard
Place...	File	CTRL-D	Places text or graphics in publication
Preferences...	Edit		Sets unit of measure, etc.
Print...	File	CTRL-P	Prints current publication
Remove pages	Page		Deletes one or more pages

Option	Menu	Shortcut Key	Description
Replace	File	CTRL-D	Closes story window and allows moving story
Reverse	Type	CTRL-SHIFT-V	Sets reverse type style
Revert	File		Restores last save of current publication
Rounded corners...	Element		Sets degree of roundness
Rulers	Options	CTRL-R	Toggles the display of rulers
Save	File	CTRL-S	Saves current publication
Save as...	File		Saves publication with new name
Scroll bars	Windows		Toggles display of scroll bars
Select all	Edit	CTRL-A	Selects an entire story or page
Send to back	Element	CTRL-B	Moves text/graphics to bottom
Set width	Type		Sets width of characters
Show index...	Options		Allows review and edit of an index
Size	Type		Sets type size
Small caps	Type	CTRL-SHIFT-H	Sets small caps type style
Snap to guides	Options	CTRL-U	Aligns items to guide lines
Snap to rulers	Options	CTRL-SHIFT-Y	Aligns items to ruler marks
Spelling...	Edit	CTRL-L	Checks and corrects spelling in story view
Strikethru	Type	CTRL-SHIFT-S	Sets strikethrough type style
Style	Type		Sets paragraph style
Style palette	Windows	CTRL-Y	Toggles display of style palette
Target printer...	File		Sets up the printer to be used
Text rotation...	Element		Rotates selected text
Text wrap...	Element		Sets how text wraps around graphics
Toolbox	Windows	CTRL-6	Toggles display of Toolbox
Topics...	Help		Provides help on selected subjects

Option	Menu	Shortcut Key	Description
Track	Type		Sets amount of space between characters
Type specs...	Type	CTRL-T	Sets all type specificatons
Type style	Type		Sets type style such as bold or italic
Underline	Type	F8 or CTRL-SHIFT-U	Sets underline type style
Undo	Edit	ALT-BACKSPACE or CTRL-Z	Reverses last action
Using PM Help...	Help		Provides help on using PageMaker Help
Zero lock	Options		Locks rulers' zero point

Keyboard Controls

Command	Key Combination	Description
All caps/lowercase	CTRL-SHIFT-K	Toggles between all caps and lowercase in Layout view only
Beginning of line	HOME	Moves to beginning of line
Beginning of paragraph	CTRL-UP ARROW	Moves to beginning of paragraph
Beginning of sentence	CTRL-HOME	Moves to beginning of sentence
Beginning of story	CTRL-PGUP	Moves to beginning of story
Beginning of word	CTRL-LEFT ARROW	Moves to beginning of word
Bottom of story	CTRL-PGDN	Moves to bottom of story
Clear manual kerning	CTRL-SHIFT-0	Removes kerning in selected text
Down a line	DOWN ARROW	Moves down one line
Down a paragraph	CTRL-DOWN ARROW	Moves down to start of next paragraph
Down a screen	PGDN	Moves down one screen in text mode or story view
End of line	END	Moves to end of line
End of sentence	CTRL-END	Moves to end of sentence
End of story	CTRL-PGDN	Moves to end of story in text mode or story view
Fit in window/ Actual size	Secondary mouse button	Toggles between "Fit in window" and "Actual size" views
Help	CTRL-SHIFT-F1	Context-sensitive help

Command	Key Combination	Description
Kern apart—coarse	CTRL-SHIFT-BACKSPACE or CTRL-keypad +[3]	Adds 1/25 em between characters
Kern apart—fine	CTRL-SHIFT-keypad +	Adds 1/100 em between characters
Kern together—coarse	CTRL-BACKSPACE or CTRL-keypad –	Removes 1/25 em between characters
Kern together—fine	CTRL-SHIFT-keypad –	Removes 1/100 em between characters
Larger point size	CTRL-SHIFT->	Increases point size by one point
Larger standard point size	F4 or CTRL->	Increases point size per menu
Left a character	LEFT ARROW	Moves left one character
Left a word	CTRL-LEFT ARROW	Moves left one word
Menu	F10 or ALT	Opens the menu
Move publication	ALT-drag	Moves publication in its window
Next line	DOWN ARROW	Moves to next line
Next page	F12	Moves to next page
Next paragraph	CTRL-DOWN ARROW	Moves to start of next paragraph
Next word	CTRL-RIGHT ARROW	Moves to start of next word
Previous page	F11	Moves to previous page
Right a character	RIGHT ARROW	Moves right one character
Right a word	CTRL-RIGHT ARROW	Moves right one word
Select character left	SHIFT-LEFT ARROW	Selects character to left
Select character right	SHIFT-RIGHT ARROW	Selects character to right
Select down a line	SHIFT-DOWN ARROW	Selects text down one line
Select paragraph	Triple-click	Selects paragraph with mouse
Select range	Drag	Selects range with mouse
Select to line beginning	SHIFT-HOME	Selects text to beginning of line
Select to line end	SHIFT-END	Selects text to end of line
Select to paragraph beginning	CTRL-SHIFT-UP ARROW	Selects text to beginning of paragraph
Select to paragraph end	CTRL-SHIFT-DOWN ARROW	Selects text to end of paragraph
Select to sentence beginning	CTRL-SHIFT-HOME	Selects text to beginning of sentence
Select to sentence end	CTRL-SHIFT-END	Selects text to end of sentence
Select to story beginning	CTRL-SHIFT-PGUP	Selects text to beginning of story
Select to story end	CTRL-SHIFT-PGDN	Selects text to end of story
Select up a line	SHIFT-UP ARROW	Selects text up one line
Select word	Double-click	Selects word with mouse

Command	Key Combination	Description
Select word left	CTRL-SHIFT-LEFT ARROW	Selects word to left
Select word right	CTRL-SHIFT-RIGHT ARROW	Selects word to right
Smaller point size	CTRL-SHIFT-<	Decreases point size by one point
Smaller standard point size	F3 or CTRL-<	Decreases point size per menu
Subscript	CTRL-\	Sets subscripted type style
Superscript	CTRL-SHIFT-\	Sets superscripted type style
Top of story	CTRL-PGUP	Moves to start of story in text mode or story view
Up a line	UP ARROW	Moves up one line
Up a paragraph	CTRL-UP ARROW	Moves up one paragraph
Up a screen	PGUP	Moves up one screen in text mode or story view

Special Characters

PageMaker and the Adobe Type Manager offer a large number of special characters. Some of the more useful English language ones are shown here.

Character	Key Combination	Description
Bullet	CTRL-SHIFT-8	Adds • character
Closing double quotes	CTRL-SHIFT-]	Adds " character
Closing single quote	CTRL-]	Adds ' character
Copyright mark	CTRL-SHIFT-O	Adds © character
Discretionary hyphen	CTRL--	Adds hyphen if word breaks
Em dash	CTRL-SHIFT-=	Adds dash equal to current point size
Em space	CTRL-SHIFT-M	Adds space equal to current point size
En dash	CTRL-=	Adds 1/2 em dash
En space	CTRL-SHIFT-N	Adds 1/2 em space

Character	Key Combination	Description
Nonbreaking hyphen	CTRL-SHIFT--	Adds a nonwordbreaking dash or hyphen
Nonbreaking slash	CTRL-SHIFT-/	Adds a nonwordbreaking slash
Nonbreaking space	CTRL-SPACE	Adds nonbreaking space character
Opening double quotes	CTRL-SHIFT-[	Adds " character
Opening single quote	CTRL-[	Adds ' character
Page number marker	CTRL-SHIFT-3	Adds page number marker to master pages
Paragraph mark	CTRL-SHIFT-7	Adds ¶ character
Registered trade mark	CTRL-SHIFT-G	Adds ® character
Section mark	CTRL-SHIFT-6	Adds § character
Thin space	CTRL-SHIFT-T	Adds 1/4 em space

Toolbox Tools

If the Toolbox is on the screen, it is easy to click on the tool you want. If, for some reason, you need to remove the Toolbox to see your publication, you can still change tools. The key combinations to do this are shown here.

Tool	Key Combination	Description
Box tool	SHIFT-F5	Draws boxes with square corners
Circle tool	SHIFT-F7	Draws circles or ovals
Cropping tool	SHIFT-F8	Trims graphics
Line tool	SHIFT-F2	Draws any type of line
Oval tool	SHIFT-F7	Draws ovals or circles
Perpendicular-line tool	SHIFT-F3	Draws lines at 45-degree increments
Pointer / Other tool	F9	Toggles between pointer and other tool in use
Rounded-corner tool	SHIFT-F6	Draws boxes with rounded corners

Character	Key Combination	Description
Square-corner tool	SHIFT-F5	Draws boxes with square corners
Text tool	SHIFT-F4	Enters or edits text

Footnotes

1. An ellipsis (...) means that this command opens a dialog box.

2. "Toggle" means that the current state is reversed. If a setting is on, it is turned off by selecting the toggle, and vice versa.

3. "Keypad" means the numeric keypad on the far right of most keyboards.

Index

PageMaker 4 Menu Options
(arranged alphabetically)

Option[1]	Menu	Shortcut key	Description
25% size	Page	CTRL-0	Changes display size to 25% of actual
50% size	Page	CTRL-5	Changes display size to 50% of actual
75% size	Page	CTRL-7	Changes display size to 75% of actual
200% size	Page	CTRL-2	Changes display size to 200% of actual
400% size	Page	CTRL-4	Changes display size to 400% of actual
About PageMaker...	Help		Provides version and registration data
Actual size	Page	CTRL-1	Changes display size to actual size
Align center	Type	CTRL-SHIFT-C	Aligns text at center
Align left	Type	CTRL-SHIFT-L	Aligns text on left
Align right	Type	CTRL-SHIFT-R	Aligns text on right
Alignment	Type		Sets how text will be aligned
Auto leading	Type	CTRL-SHIFT-A	Applies 120% leading to text
Autoflow	Options		Toggles[2] flowing entire story
Bold	Type	F6 or CTRL-SHIFT-B	Sets bold type style
Book...[3]	File		Groups several PageMaker publications
Bring to front	Element	CTRL-F	Moves text/graphics layer to top
Change...	Edit	CTRL-9	Searches for and replaces text, fonts, styles
Clear	Edit	DEL	Deletes selection—not to Clipboard
Close	File		Closes current publication
Close story	Story	CTRL-SHIFT-E	Closes current story window
Color palette	Windows	CTRL-K	Toggles display of color palette
Column guides...	Options		Sets up columns and their spacing
Commands...	Help		Provides help on menu commands
Copy	Edit	CTRL-INS or CTRL-C	Copies selection to Clipboard
Copy master guides	Page		Copies guide lines from master pages
Create TOC...	Options		Creates a table of contents
Create index...	Options		Creates an index from a set of entries
Cut	Edit	SHIFT-DEL or CTRL-X	Deletes selection to Clipboard

© 1990 Martin S. Matthews and Carole Boggs Matthews, *Using Pagemaker 4 for the PC, Third Edition*

Option[1]	Menu	Shortcut key	Description
Define colors. . .	Element		Creates colors to apply to text or graphics
Define styles. . .	Type	CTRL-3	Defines paragraph styles
Display master items	Page		Toggles display of master page items
Display style names	Options		Toggles display of style names in story view
Display	Options		Toggles display of special characters in story view
Edit story/layout	Edit	CTRL-E	Toggles between layout view and story view
Exit	File	CTRL-Q	Leaves PageMaker
Export. . .	File		Saves text in word processing file
Fill	Element		Sets fill density and pattern
Find. . .	Edit	CTRL-8	Searches for text, fonts or styles in story view
Find next. . .	Edit	CTRL-SHIFT-9	Searches for next occurence in story view
Fit in Window	Page	CTRL-W	Changes display size to fit in window
Font	Type		Sets typeface
Force justify	Type	CTRL-SHIFT-F	Spreads text evenly between margins
Go to page. . .	Page	CTRL-G	Displays another page
Guides	Options	CTRL-J	Toggles display of guide lines
Hyphenation. . .	Type	CTRL-H	Determines if and how words will be hyphenated
Image control. . .	Element		Sets contrast, etc., of graphic
Import. . .	Story		Imports text in story view
Indents/tabs. . .	Type	CTRL-I	Sets indent and tab positions
Index. . .	Help	F1	Opens the Help Index
Index entry. . .	Options	CTRL-;	Creates an index entry
Insert pages. . .	Page		Adds one or more pages
Italic	Type	F7 or CTRL-SHIFT-I	Sets italic type style
Justify	Type	CTRL-SHIFT-J	Aligns text on both left and right
Leading	Type		Sets amount of space between lines
Line	Element		Sets line width and style
Link info. . .	Element		Supplies information on file links
Link options. . .	Element		Determines how linked items are stored & updated

Option[1]	Menu	Shortcut key	Description
Links. . .	File	CTRL-SHIFT-D	Manages links with text or graphics files
Lock guides	Options		Locks guide lines in place
New story	Story		Creates new, untitled, story window
New. . .	File	CTRL-N	Creates new publication
No track	Type	CTRL-SHIFT-Q	Turns off any kerning
Normal style	Type	F5 or CTRL-SHIFT-SPACE	Sets normal type style
Normal width	Type	CTRL-SHIFT-X	Sets normal character width
Open. . .	File	CTRL-O	Opens existing publication
Page setup. . .	File		Sets margins and other page options
Paragraph. . .	Type	CTRL-M	Sets paragraph specifications
Paste	Edit	INS or SHIFT-INS or CTRL-V	Inserts contents of Clipboard
Place. . .	File	CTRL-D	Places text or graphics in publication
Preferences. . .	Edit		Sets unit of measure, etc.
Print. . .	File	CTRL-P	Prints current publication
Remove pages	Page		Deletes one or more pages
Replace	File	CTRL-D	Closes story window and allows moving story
Reverse	Type	CTRL-SHIFT-V	Sets reverse type style
Revert	File		Restores last save of current publication
Rounded corners. . .	Element		Sets degree of roundness
Rulers	Options	CTRL-R	Toggles display of rulers
Save	File	CTRL-S	Saves current publication
Save as. . .	File		Saves publication with new name
Scroll bars	Windows		Toggles display of scroll bars
Select all	Edit	CTRL-A	Selects an entire story or page
Send to back	Element	CTRL-B	Moves text/graphics to bottom
Set width	Type		Sets width of characters
Show index. . .	Options		Allows review and edit of an index
Size	Type		Sets type size
Small caps	Type	CTRL-SHIFT-H	Sets small caps type style
Snap to guides	Options	CTRL-U	Aligns items to guide lines
Snap to rulers	Options	CTRL-SHIFT-Y	Aligns items to ruler marks

© 1990 Martin S. Matthews and Carole Boggs Matthews, *Using Pagemaker 4 for the PC, Third Edition*

Option[1]	Menu	Shortcut key	Description
Spelling. . .	Edit	CTRL-L	Checks and corrects spelling in story view
Strikethru	Type	CTRL-SHIFT-S	Sets strikethru type style
Style	Type		Sets paragraph style
Style palette	Windows	CTRL-Y	Toggles display of style palette
Target Printer. . .	File		Sets up the printer to be used
Text rotation. . .	Element		Rotates selected text
Text wrap. . .	Element		Sets how text wraps around graphics
Toolbox	Windows	CTRL-6	Toggles display of Toolbox
Topics. . .	Help		Provides help on selected subjects
Track	Type		Sets amount of space between characters
Type specs. . .	Type	CTRL-T	Sets all type specifications
Type style	Type		Sets type style such as bold or italic
Underline	Type	F8 or CTRL-SHIFT-U	Sets underline type style
Undo	Edit	ALT-BACKSPACE or CTRL-Z	Reverses last action
Using PM Help. . .	Help		Provides help on using PageMaker Help
Zero lock	Options		Locks rulers zero point

Notes:

1. Options are chosen in two ways:
   a. by selecting the menu and choosing the option with the mouse or the keyboard or
   b. by pressing the shortcut keys shown.

2. "Toggle" means that the current state is reversed. If a setting is "on," it will be turned "off" by selecting the toggle, and vise versa.

3. An ellipsis (. . .) means that this command opens a dialog box.

Computer Books

— Tear off for Bookmark

▼

You're important to us...

We'd like to know what you're interested in, what kinds of books you're looking for, and what you thought about this book in particular.

Please fill out the attached card and mail it in. We'll do our best to keep you informed about Osborne's newest books and special offers.

▶ *YES, SEND ME A FREE COLOR CATALOG*
of all Osborne/McGraw-Hill computer books.

Name:_____ Title:_____

Company:_____

Address:_____

City:_____ State:_____ Zip:_____

I'M PARTICULARLY INTERESTED IN THE FOLLOWING *(Check all that apply)*

I use this software:
❏ Lotus 1-2-3
❏ Quattro
❏ dBASE
❏ WordPerfect
❏ Microsoft Word
❏ WordStar
❏ Others_____

I use this operating system:
❏ DOS
❏ OS/2
❏ UNIX
❏ Macintosh
❏ Others_____

I program in:
❏ C
❏ PASCAL
❏ BASIC
❏ Others_____

I chose this book because...
❏ Recognized author's name
❏ Osborne/McGraw-Hill's reputation
❏ Read book review
❏ Read Osborne catalog
❏ Saw advertisement in _____
❏ Found while browsing in store
❏ Found/recommended in library
❏ Required textbook
❏ Price
❏ Other_____

I rate this book:
❏ Excellent   ❏ Good   ❏ Poor

Comments_____
_____

Topics I would like to see covered in future books by Osborne/McGraw-Hill

include:_____
_____

Print **ISBN** from the back cover here: 0-07-881_ _ _ _ - _

Osborne McGraw-Hi[ll]

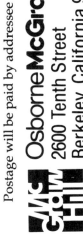

Compu[ter]
Boo[ks]

(800) 227-0900

No Postage
Necessary
If Mailed
in the
United States

BUSINESS REPLY MAIL

First Class   Permit NO. 3111 Berkeley, CA

Postage will be paid by addressee

 **Osborne McGraw-Hill**

2600 Tenth Street

Berkeley, California 94710–9938